Queenship and Power

Series Editors
Charles E. Beem, University of North Carolina, Pembroke, NC, USA
Carole Levin, University of Nebraska, Lincoln, NE, USA

This series focuses on works specializing in gender analysis, women's studies, literary interpretation, and cultural, political, constitutional, and diplomatic history. It aims to broaden our understanding of the strategies that queens—both consorts and regnants, as well as female regents—pursued in order to wield political power within the structures of male-dominant societies. The works describe queenship in Europe as well as many other parts of the world, including East Asia, Sub-Saharan Africa, and Islamic civilization.

More information about this series at
https://link.springer.com/bookseries/14523

Carole Levin

The Reign and Life of Queen Elizabeth I

Politics, Culture, and Society

Carole Levin
Willa Cather Professor of History
Emeritus
University of Nebraska
Lincoln, NE, USA

ISSN 2730-938X ISSN 2730-9398 (electronic)
Queenship and Power
ISBN 978-3-030-93008-0 ISBN 978-3-030-93009-7 (eBook)
https://doi.org/10.1007/978-3-030-93009-7

© The Editor(s) (if applicable) and The Author(s), under exclusive license to Springer Nature Switzerland AG 2022
This work is subject to copyright. All rights are solely and exclusively licensed by the Publisher, whether the whole or part of the material is concerned, specifically the rights of translation, reprinting, reuse of illustrations, recitation, broadcasting, reproduction on microfilms or in any other physical way, and transmission or information storage and retrieval, electronic adaptation, computer software, or by similar or dissimilar methodology now known or hereafter developed. The use of general descriptive names, registered names, trademarks, service marks, etc. in this publication does not imply, even in the absence of a specific statement, that such names are exempt from the relevant protective laws and regulations and therefore free for general use.
The publisher, the authors and the editors are safe to assume that the advice and information in this book are believed to be true and accurate at the date of publication. Neither the publisher nor the authors or the editors give a warranty, expressed or implied, with respect to the material contained herein or for any errors or omissions that may have been made. The publisher remains neutral with regard to jurisdictional claims in published maps and institutional affiliations.

Cover illustration: incamerastock/Alamy Stock Photo

This Palgrave Macmillan imprint is published by the registered company Springer Nature Switzerland AG
The registered company address is: Gewerbestrasse 11, 6330 Cham, Switzerland

My wonderful family and friends made all the difference during my misadventures during my three months in Washington DC to do research for this project in 2019. On the first day, I tripped on a loose brick and fractured my elbow, and a few weeks before I was leaving, I was as a pedestrian hit by a car. The help and love I received made all the difference.

This book is for
Rohana, David, Erika, Nancy, and Renee
with so much love

Acknowledgments

I loved working on this book, and I have so many people to thank. I am deeply grateful to Sam Stocker, my editor at Palgrave, for all his help and support.

I spent three months in Washington DC at the Folger Shakespeare Library in 2019. The Folger is such a wonderful place to do research, and the kindness of the staff, especially with my misadventures, meant everything.

As I was working on this book, my life and the lives of everyone changed drastically in March 2020. Working on this book in the midst of a pandemic meant a number of added difficulties. I am so grateful for the help from Lia Markey at the Newberry Library. I appreciate all the support from the University of Nebraska, especially the staff at Love Library. I also am grateful to Jess and Jason during this trying time for helping me keep my body strong so my mind could keep focused.

Many thanks to Courtney Herber, who was so helpful in the research and preparation of this book, Jack Ellis, who gave me such useful technical help, and especially Jaime Rea Moore, who provided such valuable research assistance and meticulous help in preparing the manuscript.

I am deeply grateful to Jo Eldridge Carney for her help on this book project and for so much else over many years of friendship and shared scholarly interests.

Good friends and generous scholars Pamela Starr and Linda Austern were so helpful on music at Elizabeth's court. Estelle Paranque provided her expertise on the French monarchy and dear friendship.

So many friends were pillars over the years that I worked on this book. When I wrote about Elizabeth's friends I thought about my own friends and my gratitude for them: Elaine, Pamela, Mary Ann, Anya, Ilona, Mary Ellen, Pat, Jane, Marcia, Michele, Musa, Marguerite, Harriet, Dean, Nicki, Lisa, Donald, Tim, Nate, Alicia, Kaley, Alyson, Cassie, Chelsea, Catherine, Alan, Katy, Patty, John, Gerald and Stas, Joye, Todd and Colleen, Sue, Helen, Tess, Bob, Gina, Charles, Cinzia, Nan, Rick and Casey, Judith, Jillian, Karolyn,

Linda, Jess, Valerie, Ellie, Emily, Christina, Richie, Tony, Rick and Payiotis, Joye, Mark, Christine and Brock. I have also been thinking about my oldest friends, especially Banisa, and one of my newest friends, Sal. Thank you to everyone for so much love, help, and support.

"I count myself in nothing else so happy as in a soul remembering my good friends"

William Shakespeare

PRAISE FOR
THE REIGN AND LIFE OF QUEEN ELIZABETH I

"There is no such thing as too many books on Elizabeth I and Carole Levin once more proves it. This textbook is the pinnacle of Elizabethan studies. Thoroughly researched with new primary evidence, scholars and students alike will find it indispensable for the study of Elizabeth I's reign. This is undoubtedly a significant contribution to our understanding not only of the queen herself but of the politics and culture of her reign and as usual Carole Levin shows what a groundbreaking scholar she truly is."

— Estelle Paranque, *New College of the Humanities, London, UK*

"This lively and comprehensive book provides a wealth of information about the queenship of Elizabeth I, but it is also accessible, engaging, entertaining, and often surprising. Researched with a detective's painstaking attention to archival detail that characterizes all of Levin's work, *The Reign and Life of Queen Elizabeth I* demonstrates that there are still new revelations to be uncovered about this fascinating monarch. Information about Elizabeth and the wide net she cast that has been neglected or overlooked is highlighted here, alongside attention to events and issues that were relevant in the sixteenth century and still resonate today. Students and scholars at every level and early modern enthusiasts in general will find this book an invaluable resource for opening up fresh doorways to Elizabeth and her world."

—Jo Carney, *The College of New Jersey, USA*

"A result of Levin's nonpareil archival research and decades of her seminal scholarship on Queen Elizabeth I, this book situates meticulously researched facts about Elizabeth's queenship within broader political, religious, social, and cultural issues, developments, and events. *The Reign and Life of Queen Elizabeth I* is both an encyclopedia and textbook, and it will serve as an invaluable asset for teachers, students, and scholars alike. This book is a treasury of new information that clarifies and illuminates the historical record and brings Elizabeth's world to life like never before."

—Anna Riehl Bertolet, *Auburn University, USA*

"An elegant journey through Elizabeth I's reign, queenship, and life, this volume is divided into sections that explore privy councilors, ranking statesmen and churchmen, and personal friends. Fresh substance and original insights encountered here prove there is still more to learn about this Tudor queen. Its format makes it useful in the classroom with a variety of independent essays. A crowning achievement of scholarship and archival sleuthing."

—Renee Bricker, *University of North Georgia, USA*

Contents

1	Introduction: Elizabeth I	1

Part I Politics and Religion

2	The Coronation	13
3	The Privy Council	19
4	Elizabeth's Parliaments	49
5	The Archbishops of Canterbury	59
6	Courtships and Favorites	69
7	Potential Heirs to Elizabeth's Throne	91
8	Ambassadors at Elizabeth's Court	111
9	Assassination Attempts, Plots, and Rebellions	139
10	The Spanish Armada	167

Part II Society and Culture

11	Elizabeth's England and Others	177
12	Mirrors	209
13	Dreaming Elizabeth	215
14	Women Friends of Queen Elizabeth	229
15	Slander Gossip Rumors	241
16	Elizabeth's Pleasures	259

Bibliography 289

Index 295

Chronology

1533	Birth of Queen Elizabeth.
1536	Execution of her mother Anne Boleyn.
	2nd Act of Succession. Elizabeth, with older sister Mary, declared illegitimate by Parliament and excluded from rights to the throne.
1537	Birth of Edward VI.
1543	3rd Act of Succession, restoring Mary and Elizabeth's claims to the throne, but not restoring their legitimacy.
1547	Death of Henry VIII of England. Accession of Edward VI.
1553	Death of Edward VI, his will excluded his two sisters
	Lady Jane Grey was proclaimed Queen.
	Ten days later, Mary Tudor proclaimed Queen.
1554	Elizabeth was sent to the Tower of London, Later under house arrest.
1558	Mary I died. Elizabeth ascended the throne.
1559	Coronation of Elizabeth I.
	Elizabeth's Acts of Supremacy and Uniformity passed.
1561	Widowed Mary Stuart returned to Scotland from France.
1562	Elizabeth was seriously ill with smallpox.
1563	Thirty-Nine Articles issued.
1565	Mary Stuart married Henry Stuart, Lord Darnley, murdered in 1567.
1566	Birth of James VI of Scotland (and later I of England).
1567	Mary married James, Earl of Bothwell, presumed murderer of Darnley; forced to abdicate. Infant son James was proclaimed King of Scotland.
1568	Mary fled to England.
1569	The Northern Rebellion.
1570	Elizabeth was excommunicated by Pope Pius V.
1571	The Ridolfi Plot to assassinate Elizabeth.
1572	Duke of Norfolk executed for treason for his involvement in the Ridolfi Plot.
1581	Francis Drake brought back great wealth from his world voyage; knighted; Spain enraged.
1579, 1581	Francis, Duke of Anjou visited England, hoping to marry Elizabeth.
1583	Throckmorton plot to assassinate Elizabeth and put Mary Stuart on the throne. Following year Throckmorton executed.

1584	Assassination of William of Orange.
	The Bond of Association formed: loyal subjects pledged Elizabeth assassinated the person for whom the assassination was performed would be executed.
1585	Robert Dudley, Earl of Leicester left England for the Netherlands to lead forces there against the Spanish; returned to England in 1586.
1586	Babington Plot to assassinate Elizabeth and put Mary Stuart on the English throne.
1586	Trial of Mary Stuart.
1587	Mary Stuart was executed for treason.
1588	Defeat of the Spanish Armada. Elizabeth delivered Tilbury speech.
	Death of Robert Dudley, Earl of Leicester.
1590	Death of Sir Francis Walsingham.
1591	Death of Sir Christopher Hatton.
1598	Death of William Cecil, Lord Burghley.
1598	Death of Philip II of Spain.
1599	Robert Devereux, Earl of Essex sent to Ireland to suppress the rebellion; failed, returned to court without permission.
1601	Essex rebellion.
	Essex executed.
	Elizabeth delivered Golden Speech.
1603	Queen Elizabeth died. James VI of Scotland proclaimed James I King of England.

List of Figures

Fig. 2.1	Queen Elizabeth wearing crown private collection	14
Fig. 3.1	Burghley, Elizabeth, Walsingham private collection	20
Fig. 5.1	Elizabeth with Bishops private collection	60
Fig. 6.1	Duke of Alençon, later Anjou private collection	81
Fig. 6.2	Robert Dudley, Earl of Leicester private collection	83
Fig. 7.1	Mary Stuart private collection	103
Fig. 8.1	Elizabeth receiving the French ambassadors private collection	112
Fig. 8.2	St. Bartholomew's Day Massacre	128
Fig. 8.3	Spanish ambassador expelled from England private collection	134
Fig. 9.1	Somerville attempted assassination private collection	150
Fig. 9.2	Babington plot private collection	153
Fig. 10.1	Spanish Armada Private Collection	168
Fig. 10.2	Elizabeth in procession to St. Paul's private collection	172
Fig. 10.3	Elizabeth surrounded by her people private collection	173
Fig. 11.1	Lopez private collection	201
Fig. 13.1	Anne Boleyn private collection	217
Fig. 13.2	Elizabeth signing death warrant private collection	220
Fig. 14.1	Elizabethan women private collection	230
Fig. 16.1	Elizabeth watching play private collection	284

CHAPTER 1

Introduction: Elizabeth I

This book provides a thorough discussion of various aspects of the life of Queen Elizabeth and her reign. The book is divided thematically into several sections. Part I focuses on aspects of the complex political trajectory of Elizabeth's long rule, including the many assassination plots and attempts, her various courtships and court favorites, the many members of her Privy Council, her relationship with Parliament, and the ever-present pressures of religious conflict. Some of the units, such as the one of Elizabeth's coronation, are stand-alone essays, but most of the more extensive units are subdivided. Part II is concerned with the cultural and social landscape of the Elizabethan era, including units on foreigners in England, especially those with connections to the court; the queen's friends; slander, rumor, and gossip about the queen; her own dreams and others about her; and the activities that amused and interested the queen. While these units are organized around discrete themes, cross-references have been included to show the considerable connections among the various subjects. I have modernized the spelling so that the book is more accessible. Scholarship on Queen Elizabeth I is extensive, but this book demonstrates that a study of her reign can continue to reveal new and fascinating information about her queenship and her surrounding world. The rest of the introduction provides the reader with a biography of Elizabeth.

There was great excitement in September 1533 as Henry VIII's second queen, for whom he had broken with the Catholic Church, was about to give birth to a child that Henry was sure would be his son. Convinced that he must have a legitimate male heir, the Tudor king had declared his marriage to Catherine of Aragon invalid and their daughter Mary, the sole child of the union to survive infancy, a bastard. But on September 7 Anne Boleyn gave birth to another daughter, this one named Elizabeth. In less than three years Anne Boleyn was dead, executed by her husband with five other men, one of whom was her own brother, who were named, most improbably, as her lovers. Elizabeth too was declared a bastard. Only ten days later Henry married Jane Seymour. By the Second Act of Succession of June 1536, it became treason to declare Elizabeth an heir to the throne. In October 1537 Henry finally had the son he craved, though Jane died soon after the birth. While Henry married three more times, Edward was his last child.

Before she was three years old Elizabeth went from the title of Princess and heir to the throne, to being declared a bastard. As a child she focused on her studies and the affection of her governess, Kat Ashley. If she did not know her mother's fate before, she surely learned about it when Henry also had his fifth wife Katherine Howard, a cousin of Elizabeth's mother Anne Boleyn, executed for having taken lovers. No doubt the gossip about Katherine also included Anne Boleyn's fate as well. Elizabeth, eight years at the time of her stepmother's execution, declared that she would never marry. It was not until the third act of succession in July 1543 toward the end of Henry's reign that, while still considered illegitimate, Elizabeth and Mary were restored to the succession after Edward. This was also ratified by Henry VIII's last will.

Elizabeth, whatever her status, received an excellent education that she took very seriously. Her tutor Roger Ascham stated that the young Elizabeth worked as hard on her studies as any man, and that she also had an excellent memory for anything she learned. In her sister Mary's reign, the Venetian ambassador wrote of Elizabeth's skill in languages, calling her a good scholar of Greek and Latin, adding that she could speak Latin, French, Spanish, and Italian.

Elizabeth's life was difficult during the reign of her father and became more so in the reigns of her half-brother Edward VI (1547–1553) and half-sister Mary I (1553–1558). After her father's death she lived with her last stepmother, Katherine Parr. But scandalously soon after her husband's death, Katherine married Thomas Seymour, younger uncle to the new king. The older Seymour brother, Edward, became Duke of Somerset and Lord Protector to the nine-year-old king. While in the dowager queen's household, Elizabeth had to deal with Seymour's sexual advances. The situation eventually became fraught enough that Katherine, pregnant with her first child, suggested it would be better for Elizabeth to live elsewhere. While the two maintained a friendly correspondence, Elizabeth never saw Katherine Parr again, as she died soon after giving birth to a daughter. Rumors spread that the new widower would marry Elizabeth, and some even claimed that Elizabeth was pregnant with Seymour's child.

While Elizabeth in fact was very cautious about any connection with Seymour, his behavior became increasingly dangerous, with counterfeiting money and plans to kidnap the young king. In, January 1549 he was arrested and sent to the Tower, as were members of Elizabeth's household. Both her governess Katherine Ashley and her treasurer Thomas Parry were lodged in the

Tower and in terror gave information about the goings on between Thomas Seymour and Elizabeth when she lived in the Dowager Queen's household.

The Lord Protector dispatched Sir Robert Tyrwhit and his wife to Hatfield to take charge of Elizabeth's household and wring a confession from her. Elizabeth refused; she wanted her innocence publicly proclaimed and her servants freed and returned to her. While Seymour was executed on March 20, 1549, Elizabeth at the age of fifteen survived through her intelligence and prudence. Elizabeth was intensely loyal and committed herself to protecting Ashley and Parry and having them return to her household.

The Duke of Somerset soon after lost his power and then his head. He was executed January 22, 1552, and John Dudley, Duke of Northumberland, became the most influential man in the reign of the young king. Elizabeth did well for the rest of her brother's reign, and William Cecil, Principal Secretary of State under the Duke of Northumberland, also was employed by Elizabeth as he supervised her accounts. This was the beginning of a very important working relationship that would continue for almost half a century. But in the spring of 1553 the fifteen-year-old Edward VI was very ill. The young king, either of his own initiative, or at Northumberland's suggestion, removed both of his sisters from the succession in favor of his cousin, Lady Jane Grey, granddaughter of Henry VIII's younger sister Mary, and recently married to Northumberland's youngest son Guildford. The reason given was that Mary was a Catholic and while Elizabeth was not, she might marry a foreign Catholic.

Since Edward was not yet of age and Henry's Act of Succession had the force of Parliament, this was illegal. Northumberland had hoped to have the king's two sisters under his control at the death of the king, but he failed, and many were deeply unhappy after Edward's death on July 6 to have Jane pronounced the next monarch. Mary proclaimed herself queen, Northumberland's troops deserted him, and she became queen without a battle. Mary was the old king's daughter and rightful heir and even those who were anti-Catholic supported her rightful succession. This meant unless Mary had a child of her own Elizabeth was the next heir.

Mary was the first queen regnant in England and Elizabeth learned a great deal about what to do, and what not to do, from watching Mary rule. Mary soon restored the realm to its obedience to Rome and, at the age of thirty-seven, was eager to marry so that she might produce an heir. The queen pressured Elizabeth to convert to Catholicism and attend Mass. While Elizabeth attended Catholic religious ceremonies on occasion she did so with clear reluctance.

While at first Mary welcomed Elizabeth warmly, the relationship between the two sisters worsened, and finally in December of 1553 Mary allowed Elizabeth to leave court. Mary announced that she would marry her cousin Philip of Spain, son of Charles V, a decision highly unpopular with many of the English people. A February 1554 rebellion against the marriage led by Sir Thomas Wyatt failed, and Elizabeth was in even more danger than she had been in her brother's reign, as any evidence of her collusion would lead to her death. Some of Mary's advisors, especially the Spanish ambassador Simon Renard, argued that such evidence was unnecessary. For the safety of Mary and her future husband Philip, Elizabeth should die, just as Lady Jane had already been executed after the Wyatt rebellion. Though Elizabeth was for a time in the Tower she managed to survive this crisis as well, and Philip came to believe it preferable to have Elizabeth as a potential ally.

In July 1554 Mary married Prince Philip. Within a few months many were convinced that she was pregnant. What proved to be a phantom pregnancy was disheartening for the queen. In February 1555 she began heresy trials, and over the course of three years more than three hundred people were burned to death. This policy was extremely unpopular. About 800 Protestants also fled the country. Philip convinced Mary to join in his war against France, and Calais, the last English holding at the end of the Hundred Years War, was lost in January 1558, which also greatly troubled the English. Elizabeth last saw Mary in February. On November 17 Mary died and Elizabeth was now queen of England.

In 1558 the country had a surprisingly smooth transition to Elizabeth, given the crises that had happened only five years earlier when Edward VI had died and Mary's hostility to Elizabeth as her heir. There was a rush of relief over the death of Mary and the endings of the burning of heretics. Many of the English, distressed by Mary's religious persecution and losing the war with France, were delighted with their new young queen, though some worried that her reign would be short and chaos would follow. There was deep anxiety over whether the reign of a twenty-five-year-old woman would be any more successful than the previous woman's rule.

Sir Thomas Smith, scholar, diplomatic, and for some years one of the Principal Secretaries, later wrote that when Elizabeth acceded the throne England was the weakest he had ever known, and he felt ashamed of both his country and his countrymen. Elizabeth began her rule working hard to put England on stronger footing. Her first step was to appoint Sir William Cecil, a man of great experience and commitment, as her Principal Secretary of State. He would be the most important man in her government largely due to Elizabeth's trust in him.

Elizabeth had a long and fruitful partnership with Cecil. He greatly influenced foreign policy from 1558 to 1572 while he was Principal Secretary. When he became Lord Treasurer and Baron Burghley, and Sir Francis Walsingham succeeded him as Secretary from 1573 to 1590, Elizabeth still consulted Cecil on foreign as well as domestic policy, and most ambassadors and agents continued to correspond with him as well as with Walsingham. Her other early appointments included Robert Dudley, son of the executed Duke of Northumberland, as Master of the Horse. He was eventually created Earl of Leicester. Her relationship with Dudley was based on personal affection, and for years he tried, though unsuccessfully, to convince her to marry him.

Sir Francis Knollys became the Vice-Chamberlain, and Nicholas Bacon her Lord Keeper. Elizabeth kept less than a third of Mary's councilors for her Privy Council and decided on a smaller one. She also excluded virtually all clergymen. The only one of note in her Council in her whole reign was John Whitgift, Archbishop of Canterbury, whom she appointed in the 1580s. She also had a completely new list of women of the Privy Chamber and ladies-in-waiting, as it was important to have women, especially at the beginning of the reign, she could trust. She kept many women who had been so loyal to her before she became queen, particularly Kat Ashley who became Chief Gentlewoman of the Privy Chamber. As her reign progressed, Thomas Radcliffe, the Earl of Sussex, Sir Christopher Hatton, and Sir Francis Walsingham became members of the Privy Council; Walsingham especially was a critical advisor to her.

Elizabeth's coronation was symbolically most important. The coronation procession included many pageants and Elizabeth publicly expressed her enjoyment of them all. It was difficult to find a bishop willing to perform the coronation ceremony. Finally, Owen Oglethorpe, Bishop of Carlisle, agreed. Elizabeth insisted that her coronation oath be administered from an English Bible, which William Cecil held up.

Elizabeth had many palaces. While Whitehall was her main base, she also was frequently at Hampton Court or Richmond. Many summers Elizabeth went on progress through some of the counties either visiting her rural properties or her wealthy subjects, who paid dearly for the honor.

As a new queen what was most important to Elizabeth was that she was queen of all of the English, not just the Protestants, and that she worked hard to bring about national unity. While Elizabeth may have hated her half-sister and all for which she stood, Elizabeth did not seek revenge on those who had supported her, nor did she allow those who had returned to power to take retribution. She wanted a united aristocracy behind her and managed to rally most of them to her cause. She wanted to be queen of an independent England, to encourage old industries to grow and to develop new industries, so the country would no longer be so dependent on imports from abroad. She wanted to encourage trade, and as the reign progressed that trade spread to Russia and the Middle East. She wanted to be queen of a strong England that remained peaceful and not feel threatened by the great Catholic powers on the continent, France and Spain.

Elizabeth cared about her subjects and was proud of how they cared about her. As her earlier biographer William Camden stated, "So far was she from giving way to any suspicion against her people, that she was many times wont to say, that she could believe nothing of her people which parents would not believe of their children" (Camden, 233).

There were two vital issues at the beginning of the reign. One was the succession, which her advisors and the English people hoped would be easily solved by getting the queen married—the question was to whom—and giving birth to a child, preferably male. Elizabeth had a variety of suitors: her former brother-in-law, Philip II; Philip's cousin, the Archduke Charles; James Hamilton, the Scottish Earl of Arran; Eric XIV of Sweden; and the sons of Catherine de Medici, both Henri Duke of Anjou, later Henri III; and François, Duke of Alençon, later Duke of Anjou. While at the beginning of her reign there was a strong popular interest in Erik of Sweden, Elizabeth expressed no enthusiasm; she also quickly declared it was impossible to consider marrying Philip. Robert Dudley was also a forceful suitor for her hand, but the shocking death of his wife Amy Robsart in 1560 made the possibility of this match quite problematic. Each suitor, however, also had many critics. Courtship and marriage negotiations continued for more than twenty years into the reign. But if no one could agree on the right husband for Elizabeth, and she had no child of her own, the succession was unsettled. According to the third act of succession and Henry VII's will, the descendants of Henry's older sister Margaret were excluded, and after Elizabeth the next heirs would be the descendants of his younger sister Mary, which included the younger sisters of the executed Jane Grey. Though Elizabeth claimed God would take care of England, her Parliaments, Council, and her subjects thought she should provide some care as well.

The other major issue at the beginning of the reign was religion. While Catholic Mary had ruled, Elizabeth had been the hope of the reformers, a hope only partially justified from their perspective once she became queen. After the constant changes the English people had seen in regard to religion, Elizabeth attempted a broadly based compromise. In 1559 Parliament defined the official religion of England and its relationship to the state in a series of statutes that began with Acts of Supremacy and Uniformity. Elizabeth's title was Supreme Governor of the Church, rather than Supreme Head of the Church, which had been held by her father and brother. For many members of Parliament, it would be blasphemy to have a woman Head of the Church. But Elizabeth agreed to the title, she said, because Christ was the Supreme Head of the Church, not a human being. And as Supreme Governor of the Church she did what she thought best.

Mass was yet again abolished. The Act of Uniformity returned England to the Edwardian Protestant form of worship. The form of the new service determined by the Act of Uniformity was the 1552 Book of Common Prayer with some alterations that allowed the sacrament of the Eucharist interpreted in many ways; people could understand Christ's words at the Last Supper any way they wished. The service was again in English, instead of the Latin of Mary's reign. In 1563, Convocations, the assembly of clergy, produced the Thirty-Nine Articles, which provided the Elizabethan Church with a doctrinal basis, with Parliamentary ratification in 1571. For Elizabeth this was now settled, and she wanted no further changes. But some Protestants felt that she had not taken the Church Settlement far enough.

As queen, Elizabeth regularly attended morning services in the royal chapel, and she wrote her own private prayers for her daily worship. While she defined herself publicly as a Protestant, Elizabeth also wanted some Catholic ceremonial and traditions within her Church both for personal and for political reasons. She loved elaborate Church music. She refused to believe that all images were idolatrous. She also wanted the Catholic powers to tolerate her and not launch a Holy Crusade against England, and she wanted the Lutheran Princes in Germany to support her so wanted to maintain a moderate position. Some elements of Church of England—such as vestments, crosses, and candlesticks—were similar to Catholic ritual. Elizabeth needed to reassure both Lutherans and Catholics that England was not a Calvinist country, and Elizabeth herself did not want an English Calvinist Church. At the beginning of her reign she argued successfully with the Archbishop of Canterbury and other church leaders over her use of a silver crucifix and candles in her royal chapel. Elizabeth insisted that the clergy wear vestments similar to those of Catholic priests, and she required them to continue many traditional ceremonies, such as the making of the sign of the cross in baptism and requiring parishioners to kneel for communion. Marriage for clergy was legal, but Elizabeth opposed the idea, especially for bishops. Having arrived at that Settlement, Elizabeth was satisfied, even if she did not find it ideal, and wanted it left alone. She did not desire the thorough reform in the Church that many of her divines and returned Marian exiles wanted. This was probably wise not only because of Elizabeth's own inclinations but because on her accession the majority of the population were still Catholic in belief in terms of their theology, though not in terms of obedience to the pope. Elizabeth's Protestant regime had to convince the people to leave their traditional beliefs and through preaching and education convert the country to Protestantism. Elizabeth's government was outstandingly successful at this task. As her reign progressed, however, she found she had to resist pressure from two different sides: Catholics and Puritans, who were Calvinist in their leanings.

She was able to work well with some of the church hierarchy and had a particularly fruitful relationship with her last Archbishop of Canterbury, John Whitgift; she had, however, problems with many of her bishops, some of whom felt Elizabeth did not support them adequately and she mistrusted the more zealous Protestants among them. She was in especial conflict with Edmund Grindal, who became Archbishop of Canterbury in 1575 with the support of both Burghley and Walsingham. The conflicts became so intense that in 1577 Elizabeth ordered him suspended from exercising his office. While he was not dismissed as archbishop, the suspension was never lifted; effectively the Church had no active leader until his death in 1583 when he was replaced with Whitgift.

The problems of religion and the succession were interconnected, especially since Elizabeth remained unmarried and refused to name an heir. By primogeniture, Elizabeth's Catholic cousin, Mary Stuart, queen of Scotland and the granddaughter of Henry's older sister Margaret, was the next heir. Some who refused to recognize the legality of Henry's marriage to Anne Boleyn argued that Mary Stuart was the rightful queen. Mary had been raised at the French court and eventually became the consort of Francis II. But after Francis' death in December 1560, Mary returned to Scotland. After the murder of her second husband, Henry Stuart, Lord Darnley, and the suspected complicity of her third husband James Hepburn, Lord Bothwell, Mary was imprisoned and forced to abdicate; she managed to escape and fled to England in 1568.

Elizabeth's problems with Catholic resurgence intensified when Mary Stuart arrived in England, presenting Elizabeth's government with what seemed an insoluble problem. Elizabeth did not want to return Mary to Scotland as queen with full power, nor did she want to see the Scots execute Mary. Allowing her to go on to France or Spain could enable Mary to return to Scotland with an army, which could be turned against England. Elizabeth felt she had no choice but to keep Mary in confinement. It turned out to be for nineteen years.

Mary's presence in England undermined the delicate religious balance, leading to the Northern Rebellion in 1569 headed by the Earls of Northumberland and Westmoreland. During Mary's captivity there were numerous plots to assassinate Elizabeth, free the Scottish queen, and place Mary on the English throne with the aid of foreign invasion. In the 1571 Ridolfi Plot conspirators hoped to have Mary marry Thomas Howard, Duke of Norfolk, and crown them king and queen of England after Elizabeth and Cecil were assassinated. The following year Norfolk was executed. By 1584 Protestants were so upset over the Scottish queen, they formed the Bond of Association, where signatories threatened Mary with death if Elizabeth was assassinated.

Other events greatly worried the English and demonstrated the connections between religion and politics. In 1570 Pope Pius V excommunicated Elizabeth, released all her subjects from any allegiance to her, and even threatened excommunication to any who obeyed her. This was frightening, though most English Catholics continued to be loyal to the queen. Another incident that greatly troubled the English was the massacre of thousands of Protestants in Paris on St. Bartholomew's Day August 24, 1572. Elizabeth put her whole court in mourning. In July 1584 the Protestant leader in the Netherlands, William the Silent, Prince of Orange was assassinated by Balthasar Gerard, a Catholic zealot, after Philip II of Spain put a price on William's head. The problems with Mary Stuart demonstrated the impact of religious division on international politics.

The 1586 conspiracy led by the young highly born Anthony Babington was yet another attempt to assassinate Elizabeth. Mary was put on trial for her involvement. After some months Elizabeth finally signed Mary's death warrant and the Scottish queen was executed on February 8, 1587. Mary Stuart's execution helped to convince Philip of Spain that he could conquer England and restore it to Catholicism without having a French queen as a result. Philip finally committed himself to the invasion in 1587, but the Spanish Armada was delayed for over year when Sir Francis Drake destroyed much of the Spanish fleet at Cadiz. In the summer of 1588, after many delays, Philip II launched the Armada under the command of Alonso Pérez de Guzmán y de Zúñiga-Sotomayor, Duke of Medina Sidonia. Against the advice of some of her councilors that she should stay safe in London, Elizabeth went to Tilbury Camp to encourage the assembled troops. There was great fear that the Armada might not be stopped at sea and there would be an invasion on land. The speech Elizabeth gave, stating that she had the heart and stomach of a king, was one of the most famous of her reign, though there are debates over what exactly she said. The English naval force was under the command of Charles Howard, Baron Howard of Effingham and later Earl of Nottingham, and Sir Francis Drake. There were eight hours of intense fighting, and then the Spanish decided to break off from the battle and retreat after a change in wind direction. Thus, a combination of English naval skill and bad weather foiled the invasion. There was great celebration and relief, and the English and their queen celebrated elaborately at St. Paul's on August 20, 1588 to give thanks to God for this great Protestant victory.

Though this was a high point for Elizabeth, in a number of ways, the final fifteen years of Elizabeth's reign after the defeat of the Armada were difficult. Her most trusted advisors died. To her great personal grief, she lost Robert Dudley, Earl of Leicester, in 1588 soon after the Armada victory. Walsingham died in 1590. Burghley's death in 1598 was also especially difficult for Elizabeth. The economy suffered from the drain of the long, expensive struggle in Ireland that had been going on since the 1560s but finally reached crisis proportions in the later 1590s as Hugh O'Neill, Earl of Tyrone led a rebellion. Continued support to the Netherlands was also costly.

These foreign policy expenses were especially problematic as the 1590s suffered from bad harvests and inflation. Ongoing struggles with Puritans over the religious settlement were also divisive, as were the factions in Elizabeth's court. With the deaths of the Earl of Leicester and Sir Francis Walsingham, and William Cecil's declining health, there were serious power struggles among some of the younger men at court for Elizabeth's favor, especially Robert Devereux, Earl of Essex and Sir Robert Cecil, Burghley's second son. These factions, with clear ideological components, hardened and became detrimental to Elizabeth's ability to rule.

In 1594 the Earl of Essex accused Elizabeth's physician, Roderigo Lopez, of Portugese Jewish background though outwardly an Anglican, of planning to poison the queen. Though the evidence may have been problematic, he was found guilty and executed. At his trial the Attorney-General Sir Edward Coke spoke extensively about his secret Judaism. That spring the late Christopher Marlowe's play, *The Jew of Malta*, first performed in 1592, was performed to sell-out crowds, and William Shakespeare composed *The Merchant of Venice*. Anti-Jewish sentiment was paralleled by a belief that the relatively few Africans in England were one cause of the economic problems because they were allegedly taking jobs away from the English. In 1601 Elizabeth ordered blacks in England to return to Africa, though this did not happen. In 1563 Parliament had passed the second witchcraft statute, more severe than the earlier one of 1542, though less than the 1604 one passed by her successor James I. Prosecutions occurred throughout the reign, most intensely in the 1590s.

Her relationship with her last favorite, the Earl of Essex, was especially difficult, and he perceived himself as Robert Cecil's enemy. While Cecil saw England's position as one of defense, Essex believed his country's natural role was the champion of Europe against Spain at whatever cost. Alternately Essex cajoled and threatened Elizabeth to adopt his policies, award him more power, and reward his followers. Essex's aggression came to a head over who would go to Ireland in 1599 to fight the increasingly successful Hugh O'Neill, Earl of Tyrone. Essex's campaign there to subdue the rebels was disastrous. The disgrace he faced when he returned to England without leave eventually led him to stage a rebellion against the queen in 1601. It failed, and Essex was executed.

But a flowering in literary cultural development also marked the latter part of Elizabeth's reign. The work of such men as Edmund Spenser and William Shakespeare must have drawn inspiration from the extraordinary woman who ruled England both as a Virgin Queen and mother of her people. And while literature, and especially drama, was most remarkable, architecture, music, and portrait painting also flourished. Overseas trade expanded along with burgeoning interest in expansion and colonization, especially by Sir Walter Raleigh and his older half-brother Sir Humphrey Gilbert, though this also signified the beginning of involvement in the slave trade.

Elizabeth aged visibly after the Essex rebellion and his subsequent execution. She held the final Parliament of her reign that same year. On November 30, 1601, Elizabeth addressed members of the House of Commons in what became known as her "Golden Speech," where she stated that the glory of her crown was the love of her subjects. She also assured them that while there might have been rulers mightier and wiser than she, they had never had, or would have, any that loved them more.

Though her physicians could not name a specific complaint, by the beginning of 1603 her health began to fail; she died on March 24, 1603. Elizabeth had always refused to name an heir stating God would protect England. Though had she died earlier there might well have been strife and bloodshed, her cousin James VI of Scotland, Mary Stuart's son, peacefully ascended the throne of England.

PART I

Politics and Religion

CHAPTER 2

The Coronation

Elizabeth became queen on November 17, 1558. Messengers went to Hatfield to inform her, while Nicholas Heath, Mary I's Chancellor and the Archbishop of York, informed Parliament. Five days later Elizabeth left Hatfield for the Charterhouse just outside the city of London's walls. The Lord Mayor, with other dignitaries, met her to congratulate her. But when Edmund Bonner, the Bishop of London, who had encouraged the burning of the heretics in Mary's reign, came to kiss her hand, she showed her disgust by snatching it away and turning from him. Soon the Council asked him to resign his bishopric, but he refused and was imprisoned for refusing to take the Oath of Supremacy. While there were many calls for his execution Elizabeth refused; he stayed under constraint, however, until his death in 1569.

After six days at the Charterhouse Elizabeth entered London to great cheers. As the new queen she arranged for a formal funeral worthy of a monarch for Mary. She asked John White, Bishop of Winchester, to preach the funeral sermon, but was not pleased when he stated that a living dog was preferable to a dead lion. Clearly, he was referring to the new queen Elizabeth as a dog but the dead queen Mary as the noble lion. He was placed under house arrest for one month. Elizabeth spent Christmas at Whitehall and at the church service insisted that the Host not be elevated, to the great dismay of many of Mary's Catholic bishops. Two days later she issued a proclamation that church services should be conducted in English (Fig. 2.1).

One of the most immediate issues facing Elizabeth and her advisors was planning her coronation. It would be only the second coronation of a queen regnant, the first being Mary five years earlier. Elizabeth already knew the astrologer John Dee and asked him to cast her horoscope to determine the

Fig. 2.1 Queen Elizabeth wearing crown private collection

most auspicious day for her coronation; he named Sunday January 15. At least in this instance Dee was successful at his craft, as Elizabeth had a long and often successful reign. Robert Dudley, whom Elizabeth had immediately appointed her Master of the Horse, may well have been involved in coronation planning, and he had long known Dee.

One difficulty for the coronation was which bishop would agree to perform the ceremony given the great anger with the religious changes she had wrought. There was at that time no Archbishop of Canterbury, as Reginald Pole had died within twelve hours of his cousin Queen Mary. Nicholas Heath, Archbishop of York, refused as did others of Mary's bishops. Owen Oglethorpe, Bishop of Carlisle, finally agreed as Oglethorpe argued that Elizabeth would be pushed further into the arms of the heretics if no bishop assented. Elizabeth insisted that her coronation oath be administered from an English Bible.

On January 12 Elizabeth left Whitehall and took a royal barge down the Thames River to the Tower of London, beautiful music being played for her while she traveled. The Tower was where the monarch traditionally stayed prior to the coronation, symbolizing the new ruler's control of the nation. A few years earlier she had been lodged in the Tower as a prisoner fearing she would die; now she was waiting for what was surely the most important day of her life. That night was the first in a series of coronation feasts. They feasted in the Tower the following night, with dancing as well.

Twenty-five years earlier her mother Anne Boleyn had been brought through the London streets on the way to her coronation. Henry's queen had been pregnant so even though for her first time she was in her mother's womb, in a sense Elizabeth had already experienced being carried through the streets. The next part of the coronation celebration was a procession through London and the entertainments as on January 14 Elizabeth moved through the city.

As she got into her gold adorned chariot, Elizabeth, dressed in cloth of gold with her hair hanging loose and with a gold circlet, looked to the sky and gave God her enthusiastic thanks for being so merciful in saving her for this joyful time. On horseback Robert Dudley accompanied Elizabeth's chariot as it moved through the London streets. She stopped frequently to talk with people, especially at every pageant and exhibit, where she would give thanks. Much of the rest of court rode behind them. At Fenchurch a gorgeously dressed little boy presented the official welcome of the city to the queen. Elizabeth listened with rapt attention. People swarmed the queen's procession as she went through the streets of London; many people gave the new queen gifts. For example, a poor woman handed the young queen a branch of rosemary, for remembrance, which not only symbolized memory but also faithfulness. As she traveled there were many entertainments, often with life-sized figurines against diorama-like backgrounds.

At Gracechurch Street's main gate were three stages. On the lowest were actors portraying Henry VII and his wife Elizabeth of York; on the next was Henry VIII and Elizabeth's mother Anne Boleyn. At the top was a representation of Elizabeth standing on her own. There was music and more speeches, and many garlands of red and white roses with a pageant celebrating the uniting of Lancaster and York.

The next pageant was at Cornhill, where a child representing Elizabeth had a sign saying "the Seat of Worthy Governance" (Seccombe, 375). With the actual queen and the model queen watching, four people representing Virtues stamped on their opposite Vices under their feet: Pure Religion stamped on Superstition and Ignorance; the one representing Love of Subjects got to tread on Rebellion and Insolency; Wisdom stood upon Folly and Vain-Glory, while Justice got to stamp on Adulation and Bribery.

When Elizabeth came to the upper end of Cheapside the Lord Mayor presented her with the city's gift: a purse made of crimson satin embroidered in gold. A thousand marks of gold was inside. Elizabeth eloquently thanked everyone; the crowd was jubilant. Elizabeth smiled when someone recalled the old king, Henry VIII. When Elizabeth heard that the next pageant represented Time, she told the crowd that she praised God that Time had brought her to where she was that day. Father Time, an old man with artificial wings and carrying a scythe, presented the queen with his daughter Truth, who wore white silk; she handed Elizabeth an English Bible. The new queen kissed the book and brought it to her breasts.

At Ludgate Elizabeth was presented with a figurine in a seat dressed in Parliamentary robes, a crown, and scepter. A sign stated that this was the Biblical Deborah, judge and restorer of Israel. On either side were six other figurines representing the nobility, the clergy, and the common people. Another sign explained that Deborah was with her estates, consulting about good government. A child explained that this pageant was to remind people that God had before sent women to nobly rule.

Elizabeth then went on to Temple Bar, and passed the Children of Christ's Hospital, where children stood with the hospital's governors and one child gave an oration for Elizabeth, who paid great attention. She told the children that she was very thankful for the presentation, telling them that "we are all orphans"—the children and her—a fascinating way to bring solidarity with them and an insight into how she understood herself. Elizabeth ended up at Whitehall where she spent the night, agreeing there to free some prisoners. During the procession she assured the people "that I will be as good unto you as ever queen was to her people," adding "And persuade yourselves that for the safety and quietness of you all I will not spare, if need be, to spend my blood" (Elizabeth I, *Collected Works*, 54).

The next morning the procession went from Whitehall to Westminster for the ceremony itself. When Elizabeth entered, her cousin Margaret, Countess of Lennox, the daughter of Henry VIII's older sister Margaret, carried her train. Elizabeth sat across from the high altar where she listened to a sermon. Elizabeth then took oaths offered by Bishop Oglethorpe to keep the laws and customs of England. When the bishop administered the coronation oath, it was with an English Bible as she had insisted, which William Cecil held up. Elizabeth was anointed with holy oil. She then received the symbols of power: gloves, sword, scepter, and the orb. The bishop crowned her and put the scepter in her hand. When Elizabeth left the Abbey, she was smiling widely and greeting the people who cheered her. This had been a wonderful moment for her.

Elizabeth then dined at a beautifully decorated Westminster Hall with two hundred guests. The banquet was organized by her cousin Thomas Howard, Duke of Norfolk, dressed in silver tissue, and Henry FitzAlan, Earl of Arundel, in cloth of gold. Everything Elizabeth ate Norfolk or Arundel carved for her. The seating for the guests was done with strict precedence to rank. There were four enormous tables. Elizabeth changed for the banquet into a dress of purple velvet. She sat down at the high table at about 3 p.m. after publicly washing her hands. The servants were all dressed in red and as food was served beautiful music was played.

During the feast Sir Edward Dymoke rode in wearing a full suit of armor and three times proclaimed that if there were any who denied that his sovereign Queen Elizabeth was not the legitimate Queen of England, he would maintain it to the death. Each time he threw down his gauntlet as he spoke. When no one challenged him, Sir Edward told the queen he was taking his leave, and Elizabeth drank to his health and rewarded him with a silver-gilt cup worth 200 crowns. Being the monarch's champion had been in the Dymoke family for centuries. Dymoke had earlier participated at the coronations of Edward VI and Mary. After the banquet there was dancing. Elizabeth did not leave to return to Whitehall until 9 p.m. There was supposed to be a joust the next day, but it was postponed as all the celebrations had exhausted Elizabeth.

CHAPTER 3

The Privy Council

When Elizabeth became queen in 1558, the Privy Council, whose main function was to support the monarch's decisions on a range of domestic and international issues, had about fifty members. But Elizabeth believed that too many different opinions would not be useful, and reduced the number of members to nineteen, and later to eleven. It was solely up to the Queen to appoint members. She continued to have some nobles on the Privy Council but also appointed talented men of gentry background. Many of the men who were Privy Councilors also served in Parliament, either in the House of Commons or the House of Lords. Some members were greatly honored by being named a knight of the Order of the Garter. There were twenty-four members at any time. Beyond that, the king and his oldest son were automatically members, but this was not an issue in the reign of Elizabeth. Early in Elizabeth's reign the Council met at least weekly, sometimes three times a week; by the end of the reign it was meeting almost every day (Fig. 3.1).

The Privy Council also sat judicially as the Court of Star Chamber on Wednesdays and Fridays; on these days Councilors commuted by horse or barge to Westminster. This was a special court set up in the late fifteenth century that had no jury, just the council members and sometimes the ruler as judges. It was originally established to provide fair enforcement of the law for people who were so socially or politically powerful that other courts might be hesitant to convict them of their crimes. By the time of Charles I, its proceedings were viewed as arbitrary and used to oppress those in opposition. Parliament ended it at the beginning of the Civil war.

Privy Council meetings were run by the Principal Secretary. By the end of Elizabeth's reign the position was known as the Secretary of State, though the

Fig. 3.1 Burghley, Elizabeth, Walsingham private collection

term Principal Secretary was also used into the late seventeenth century. There were times during Elizabeth's reign when there were two principal secretaries. The Principal Secretary would begin the meetings with a list of issues that needed to be discussed, though this was not like a modern agenda that would be circulated to members.

There were also Clerks of the Privy Council, essential in making sure that the Privy Council was run efficiently. When Elizabeth became queen there were three clerks; a fourth was added in 1576. They were not all on duty at the Council at the same time but relieved each other; the four of them helped everything to run smoothly. Clerks were paid a salary of £50 a year. The clerks took notes so they could later aid the Principal Secretary with the letters or instructions he had to send out. This position was considered important, and most of the clerks were very talented, possessing both linguistic and diplomatic skills. Several of them also served as ambassadors and many were knighted as a reward for service. When delicate issues of foreign policy were discussed sometimes the clerks would be excused from the meetings. All notes from the meetings were kept in a large chest.

There was also the Keeper of the Council Chamber. He prepared the room where the meetings would take place. He could bring in freshly cut flowers and replace the cushions when necessary. He made sure there were supplies, such as blank pre-bound volumes and pens and ink. He was also responsible for keeping the chest safely guarded and properly moved when the court traveled.

The most significant members of the Council—William Cecil, Lord Burghley, Sir Francis Walsingham, Robert Dudley, Earl of Leicester, Thomas Radcliffe, Earl of Sussex, and Sir Christopher Hatton—attended meetings most often, served on committees, made reports to other members, and had the ear of the queen. Writing soon after her death, John Clapham stated that "and as she was beloved of the common people, so was she no less honored by her nobility and especially by her privy councilors.... A rare thing that a woman sitting in council amongst the gravest and best experienced men of her time should be able to examine and individually to control their consultations" (Clapham, 69–70). While Elizabeth listened to her Councilors, she believed she should make the final decisions.

Principal Secretaries

Sir William Cecil, Later Lord Burghley (1520–1598)—Served from 1558–1572; 1590–1596, Member 1558–1598

The very first day of her reign, Elizabeth made Cecil her Principal Secretary. He was a devoted Protestant and completely loyal to his queen. Forty-two years old when Elizabeth became queen, Cecil had been active at Court in the reign of her younger brother Edward, first working for Edward Seymour, Duke of Somerset and then for John Dudley, Duke of Northumberland. Cecil was able to make peace with Mary but was much less involved in public affairs during the Catholic queen's reign. During this time, however, he also got to know Elizabeth. In 1550 he became her surveyor.

Clearly by the time Elizabeth became queen she had great trust in him. She told Cecil at her first Council meeting: "I give you this charge that you shall be of my Privy Council and content to take pains for me and my realm. This judgment I have of you that you will not be corrupted by any manner of gift and that you will be faithful to the state; and that without respect of my private will, you will give me that counsel which you think best and if you shall know anything necessary to me of secrecy, you shall show it to myself only" (Elizabeth I, *Collected Works*, 51). Mary's final Principal Secretary, John Boxall, co-operated with Cecil to aid the transition, though Boxall was later imprisoned in 1560 for some years after his refusal to take the Oath of Supremacy. Cecil remained as Principal Secretary until July 1572. He handled all the routine matters of the Council and managed the Council's relationship with the queen. He was responsible for the administration of the queen's foreign policy and concerned with national defense issues and finances. In 1571 Elizabeth made Cecil Lord Burghley, the only one of Elizabeth's ministers to receive a peerage. In 1572, he also became a Knight of the Garter. That year he left the position of Principal Secretary to become Lord Treasurer, administering all royal finances. He continued as a member of the Privy Council and continued much of his other work as well. His own two main secretaries were Michael Hicks and Vincent Skynner. In 1590, after the death of Sir Francis Walsingham, he was the Acting Secretary until July 1596 when his son Robert took over. Given Burghley's health at the time, it is quite likely that he had substantial help from Robert.

Cecil was educated at Cambridge University where he became good friends with the classical scholar John Cheke. Cecil's first wife was Cheke's sister Mary, whom he married in 1541 and they had one child Thomas, but Mary died only two years later. He then married Mildred Cooke, the eldest daughter of Anthony Cooke, in 1546. It was a very happy marriage until her death in 1589, and Cecil greatly appreciated his wife's wisdom and advice. At the end of his life, in 1598, the queen was extremely worried about Burghley's health, and sent him a cordial with wishes for his recovery, saying she prayed every day for his longer life, or else, she would need a cordial too. Elizabeth came to visit him and served him broth at his bedside. As he was dying, he told his son, "Serve God by serving the Queen" (Doran, *Elizabeth I & Her Circle*, 243). Soon after the death of the queen John Clapham wrote of Burghley, "His credit with the Queen was such as his wisdom and integrity well deserved" (Clapham, 79).

Sir Thomas Smith (1513–1577)—Served as Secretary 1572–1576, Member 1571–1576

Smith was an early Protestant and in Edward VI's reign served as a Clerk of the Privy Council. While he went into retirement in Mary's reign, he was welcomed back to court by Elizabeth at the encouragement of William Cecil, a close friend. Smith served as ambassador to France, from 1562–1566, though it was difficult as he came into conflict with the previous ambassador, Sir Nicholas Throckmorton, who stayed in France for a time past his recall. In 1571 Smith became a member of the Privy Council and then was briefly sent back to France. In 1572 when the new Lord Burghley became Lord Treasurer, Smith became Principal Secretary. But Smith never achieved the power that Burghley had, and though now Lord Treasurer, Burghley continued in his work of formulating policy. Smith was often irritated that the queen refused to sign papers until she had discussed the issues with Burghley. Smith was the author of *De Republica Anglorum: the Maner of Governement or Policie of the Realme of England*, published after his death in 1577.

Sir Francis Walsingham (1532–1590) Served as Secretary and Member End of 1573–1590

For the last years of Smith's term as Secretary Walsingham also held the office, and he became one of the most powerful men at Court, holding the office until his death. As a dedicated Protestant, Walsingham fled England in the reign of Mary I, returning in the early reign of Elizabeth. In 1570 he became the ambassador to France, and was there during the St. Bartholomew's Day Massacre, when thousands of French Protestants were slaughtered in Paris. The massacre began with orders from Charles IX and the queen mother Catherine de Medici for the murders of many leading Protestants and then escalated. Walsingham did all he could to shelter people in his embassy. After the massacre he repeatedly requested that he return to England, which he was allowed to do in 1573. By the end of the year he was appointed a member of the Privy Council and Principal Secretary. As Secretary he developed a highly effective spy system to keep Elizabeth safe, especially with Mary Stuart living in England under house arrest and involved in plotting against Elizabeth. Walsingham supported Mary's execution as early as 1572 in response to the Ridolfi Plot (see Chapter 9). He was one of the commissioners at Mary's trial in 1586 after the Babington Plot. During the trial, Mary accused him of faking evidence against her, but he was able to amply demonstrate her guilt.

Walsingham and Ursula St. Barbe had one surviving child Frances who married Sir Philip Sidney in 1583 when she was fifteen. After his death, she subsequently married first Robert Devereux, Earl of Essex and then Richard Burke, fourth Earl of Clanricarde. They were married until her death in 1632. Her father, who despite his ill health in his last years, continued working until his death in April 1590.

Thomas Wilson (1524–1581) Member and Second Secretary 1577–1581

Thomas Wilson, a committed Protestant, left England when Mary became queen, but she summoned him back in 1558. When he refused to return Cardinal Reginald Pole, Archbishop of Canterbury, proclaimed him a heretic to the Roman Inquisition. Wilson was arrested and tortured but escaped when a mob destroyed the building where he was kept. He returned to England at the beginning of Elizabeth's reign and served at various times as ambassador to Spain, Portugal, the Netherlands, and France. He was appointed to the Privy Council in 1577 and became second Secretary under Walsingham with the replacement of Smith. Wilson was also the author of a number of works, including *The Rule of Reason*, and *The Arte of Rhetorique*.

William Davison (d. 1608) Served as Secretary 1586–1587

By the mid-1570s William Davison was working with Walsingham, who thought highly of him. In the 1570s and '80's Davison was sent on missions to Scotland, Brussels, and the Netherlands. Davison became a member of the Privy Council in the fall of 1586. Once he had become a Privy Councilor, he also became one of the commissioners for Mary Stuart's trial. Davison married Catherine Spelman about 1570 and they had two daughters and four sons who lived to adulthood.

Davison was secretary for only six months from September 1586–February 1587, which might suggest that he was appointed to protect Burghley and Walsingham during the period of the trial of Mary Stuart and the pressures on Queen Elizabeth to sign Mary's death warrant. From mid-December to mid-February Walsingham was ill and away from court and Burghley had an accident as he was riding in January that kept him in bed for more than a month. Though Davison was very junior to both of these men, it was Davison who had the job of convincing the queen to sign Mary Stuart's death warrant. Though Elizabeth eventually signed it she told him not to send it on without her express consent, but once Burghley learned about it, he convinced members of the Council to sign off on it and send it themselves to spare Elizabeth. The queen was furious when she heard of Mary Stuart's execution, and she sent Davison to the Tower. At the end of March, he was tried in Star Chamber. The verdict was that he had abused Elizabeth's trust. He was suspended—never formally dismissed—from the office of Secretary, sent back to the Tower, and a large fine was levied. He was released from the Tower in October 1588 and never paid his fine. Moreover, he continued to be paid his salary as Secretary until the end of his life, dying in 1608.

Robert Cecil (1563–1612) Served as Secretary 1596–1612, Member 1593–1612

The son of William Cecil and his second wife Mildred, Robert Cecil was born with some deformities, being very short and hunchbacked. But Cecil had a great intellect and was deeply loved by both his parents. Cecil was named to the Privy Council in 1593 but after the death of Walsingham, Cecil worked very hard to help his father who had once again been tasked with being Secretary. Some scholars argue that the younger Cecil was effectively the Secretary some years before his formal appointment in 1596. In her last decade the queen depended on Robert Cecil a great deal, and he headed a faction strongly opposed to that of Robert Devereux, Earl of Essex. In 1598 Cecil went to France to negotiate with Henry IV of France. Cecil was deeply involved in matters of national security and in keeping his queen safe, a role for which he had been trained by his father and Walsingham. In August 1589 he married Elizabeth Brooke, a goddaughter of Queen Elizabeth. Cecil was very much in love with Elizabeth, and it appears to have been a happy match, cut short by her death only eight years later. Cecil's fortunes continued to rise in the next reign when James gave him the title of Earl of Salisbury. Cecil continued as Secretary until his death in 1612.

Sir John Herbert (c.1540–1617) Served as Secretary 1600–1606, Member 1600–1619

John Herbert was educated at Oxford and became known for his proficiency in several languages, so he was sent on several diplomatic missions to such places as Denmark, Poland, and the Netherlands. At court he was very much in the Cecil circle. In 1590 he was appointed a Clerk to the Privy Council. He accompanied Robert Cecil to France in 1598 and the two became very close. He was appointed a member of the Privy Council in 1600 and became the second Secretary, working closely with Cecil. After Cecil's death, Herbert withdrew from public life.

SOME OF THE CLERKS OF THE PRIVY COUNCIL

Bernard Hampton (d. 1572) Clerk, 1551–1572

Bernard Hampton was a Clerk of the Privy Council for the last two years of the reign of Edward VI and during Mary's reign. He was fluent in Spanish and was named Spanish secretary to the Council during Mary's reign. This skill was useful in Elizabeth's reign as well, as Elizabeth appointed Hampton to work with the Spanish ambassador Guerau de Spes on some issues dealing with a ship convoy. De Spes was pleased that he was working with Hampton rather than Cecil because, as he wrote to Philip II, he considered Hampton a friend. Because of their friendly relationship several months later the Privy Council asked him to deal with de Spes again over some letters. That Hampton got along pleasantly with de Spes never put his clear loyalty into question, and he did a lot of work for William Cecil beyond his position as a clerk, including helping with Parliamentary committees. Of the three clerks at the beginning of Elizabeth's reign, he was the one who lasted the longest, dying in 1572. The following year his widow Catherine was given a lease of land for 21 years in consideration of his long service as a Clerk of the Privy Council for the same number of years.

Francis Allen (c.1518–1570), Clerk 1553–1570

Francis Allen may have attended Cambridge University. In 1540 he became a licensed public notary and was described as a scholar. By 1543 he was a secretary to Bishop Stephen Gardiner, the Chancellor of the University. Gardiner was in the Tower from 1548 through the rest of Edward VI's reign, and, at some point during this time, Allen became part of the household of Princess Mary. He accompanied her to London when she became queen. Soon after her accession he was awarded a grant for life because of his service to the queen and was also appointed a Clerk of the Privy Council. He stayed in this position after the accession of Elizabeth, dying in 1570.

William Smith, Clerk 1553–1566

William Smith had been in Mary's service before she became queen and he was also named a Clerk of the Privy Council, a position he kept in the reign of Elizabeth. Nothing else appears to be known about him.

Edmund Tremayne (c.1525–1582), Clerk 1571–1582

In Mary I's reign, Tremayne was in the service of Edward Courtenay, Earl of Devon. He was sent to the Tower in March 1554 as a suspect in the Wyatt rebellion. Tremayne was tortured but refused to provide any evidence against either Courtenay or Princess Elizabeth. He was released in January 1555 and spent some time on the continent. Once Elizabeth became queen, Tremayne's fortunes shifted. He was a Member of the 1559 Parliament and some later ones, and he was given a number of appointments, including being tasked to write a report on Ireland in 1569. In May 1571 he became Clerk of the Privy Council.

Tremayne's cousin was Sir Francis Drake, and the queen asked Tremayne to inventory the treasure unloaded from the *Golden Hind* in October 1580. So that the Spanish would not know the complete inventory Tremayne and Drake were very careful about what they listed and Elizabeth told Tremayne to let Drake take some of the treasure for himself before there was any accounting. In the end, only the queen and Drake knew just how much treasure Drake had brought back, much of it taken from the Spanish. When Bernadino de Mendoza, the Spanish ambassador, charged Drake with cruelty toward the Spanish, Elizabeth tasked Tremayne with investigating the allegations, and he then declared his cousin innocent.

Robert Beale (1541–1601), Appointed Clerk 1572

Robert Beale seriously studied law from about the age of twenty. Though he never received a degree he had excellent training and was a very able worker. As a committed Protestant, he had been among those who fled England when Mary I was queen. In Elizabeth's reign he was in Paris in the early 1560s when Sir Henry Norris was ambassador. When the post was taken over by Sir Francis Walsingham, Beale stayed on as his formal secretary. Beale married Edith St. Barbe, the sister of Walsingham's wife Ursula. Sir Thomas Smith had high praise for Beale, and Walsingham also was impressed by his work. When Walsingham returned from France, the queen appointed Beale to be a Clerk of the Privy Council, and for most of his tenure working for the Privy Council, Beale was the leading clerk. He wrote a book about his duties: *A treatise of the office of a councellor and principall secretarie to her majestie.* As well as his work as clerk, he had several diplomatic appointments, such as serving as special ambassador to the Low Countries in 1576. Beale was so highly regarded that at times when Walsingham was absent from court, he served as acting principal secretary.

Henry Cheke (c.1548–1586) Appointed Clerk 1576–1581

Henry Cheke was the eldest son of Sir John Cheke and Mary Hill, who had long been in service to Elizabeth. William Cecil's first wife Mary was John Cheke's sister and having Lord Burghley as his uncle proved important, especially with Cheke's father's early death in 1557. He often asked his uncle to help him find work at court, especially as his finances were in great difficulty. In 1576 he was appointed Clerk to the Privy Council, which provided good experience as well as income. He left that post in 1581 when he was appointed secretary to the Council of the North.

Sir Thomas Wilkes (c.1545–1598) Appointed Clerk 1576

Thomas Wilkes received a B.A. from Oxford in 1573, and soon after was appointed as secretary to the new ambassador to France, Valentine Dale. In 1576 he was appointed as a Clerk of the Privy Council. In 1586–1587 Elizabeth sent him to the Netherlands to report on Robert Dudley, the Earl of Leicester's term as Governor-General. Wilkes was not impressed, and Leicester was furious with him. When both were back at court, Leicester managed to have Wilkes suspended from his role as Clerk, and he was not able to resume his clerkship until after Leicester's death in September 1588. In 1590 he was again sent to the Netherlands, and Elizabeth knighted him for his service in 1591. He made further diplomatic trips to the Netherlands and France in the 1590s. He died while traveling with Robert Cecil to France for another diplomatic mission.

Sir William Waad (1546–1623) Appointed Clerk in 1583

William Waad was the son of Armagil Waad, who had served as a Clerk of the Privy Council in the reign of Edward VI. William Cecil had been a friend of his father and sponsored Waad's continental travel in the 1570s. Waad was deeply loyal to Lord Burghley and sent him many helpful letters during his travels, eventually becoming part of the French embassy and gathering intelligence for Burghley. Waad's excellent language skills, including French, Italian, and Latin, as well as his negotiation skills, meant he was frequently sent abroad for the government. Burghley and Walsingham worked to have him appointed a Clerk of the Privy Council in 1583. He continued to go on difficult diplomatic missions, including to Spain in 1584 to explain the reasons for ambassador Bernardino de Mendoza's expulsion, and in 1585 to demand, unsuccessfully, the return of conspirator Thomas Morgan. In 1587 he was sent to France after the execution of Mary Stuart to discuss the situation with Henri III. After 1587 he stayed in England where his work as clerk had him investigating dissidents and subversives. Waad also served in Parliament. By the end of Elizabeth's reign, he was strongly allied with Robert Cecil and continued his service in James's reign.

Anthony Ashley (1552–1628) Appointed Clerk 1587

Anthony Ashley traveled when he was young and learned several foreign languages. He then trained at the Middle Temple. His father was in service to Christopher Hatton, who secured for him the post of Clerk of the Privy Council. He also served in Parliament. At the request of the Privy Council he translated and supplemented Lucas Waghnaer's collection of maritime charts, published in 1588 as *The Mariners Mirrour*. A few years after Hatton died in 1591, Burghley accused Ashley of fraud and embezzlement, and late in the reign he was suspended from his position but was reappointed with James' accession.

Sir Daniel Rogers (c.1538–1591) Appointed Clerk 1587

Daniel's father, John Rogers, was burnt as a heretic in Mary's reign. Early in Elizabeth's reign Rogers received a B.A. and M.A. from Oxford. He then went on to Paris for most of the 1560s studying and serving as a steward in Sir Henry Norris's ambassadorial household, and then working for Walsingham when he replaced Norris. He was part of Walsingham's circle for the next two decades. During the 1570s Rogers went on numerous diplomatic missions to the Netherlands. In 1587 he became a Clerk of the Privy Council, a position he held for the rest of his life, though he was also often sent on diplomatic missions.

Sir Thomas Smith (c.1556–1609) Appointed Clerk 1595–1605

Thomas Smith was no relation to the Thomas Smith who served as Secretary of the Council from 1572–1576. Through the Earl of Leicester's patronage, he was appointed secretary to Leicester's stepson, Robert Devereux, Earl of Essex, possibly as early as 1585–1586. He traveled regularly with Essex; while Essex was leading an army in Normandy in 1591, he often sent Smith back to England to calm Elizabeth's anger over his actions. Smith assumed many delicate tasks for Essex who greatly trusted him. In September 1595 Essex managed to have Smith appointed a Clerk of the Privy Council. But as a Clerk Smith also had to develop a good working relationship with Robert Cecil, and by 1599 he was clearly looking to Cecil for patronage. Cecil's support of Smith was important in James' reign, where Smith was appointed to a variety of offices.

Sir Thomas Edmondes (d. 1639) Appointed Clerk 1601

Thomas Edmonds came from Plymouth and apparently was at court from the 1580s. Walsingham appointed Edmonds to be secretary to Sir Henry Unton during his embassy to France 1591–1592. While Unton returned home in June 1592, Edmonds remained in France as the English chargé d'affaires until 1596. When Unton returned as ambassador in late 1595 Edmondes was again his secretary for a few months but, in the summer of 1596, he was recalled to England. Edmondes was again dispatched to Paris in September 1597, and he was again chargé d'affaires from May 1598 until Henry Neville arrived as resident ambassador in May 1599. Edmondes was Elizabeth's representative at the conference at Boulogne, which attempted to negotiate peace between Spain and England. Henri IV of France also participated. Though the attempt to end the long, languishing Anglo-Spanish war failed, the French king wrote to Elizabeth of his admiration for Edmondes. Elizabeth agreed with Henri's assessment, and appointed Edmondes Clerk of the Privy Council in 1601. Edmondes was knighted by James I in May 1603 and continued his impressive diplomatic career. In 1617 he became a member of the Privy Council.

Members—Listed Chronologically

Members Who Had Been Appointed Prior to the Reign of Elizabeth and Were Reappointed in November 1558

William Paulet, Marquess of Winchester (c.1475–1572), Member 1536–1572

The Marquess of Winchester served on Henry VIII's Privy Council as well as those of all three of his children. He also served as Lord Treasurer for Edward VI and Mary, as well as for Elizabeth. In Elizabeth's reign he worked diligently to have the office of the Lord Treasurer be the central office for royal finances and the advisor to the Privy Council on all financial matters. Winchester helped to make the office of Lord Treasurer a central post instead of the unimportant position it was earlier in the century. He initiated a number of financial reforms. Elizabeth thought highly enough of him that early in her reign she joked that if only he were a young man—by this time he was in his early 80s so she could joke safely—she would consider him the best match for her in England. Winchester retired to Basing House in the summer of 1570, dying there in 1572 at the great age of ninety-seven.

Sir William Petre (1506–1572) Member of Council 1544–1572

William Petre served on the Privy Council in the reigns of Henry VIII, Edward VI, and Mary, and stayed on as member for Elizabeth; the queen trusted him enough that Katherine Grey, after her marriage to Edward Seymour, Earl of Hertford, was kept under house arrest at Petre's home, Ingatestone.

Sir Ralph Sadler (1507–1587) 1537–1533, 1558–1587

Ralph Sadler was a member of the Privy Council for Henry VIII and Edward VI, but, as a committed Protestant, was removed from the Council by Mary. When Elizabeth became queen, he was one of the first she named for the Privy Council, doing it only three days after her accession. Sadler was part of the delegation in York to discuss what should be done with Mary Stuart when she fled to England in 1568. At first sympathetic, he was less so after the introduction of the Casket Letters used to demonstrate Mary's involvement in the murder of her second husband Henry Stuart, Lord Darnley. Sadler sent a précis of the letters to William Cecil, believing they proved Mary's guilt. The veracity of the Casket letters has been debated for centuries. With Thomas Radcliffe, Earl of Sussex, he led the queen's army to suppress the Northern Rebellion of 1569. Sadler was one of those tasked with investigating Mary and Thomas Howard, Duke of Norfolk's role in the Ridolfi Plot of 1572. Several times he guarded Mary, particularly when George Talbot, Earl of Shrewsbury, had to be at Court, and though he treated her kindly, he forcefully argued for her execution in Parliament because of the danger she posed to Elizabeth.

Around 1530 Sadler met Helen Barre while in Cromwell's service; they fell in love and soon married, having seven surviving children. Barre, already the mother of two small children, was a laundress in the Cromwell household. Some years earlier, Barre's husband Matthew, a London tradesman known most for his drinking, had deserted her. She had done everything she could to find out what had happened to him to no avail, and eventually learned that he was dead. But in November of 1545, they learned that he had gone to Ireland and had now returned; he was very much alive. One of Wriothesley's servants heard Barre bragging in a pub that he was the real husband of Lady Sadler. Barre was interrogated and he was able to prove that he was Helen's husband. Sadler loved his wife deeply and was greatly disturbed. The next month through a private bill in Parliament their children were legitimized, and Helen stayed with Sadler even though she was legally Barre's wife. Barre disappeared again. We do not know when she died, but Sadler was almost eighty when he died in 1587, known as one of the wealthiest subjects in England.

Henry FitzAlan, Earl of Arundel (1512–1580) 1546–1580

Henry FitzAlan, Earl of Arundel, served on the Privy Council for Henry VIII and his three children. At the beginning of Elizabeth's reign, he pursued a marriage with her, but this went nowhere (see Chapter 6).

During his time on the Privy Council in Elizabeth's reign he consistently argued against military engagements. Arundel was criticized for being on the edge of the Northern Rebellion, as the rebel leaders claimed that Arundel had thought it a good idea. Arundel was confined briefly, but he returned to the Privy Council in March 1570 where he advocated for leniency in the treatment of Mary Stuart. He was again under house arrest after September 1571 because of concern that he had been part of the Ridolfi Plot (see Chapter 9) but he was released late in 1572 and the following year returned to the

Council once again. By 1579 his health was problematic as he was greatly troubled with gout. He only attended the Council twice that year and died in 1580.

Nicholas Wotton (c.1497–1567) Member 1546–1567
Nicholas Wotton was another member of the Privy Council who served under Henry VIII and all of his children. In Elizabeth's reign Wotton worked on the negotiations with Scotland that resulted in the Treaty of Edinburgh in 1560. As a member he worked on commercial and legal matters, as well as dealing with some foreign ambassadors. By the summer of 1566 he was in ill health and died the following year.

Francis Talbot, Earl of Shrewsbury (1500–1560) 1549–1560
Francis Talbot, Earl of Shrewsbury, was a member of the Privy Council in the reigns of Edward VI, Mary, and Elizabeth. Though a Catholic, he was very loyal and supported his monarchs' religious choices. Elizabeth reappointed him to her Council, but he died in 1560.

Edward Feinnes de Clinton, Earl of Lincoln (1512–1585) 1550–1585
Edward Feinnes de Clinton was a member of the Privy Council in the reigns of Edward, Mary, and Elizabeth. When Elizabeth became queen, she immediately confirmed him as a member. He also served as her Lord Admiral. His third wife Elizabeth Fitzgerald, widow of Sir Anthony Browne, was close to Elizabeth, and was a member of her Privy Chamber from 1559–1585. Clinton was one of the lieutenant-generals who led the forces to suppress the rising of the northern earls. In 1572 he was created to Earl of Lincoln as recognition for his long service. He stayed at Court as Lord Admiral and a member of the Privy Council until his death in 1585.

Sir John Mason (1503–1566) Member 1550–1566
Henry VIII appointed John Mason a Clerk of the Privy Council in 1541 and he became a member in the reigns of his three children. In the last year of her reign Mary appointed him treasurer of the chamber, and Elizabeth maintained him in this post as well as having him continue as a member of the Privy Council. In Elizabeth's Council Mason strongly warned against the perils of foreign military adventures and urged Elizabeth to pursue peace with other countries instead. He attended Council meetings through 1565, dying the following year.

Nicholas Heath, Archbishop of York (c.1501–1578), Member 1553–1559, When He Was Removed
Nicholas Heath supported Henry VIII's break with Rome, and preached against Elizabeth Barton, the Holy Maid of Kent. He became Bishop of Rochester in 1540. In Edward VI's reign, however, he was imprisoned because he refused to remove altars and images in his churches. When Mary became

queen, he agreed that England would do better as a Roman Catholic nation and joined the Privy Council at the beginning of her reign. In 1555 she appointed him Archbishop of York, and after Stephen Gardiner's death he served as her Chancellor. When Mary died, he immediately proclaimed Elizabeth the new queen in the House of Lords. Elizabeth briefly continued him as a member, but she was distressed when he refused to crown her, as she would not have the coronation service with the elevation of the Host. After refusing to take the Oath of Supremacy, he was dismissed as archbishop and from the Council. He was then sent to his estates in retirement, where he lived for almost twenty more years.

William Herbert, Earl of Pembroke (1507–1570) Member 1553–1570
As soon as Elizabeth's reign began, William Herbert, Earl of Pembroke, was immediately part of her Privy Council. When the new queen entered London, Pembroke bore the sword before her. Pembroke was seriously ill in 1560 and 1564, but in 1568 he was made Lord High Steward of the Royal household. Elizabeth was upset he supported the marriage of Mary Stuart with Thomas Howard, Duke of Norfolk, but he was able to convince the queen that he was not involved in any plot against her. He died in 1570.

Edward Stanley, Earl of Derby (1509–1572) Partial Member in 1551, Member 1553–1572
Edward Stanley, Earl of Derby, was a partial member of the Privy Council in Edward's reign and a full member in Mary's. Elizabeth kept him on the Privy Council, and he supported the Church of England settlement, though he did not want to see Catholics ill-treated. When the Earls of Northumberland and Westmoreland were rebelling in 1569, they contacted Derby hoping for his support, but he reported it to Elizabeth instead. While his two younger sons were involved in plots supporting Mary Stuart, the Earl and his oldest son Henry, Lord Strange, who married Margaret Clifford, a cousin of the Tudors, stayed loyal to Elizabeth (see Chapter 7). Derby believed in charity and was said to feed sixty poor people every day, increasing it to 2700 on Good Friday. He died in 1572.

William Howard, Lord Howard of Effingham (c.1510–1573) Member 1554–1573
William Howard was the fourth son of Thomas Howard, 2nd Duke of Norfolk. Mary gave him the title Baron Howard of Effingham and appointed him Lord Admiral and a member of her Privy Council. Though loyal to Mary, Howard also was vocal in his support of Elizabeth as Mary's heir. When Elizabeth became queen, he was immediately confirmed as a member of her Privy Council and also made her Lord Chamberlain. He served Elizabeth in several other roles including ambassador to France. In 1572 Howard was too ill to discharge his duties as Lord Chamberlain. Elizabeth replaced him with

Thomas Radcliffe, Earl of Sussex, and appointed Howard as Lord Privy Seal, a well paid but sedentary office. He died the following year.

Sir Ambrose Cave (c.1503–1568) Member 1558–1568
Ambrose Cave, who was related to William Cecil, grew up in Northamptonshire. Around 1546 Cave joined Princess Elizabeth's household as a manager of her estates. After Mary's death, he immediately made his way to Hatfield, and was named one of her first Privy Councilors. He worked to enforce the Acts of Uniformity and Supremacy. He also served in Parliament. To demonstrate his love and loyalty for Queen Elizabeth, Cave had his portrait painted wearing a yellow garter on his left arm. He stated that Elizabeth had dropped it while she was dancing, and he had sworn to wear it the rest of his life.

Sir Thomas Parry (c.1515–1560) Member 1558–1560
Thomas Parry entered Princess Elizabeth's service later in the reign of Henry VIII, and by 1548 he was named her cofferer, her business manager. At that time Elizabeth was living in the household of her stepmother Katherine Parr. That year Kat Ashley, Elizabeth's governess and principal gentlewoman shared her concerns about Katherine's husband Thomas Seymour's inappropriate attention to Elizabeth. After the death of Katherine Parr, Seymour considered marrying Elizabeth, though she did not encourage this. He was involved in several dangerous situations leading to his imprisonment in the Tower. Parry and Ashley were also arrested and examined about all that had passed between Seymour and Elizabeth. Elizabeth was very loyal to them and took them back into her household afterward. Three days after Elizabeth became queen Parry became Comptroller of her household and a member of the Privy Council. He also served in the 1559 Parliament. He died suddenly in 1560.

Sir Edward Rogers (1498–1568) Member 1558–1568
Edward Rogers was a determined Protestant. In Mary's reign he was sent to the Tower for complicity in the Wyatt rebellion. He was severely fined but finally released, and then left England. He returned in 1558 and right after her accession Elizabeth appointed Rogers as her vice-chamberlain, Captain of the Guard, and named him a member of the Privy Council. Soon after, he became Comptroller of the Household. He also served in Parliament on several occasions. Rogers was a committed, hardworking member and attended the Council regularly until 1567; he died in 1568.

Sir Richard Sackville (c.1506–1516–1566) Member 1558–1566
Richard Sackville was born sometime between 1506 and 1516. His mother was Anne Boleyn's cousin, making him a relative of Queen Elizabeth. When Elizabeth became queen he was appointed a Privy Councilor and under-treasurer of the Exchequer. For the rest of his life he worked to bring order to the kingdom's finances and financial courts. He was also guardian of Elizabeth's cousin Margaret Stuart, Countess of Lennox, daughter of Henry VIII's

older sister Margaret. Sackville died in 1566 and in his will left valuable jewelry to the queen.

Francis Russell, Earl of Bedford (1527–1585) Member 1558–1585
Francis Russell was knighted at Edward VI's coronation. During Mary's reign he became close friends with William Cecil and a supporter of Elizabeth, who named him a member of the Privy Council only four days after she became queen. He was sent to Paris as special envoy after the death of Francis II in 1560. He was also involved in the diplomacy around Mary Stuart's second marriage to Henry, Lord Darnley. The queen sent Bedford to be her representative at the baptism of Mary's son James. Bedford strongly supported Mary's half-brother James, Earl of Moray, and met with him when he was in Scotland for the ceremony. Bedford was also an ally of Robert Dudley, especially after his daughter Anne became the third wife of Robert's brother Ambrose in 1565. His daughter Margaret married George Clifford, Earl of Cumberland. Both Anne and especially Margaret were important literary patrons. Both women became close friends of Queen Elizabeth. He died in 1585.

Sir Nicholas Bacon (1510–1579) Member 1558–1579
Coming from a fairly humble background, Nicholas Bacon attended Cambridge University, where he made connections important to his intellectual development as well as his later career. His second wife was Anne Cooke, known for her fine education, strong Protestant beliefs, and important religious translations. They cared deeply about each other and their children. They had two sons, Anthony and Francis. This marriage gave him even more important connections, as William Cecil was married to Anne's older sister Mildred.

When Elizabeth became queen, she knighted Bacon, named him a Privy Councilor and the Lord Keeper of the Great Seal, which meant that he presided over the House of Lords. He was also appointed head of the Court of Chancery. In matters of religion, he called for moderation and tolerance, a view supported by his queen. Though he usually got along well with Elizabeth, in 1563 she was furious when John Hales circulated a pamphlet arguing that the disgraced Katherine Grey, now Katherine Seymour, was the closest heir to the throne. She learned that Bacon had aided Hales in his research and banished him from the court and the Privy Council. In the spring of 1565, Cecil helped Bacon regain his previous standing. Bacon, with Cecil, was also committed to protecting England against Catholic forces on the continent. Though his health worsened in the 1570s, Bacon stayed involved in the Privy Council and the Chancery. He died in 1579. His widow Anne continued her support of Puritanism and advocated for her sons.

William Parr, Marquess of Northampton (1513–1571) Member, 1545–1548, 1558–1571

Loyal and greatly appreciated by Queen Elizabeth, William Parr had at times an illustrious career beginning in the reign of Henry VIII, including serving at times on the Privy Council.

In December 1558 Elizabeth restored him to the Privy Council and he held several appointments and was involved in several negotiations with the French in the early years of the reign. He was a commissioner for several royal visitations and one of his last duties was to serve on the commission for the trial of Thomas Howard, Duke of Norfolk, over his involvement in the Ridolfi Plot. But he was also well known for his problematic marriages. His mother arranged a marriage for Parr in 1527 when he was only fourteen to Anne Bourchier, one of the wealthiest heiresses in England at the time; she was only ten. The two did not live together until 1539, and the marriage was unhappy. There was an enormous scandal in 1541, when Anne eloped with John Lyngfield. In 1543, now Henry VIII's brother-in-law, Parr successfully asked Parliament to agree to a separation on the grounds of adultery. Parr also kept control of all of Anne's inheritance. In 1543 Parr began to court Elizabeth Brooke, a lady at court, though he was still officially married. Five years later Parr, feeling in a strong position politically and eager to remarry, asked for a commission to examine the legality of his marriage to Anne. But impatient, Parr secretly married Elizabeth anyway before a ruling was made. He was expelled from the Privy Council and ordered to separate from Elizabeth. He was forgiven a few years later, and in 1551 he was able to get a private act of Parliament passed that annulled his first marriage, allowing him to live openly with Elizabeth. When Mary became queen, she took away his lands and titles and rescinded his divorce, making his first wife one of her ladies. Under Queen Elizabeth his divorce was again accepted. The queen was very fond of his second wife Elizabeth, who died in 1565. Anne Bourchier died in early 1571. That year Northampton married Helena Snakenborg, who had come from Sweden with the Princess Cecilia and stayed in England when the Swedish delegation left (see Chapter 11). Northampton had fallen in love with her, but the marriage only lasted a few months as he died later that year. Valued by the queen, she paid for his lavish funeral.

Sir Francis Knollys (1512–1596) Member 1559–1596

Francis Knollys was a very committed and devout Protestant which shaped his life and career. In 1540 he married Katherine Carey, the daughter of Mary Boleyn, and thus first cousin to Elizabeth. During Mary's reign he took his family to the continent where they could live in Protestant communities. He returned to England when Elizabeth became queen and she soon appointed him to her Privy Council and made him Vice-Chamberlain of the Household. In 1568, when Mary Stuart arrived in England, Elizabeth appointed Knollys her guardian. Knollys told William Cecil how dangerous he considered Mary and urged the queen to see Mary disgraced for her actions and to support

James, Earl of Moray as regent in Scotland. By the end of 1568 Mary was transferred to the care of George Talbot, Earl of Shrewsbury. Knollys also handled the crown business in the House of Commons until 1572, though he was a Member of Parliament for most of the reign. In 1570 he was promoted to Treasurer of the Household. Knollys died in 1596.

Robert Dudley, Earl of Leicester (c.1532–1588) Member 1562–1588
Robert Dudley was close to Elizabeth from the beginning of her reign and became a member of the Privy Council in 1562. He played an active role in the Council until his death in 1588 (see Chapter 6).

Thomas Howard, Duke of Norfolk (1538–1572) Member 1562–1572
Thomas Howard was only nine when his father Henry, Earl of Surrey was executed on January 19, 1547 on the order of Henry VIII. The king died before the execution of his grandfather, Thomas, Duke of Norfolk, could be carried out, and the new regime decided to keep Norfolk in the Tower. When Mary became queen, Norfolk was freed, and with her first Parliament his grandfather was restored to the dukedom of Norfolk, and Thomas became Earl of Surrey and his grandfather's heir. In August 1554 with his grandfather's death, he was now Duke and Earl Marshall himself at sixteen. With Elizabeth as queen, he expressed his loyalty to the Church of England. He was a cousin of Elizabeth on her mother's side and the only Duke in England. Elizabeth saw him as someone who would naturally play a prominent role at court. As Earl Marshall he organized Mary's funeral in December of 1558 and was involved in planning Elizabeth's coronation. He became a Knight of the Garter in April 1559. Elizabeth appointed him to the Privy Council in 1562. Norfolk was strongly opposed to Robert Dudley as a potential husband to the queen, and the two men had an intense rivalry. Norfolk, along with Thomas, Earl of Sussex, and Sir Ralph Sadler, were the commissioners examining Mary Stuart in 1568 in York and then Westminster about her involvement in her husband Henry, Lord Darnley's death. There was no clear verdict and Mary stayed in England under modified house arrest. Soon there were plots to have Norfolk, who was thrice widowed, marry Mary. Elizabeth was furious when she learned about this in 1569 and warned Norfolk. He was held in the Tower and then under house arrest. He begged the queen's forgiveness and promised to never meddle in a marriage plot again. Instead, however, he became involved in the Ridolfi Plot to have Elizabeth murdered so that he and Mary Stuart would rule England, and in January 1572 he was found guilty of treason. Elizabeth was very reluctant to have him executed, but finally agreed and Norfolk died by beheading June 2, 1572 (see also Chapter 9).

Sir Walter Mildmay (1521–1589) Member 1566–1589
Walter Mildmay's background was modest but his skills allowed him to serve the Tudors.in the administration of royal finance. Though a committed Protestant, in Mary's reign he served as a financial administrator, and served

Elizabeth faithfully in many financial matters, particularly in the role of Chancellor of the Exchequer, working with William Paulet on numerous reforms. He also worked with William Cecil, a close friend and ally. Elizabeth appointed him to the Privy Council in 1566. He was also a regular member of Parliament and a skilled orator, consistently praising the queen in his speeches there. He was also a committed Protestant who believed in education, establishing Emmanuel College at Cambridge in 1584, hoping to train ministers to preach well.

Sir James Croft (c.1518–1590) Member 1570–1589
In Mary's reign James Croft was involved in Thomas Wyatt's rebellion and was in the Tower sentenced to death. Mary's government hoped he would incriminate Elizabeth, but he refused, and the sentence of death was never carried out. When she became queen Elizabeth was always grateful for this loyalty, and he was appointed Governor of Berwick and instructed to settle border disputes with the Scots. But he got into trouble over the lack of discipline at Berwick, and was dismissed from his office and briefly imprisoned. He soon began to rebuild his career. From 1563 he represented Hertfordshire in every Parliament until his death. In January 1570 Elizabeth appointed him as Comptroller of the Household, a clear sign that she had restored Croft to favor. A few months later he was also appointed a member of the Privy Council, and he attended regularly. In March 1587 he was the only commissioner in the Star Chamber trial of William Davison who had the courage to speak up for the former secretary. The following year he was part of a team negotiating with Alexander Farnese, Duke of Parma, but he met secretly with the Duke, leading to his brief imprisonment on his return. Elizabeth, however, forgave his zeal for attempting to make peace and he was back in the Council at the beginning of 1589, dying in 1590.

Thomas Radcliffe, Earl of Sussex (1527–1583) Member 1570–1583
Thomas Radcliffe, Earl of Sussex, was sent to Ireland in the reign of Mary. He returned.to England upon Mary's death and pledged his loyalty to the new queen, pleading to be released from the governorship. But Elizabeth sent him back, now promoted to the full dignity of Lord Lieutenant. But the situation there was very difficult, and he was recalled in 1564, in ill health. Back at court, he allied himself with Thomas Howard, Duke of Norfolk, and strongly encouraged the marriage of Elizabeth with the Archduke Charles, to the anger and dismay of Robert Dudley. Elizabeth sent Sussex to Vienna to discuss the marriage. His hard work to encourage the marriage ultimately came to naught (Chapter 6). In July 1568 soon after Mary Stuart had fled to England, he was appointed President of the Council of the North. Sussex was appointed one of the commissioners, along with Thomas, Duke of Norfolk and Sir Ralph Sadler, to investigate Mary's role in the murder of her husband, Lord Darnley. He took the role seriously and agreed with the queen that a formal judgment or trial would not be politically strategic, but that it was essential Mary be kept in

England. There was suspicion about him during the Northern Rebellion, especially as his half-brother Egremont Radcliffe had joined the rebels. But Sussex loathed his half-brother and fought vigorously against the rebels. To show her confidence in Sussex, in July 1570 Elizabeth appointed him Chamberlain of the Household and then made him a member of the Privy Council. Sussex was a diligent Council member and became a close ally of William Cecil. As Lord Chamberlain Sussex was in frequent attendance to the queen, both at court and during her progresses.

George Talbot, Earl of Shrewsbury (c.1522–1590) Member 1571–1590
When Elizabeth became queen, George Talbot, who became Earl of Shrewsbury in 1560, was named a Knight of the Garter and was appointed joint lieutenant-general in the north. His first wife Gertrude, whom he married in 1539 and with whom he had seven children, died in 1567. Later the same year he married the thrice-widowed Bess of Hardwick with whom he was deeply in love. The marriage, however, ended in great bitterness and accusations against her that led to a separation. Shrewsbury, who at first called Bess his sweetheart and jewel, eventually came to describe her as a wicked woman. Two years after his second marriage Elizabeth appointed Shrewsbury to be custodian for Mary Stuart, which proved very difficult for Shrewsbury and exacerbated the problems with Bess. Although he was appointed to the Privy Council in 1571, he could attend only rarely because of the guarding of Mary. He was relieved of this duty in 1584, to his great relief. He died six years later in 1590 (see Chapter 9).

Ambrose Dudley, Earl of Warwick (c.1530–1590) Member 1573–1590
For supporting his father John, Duke of Northumberland in his attempt to place Lady Jane Grey on the throne, Ambrose was found guilty of treason and lodged in the Tower but was later released and pardoned partly due to the endless endeavors of his mother Jane. His prospects improved under Elizabeth, who gave him the titles of Baron Lisle and Earl of Warwick. Warwick had several military appointments in the 1560s, but he was wounded in the leg in 1563 and his health began to decline. In 1572 he became a member of the Privy Council and was at first an active member, but his attendance declined after 1578 as his health further deteriorated. Warwick and his brother Robert were very close, and Robert said he loved his brother as much as he loved himself. They spent much time together, and Warwick served as godfather in 1574 for his brother's illegitimate son Robert Dudley, the son of Douglas Sheffield. He was also a witness to his brother's 1578 secret second marriage to Lettice Knollys, the widow of Walter, Earl of Essex.

Warwick was greatly grieved with the unexpected 1588 death of his brother Robert, who left him all his lands, except for those in the Countess of Leicester's jointure. Unfortunately, Warwick also inherited his brother's debts. In January 1590 his leg was so badly infected it had to be amputated. Warwick died the next month, with his wife Anne in the room with him so tearful she could not speak.

Sir Henry Sidney (1529–1586) Member 1575–1586
Henry Sidney was a close companion to Edward VI and in 1551 married Mary Dudley, daughter of John, Duke of Northumberland. Despite this connection, Queen Mary pardoned Sidney and he served her in various capacities. In 1554 her husband Philip was godfather to Henry and Mary's son, named for him. In Elizabeth's reign, he was strongly allied with his brother-in-law Robert Dudley. In 1560 he was appointed president of the Council of the Marches of Wales, a post he held for the rest of his life. Two years later Sidney was with Dudley when they went to support the French Protestants at Le Havre and was ordered to stay behind when the queen wanted Dudley back at court. During that time some people caught smallpox, including the queen. Sidney's wife Mary nursed Elizabeth devotedly. While the queen recovered with few scars, Mary, from caring for the queen, also became ill and was terribly scarred. Henry later wrote that he had left a woman he thought the most beautiful and returned to one who looked terrible because of her service to the queen. Mary did not hide herself away, despite the scarring. In 1565 Sidney was sent back to Ireland as Lord Deputy, with his wife accompanying him, where he hoped to establish effective royal authority. But Ireland was difficult for anyone to control in Elizabeth's reign, and so this proved for Sidney. He was finally released from the position in 1571. His second time in Ireland, 1575–1578, was no better, and he appreciated his recall so he could reassume his seat on the Privy Council, to which he had been appointed in 1575. In the mid-1580s Mary was ill and Henry was considering whom he might marry after her death; however, he died in May 1586 and his wife Mary did not succumb until a few months later.

Henry Carey, Lord Hunsdon (1526–1596) Member 1577–1596
The son of Mary Boleyn, Elizabeth's cousin Henry Carey served as a Gentleman of the Queen's Household throughout Mary's reign. When Elizabeth became queen, she knighted him and named him first Baron Hunsdon. Since his mother had been Henry VIII's mistress before he married her sister, some thought Henry Carey might have been Elizabeth's half-brother as well as her cousin, but Elizabeth never recognized him as such, and most scholars today consider it unlikely, as the affair had ended considerably before his birth. In 1564 Carey went to France to bring Charles IX the Order of the Garter. In 1568 Elizabeth appointed him governor of Berwick, and he strongly disapproved what he saw as Elizabeth's leniency to Mary Stuart after she fled to England. He was away when the Northern Rebellion broke out, and quickly rushed north to deal with the rebellion, pleasing Elizabeth with his bravery. He soon assumed more responsibilities in the north. In 1577 the queen appointed him to the Privy Council, and he attended whenever he was at court, though he was often sent back to the North for specific negotiations with Scotland.

On the Privy Council he was considered the expert on Scotland. In 1585 he became the Lord Chamberlain of the Household and was still active at court after the Armada. His last Council meeting was late June 1596, only a few weeks before his death. Elizabeth appears to have cared deeply for her cousin and paid for his funeral at Westminster Abbey. Hunsdon was also significant as a patron of the theater. Beginning in the 1560s he had a company of players, who eventually became the Lord Chamberlain's Men (see Chapter 16).

Sir Christopher Hatton (1540–1591) 1577–1591
In 1577 Christopher Hatton was appointed to the Privy Council, received a knighthood, and was named Vice-Chamberlain of the Household. He took his position on the Council very seriously—he attended extremely regularly, in fact, as much as Burghley and Walsingham. He was involved in discussions about the queen's potential marriage with the Duke of Anjou. In the autumn of 1579 Hatton was named to a seven-man commission that also included Burghley and Walsingham to negotiate with Anjou's representative, Jean de Simier, on articles for a marriage treaty; by 1580, however, Elizabeth announced that public antipathy made the marriage impossible. But the matter was not dropped, negotiations continued, and Hatton continued to be part of the conversations about it in the Council (see Chapter 6).

Sir Thomas Bromley (c.1530–1587) Member 1579–1587
Thomas Bromley studied law and served often as a Member of Parliament. William Cecil thought highly of Bromley and in 1569 he was appointed solicitor-general; he had a significant role two years later in the trial of Thomas Howard, Duke of Norfolk. He also was sent to examine Mary Stuart. In 1579 he was named Lord Chancellor, knighted, and appointed to the Privy Council. In June 1585 Henry Percy, Earl of Northumberland, in the Tower because he was implicated in the Throckmorton plot, (see Chapter 9) was found dead. Bromley was part of the inquiry commissions and he concluded that the earl had committed suicide. Bromley also examined Anthony Babington for his part in the plot to assassinate Elizabeth and was part of the commission sent to Fotheringay for the trial of Mary Stuart.

Charles Baron Howard of Effingham and Later Earl of Nottingham (1536–1624) Member 1584–1619
Elizabeth thought highly of her cousin Charles Howard both for his loyalty to her in Mary's reign and because she found him charming. Howard played an important role in suppressing the Northern rebellion. Elizabeth knighted him and in 1575 he received the Order of the Garter. In 1584 he became Lord Chamberlain and a Privy Councilor, and the following year was named Lord Admiral. He was one of the commissioners for the 1586 trial of Mary Stuart and as war with Spain loomed worked on the defense of England and was naval commander during the Spanish Armada. In 1597 Elizabeth gave Howard the title of Earl of Nottingham. One of his last services for the queen

was to be a commissioner at the Earl of Essex's treason trial in 1601. The earl went on to a distinguished career in the reign of her successor, James I, dying in 1619.

Sir Amias (or Amyas) Paulet (c.1532–1588) Member 1585–1588
Amias Paulet, a committed and serious Protestant, spent much of his career on the Isle of Jersey. From 1556 to 1571 he was the deputy for his father, the lieutenant governor. By 1572 he was the sole governor, and harbored Huguenots who fled France after the St. Bartholomew's Day Massacre. From 1576 to 1579 he was the resident ambassador in Paris, where he greatly distrusted Henri III and queen mother Catherine de Medici. In January 1585 Burghley, Walsingham, and the queen decided that he would be excellent as the next keeper of Mary Stuart. They wanted a close eye kept of her, given the number of plots in which she had been involved. He was also that year named a member of the Privy Council but could not attend meetings due to his careful guarding of Mary. Though she thought her correspondence with Anthony Babington was secret, Walsingham and Paulet knew about it, and he searched her rooms for evidence at her trial. Paulet was greatly irritated that Elizabeth took so long to sign the death warrant for Mary. Davison suggested that Paulet just have Mary murdered, but he absolutely refused. Soon after Mary's execution in February 1587 he was appointed the Chancellor of the Order of the Garter as a reward for his diligent work. Paulet attended the Privy Council in January of 1588 but unfortunately his health was failing, and he died that September.

Henry Stanley, Earl of Derby (1531–1593) Member 1585–1593
The eldest son of Edward, Earl of Derby, Henry Stanley, Lord Strange made what would have been an excellent and prestigious marriage when in 1555 he wed Margaret Clifford, granddaughter of Henry VIII's younger sister Mary (see Chapter 7). In 1572 he became earl and was a member of the queen's Council of the North. In January 1585 he went to France to bestow the insignia of the Order of the Garter on Henri III, and later that year became a member of the Privy Council. He was also part of the commission to try Mary Stuart. In 1589 he served as lord steward for some treason trials. Derby had financial difficulties, still ongoing when he died in 1593.

William Brooke, Lord Cobham (1527–1597) Member 1550–1553, 1586–1597
William Brooke was a member of the Privy Council during Edward VI's reign. On his father's death in 1558 he became Lord Cobham, and the day after she became queen, Elizabeth made him the special ambassador to Philip II to inform him of Mary's death. Cobham was soon appointed Lord Warden of the Cinque Ports and Constable of Dover Castle. His close friendship with his distant relative William Cecil, which endured for forty years, certainly helped Cobham's career. But his friendship with Thomas, Duke of Norfolk

was more problematic, and he was on the edge of the Ridolfi plot, which led to seven months of house arrest at Burghley House. He was granted the Order of the Garter in 1584 and rejoined the Privy Council in 1586. In 1589 his daughter Elizabeth married Burghley's son Robert. Cobham supported Burghley during the last months of his life, faithfully attended the Council, and supporting the Cecils against the Earl of Essex. Cobham is known in theater history for insisting that Shakespeare's character John Oldcastle—an ancestor of his—be renamed, hence the name of the character, Falstaff, Prince Hal's large carousing friend.

Thomas Sackville, Lord Buckhurst, Earl of Dorset (c.1536–1608) Member 1586–1608

Thomas Sackville not only played many political and administrative roles in Elizabeth's court; he was also a poet. Through his mother Margaret Boleyn, he was related to Queen Elizabeth. He served in Parliament and was also in 1560 the co-author of the play, *Gorboduc* (see Chapter 16). Both that and his other works demonstrate that he believed contemporary political lessons could be understood from a study of history. In 1567 he was knighted and created Baron Buckhurst. Two years later he was appointed to be joint Lord Lieutenant of Sussex. In 1571 Elizabeth sent him to Paris to discuss her potential marriage to Henri, Duke of Anjou. Buckhurst also served as a commissioner for the Duke of Norfolk's trial. Lord Burghley secured his appointment to the Privy Council in 1586. Buckhurst became known for his courage and ability to avoid factions at court. He was a member of the commission for Anthony Babington's trial. When Buckhurst was sent to the Netherlands in 1587, he wrote to his queen that the soldiers were starving, and it was imperative that they be paid. Leicester tried to undermine him, and upon his return he was placed under house arrest. With the support of Burghley and Walsingham Buckhurst regained the confidence of the queen, and he worked hard on England's defense at the time of the Armada. In 1589 he became a Knight of the Garter. After Christopher Hatton's death, Buckhurst was also appointed Chancellor of the University of Oxford. He served on the commission that tried the queen's physician, Roderigo Lopez, for treason. When Lord Burghley died, despite Essex's opposition, Elizabeth expressed her trust in Buckhurst and appointed him Lord Treasurer. As the Lord Steward, in 1601 Buckhurst oversaw the trials of the Earl of Essex and his ally Henry Wriothesley, Earl of Southampton (see Chapter 9). After the queen's death Buckhurst continued his successful career under James.

John Whitgift, Archbishop of Canterbury (c.1531–1604) Member 1586–1604

In Elizabeth's reign, as a strong Protestant, Whitgift was soon ordained, and developed a reputation for his preaching, especially as he often denounced the pope as the Antichrist. Whitgift believed deeply in the Elizabethan religious settlement as enacted, and he and Puritans were very hostile to each other.

Elizabeth was very impressed with Whitgift, and in 1577 he was appointed Bishop of Worcester. In 1583 he became her third Archbishop of Canterbury. Elizabeth had gotten along well with Matthew Parker, her first archbishop, but when he died in 1575 the next archbishop of Canterbury was Edmund Grindal. There were deep conflicts between the queen and Grindal, and she was relieved when he died in 1583. For Elizabeth, Whitgift was the perfect replacement. But the Puritans and their sympathizers in the Privy Council were deeply concerned. Elizabeth greatly appreciated Whitgift's work against religious radicals, and he was the only archbishop appointed a member of her Privy Council, which happened in 1586. One of his close allies was Sir Christopher Hatton. Much of his time was spent suppressing Puritans. His relationship with Elizabeth continued to be close; he was at her bedside when she died in March 1603 and acted as the chief mourner of her funeral. He died the following year (see Chapter 5).

Sir John Wolley (d. 1596) Member 1586–1596
John Wolley was educated at Oxford. He was eloquent and learned, and in 1568 became Elizabeth's Latin Secretary. Wolley was highly competent, and by 1586 he was preparing reports for debates in the House of Commons. That year he was also appointed a member of the Privy Council. Wolley served as one of the commissioners at Mary Stuart's trial. Between 1587 and 1590, when Sir Francis Walsingham was often ill, he assumed many of the duties of his office. He was also a member of Parliament from 1571 until his death and saw his role as defending royal prerogatives. Elizabeth, grateful for his loyal service, appointed him to several well-paying positions, such as Chancellor of the Order of the Garter.

Sir Thomas Heneage (c.1532–1595) Member 1587–1595
First elected to Parliament in 1553, Thomas Heneage served in at least eleven Parliaments during Elizabeth's reign. In 1561 Elizabeth appointed him steward of Hatfield and then appointed him and his wife Anne Poyntz, whom he married in 1554, Gentleman and Gentlewoman of the Privy Chamber. Heneage was able and charming and had a deep friendship with the queen, which upset Robert Dudley in the 1560s, leading to Dudley's flirtation with Lettice Knollys, Countess of Essex, whom he married more than a decade later. Heneage worked well with most of the men at court and did not become embroiled in factions. He had several positions at court; in the 1570s Elizabeth named him Treasurer of the Privy Chamber and in 1587 he became Vice-Chamberlain of the Household and a member of the Privy Council. Elizabeth so valued him that she publicly rebuked Sir Edward Hoby in 1593 after he insulted Heneage while both were serving in Parliament. Heneage took his role as privy councilor very seriously, attending as many as one hundred council meetings a year until his health began to fail. He died in 1595.

Sir John Fortescue (1533–1607) Member 1589–1607
John Fortescue's father Sir Adrian was executed for treason in 1539 for reasons that were never clearly articulated. John was distantly related to Elizabeth through his father's mother, but when his mother Anne Rede remarried in 1540, he was brought closer to Elizabeth's circle, as her second husband was Sir Thomas Parry, who later became the cofferer of the princess's household. In 1555 Fortescue was also a member of Elizabeth's household. No doubt due to his stepfather's influence, soon after Elizabeth became queen, he was appointed Keeper of the Great Wardrobe, a post he held for the rest of his life. Fortescue was responsible not only for the care of the royal clothing, but also armor and state documents. In 1588 he was appointed to the Privy Council and became under-treasurer and Chancellor of the Exchequer. In 1593 he was appointed keeper of Hatfield House.

Sir John Perrot (1528–1592) 1589–1590, Removed from Council and Charged with Treason
Though there were rumors and legends that John Perrot was a bastard son of Henry VIII, there is no concrete evidence to support this claim. Perrot was intelligent and strong-minded. He knew Welsh, French, Spanish, Italian, and Latin. But he was also quarrelsome and violent as well as being a spendthrift. In Mary's reign he was suspected of being involved in plots against the queen leading to his imprisonment. Perrot's situation improved when Elizabeth became queen, and she asked him to be one of the four gentlemen to carry the canopy of state at her coronation. He was given numerous profitable positions in her early reign, but his behavior made him many enemies. Perrot married twice but also had at least four illegitimate children, which led to further conflicts. One of the mothers of an illegitimate child was Elizabeth Hatton, herself illegitimate daughter of Sir Christopher Hatton. Hatton was upset with how Perrot treated his daughter, and this was exacerbated by Perrot's contempt for Hatton, who echoed the claim that Hatton only got his place at court because he was a good dancer.

In 1571 Queen Elizabeth sent Perrot to Ireland, a typically difficult appointment. He left Ireland two years later without the queen's permission and briefly retired from public life until the following year, when Elizabeth appointed him to the Council of the Marches of Wales. The queen sent Perrot back to Ireland in 1584 as Lord Deputy and he stayed for the next four years. In 1589 he was appointed to the Privy Council. It turned out it was only for a short time. Perrot fought with his replacement in Ireland, Sir William Fitzwilliam. Perrot accused Fitzwilliam of corruption, and in return, Fitzwilliam accused Perrot of treason. Fitzwilliam claimed that Perrot had been involved with such traitors as Brian O'Rourke and Sir William Stanley, and that he had conspired with Philip II to murder Elizabeth, for which he would be granted Wales, the last a highly unlikely scenario. There were more and more accusations as other enemies of Perrot came forward. He was removed from the Council, and in 1591 sent to the Tower and charged with treason, being put on trial the following year. The treason charges included helping known traitors, encouraging O'Rourke's rebellion, and sending Philip II and Stanley treasonable letters. He was also charged with describing the queen with contemptuous words, something of which he was certainly guilty. His former secretary Philip Williams testified that Perrot informed him about Elizabeth "she may command what she will, but we will do what we list," meaning what he wanted. Perrot added, "Ah, silly woman, now she shall not curb me, she shall not rule me... God's wounds, this is it to serve a base bastard pissing kitchen woman" (Perrot, Sir John, ODNB). Perrot was found guilty and sentenced to die. But he stayed in the Tower the next few months and died in November before the sentence could be carried out—or, as he had hoped, Elizabeth could pardon him.

Sir John Puckering (1544–1596) Member 1592–1596
After studying at Lincoln's Inn, John Puckering was called to the bar in 1567. In 1569 he was the under-treasurer of Lincoln's Inn, and its governor by 1575. Two years later he was named a member of the Council in the Marches of Wales and a Justice of the Peace in Wales and border counties. In 1578 he was the Chief Justice of the Carmarthen circuit, though also retaining his London practice. Though Puckering was new to Parliament in 1584, he was chosen as speaker of the House of Commons. In 1585 Elizabeth appointed him to be the queen's serjeant-at-law and the following year he was involved in the prosecution of some of the Babington conspirators. The last state trial he prosecuted was the treason trial of John Perrot. In May 1592 Puckering was knighted, appointed to the Privy Council, and became Lord Keeper of the Great Seal. He died in 1596 and was buried at Westminster Abbey.

Robert Devereux, Earl of Essex (1565–1601) Member 1593–1600,
Removed from the Council
Robert Devereux, Earl of Essex became upset in 1593 that Robert Cecil had been appointed to the Privy Council when he himself was not a member, so to placate him Elizabeth also named him a privy councilor. His failure in Ireland and his return to court without permission led him to be expelled from Council in 1600, and to his rebellion and execution the following year (see Chapters 6 and 9).

Sir Thomas Egerton, Baron Ellesmere, First Viscount Brackley
(1540–1617) Member 1596–1614
Thomas Egerton was the natural son of the landowner Sir Richard Egerton and Alice Sparke, a servant girl. Egerton was brought up in the household of Thomas and Katherine Ravenscroft. After attending Oxford, he was admitted to Lincoln's Inn. In 1581 Elizabeth appointed him solicitor-general; also in that decade he served in Parliament. Egerton worked on the prosecutions of recusants and Jesuits, as well as the Babington conspirators, Mary Stuart, and later John Perrot. In 1592 Egerton was appointed Attorney-General. Two

years later he was knighted and appointed Master of the Rolls of the Court of Chancery. When John Puckering died in 1596, Elizabeth chose Egerton to succeed him as Lord Keeper and he also became a member of the Privy Council. He was one of the few members in the council chamber in July 1598 when in the heated discussion of who to send to Ireland, the Earl of Essex insulted Elizabeth, and she boxed his ears. After Elizabeth's death he became even more important in the reign of James.

Sir William Knollys, Baron Knollys, Earl of Banbury (c.1545–1632) Member 1596–1532
William Knollys was the son of Francis Knollys and his wife Catherine Carey, the daughter of Mary Boleyn, thus making William Elizabeth's cousin. He served in the army that suppressed the Northern Rebellion and aided his father in guarding Mary Stuart at Bolton Castle when she first fled to England. His older brother Henry died in 1582 making William the heir. In 1585 Elizabeth sent him to Scotland as ambassador-extraordinary. He also served in the Netherland under the Earl of Leicester, who, having married Lettice Knollys, widow of Walter, Earl of Essex, was Knollys' brother-in-law. He also served in the House of Commons. His father died in 1596 and Elizabeth gave him his father's office of Comptroller of the Household and also named him a privy councilor. Though the Earl of Essex was his nephew, he had nothing to do with his plots, and testified against him during his trial. His last appointment under Elizabeth was Treasurer of the Household in 1602. He went on to be created Baron Knollys under James, and Charles I granted him the title Earl of Banbury.

Roger Lord North (1531–1600) Member 1596–1600
There is a portrait of the young Roger North, which hung for centuries at Wroxton, dressed for a tournament with a red silk scarf tied around his left arm. The tradition is that it was Princess Elizabeth who tied it. Certainly, Elizabeth had a long and trusted friendship with him, and as soon as she became queen, she named him a Gentleman of the Chamber, knighting him at her coronation. For many years they played cards together, and North was tactful enough that the queen usually won. His father had warned him before his death in 1564 to avoid pride and profligacy, and North followed this advice for the rest of his life. In 1567 he accompanied Thomas Radcliffe, Earl of Sussex, to Vienna for a final attempt to negotiate the marriage of Elizabeth with the Archduke Charles. He also accompanied Sir Francis Walsingham to France to secure greater toleration for the Huguenots. Most important was when the queen sent him back to France in 1574 as a special ambassador to congratulate Henri III on his accession. He was also there to negotiate a renewal of the April 1572 Treaty of Blois, an Anglo-French treaty against Spain, and to again urge more toleration for the Huguenots, especially significant after the St. Bartholomew's Day Massacre, which occurred four months after the signing of the treaty. North was charming and effective, but he refused to ignore the

queen mother Catherine de Medici's insult of a fool dressed as Henry VIII. The Earl of Leicester and Roger North became close friends in the 1560s. North and his son served in the Netherlands with Leicester in 1585 before returning to England to help in the defense of the realm before the Spanish Armada. In 1596 Lord North was named Treasurer of the Household and a Privy Councilor. He once wrote that he desired Elizabeth to know that he lived only to serve her. He died in 1600 and left in his will £100 to the queen in acknowledgment of his love and duty toward her.

George Carey, Lord Hunsdon (1548–1603), Member 1597–1603
The son of Henry, first Baron Hunsdon, and thus also a cousin of Queen Elizabeth, George Carey was sent on a mission to Scotland in 1569 and was knighted the following year. He was sent on further missions to the Netherlands and Scotland. During the Spanish Armada he dispatched munitions and ships to Lord Admiral Howard. His father died in 1596, and he was appointed to his father's offices of Captain of the Gentlemen Pensioners; the following year he was named Lord Chamberlain and a member of the Privy Council. In 1599 he argued that the Earl of Essex's army in Ireland was a threat to the nation. He continued the support his father's theater company, The Lord's Chamberlain's Men. He died in September 1603, only six months after his queen.

Sir John Stanhope (c.1540–1621) Member 1601–1621
John Stanhope built a career by frequently serving in Parliament in Elizabeth's reign. In 1569 he helped to suppress the Northern Rebellion. He was appointed Vice-Admiral for Yorkshire and became a member of the Council of the North. Around 1577 he became a Gentleman of the Privy Chamber. In the 1590s he and Robert Cecil were close allies. Stanhope was knighted in 1596, the year he was appointed Treasurer of the Chamber. Five years later he came Vice-Chamberlain of the household and was named to the Privy Council. He rose to even greater heights in the reign of James I.

Edward Somerset, Earl of Worcester (c.1550–1628) Member 1601–1628
The only son of William Somerset, Earl of Worcester, Edward was raised to have great loyalty to the Tudors. After his father's death in 1589 he became Earl of Worcester and the following year he went to Scotland to congratulate James VI on his marriage to Anna of Denmark. The Scottish king and Somerset became good friends. He was elected a Knight of the Garter in 1593 and four years later Elizabeth named him Deputy Master of the Horse. The master was the Earl of Essex, and Worcester was one of four men sent to the earl in February 1601 to investigate why men were assembling at Essex House. Worcester and the others were kept under guard while Essex attempted to raise London against the court, and Worcester testified against Essex. In April he became Elizabeth's Master of the Horse and was appointed to the Privy Council. He rose to even greater favor under James I.

Gilbert Talbot, Earl of Shrewsbury (1552–1616) Member 1601–1616
On November 1, 1567 there was a double wedding. George Talbot, Earl of Shrewsbury married the thrice-widowed Bess of Hardwick. Her daughter Mary Cavendish married his son Gilbert. He was fifteen and she was eleven years old. They had two sons and three daughters. His father died in 1590 and Gilbert became the new earl. He was banned from court in 1594 and 1595 because of his ill-treatment of his tenants. Talbot was notorious for his quarrels and the costly litigation in which he engaged. He served as a commissioner at the trial of the Earl of Essex and the following year, in 1601, he was named as a privy councilor.

Sir Edward Wotton (1548–1628) Member 1602–1628
As a young man Edward Wotton spent several years on the continent and became fluent in Italian, Spanish, and French. These language skills held him in good stead when he returned to England in 1575. In 1577 he and Philip Sidney were sent to congratulate the newly elected Holy Roman Emperor Rudolf II. They also made a diplomatic visit to William the Silent, Prince of Orange. Soon after Sir Francis Walsingham sent him to escort Charles Phillippe de Croye, a councilor of the state in Brussels, to London so he and the queen could discuss the crisis in the Netherlands. In 1579 he became the special envoy to Portugal. He was special ambassador to Scotland in 1585. The following year as special ambassador to France he presented Henri III with the evidence of Mary Stuart's complicity in the Babington Plot. In 1589 he was named a Gentleman of the Privy Chamber, and two years later he received his knighthood. At the end of Elizabeth's reign in December 1602 he was appointed to the Privy Council and became Comptroller of the Household. He received new titles from James I.

CHAPTER 4

Elizabeth's Parliaments

In the Tudor period, most serious policy decisions were made by the monarch with the advice of key members of the Privy Council. But some important issues had to be ratified by Parliament, as it began to gain more power; this led eventually to the conflict between the king and Parliament in the seventeenth century. In part because of developing political support for the break with Rome, Henry VIII, under the advice of Thomas Cromwell, called Parliament more often. The Reformation Parliament sat from 1529 to 1536, for example, and it gained more power than it had in the centuries previously. It was the monarch who made the decision to call for elections for Parliament to meet. In Elizabeth's reign there was a new Parliament about every three to four years and most lasted from two to four months. One of the important reasons a monarch would call Parliament would be financial—the need for special subsidies.

When Elizabeth's half-sister Mary became queen, her Parliament passed an act that stated that the regal power in England was in the queen as fully and absolutely as it was in any previous kings, and this was then true for Elizabeth as well.

Parliament, then as now, was made up of two sections, the House of Lords, the upper house, and the House of Commons, the lower house. Those who sat in the House of Lords were bishops and hereditary titled aristocrats, dukes, earls, and barons. They met in the parliament chamber in Westminster Palace. Those who sat in the House of Commons were elected, and male landholders had the right to vote if they owned a 40-shilling freehold. All Members of Parliament were substantial landowners. Sometimes a powerful counselor of the queen or an aristocrat could control an election. Commons had acquired a new and permanent home in St. Stephen's Chapel in the reign of Edward VI.

Though the members of the House of Commons elected the Speaker at the beginning of the session, the Speaker was always the crown's nominee. Some members of her Privy Council also served in Parliament, so Elizabeth had a clear voice in Parliament that protected her interests. Elizabeth worked with her Parliaments but wanted Parliament to know she was the senior partner. She expressed her view of the role of Parliament by instructing the House of Commons that they should not meddle in matters of state unless she asked them to but should instead occupy themselves in other matters that concerned the commonwealth, which meant the common good of the people.

While she often had a tense relationship with some of her Parliaments, especially the House of Commons, she also worked to charm the members. After the religious settlement she did not want Parliament to address the issue again. Though throughout the reign there was fear of Catholics, Elizabeth also worried greatly about Puritans who wanted to redo the Church settlement. Nor did she want to be pressured to marry or name an heir. These issues kept coming up in Parliament and Elizabeth kept refusing to deal with them, stating the members had no business discussing such things. As the reign progressed, the issue of the succession became an increasing concern. The brothers Paul and Peter Wentworth were thorns in Elizabeth's side in many Parliaments because of their insistence that Elizabeth must name a successor or let Parliament do so. Paul even warned the queen that if she did not name an heir her people would no longer see her as a mother of her country but rather as a parricide who would prefer for England to die with her than survive her. Tied to this were their demands for freedom of speech. Paul Wentworth asked in the House of Commons "Whether her Highness's commandment, forbidding the Lower House to speak or treat any more of the succession and of any their excuses in that behalf, be a breach of the liberty of the free speech of the House or not?" (Neale, *Elizabeth I and Her Parliaments, 1559–1581*, 152). His older brother Peter was several times sent to the Tower for his comments about the succession and the right to speak openly in Parliament.

While Mary Stuart was in England and there were conspiracies against Elizabeth, Parliament also wanted to deal more firmly with the Scottish queen than Elizabeth, though there was no constant conflict between Elizabeth and Parliament. The queen, not wanting direct confrontation, would often give evasive replies or what she herself described as her "answer-answerless" (Neale, *Elizabeth I and Her Parliaments, 1584–1601*, 129).

Toward the end of Elizabeth's reign there was more friction as the House of Commons became increasingly worried about the succession. There were also severe problems in the 1590s with drought and bad harvests, continued war with Spain, and discord in Ireland. Many of these issues were costly and needed funding, which could cause a clash between the government and Parliament. But Elizabeth was careful to do all she could to avoid direct conflict.

Parliament 1559

The important reason that Parliament was called in 1559 was to establish the uniform religion for Elizabeth's reign. She was also concerned that England should continue to maintain the navy and its coastal defense. Elizabeth's first Parliament passed the Act of Supremacy, reviving the antipapal statutes of Henry VIII, which made Elizabeth the Supreme Governor of the Church, but not Supreme Head as her father and brother had been. Many members of Parliament were uncomfortable with the idea of a woman as "supreme head." Archbishop of York Nicholas Heath argued emphatically in the House of Lords that a woman was unqualified to be the supreme head of the church in the realm of England. Elizabeth agreed to the title of Supreme Governor instead, but in fact did not relinquish any power, though she often worked through the bishops who were loyal to her.

Parliament also passed the Act of Uniformity, which established the Elizabethan Religious Settlement. This act established the forms of worship using the various prayer books issued under Edward VI, especially the one of 1552. This new prayer book was ordered to be used by every English church. All services were again in English, but alterations to the Book of Common Prayer allowed people to interpret the sacrament of the Eucharist in such a deliberately vague fashion that it could be widely acceptable. Though England was now a Protestant nation, there were efforts at compromise after the years of violent upheaval in previous reigns. If people did not attend church services they were fined, and this money was used to help the poor.

Setting a precedent for later Parliaments as well, Parliament also petitioned Elizabeth to marry and settle the succession. Though she told Parliament she understood that they wanted to advise her, it was not their place to do so. This was a dance she did with Parliament again and again. She told the 1559 Parliament: "And reproach me no more that I have no children: for every one of you, and as many as are English, are my children and kinsfolks" (Elizabeth I, *Collected Works*, 59).

1563 Parliament, with Second Session 1566–1567

The 1563 Parliament was called after Elizabeth had almost died of smallpox. Her Council wanted more support in pressuring Elizabeth to marry or to name a successor. This issue was also important to members. Its first session was from January to April 1563. A petition to the queen from the Commons stated how "almighty God to our great terror and dreadful warning lately touched your highness with some danger of your most noble person by sickness" so, they told her, she had to marry or name an heir (Elizabeth I, *Collected Works*, 73). Elizabeth told Parliament that naming a successor would only cause more problems with an heir who would be the focus of plots and would cause the developments of serious factions. She forbade Parliament from discussing the matter further. This Parliament also passed *An*

Act Against Conjurations, Enchantments and Witchcrafts. There had been an earlier Witchcraft Act in 1542, in Henry VIII's reign, but it was repealed early in Edward's reign. Before the break with Rome the crime of witchcraft had been dealt with by the Church, but with the Reformation this changed. The Elizabethan Act was in some ways more merciful than its predecessor; lesser crimes achieved through witchcraft were punishable by a term of imprisonment. But any spell that caused someone to be killed would be punishable by death. The Act also outlawed treasure hunting and offering fantastical prophesies, especially if they related to sedition. This Act was repealed in 1604 early in the reign of James I and replaced with a much harsher one.

The birth of Mary Stuart's son James in June 1566 heightened tensions about the succession, which were expressed during the second session from September 1566 to January 1567. Despite many attempts by the privy councilors, and Elizabeth herself, both Houses of Parliament brought up petitions for Elizabeth to settle the succession and marry quickly. Elizabeth eventually promised that she would settle the succession when she and her Council believed the time was right. Paul Wentworth was angry that Elizabeth refused to engage with Parliament on the question of marriage and the succession; he argued that she could not order Commons not to discuss these issues as the Commons had freedom of speech. This was a conflict that would also come up again. Elizabeth was very clear about her views, telling Parliament in 1567. "As to liberties, who is so simple that doubts whether a prince that is head of all the body may not command the feet not to stray when they would slip?" (Elizabeth I, *Collected Works*, 105).

PARLIAMENT OF 1571, NOT DISSOLVED UNTIL 1583, SEVERAL SESSIONS

Paul's older brother Peter was impassioned on the question of free speech in the next Parliament of 1571. In that Parliament also some religious radicals attempted to revise the official prayer book. Elizabeth refused to accept this. Elizabeth told this Parliament, when they asked her to marry, that they had no right to discuss the matter.

After the 1571 Parliament the queen had to summon Parliament again the next year in 1572 because her Privy Council was so concerned about the Ridolfi Plot (see Chapter 9) and Mary Stuart. The Privy Council wanted support from Parliament about dealing with Mary Stuart. The Treason Bill, passed in 1571, was officially called *For the preservation of the Queene's Majestie in the royall estate and crowne of this realme*. Any speech about the deposition or causing Elizabeth's death was treason. The bill also made any speech that indicated that Elizabeth was not the lawful queen, or that she was a "heretic, schismatic, tyrant, infidel, or usurper" was treason (Neale, *Elizabeth I and her Parliament, 1559–1581*, 226).

Parliament was almost universal in calling for the execution of Mary Stuart. While a few Parliament members, particularly Arthur Hall, advocated for leniency toward her, almost everyone else united in advocating for Mary's death. The Lords and Commons came together in committee and petitioned Elizabeth to execute Mary. Peter Wentworth pushed strongly for the execution not only of Mary Stuart, but also of Thomas Howard, Duke of Norfolk. He became frustrated that Elizabeth was not willing to agree on Mary Stuart's execution and was delaying that of Norfolk. Elizabeth refused to agree to Mary's execution, but the pressure of Parliament did make her agree to that of Norfolk. Wentworth angrily argued that when the queen refused to follow the advice of Parliament, she was abusing her people.

This Parliament had a number of sessions, not being finally dissolved until 1583, and on the first day of the new session in 1576 Wentworth argued for free speech, claiming that constant acquiescence to the queen was dangerous for both her and the state. Wentworth was taken into custody and sent to the Tower. Two days before the end of the session Elizabeth ordered his release. Safety for the queen dominated the sessions of this Parliament. Wentworth was in and out of the Tower for the rest of his life, dying there in 1597.

Also, in the 1576 session there was an argument between the House of Lords and the House of Commons over Lord Stourton's Bill. The bill was the culmination of several generations of problems in the Stourton family. William Stourton, 7th Baron Stourton was married to Edmund Dudley's daughter Elizabeth. Their eldest son was Charles. Their marriage was unhappy, and William Stourton had a long-term relationship with Agnes Rice. His death in 1548 left much of the Stourton estates to Agnes, leading to years of litigation between the new baron Charles and Agnes. Charles was very quarrelsome in many aspects of his life, and he had also fought with his widowed mother Elizabeth over her marriage to Edward Ludlow. Charles vehemently opposed her remarriage because he feared he would lose some of his estates. Elizabeth was supported by their neighbor William Hartgill, who had served in Parliament, leading to a feud between Stourton and Hartgill. Charles Stourton and four of his servants murdered Hartgill and his son in 1557. Stourton was found guilty of the murders and was hung—with a silken cord because of his rank. Charles's son John was a small child at the time, and his mother Anne worked to retain custody of her son and have the title, wealth, and land confiscated by the crown restored. The 1576 bill was an attempt by the now adult Lord Stourton to uphold his right to control the Stourton lands. It was introduced into the House of Lords with the endorsement of the queen. But the bill stalled over whether Stourton could bring writs of errors against those who had exchanged lands with his father. The Lords supported Stourton but members in Commons, especially Walter Mildmay and Thomas Norton, argued that the bill should have a proviso that would protect people who had made land deals with Charles. The Lords told the House of Commons they should not meddle in a bill that had the queen's support. Commons stayed firm and the bill did not become law, demonstrating its growing power and confidence.

The Sedition Act of 1581 was also something passed by Parliament to offer further protection to the queen. It superseded an earlier act of 1555 that had been passed to protect Mary I from hostile gossip and words. The Act had severe penalties—either time in the pillory with the loss of both ears or a fine of £200 and imprisonment for the first time someone who shared seditious, slanderous news, rumors, or stories against the queen. If someone did this a second time or published a book with such seditious slander or encouraged insurrection it was a capital crime. There was some concern in the House of Commons that the law could be used against Puritans and wanted it clearly stated that the slander had to be proved, not only suspected.

1584 Parliament

The 1584 Parliament was also summoned because of yet another Catholic conspiracy, the Throckmorton Plot (see Chapter 9), a plan to assassinate Elizabeth and make Mary Stuart queen. Though the plot was discovered and stopped, it caused great worry for the queen's safety. There were even more fears because that year Balthasar Gérard assassinated the Protestant leader in the Netherlands William the Silent. Before Parliament started, Lord Burghley and Sir Francis Walsingham convinced the Privy Council of the necessity of the Bond of Association, which pledged its signers that if there was an attempt on the queen's life, they would not only kill the assassin but also the person the assassins were supporting to take over the realm. It was necessary because "it has been manifest that the life of our gracious sovereign Lady, Queen Elizabeth, hath been most traitorously and devilishly sought." Those who signed pledged that if there was an attempt that led to the "untimely death of her majesty so wickedly procured," that the person that this was done for would be pursued to the death (Elizabeth I, *Collected Works*, 184, 185). Not only did members of the Privy Council sign the bond but many other men as well, including members of Parliament.

This was obviously aimed at convincing plotters who wanted Mary Stuart as queen that it would be fatal to their cause to make an attempt on Elizabeth's life. To reinforce the Bond, it was important to have Parliamentary legislation. This was achieved with the 1585 Queen's Safety Act. To protect the queen the act established there would be a tribunal made up of peers and members of the privy council to investigate any invasion or rebellion or any attempt to injure the queen. Any guilty person would be punished by death. It took a while for this to pass because of disagreement for what this would mean for Mary's son, James VI of Scotland. There was also a great shock when members learned that William Parry, MP for Queenborough, was involved with Catholic conspirators (see Chapter 9). He was the only serving MP who was executed—March 2, 1585—in Elizabeth's reign.

1586 Parliament

The 1586 Parliament was also called because of Mary Stuart and her involvement in the Babington Plot (see Chapter 9). The Privy Council again wanted the support of Parliament to convince the very reluctant Elizabeth that she must have Mary executed. Four privy councilors, Sir Christopher Hatton, Sir Walter Mildmay, Sir Ralph Sadler, and John Wolley were all members of the House of Commons and gave speeches arguing for the execution of the Scottish queen. Elizabeth was reluctant to do so though in her speeches to this Parliament she recognized what Mary had done. "Considering the manifold dangers intended and practiced against me, which through the goodness of almighty God I have always escaped," she contended that it was miraculous that she was still alive. She expressed her grief that "most of all that one of mine own sex, state, and kin should be consenting thereunto, and guilty thereof." Mary "with so foul treasons hath stained her estate and blood," might seem to make Elizabeth take revenge, but she assured Parliament "I bear her no malice," if Mary would confess and repent. But the Scottish queen "utterly refused and steadfastly denied her guiltiness." But Elizabeth was still not willing to make a commitment to the execution. "To your petition I must pause and take respite before I give answer" (Elizabeth I, *Collected Works*, 186, 187). Pressured by the Privy Council as well as Parliament and her closest advisors, Elizabeth finally signed Mary's death warrant, though she ordered that it not be sent on. But once it had her signature on it, the Privy Council met and agreed to dispatch it; Mary Stuart was executed in February 1587.

1589 Parliament

The 1589 Parliament, called after the defeat of the Spanish Armada the previous year, was particularly concerned with religion, specifically the fear that the more radical Puritans were just as dangerous as the Catholics. Parliamentarians were also concerned with foreign policy. Sir Christopher Hatton, recently appointed Lord Chancellor, opened Parliament. He gave a patriotic speech about England's victory over Spain, and the dangers of the Catholics. But this Parliament was also concerned with radical Puritans. While Parliament was in session Richard Bancroft gave a powerful and widely reported sermon at St. Paul's Cross, attended by many members of Parliament. At the beginning of the 1580s Bancroft had entered the service of Hatton as a chaplain. By the time of his sermon, he was a canon of Westminster. He preached that the Puritans were enemies of the Church of England.

1593 Parliament

The 1593 Parliament was also concerned with Spain and fear of other invasions. It was claimed of Philip II "that he was thereby more furiously enraged than ever before... He breathed nothing but bloody revenge" (Neale, *Elizabeth I and Her Parliaments, 1584–1601*, 246). Peter Wentworth again brought up freedom of speech in relation to the succession, wanting both Houses to force the queen to name a successor. He had written his *A pithie exhortation to her Maiestie for establishing her successor to the crowne*. In it he warned the queen that if she did not name a successor "your Grace shall then find such a troubled soul and conscience, yea, ten thousand Hells in your soul, even such bitter vexation of soul and heart," adding that after her death "you shall leave behind you such a name of infamy throughout the whole world" (Neale, *Elizabeth I and Her Parliaments, 1584–1601*, 254). It is hardly surprising that his colleagues were very doubtful about his plan to present a fair copy of his manuscript to the queen and tried to dissuade him. He was brought before the Privy Council and again sent to the Tower, where he stayed until his death in 1597. The 1593 Parliament was also concerned about Catholics, with Jesuits still coming into the country. There were also conflicts over the Puritans' desired reforms of the Church of England. Some wanted to get rid of the church hierarchy and opposed some of Elizabeth's more moderate advisors. They were very critical of Elizabeth as Supreme Governor of the Church. Elizabeth at this time believed Protestant nonconformity, like Catholicism, was a great danger to the state.

1597 Parliament

The 1597 Parliament was called at a time of great crisis. There had been four years of bad harvests. Food was scarce and inflation soared. The cost of flour had tripled by August of that year. The speaker of the House of Commons stated, "The eyes of the poor are upon this Parliament, and sad for the want they yet suffer" (Neale, *Elizabeth I and Her Parliaments, 1584–1601*, 341). There had also been a rebellion in Ireland led by Hugh O'Neill, Earl of Tyrone since 1594 and the continued need for defense against Spain. Bills to take land away from pastures so they could be used as food-producing land were finally passed but a bill to reduce the cost of corn was not. Bills were passed to deal with poor relief and the homeless. There were additional taxes for defense and to pay for costs for dealing with Ireland.

1601 Parliament

The 1601 Parliament was Elizabeth's final Parliament, and the queen understood that it might be when she called it in September. It assembled at the end of the next month and was dissolved on December 19. The government had a desperate need for additional funding. War with Ireland was costly, especially with the Spanish support that Philip III was sending. Just as Parliament was about to meet news came to London that the Spanish had landed at Kinsale. Robert Cecil stated that £300,000 was needed and Parliament voted unanimously to have the first installment of this collected by the next February. But members in the House of Commons also had serious issues they insisted on bringing up. There had been monopolies since the time of Edward III and Elizabeth made much more use of them. These were given to a courtier or merchant who then had the sole right to manufacture to sell a specific invention or item. Granting monopolies could promote a business but it was also a way for Elizabeth to reward someone or gain money if she were paid for the monopoly. From the 1580s onward the queen granted more and more monopolies, and for some courtiers it became a source of income for no real work. The most famous example is that of the Earl of Essex. Soon after he came to court Elizabeth granted him the monopoly in sweet wine, which was a significant source of income for the extravagant earl. In October 1600, after Essex's disastrous sojourn in Ireland, Elizabeth refused to renew the monopoly, which was devastating to Essex financially. It was one of the events that led to his rebellion (see Chapter 9).

For the Members of Parliament, what made the monopolies so problematic was that the person with complete control over supplying the product could control the price, which meant prices kept going up. This became a growing problem as the reign progressed. Concern about monopolies was first mentioned in the 1571 Parliament. Protests were much stronger in the 1597–1598 Parliament. By the 1601 Parliament there was a real campaign against them, and much talk in the streets of London against monopolies.

With such widespread anger, Elizabeth decided that she had to deal with the problem. The queen admitted some of the grants she had made had been a mistake, though she still maintained that she had the right to do so. Some were revoked and others put under the jurisdiction of the common law courts. While Parliament was still in session a Proclamation announcing these steps was issued. Elizabeth gave a speech on the monopolies to a delegation of about 140 Members that eased the tensions. "For above all earthly treasures I esteem my people's love…. That my grants should be grievous unto my people and oppressions to be privileged under color of our patents, our kingly dignity shall not suffer it. Yes, when I heard it I could give no rest unto my thoughts until I had reformed it." Her comments, known as "the Golden Speech" was, however, about so much more than monopolies. She told Parliament—but it was aimed at all her subjects—"To be a king and wear a crown is a thing more glorious to them that see it than it is pleasant to them that bear it. For myself, I was never so much enticed with the glorious name of a king or royal authority of a queen as delighted that God hath made me His instrument to maintain His truth and glory, and to defend this kingdom (as I said) from peril, dishonor, tyranny, and oppression." Elizabeth went on to state that "there will never queen sit in my seat with more seal to my country, care to my subjects, and that will sooner with willingness venture her life for your good and safety, than myself. For it is not my desire to live nor reign longer than my life and reign shall be for your good." She ended her speech by claiming, "and though you have had and may have many princes more mighty and wise sitting in this seat, yet you never had nor shall have any that will be more careful and loving" (Elizabeth I, *Collected Works*, 340, 341). It was a fine conclusion to her last Parliament—and truly to her reign.

CHAPTER 5

The Archbishops of Canterbury

When Elizabeth became queen the Catholicism and obedience to the pope that had been restored under Mary was again swept away. To establish the Anglican Church under Elizabeth the position of the Archbishop of Canterbury was critical. Elizabeth was fortunate that Mary's Archbishop of Canterbury, Reginald Pole, had died twelve hours after Mary. As a result, she did not have to worry about how to deprive the Archbishop of Canterbury as she did Nicholas Heath, the Archbishop of York, who was Mary's Chancellor. He had proclaimed Elizabeth's accession, but he had refused to take the Oath of Supremacy. Heath was deprived of his position in July 1559 (Fig. 5.1).

Not only was the Archbishop of Canterbury the highest churchman of the realm, but with the political and social significance of religion, the archbishop had a lot of influence in a wide range of ways. It was critical to the queen that she could work well with her archbishop; when she could not, the problems were serious. As soon as she became queen, Elizabeth knew she had to find the right Archbishop of Canterbury, and for her that was Matthew Parker. The queen had terrible problems with her second archbishop, Edmund Grindal. The one with whom she got along best, was her final archbishop, John Whitgift, though he alienated a number of others. Being able to work well with her Archbishop of Canterbury was very important as she had problems with many of her bishops. Some of her bishops felt Elizabeth did not support them adequately, while she mistrusted the more zealous Protestants among them.

Fig. 5.1 Elizabeth with Bishops private collection

Matthew Parker, Archbishop of Canterbury 1559–1575

Matthew Parker was born in 1504. His father William was a successful weaver. His mother Alice Monins may have been a relative of Anne Boleyn. He started at Cambridge University when he was sixteen and was introduced to new reformed ideas. In late 1534, through his preaching, Parker came to the attention of the queen, Anne Boleyn, and the next year he was appointed one of her chaplains. That year he preached before the infant Elizabeth, and later preached before the king. Anne clearly trusted Parker; a few days before she was arrested in May 1536, knowing something terrible was in store, she entrusted her daughter to Parker's spiritual care. This was the final time that Anne and Parker spoke, and for the rest of his life he felt a great sense of obligation to both Elizabeth and her mother.

Parker managed to survive the death of Anne Boleyn and became one of Henry VIII's chaplains in 1537. Two years later Parker gave a sermon for Prince Edward, and for the young Elizabeth in 1540. His administrative skills were demonstrated when he also served as Dean of Stoke by Clare in Suffolk and as Master of Corpus Christi College at Cambridge University and Vice Chancellor, to which he was elected to in 1545. He also received ecclesiastical preferment in the later reign of Henry VIII and the reign of Edward VI.

Parker married Margaret Harlestone in 1547 early in the reign of Edward VI, even though clerical marriage was not legalized until December 1549. It was apparently a very happy marriage, and Parker's colleagues thought highly of her. Margaret died in 1570. They had two surviving sons, each of whom married bishops' daughters. When Mary became queen, he was in trouble, not only as a reformer but also because he was married. By the spring of 1554 he had lost his various offices and at times went into hiding.

As soon as Elizabeth became queen, she knew she wanted Matthew Parker to become her Archbishop of Canterbury. Parker worried that he would disappoint her as archbishop; nor was he in good health. He offered what was needed in the archbishop: he should not be arrogant, fainthearted, or covetous; Elizabeth thought that described Parker. In May of 1559 Parker was told that the queen would not take no for an answer. It is very possible that Anne Boleyn's request over twenty years earlier was what finally made Parker agree to take the position. Elizabeth really valued her archbishop, and they for the most part worked together well, but there were a few problematic issues, and one was his marriage. At the beginning of her reign ministers assumed she would immediately restore clerical marriage, but she hesitated, and when she did she made the process more difficult. Elizabeth disliked the fact of married clergy, but Parker defended it to the queen. In 1567 Parker published *Defence of Priestes Mariages* (1567). Elizabeth respected Parker enough that despite her dislike of clerical marriage, she attended feasts in her honor hosted by the archbishop and his wife, though she may not have been as polite to Margaret as she could have been.

Many reformers considered the Anglican Church Settlement as a starting point, not the end. Some, like Parker, wanted the change to continue gradually, while others wanted more radical change. This caused some conflict for Elizabeth throughout her reign. Elizabeth's view of Protestantism, though she was strongly committed, was somewhat conservative. For example, in the summer of 1559 Elizabeth was away from London, and during that time someone removed the crucifix and other church ornaments from the Chapel Royal. Elizabeth was very upset when she returned at the end of September, and insisted they be replaced. Parker, and other bishops, were appalled. Either Parker or Edmund Grindal, the bishop of London, wrote a formal statement against having such images in the Chapel Royal. Elizabeth prevailed, but she decided to make a concession on a related issue and abandoned her insistence that rood screens be replaced in parish churches. Rood screens were substantial, usually made from beautifully carved wood or stone and they separated the nave of the church from where the priest performed services.

Elizabeth and Parker did agree on greater toleration. According to Parliamentary statute, if someone refused to take the Oath of Supremacy a second time, it was a capital crime. Elizabeth told Parker that if someone refused to take the oath the first time, they should not be asked again, and Parker followed this directive, privately warning his bishops that they should only ask once. Some of his colleagues were unhappy with this but Parker enforced it.

This was clearly a very important issue for Elizabeth. In 1568 she told the Spanish ambassador Guzman de Silva that when she had first become queen, she had prayed that God would give her the grace so that she might "govern with clemency, and without bloodshed, keep her hands stainless" (*CSP, Spain*, II, 52). In September 1563 Elizabeth found a way to demonstrate her regard for Archbishop Parker. She had been hunting and had killed a stag and had Robert Dudley take the meat to Parker.

From the time Parker became archbishop, he and William Cecil corresponded frequently, demonstrating the intermingling of religion with politics. The two men apparently trusted each other, and Parker felt able to share his concerns. Another important issue where the queen and the archbishop were close allies was against opposition to what was known as the vestiarian controversy, a dispute over clerical dress. Part of the Elizabethan Church Settlement went back to the 1549 Edwardian prayer book's legal requirements regarding the vestments ministers had to wear, which were more conservative than those described in the 1552 prayer book. The vestments—attire worn by clergy— were similar to those of Catholic priests, which is what Elizabeth wanted. Some Protestants had fled to the continent during Mary I's reign and insisted on greater reforms, which included clergy wearing very simple clothing. These reformers would become known as Puritans and in 1563 some clergy and theologians viewed the issue as matter of conscience, seeing the priestly vestments as the hated symbols of Catholicism. They were a relatively small number, but they were men of high education and some standing. It was the first major move in the Puritans' campaign for reforming the official church. The following year Parker began to take disciplinary measures. When that did not stop the Puritans, Parker became dismayed at their rebellious behavior; before Easter 1566 thirty-seven ministers were suspended for refusing to wear the designated vestments. Some of their parishioners were very distressed. That year Parker also published a pamphlet clarifying the Church of England's official position on how ministers needed to dress to perform church services.

One Puritan leader was Thomas Cartwright, Lady Margaret Professor of Divinity at Cambridge University. He and John Whitgift, future Archbishop of Canterbury, engaged in bitter disputations. The Puritans sought advice from the Swiss reformer Heinrich Bullinger, who counseled obedience and the protests died down. But while the queen and Archbishop Parker were victorious, the Puritans continued their calls for reform. Parker stated that he knew that some were critical of his moderation, but he believed it was the best way for conciliation and to keep the queen's support.

The Puritans were not Archbishop Parker's only concern. He was very worried about the Northern rebellion in 1569 and the publication of the papal bull of excommunication against Elizabeth in 1570. Parker had a hand in writing the homily against disobedience and willful rebellion published in the second *Book of Homilies* in 1571. A book of homilies, official versions of sermons that ministers could use, had been published in Edward VI's reign, and was reissued with new sermons in 1562, with the second book in 1571.

In 1572 Parker was involved in a serious controversy. Thomas Cartwright lost his position at Cambridge for preaching Presbyterian doctrines and advocating major changes in the Church of England. Some of his adherents went even farther, describing bishops as authoritarian and tyrannical, and criticized Parker for acting like a pope and performing abominations. The hope for moderate reform was damaged by these more radical perspectives. Queen Elizabeth was also very concerned with "prophesyings," which was the name given to groups of clergy who got together to discuss a range of topics, including the need some felt for change. In 1574 Elizabeth ordered the suppression of these meetings. Parker was reluctant and wanted only to stop the most disruptive gatherings. He prevented this situation from becoming a crisis; however, "prophesyings" became an acute problem with Elizabeth and her next Archbishop of Canterbury, Edmund Grindal. The death of Parker's much beloved wife Margaret in 1570 devastated him and he had been unwell for several years; his health worsened in 1575 and he died May 17.

Edmund Grindal, Archbishop of Canterbury 1575–1583

After Matthew Parker's death, Edmund Grindal, who had been Bishop of London and then Archbishop of York, succeeded him. William Cecil, Lord Burghley had strongly encouraged the appointment. If Parker and the queen had some conflicts but also worked well together, the conflicts between Grindal and the queen became so intense, she considered forcing him out of the position.

Grindal came from St. Bees, from the west of Cumberland. He went to Cambridge and after receiving his degrees was ordained a deacon in 1544. Over twenty years later, he apologized to a group of Puritans for having said Mass. By the end of Henry VIII's reign Grindal was a Protestant reformer. His career flourished in the reign of Edward VI. In 1549 Grindal took part in a public disputation on transubstantiation. One of those who attended was Nicholas Ridley. Grindal and Ridley grew to be close friends, and Ridley, who became Bishop of London in April 1550, referred to Grindal as his dearly beloved brother. Grindal was devastated when Queen Mary ordered that Ridley be burnt as a heretic in 1555.

In 1551 Grindal was part of several private debates on transubstantiation, some hosted by William Cecil, who became a patron of Grindal's. By early 1553 people were talking about Grindal becoming a bishop; there was a plan to move Ridley to the north and for Grindal to become Bishop of London. Before any of this could be put into effect, the young king died. Grindal spent much of Mary's reign in Strasbourg, where there was conflict especially with reformers in Frankfort over the nature of English Protestantism. In these years Grindal was also helpful to John Foxe in securing documents from the Protestant underground in England that Foxe would use in his history of martyrs. He also during this period developed a strong alliance with John Calvin. As soon as Grindal heard that Mary was dead, he immediately headed back, arriving in London on January 15, 1559, the day of Elizabeth's coronation.

Many of the returned Marian exiles were upset that the Elizabethan Settlement still had what they perceived as Catholic elements. They wanted to push forward with advanced Protestant ideology. Grindal was fortunate that Cecil still had such regard for him. After Mary's Bishop of London Edmund Bonner was forced out of office, the plan of 1553 came to fruition and Grindal replaced Bonner. But as a bishop, Grindal had to enforce a religious settlement with which he really did not agree. Grindal stated that he and some others only became bishops so that others who were more conservative would not.

As a new bishop Grindal was pleased with the bargain the queen had made with Parker that she retained the cross in her own royal chapel but agreed to the destruction of what he called the monuments of superstition in the churches. Grindal and others interpreted this as liberally as possible, removing altars and burning crosses. When Grindal was appointing ministers and other staff he especially turned to other exiles.

Grindal had to deal with a real disaster in June 1561 when lightning struck St. Paul's. The fire destroyed the steeple and most of the roof. Grindal, with Cecil, worked very hard to raise funds and find the materials for rebuilding. The queen herself contributed generously. Only two years later there was a plague epidemic in London. At this difficult time Grindal ordered special times of prayers and fasting.

In 1566 Grindal faced another controversy. The vestiarian controversy that challenged Archbishop Parker became a serious crisis for Grindal. It demonstrated the difficulty of being a leader of the progressive Protestant cause, while still holding an episcopal position with clear responsibilities. Parker's crackdown became intense when in March 1566 thirty-seven clergy who refused to conform in wearing vestments were suspended and threatened with deprivation. A number of those who were suspended were Grindal's particular allies, and men to whom the more radical Protestant congregations were committed. The term Puritan started to be used at this time. Grindal tried to promote clerical conformity on dress. But he also stated that he himself would prefer not to wear the commanded clothing but felt he must, to keep order and obey the queen.

In 1570 Grindal became Archbishop of York. He set out for York in August, but illness delayed his journey, and, once he arrived in Yorkshire, he became ill again, so did not actually enter the city of York until March of the following year. Grindal at first found it very difficult. Catholic beliefs were still strong in the North. Many of the supposed Anglican Churches still had altars and crosses that he insisted, as was the law, be removed. He also worked hard on the nature of the sermons that ministers were preaching. There was the York Ecclesiastical Commission, with the powers to fine and imprison people, and Grindal brought many Catholics before it and assured Elizabeth that the people in York would obey the Church of England. But in fact, recusancy was growing. Grindal did what he could to find stronger Protestant clergy for York, including ones with more radical views. One, Melchior Smith, was able to convert an entire market town to militant Protestantism. Christopher Shute, vicar of Giggleswick for fifty years, was one of the founders of a radical group similar to Quakers.

Right after Parker's death Cecil, now Lord Burghley, told Walsingham that Grindal was the ideal candidate to be the next Archbishop of Canterbury. Elizabeth was not convinced, and it took six months of concerted effort to get her to agree. Those who wanted Grindal as the highest churchman in the realm wanted the laws against Catholics made more stringent, and to reform the church in terms of eliminating unlearned preachers. Elizabeth, however, hesitant about change, did not want to see more reform within the Church of England. Some scholars such as Patrick Collinson argue that more reform in the church would have halted the emerging Puritan movement.

Grindal's difficulties began to develop the following year. In June 1576 Lord Burghley, Sir Francis Walsingham, and the Earl of Leicester all wrote to Grindal to let him know that news had reached court about some disorders involving preachers. More specifically, there was concern about the "prophesying," a way of educating unlearned clergy by getting together to discuss issues of religion. While this was mostly authorized by bishops, and enthusiastically supported by Grindal, Elizabeth thought these discussions dangerous, and ordered them to be suppressed. Previously, under Parker, there had been attempts to quietly sidestep her commands. But now these men at court were warning Grindal that Elizabeth was taking the issue much more seriously. On June 12, when he went to court, the queen ordered him to suppress these meetings.

Grindal asked his bishops to evaluate the prophesying, and many, though not all, responded positively. Grindal wrote in defense of these meetings but also issued orders for more regulation. Elizabeth ordered Grindal to suppress the meetings. Grindal refused and in December wrote her a 6000-word letter, refusing to obey her. "I am forced, with all humility, and yet plainly, to profess that I cannot with safe conscience and without the offence of the majesty of God give my assent to suppressing of the said exercises." He also told her if it were a choice between obeying her and obeying God, "I beseech you, Madam, if I choose rather to offend your earthly Majesty than to offend the heavenly majesty of God," adding that if he did not tell her this she would be imperiled, as he was obeying God, implying that she was not. He also warned her, "Remember, Madam, that you are a mortal creature" (Collinson, *Archbishop Grindal*, 242). Elizabeth was furious. Grindal stayed away from court and Burghley and Leicester worked to protect him. Finally in May Elizabeth herself wrote to her bishops ordering the suppression. Grindal appeared before the Privy Council and refused to back down and was confined to Lambeth House. In January 1578 Secretary Thomas Wilson let Burghley know that Elizabeth wanted to have Grindal deprived of his archbishopric. Burghley was able to convince her not to take this step, but Elizabeth then suggested that Grindal resign. Grindal refused but in late 1582 he finally apologized to the queen. As he became very infirm and nearly blind Grindal started to consider his resignation but died in July 1583. Because of the conflict between the queen and the archbishop, for years the Church of England had lost its leadership.

John Whitgift, Archbishop of Canterbury, 1583–1604

John Whitgift was born sometime around 1530. His father was a prosperous merchant. Whitgift received his B.A. from Cambridge in 1554, and his M.A. in 1557. In Elizabeth's reign, as a strong Protestant, he was soon ordained, and developed a reputation for his preaching, especially as he often denounced the pope as the Antichrist. In 1563 he was appointed Lady Margaret Professor of Divinity, which he resigned in 1569 because of his other duties, such as being Master of Trinity College. Whitgift believed deeply in the religious settlement as enacted, and he and the Puritans were mutually hostile, which played out in Cambridge in the 1570s, especially in conflicts with Thomas Cartwright. Two followers of Cartwright, John Field and Thomas Wilcox, produced a pamphlet, known for its scurrilous style, for the 1572 Parliament. *Admonition to the Parliament* was a stinging criticism of the Elizabeth Church settlement. They had published it anonymously but were eventually unmasked and imprisoned. Archbishop Parker asked Whitgift to respond to the *Admonition*, and he immediately began his work. But before he could publish it, Cartwright published *A Second Admonition to the Parliaments*, which set forth more fully the need for a Presbyterian church system. Whitgift's *Answer* was published in November 1572, with a second more detailed edition that particularly addressed Cartwright's work that came out the next February. Only two months later Cartwright responded with *The Replye to an Answere of Dr. Whitgifte*. Elizabeth's government was not happy. The Privy Council instructed bishops to be very firm with nonconforming clergy, and Cartwright, fearful of being arrested, left the country. Parker suggested to Whitgift that he expand his response; Whitgift spent much of 1573 working on a thorough refutation of Cartwright's ideas. *Defense of the Aunswere to the Admonition Against the Replie of T.C.* was published in 1574. In March of that year, he preached before the queen.

Elizabeth was very impressed with Whitgift, and in 1577 he was appointed Bishop of Worcester. Whitgift was concerned with the number of Catholics there and worked hard to suppress recusancy. Whitgift took his work seriously and preached every Sunday. Only a month after Grindal's death, Whitgift was his chosen successor. In 1583 he became Elizabeth's third Archbishop of Canterbury. He was also the one with whom she worked best, though others found him too rigid.

For Elizabeth, Whitgift was the perfect replacement for Grindal. But for Puritans, and those who sympathized with them in the Privy Council, there was great concern. Whitgift immediately issued a comprehensive reform, with strict proceedings against Catholics and others who did not attend church and clear qualifications for those who would become ministers. Whitgift insisted that clergy use only the *Book of Common Prayer* in public worship, which pleased the queen but not the Puritans. At his ascension-day sermon at Paul's Cross Whitgift spoke against disobedience, whether it came from Catholics or other Protestants. A number of ministers around the country were then suspended. Burghley and Walsingham talked with Whitgift and there was a compromise about accepting ministers who were not planning to disturb the peace of the church. But the Puritans became more united against Whitgift, and as Whitgift continued, some of the Puritans' allies in the Privy Council became increasingly concerned.

Elizabeth announced a prohibition on debate about religion, but that did not stop the discussions and argument. In the House of Commons there was a bill requesting the adoption of a prayer book from Geneva, recently translated into English by Robert Waldegrave, and a Presbyterian church system. The Lords, however, reminded the Commons of the queen's prohibition. Elizabeth greatly appreciated Whitgift's work against religious radicals, and he was the only archbishop appointed to her Privy Council, which happened in 1586. One of his close allies was Sir Christopher Hatton. Much of his time was spent suppressing Puritans.

In October 1588, when many of the English were still celebrating the defeat of the Spanish Armada, the first of the Martin Marprelate tracts was published. These were the beginning of a scurrilous attack against Whitgift from Waldegrave's underground press. There were many insults, including calling Whitgift a caitiff, which meant vile, worthless, and wretched. Whitgift directed a search for the press and Richard Bancroft, his friend and chaplain—and successor as archbishop—wrote a response. More Marprelate tracts responded. Moderate Puritans were concerned about the tone of the tracts. When the press and authors were discovered, Whitgit pressed the case against them, especially Cartwright. Nine Puritans lost their livings and were imprisoned. Whitgift also moved against those who thought the Church of England so compromised that they needed to separate from it entirely. A number of separatists were arrested in the fall of 1587, including the former minister John Greenwood. Henry Barrow came to visit him in prison and was also arrested. At his trial Barrow called Whitgift a monster. While in prison Barrow was able to smuggle out writing that was then published in the Netherlands. In 1593 Whitgift moved more fiercely against the separatists, and Barrow and Greenwood were executed. Waldegrave published some of John Penry's tracts, who in 1588 then took over the press, moving it from place to place, but it was apprehended near Manchester at end of August 1589. Penry for a time escaped to Scotland. By 1592 Penry was back in England and his perspective had changed to that of Barrow and Greenwood. Penry was arrested March 1593 and executed two months later for publishing scandalous writings against the church. At the time Whitgift and others thought he was the author of the Marprelate tracts, but scholars today believe that doubtful.

While there was a great deal of controversy about Whitgift during his tenure as archbishop, Whitgift did a great deal to help the poor, which was especially important in the 1590s because of the poor harvests and inflation. He reminded the bishops to encourage the wealthy to bring hospitality to the poor and did so himself at Canterbury. Throughout his time as archbishop his relationship with Elizabeth continued to be close, and he was at her bedside when she died in March 1603. Whitgift acted as the chief mourner of her funeral. He died the following year.

CHAPTER 6

Courtships and Favorites

James Melville, Mary Stuart's ambassador to England, wrote in his memoir that very early in Elizabeth's reign when he was in Newcastle, he met an unnamed Englishman, who claimed to be a Gentleman of the Queen's Chamber. This man was very skilled in mathematics and geography, and in some less savory areas as well, such as necromancy and astrology. The Council had sent him North to draw a map of the lands that divided England and Scotland. Melville liked the man and two became very familiar with each other; the man told Melville that Henry VIII had visited a number of diviners, or fortune tellers, to learn what should happen in the future to his son Edward, and his daughters Mary and Elizabeth. The king was informed that his son would die young with no heirs, and that Mary would become queen, and after her, Elizabeth. Henry also learned that Mary would marry a Spaniard, while Elizabeth would marry either a Scotsman or a Frenchman, and both marriages would bring many strangers into England and as a result great strife. Henry was so appalled by the fate of England because of his daughters, the man told Melville, that he had both poisoned. But while they both suffered greatly, becoming terribly ill and vomiting, they suspected poison, and each had taken remedies. Because of the poison, Mary's womb was destroyed, and thus she could never have children. This is a disturbing tale, but there is absolutely no evidence that it is true. We do not know who the man was, what he actually said, or how much of Melville's tale, written much later, was embroidered. But it reveals that some viewed the earlier king as monstrous and provides an explanation for Mary's phantom pregnancies; it also suggests the strong belief about the dangers of female rule, and the dangers to the realm if a queen took a foreign husband.

© The Author(s), under exclusive license to Springer Nature
Switzerland AG 2022
C. Levin, *The Reign and Life of Queen Elizabeth I*,
Queenship and Power, https://doi.org/10.1007/978-3-030-93009-7_6

And yet, for royalty, foreign marriages were the norm. For Elizabeth, who became queen at the age of twenty-five, there was great pressure on her to marry, so there would be a king to help with the hardships of rule and a son to eventually restore a masculine succession. In February 1559 the House of Commons sent her the first of many petitions asking that she agree to marry as soon as it could be arranged.

William Cecil, the queen's Principal Secretary and close advisor, desperately wanted Elizabeth to marry. Writing to a confidant, Thomas Smith, early in her reign that if she did not, his life was not worth living. In 1570, Cecil requested an astrological discussion of a prospective marriage for the queen, probably created by Eliseus Bomelius, a Westphalian physician and astrologer who had emigrated to England as a young man and had trained at Cambridge. Bomelius, however, soon after had a falling out with Cecil, and left England for a position at the court of Ivan IV (see Chapter 11).

Elizabeth had many suitors from a range of European countries; there were also Englishmen who hoped to marry her, especially Robert Dudley. In her youth Elizabeth would not only have been a worthy object of desire because of her position. Though it may well have not been meant in a completely complimentary way, Simon Renard described the young Elizabeth in her sister's reign as "a spirit full on enchantment" (*CSP, Spain*, XI, 228). Yet despite all the pressure on Elizabeth to marry, and how much she enjoyed courtship, she was very reluctant. With foreign proposals, Elizabeth claimed that she had no faith in portrait painters and would never marry a man she had not seen. Given what she had observed as a child about her father's marriage with his fourth wife, Anne of Cleves, this is an understandable position for Elizabeth, not only about her feelings for an actual man as opposed to his portrait, but how a suitor might respond to the actual, instead of painted, queen.

But even when some suitors offered to come, she showed reluctance. In 1559, the Imperial Ambassador Baron Breuner wrote to Emperor Ferdinand II that Elizabeth disliked being pestered every day to marry for her honor's sake and for the welfare of the kingdom. But despite the pressure, there was also never any uniform agreement about whom she ought to marry; some thought that foreign husbands were hazardous as their first loyalty would be to their own country, so she ought to marry an Englishman, who would be dedicated only to the interests of England, though there was no agreement on which Englishman. Strong Protestants wanted a Protestant husband for the queen, worrying that a Catholic could endanger them, while those who kept more traditional beliefs hoped for a Catholic husband.

The lack of consensus made it easier for Elizabeth to avoid marriage altogether. Elizabeth had told Robert Dudley when she was eight years old that she would never marry, though later he repeatedly attempted to change her mind. An early suitor Sir William Pickering did not take the courtship too seriously as he said he was sure that Elizabeth intended to die a maid. Though she often told Parliament that she might marry when it was convenient, to placate them, in 1572, while she still was stating she would consider marriage, she added, "if I were a milkmaid with a pail on mine arm… I would not forsake that single state to match myself with the greatest monarch" (Elizabeth I, *Collected Works*, 170).

The earliest marriage negotiations began when she was still a baby; they continued until she was in her late forties. She also had favorites at court, though except for Dudley, she did not seriously consider marriage with any of them. And despite all the rumors (see Chapter 15) there is no evidence that she took any of these men as lovers.

1534–1535 CHARLES, DUKE OF ANGOULÊME (1522–1545)

When Elizabeth was born in 1533, she was considered the only legitimate heir to the throne, and Henry VIII very soon began to consider the most appropriate husband for her. Pope Clement VII's diplomat, Rodolfo Pio da Carpi, Bishop of Faenza, wrote that he thought that Henry "despairs of other sons, so that this last daughter may be mistress of England." England's policy "will probably depend upon the decision about the marriage" for Elizabeth. (*L&P, Henry VIII*, 8, 203). The husband Henry wanted for his daughter in these very early years was Francis I's third son, Charles, Duke of Angoulême. Francis was interested in the prospect and sent Philippe de Chabot, Admiral de Brion, to negotiate. But Henry had many demands. He wanted Francis to pressure Pope Clement to recognize the annulment of his marriage to Catherine of Aragon and to acknowledge the legitimacy of Henry's marriage to Anne Boleyn. Henry also insisted the duke, then about thirteen years of age, be raised in England. Francis objected and the negotiations fell apart. Once Anne Boleyn was executed, and Elizabeth declared illegitimate with no claim to the throne in the 3rd Act of Succession of 1536, Henry was no longer eager to arrange a marriage for his second daughter.

1542, 1559 JAMES HAMILTON, THIRD EARL OF ARRAN (C. 1532–1609)

After the birth of Mary Stuart in December 1542 and the death of her father James V immediately after, Henry VIII considered it to be an excellent plan for Mary to eventually marry his son Edward and negotiated with James Hamilton, second Earl of Arran, the Regent and next in line to the Scottish throne. Henry also offered nine-year-old Elizabeth to the earl's son James, about the same age as Elizabeth. The earl had converted to Protestantism and agreed to the plan. Soon after, however, the earl returned to his Catholic faith and alliance to the queen mother Mary of Guise, with the hope that his son would marry Mary Stuart instead. That plan failed, as Mary as a young child was raised in France to be married to the Dauphin Francis. In 1559, the second earl, by now Duke of Châtelherault, had again become Protestant and there was again discussion of Elizabeth, now queen, marrying his son, now third earl of Arran. Arran came to London in 1559 and met with Elizabeth in the palace gardens, though we do not know what passed between them. Arran returned to Scotland in December 1560, and Elizabeth then formally rejected the offer. It was fortunate for Elizabeth that it came to nothing. By 1562 Arran, drowned in dreams it was said, was violent and incoherent, raving of witches and demons.

1548 Thomas Seymour (c. 1508–1549)

After Henry VIII's death, Elizabeth lived in the household of her final stepmother, Katherine Parr. But within a few months of Henry VIII's death, Katherine married Thomas Seymour, Lord Admiral, and the younger uncle of the child king Edward VI. Seymour acted inappropriately toward the fourteen-year-old Elizabeth (see Chapter 15). At first Katherine did not take her husband's actions seriously, but that changed, especially after she became, for the first time in her four marriages, pregnant. She had a serious talk with Elizabeth and sent her to live with Kat Ashley's sister, Lady Joan Denny and her husband Sir Anthony at Chesthunt. Katherine died after giving birth to a daughter in September 1548. Seymour soon became interested in marrying Elizabeth. While Kat Ashley encouraged the courtship, Elizabeth was far more cautious and careful, unwilling to consider a marriage without the Council's consent, given the dangers to her if she married without that. Seymour had other plots ongoing as well, including piracy, counterfeiting, and an attempt to kidnap the king, which led to his arrest. While Seymour was in the Tower, so too were Kat Ashley and Thomas Parry, Comptroller of the Household. They both testified to all the goings on at Chelsea. Sir Robert Tyrwhitt was sent by the King's Council to examine Elizabeth and obtain a confession of her involvement with Seymour. Elizabeth handled herself well, and when told that people thought she was pregnant with Seymour's child, she insisted that these rumors be denied, and that Ashley and Parry be released. When Seymour was executed for treason, Elizabeth implied that, because of his vanity, he had made fatal mistakes.

1554–1556 Edward Courtenay, Earl of Devon (c. 1527–1556)

Henry Courtenay, Marquess of Exeter, was a descendent of Edward IV. He had long been a favorite of Henry VIII, but his wife Gertrude's support of Catherine of Aragon and her daughter Mary changed that. Courtenay and Thomas Cromwell fought bitterly in Council, and this led, in 1538, to Courtenay's arrest for treason. His wife and his twelve-year-old son Edward joined him in the Tower. Henry was executed, and Edward and his mother were not freed from the Tower until the beginning of Mary's reign in 1553, when Edward was given the title of Earl of Devon. Though, at twenty-seven, he was much younger than the new queen, many thought he would be a suitable consort for Mary. But Mary was only interested in pursuing a marriage negotiation with Philip of Spain. As a plot developed against the Spanish match, some conspirators discussed the plan to have Courtenay marry Elizabeth instead. Courtenay was on the edges of the conspiracy. There is no evidence that Elizabeth agreed to any of this or had any interest in marrying the earl. Thomas Wyatt's 1554 plot against the marriage of Mary and Philip of Spain failed. On February 12, Courtenay was returned to the Tower, and later held at Fotheringhay Castle in Northamptonshire. Though on April 11 Wyatt proclaimed both Courtenay and the princess completely innocent on the scaffold, Courtenay was not released for another year. He was then strongly encouraged to travel abroad. While in Italy, Courtenay still associated with disaffected expatriates. In 1556, Sir Henry Dudley, a cousin of Robert's living in France, began to plot to murder Mary and replace her with Courtenay and Elizabeth. While Courtenay did not join the conspiracy, he was aware of it. But the conspiracy went nowhere, and Courtenay died in Padua on September 18, 1556. While there were rumors that he was poisoned, he died of a fever. Though Elizabeth never had any interest in marrying Courtenay, clearly it was a popular idea in some quarters during Mary's reign.

1554 Emmanuel Philibert, Duke of Savoy (1528–1580)

Once Philip of Spain came to England in 1554 to marry Queen Mary, he worked to make Elizabeth an ally of Spain if Mary were to die without heirs. Catholics would have considered Elizabeth illegitimate with no claim to the throne, and the next heir by rights of primogeniture was the young Scottish queen Mary Stuart (see Chapter 7). Since she was being raised in France as a future queen consort, and France was Spain's traditional enemy, Philip saw Elizabeth as a potential ally. For Philip to achieve his goal he needed Elizabeth to marry his cousin Emmanuel Philibert, Duke of Savoy, and he invited the duke to England. Savoy arrived in December 1554, but Mary would not allow him to meet Elizabeth. Given certain events he was involved in on the continent, Savoy soon had to depart. But Philip did not forget the scheme, even after he had also left England. He convinced Mary to support the marriage. He and his ambassador to England, Simon Renard, exchanged several letters on the subject. Renard warned that Philip could not change the succession of Elizabeth without a rebellion, but if Elizabeth married Savoy, Renard was convinced the English people would be very pleased to have her as queen—and him as king. While Renard was correct about his warning about the succession, his other conclusion was highly doubtful, and Elizabeth had no interest in marrying Savoy. Once she became queen, Gómez Suárez de Figueroa y Córdoba, 1st Duke of Feria, Philip's confidant, and new ambassador, wrote to his king that no one in England wanted to even speak of a potential marriage between the new queen and the duke, as they feared if he were king, he would keep England perpetually at war.

1558–1561 Prince Erik of Sweden, Afterward Erik XIV (1533–1577)

In the spring of 1558, King Gustavus I of Sweden sent Dionysius Beurraeus, his son Erik's former tutor, to England with a letter from Erik to Elizabeth asking for her hand in marriage. Before even mentioning it to Queen Mary, the ambassador went to Hatfield to deliver the letter. Mary was furious and dressed down Beurraeus. She worried Philip would be angry as she had failed to compel Elizabeth to marry the Duke of Savoy the previous year. Mary was somewhat reassured when she learned that Elizabeth had informed the ambassador that she did not wish to marry. Once he had become king and Elizabeth queen, Erik would again vigorously pursue his suit, though with equal lack of success. As soon as he ascended the throne in September 1560, he strongly renewed his courtship sending his brother, John Duke of Finland, to assure Elizabeth that his love for her had not diminished. The duke spent lavishly during his visit, causing some of the populace to become excited about the match. In the summer of 1561, there were engravings of Erik and Elizabeth together for sale, which the queen ordered suppressed. When he heard she would never marry a man she had not seen, Erik made his plan to come. Elizabeth demurred and told him not to and was greatly relieved that a storm had driven him back to port when he had attempted the visit. She told his envoys that she had no desire to marry. Clearly Elizabeth had no desire to marry him. This again proved to be a wise decision, as, like Arran, Erik XIV later suffered from severe and violent mental instability, losing his throne in 1569 and then later his life.

1559 Henry FitzAlan, Earl of Arundel (1512–1580)

In November 1558, as Mary was dying, Philip's agent, Christopher D'Assonleville, wrote to the Spanish king that the common people were discussing how Elizabeth should marry Henry FitzAlan, Earl of Arundel. He was twenty-one years older than Elizabeth and a widower, but also one of the foremost nobles in England. Arundel had been supportive of Elizabeth during her sister's reign, opposing in Council Stephen Gardiner's plan to charge Elizabeth with treason after the Wyatt Rebellion. Renard feared in Mary's reign that Arundel hoped to have Elizabeth marry his son Henry, but in 1555, Henry married Anne Wentworth, widow of Hugh Rich. Unfortunately for her and his father, Henry died the following year, so, at the beginning of the new queen's reign, Arundel was looking at Elizabeth for himself.

The Italian Don Aloisio Schivenoglia ("Il Schifanoia") wrote to Ottaviano Vivaldino, the Mantuan ambassador in Brussels, that he knew some English were declaring that the queen would take Arundel as her husband because he received daily favors from the queen. But there were other candidates, such as an Englishman who was in France, whom he heard was very handsome and gallant, though he forgot his name. De Feria reported that Elizabeth made a joke about marrying Arundel, as she did not get along well with him, adding that he found the earl to be flighty with small ability. Other potential suitors disliked Arundel. Robert Dudley started a playful rumor that Arundel planned to poison him and the queen when he invited them to a banquet. William Pickering described Arundel as a knave who was both impudent and discourteous. Arundel apparently told his friends that if Elizabeth married Pickering, he would leave the country. The Imperial ambassador, Baron Casper Breuner, wrote to Emperor Ferdinand that Arundel was the only one who believed that the queen would marry him, adding that he was silly, loutish, and unattractive. He was spending a great deal of money on jewelry for Elizabeth's attendants in the hope they would speak well of him to her. Breuner also mentioned that Elizabeth was being daily pressured with petitions begging her to marry. Elizabeth, it turns out, had no intention to marry, especially not Arundel.

1559 Sir William Pickering (1516–1575)

The man whose name Schifanoia forgot was William Pickering, who was also more than twenty years older than Elizabeth, though considered far more attractive than Arundel. He served as ambassador to France in the reign of Edward VI and was known as a committed Protestant. In Mary's reign he was involved in Wyatt's rebellion, and though indicted for treason, he managed to escape to France. Pickering offered information about some of the other conspirators and received a pardon. But he did not return to England until Elizabeth had been queen for six months. At first Pickering was taken seriously as a suitor. He and Arundel quarreled, and Pickering challenged him to a duel when he heard Arundel's claim that if the queen married Pickering he would move to France. There were bets in London over the queen's marriage to Pickering. Schifanoia wrote in February 1559 that the common people were convinced that the queen would choose him. But Pickering became convinced that Elizabeth never intended to actually marry. He soon faded from view, living for the most part a quiet life, never marrying either, though he did have a daughter Hester, his heir (see Chapter 3). Pickering stayed loyal to his queen and was one of her lieutenants during the 1569 Northern Rebellion.

1559 Philip II (1527–1598)

Apparently, when in England as Mary's husband, Philip found his young sister-in-law attractive. Writing in the mid-seventeenth century, Godfrey Goodman, Bishop of Gloucester, stated that he had on good authority that when Philip was married to Mary, he was enamored with Elizabeth. After Mary's death, Philip wanted de Feria to publicly support the marriage negotiations of his cousins, Ferdinand and Charles, sons of Emperor Ferdinand I, but privately work against them, as Philip wanted to marry Elizabeth himself. In the first letter de Feria sent Philip after Elizabeth became queen, he assured him that if Elizabeth did not marry an Englishman, he was sure she would decide on Philip. But de Feria soon realized that this would be a very unpopular move. He wrote often to Philip that there was no one in England who wanted Elizabeth to marry him. But Philip insisted the marriage was necessary for the good of the Catholic Church. He did have his conditions. Elizabeth would have to convert to Catholicism, and she had to obtain secret absolution for the marriage from the pope. But when de Feria brought it up with Elizabeth, he realized quickly that she had no interest, so he stopped the conversation before she could give a negative reply. Philip soon after married Elisabeth Valois, daughter of Henri II of France. In her next conversation with de Feria about Philip's marriage, Elizabeth gave little sighs bordering on laughter, saying Philip could not have been very interested if he married someone else so quickly. Later in the reign, Philip became her implacable enemy, supporting assassination attempts and eventually sending his "Invincible" Spanish Armada against England (see Chapter 10). This courtship was well-remembered in early modern England. Diana Primrose's 1630 work *A Chaine of Pearle, Or a Memoriall of the peerles Graces, and Heroick Vertues of Queene Elizabeth of Glorious Memory* talked about Philip as Elizabeth's first suitor as queen, and the first whom Elizabeth chose not to marry.

1559 Archduke Ferdinand (1529–1595)

Once he learned that Philip was no longer seeking to marry Elizabeth, Emperor Ferdinand I, through his ambassador Baron Rabenstayn and the Spanish ambassador de Quadra, suggested a marriage with either of his two sons, his second son Ferdinand or his younger brother Charles. In April 1559, de Feria wrote to Philip that the English talked about Elizabeth marrying the Archduke Ferdinand but added he personally believed the queen would never marry anyone who would be good for her. He noted that sometimes she seems interested, behaving as a queen who would only accept a great prince, but then, de Feria adds, others tell him that Elizabeth is so enamored with Robert Dudley that she would never marry. But he returned to the possibility of marriage with the archduke. He confided that his spies at court told him Elizabeth could not bear children, so if the archduke married her and she died, he was convinced that, with Philip's help, the archduke could keep control of England.

But the following month, the new Spanish ambassador, Alvaro de Quadra, the Bishop of Aquila, reported that he gathered from William Cecil that the English were quite opposed to Ferdinand because of his extreme Catholicism, and the people feared that he would be violent toward Protestants. De Quadra also believed that some at court described Ferdinand as a young monster with a very big head to make the marriage even less appealing. Soon Ferdinand was no longer perceived an appropriate suitor. In fact, in 1557, he had secretly married Phillipine Weisner, though the marriage was only accepted by Emperor Ferdinand in 1559, with the condition that the marriage be kept secret. His younger brother Charles was a very different matter.

1559, 1563–1568 Archduke Charles, Son of Holy Roman Emperor 1559, Ferdinand and Brother to Emperor Maximilian II (1540–1590)

In 1559, when it was clear that Elizabeth had no interest in Ferdinand, Philip II and his Hapsburg cousins encouraged the suit of his younger brother Charles, who appeared to be more appealing. De Quadra wrote to Philip II that the queen had told him that she had heard from one of her fools that the Imperial ambassador's chamberlain was actually the archduke who had come in disguise to see her. De Quadra did not think that the queen really believed this; rather, it was a hint that she wanted to meet the archduke. But it then became clear that her interest had waned, and the possibility of the marriage flickered out, only to be revived later.

William Cecil was eager to revive the negotiations for the marriage in 1563. There was great concern over whom Mary Stuart might marry after her first husband Francis II died, and, indeed, one of those considered for that marriage alliance was the Archduke Charles, though Mary ultimately rejected him. Cecil wrote to the converted Protestant Christoph, Duke of Wurttemberg, asking him to press Charles's suit with Elizabeth since he knew Emperor Ferdinand, but the emperor showed little interest, believing it would lower his dignity since he had already made one attempt and had been refused. That autumn, both Cecil and Christopher Mundt, his agent in the Holy Roman Empire, assured the duke that another attempt would surely be successful. The duke mentioned it to the emperor and sent his agent to England for a more thorough discussion. While the envoy was at the English court in January 1564, both Cecil and the queen let him know how willing Elizabeth was to begin a new negotiation with the emperor to marry his son. Elizabeth stated that she might have to marry, but added she would not consider an Englishman, nor would she accept a suitor from France, Spain, Sweden, or Denmark, which left Charles as the only acceptable candidate. The duke suggested to the emperor and Charles that sending a friendly note would be a good first step, but soon after the emperor became seriously ill and everything was put on pause, with no letter sent. The emperor died on July 25, 1564.

The following spring, the new Emperor Maximilian sent Adam von Zwetkovich, Baron von Mitterburg, to London to discuss marriage negotiations for Elizabeth and his brother. When the baron arrived in May, he found the court preoccupied and distressed with the news that Mary Stuart had decided to marry her cousin, Henry Stuart, Lord Darnley. Several men at the queen's court believed this marriage would be the best way to counter Mary's marriage. The biggest supporters were Thomas Radcliffe, Earl of Sussex, and Thomas Howard, Duke of Norfolk. But Robert Dudley led a faction that was very much opposed to the marriage. Different versions of marriage treaties were discussed and drafted. There were many concerning issues for Elizabeth, particularly whether the archduke and his courtiers would be able to freely practice their own Catholic religion. Another disagreement was about who would pay for the archduke's household in England. Elizabeth argued the archduke should pay his expenses, while the emperor thought all expenses should be paid by the English crown. The emperor also wanted his brother to be crowned king and have the right of succession if Elizabeth died without heirs. Elizabeth examined her sister Mary's marriage to Philip of Spain's marriage treaty where this had not been allowed. And, finally, Elizabeth said she would make no commitment until she had already met the archduke, though the emperor thought it would be demeaning for the archduke to come, as it were, on approval. Though the queen had these concerns, William Cecil hoped they could still continue to negotiate. The Earl of Sussex suggested that a compromise would be for Charles to attend English church services publicly but be allowed to hear Mass in private. But the archduke stated that he and his entire household should openly go to Mass. Zwetkovich also had the opportunity to see that Elizabeth was a woman who had deep emotional bonds with those surrounding her. In July 1565, when Zwetkovich thought it was important to see the queen, he was told he must wait a few days. "Some few days ago a lady of the name Ashley died here. The Queen visited her before her death, for it was who had the upbringing of the Queen. Her decease grieved the Queen so much," she needed a few days before he could see her (Klarwill, 248).

While negotiations seemed at a stalemate, when the news of Mary Stuart's pregnancy reached the English court, Elizabeth agreed in February 1566 that Sir Thomas Dannett could visit the Emperor Maximilian and discuss the areas that were troublesome to the negotiations. Elizabeth said she would be willing to pay any extra costs to the archduke's household expenses that might result with his marriage, but that he must attend the Church of England services. The negotiations floundered. The emperor was insistent that the queen should pay the total cost of the archduke's expenses, and Dannett found that Charles was a more devout Catholic than the English had supposed: he attended Mass every day.

But members of Parliament were very alarmed when Mary Stuart gave birth to a healthy son in June 1566, thus strengthening the claims of the Scottish Catholics. They wanted marriage negotiations to continue or else force Elizabeth to name an heir. Elizabeth was furious when Parliament petitioned her, as she was convinced that naming a successor could endanger her throne. She did promise, though giving herself an out, that she would marry "as I can conveniently, if God take not him away with whom I mind to marry" (Elizabeth I, *Collected Works*, 95). The following year, Elizabeth sent the Earl of Sussex for further negotiations, asking him to attempt to successfully conclude the marriage negotiations but still insisting that the archduke must attend Anglican services and forego Mass. Sussex worked very hard and he and the emperor agreed on a compromise arrangement. The archduke could attend Mass in his private chambers, but no English people could be allowed to be there, and he would publicly accompany the queen to Anglican services. Charles would also agree to suspend his Catholic services for a period if there were disturbances about it. The emperor agreed to Elizabeth's terms on Charles's title and status.

But despite these concessions, there was a great divide in the Privy Council when they discussed the marriage contract. The Earl of Sussex had not returned to England and the Duke of Norfolk, who was most in favor of the marriage, was not at the Council meeting as his wife Elizabeth had just died and he was in mourning. Elizabeth agreed with those who argued it would be too divisive for Charles to hear Mass even in private. The negotiations were over. When Sussex got back to court, he was furious with Robert Dudley, who had spearheaded the opposition. It is hard to know how serious Elizabeth had been during the five long years of discussions about the marriage, but she was relieved of pressure to marry during those years as she was presumably in the midst of negotiations.

Count John Casimir Palatine, Younger Son of Frederick III, Elector Palatine 1564

In 1549, James Melville, whose older brother Robert was a baron, left Scotland for France at age fourteen to be a page of honor for Mary Stuart. He received a thorough education at the French court and eventually was at the court of the Frederick III, Elector Palatine, when, in 1564, he was called home by Mary Stuart, now back in Scotland as the ruling queen (see Chapter 8). Since Melville planned to travel through England, spending some time at Elizabeth's court to discuss with her his own queen's second marriage, Frederick's third son Count John Casimir asked Melville to bring Elizabeth his portrait and a marriage proposal. But Elizabeth was far more interested in discussing Mary's marital prospects. She expressed no interest in the count's proposal, but many years later she met him, by then Count John, when he visited England in 1579 to discuss help for the Netherlands (see Chapter 11).

Courtships with French Princes, the Sons of Catherine De Medici

For several decades of Elizabeth's reign there were less or more serious conversations and negotiations between the English queen and the French over her potential marriage to the various sons of the queen mother, Catherine de Medici.

When the members of the French government heard, in 1565, that there was new interest in the marriage of Elizabeth and the Archduke Charles, they suggested the alternative of her marrying the fourteen-year-old Charles IX. Elizabeth expressed no interest in such a marriage, but Cecil continued the negotiations for several months. Starting in 1568, there were discussions of a marriage between the queen and Henri, Duke of Anjou, afterward Henri III. The negotiations became more serious in the winter of 1570–1571 as a way to settle the French religious war and for the French to gain a strong alliance with England. But Elizabeth refused to change the terms that had been offered Charles and, more importantly, Anjou had no interest in any compromise about religion. The 1572 St. Bartholomew's Day Massacre in Paris horrified Elizabeth and the English people. She had been at Woodstock with a hunting party when she heard and put the court in deepest mourning. She sent back to London all musicians and entertainers. As an unnamed Spanish correspond wrote, "there are no more of the dances, farces, and entertainments with which they have been amusing themselves lately, as they have some less agreeable things to think about" (*CSP, Spain, Simancas*, II, 416). Not only did this harm French marriage negotiations at the time but was vividly remembered at the time of the more serious negotiations with François, Duke of Anjou (earlier Alençon), 1579–1582. In his 1579 anti-French marriage pamphlet, *The discovery of a Gaping Gulf whereunto England is like to be swallowed by another French marriage*, John Stubbes wrote that the marriage could lead to more massacres, where thousands would be killed. Stubbes was severely punished for this—losing his hand (see Chapter 8) (Fig. 6.1). This final marriage negotiations of Elizabeth's reign with Duke of Anjou became one of the most serious ones. While there was little interest when the marriage was first mentioned, it became so serious that he visited England twice, in 1579 and 1581. Lord Burghley had made it his business to find out that Elizabeth was still menstruating, and thus, he concluded, able to have a child. Elizabeth, at least for a time, took the marriage proposal seriously enough that she wrote to him in January 1580 that "For my part, I confess there is no prince in the world to whom I would more willingly yield to be his than to yourself…nor with whom I would pass the years of my life, both for your rare virtues and sweet nature" (Elizabeth, *Collected Works*, 243). Elizabeth gave Anjou a ring at the time of his second visit, promising publicly to marry him. But Elizabeth soon changed her mind, and while she publicly wept when he left, it was said that privately she danced for joy at getting rid of him (For more on the French marriage negotiations, see Chapter 8).

6 COURTSHIPS AND FAVORITES 81

Fig. 6.1 Duke of Alençon, later Anjou private collection

Favorites

Robert Dudley, Earl of Leicester (c. 1532–1588) Favorite, 1558–1588; Marriage Attempts 1561–1575

In 1566, Robert Dudley told Jacob de Vulcob, sieur de Sassy, that he had known Elizabeth since she was eight years old, and she had told him then she would never marry, adding that he had never seen her waver about this choice. He also said, however, that she told him if she changed her mind, and decided to marry one of her subjects, that it would definitely be him (Fig. 6.2).

From this comment we know that Dudley and Elizabeth knew each other as children. Dudley and Elizabeth were in the Tower in Mary's reign at the same time—Dudley as a traitor for the part he played in the attempt to put Lady Jane Grey on the throne and Elizabeth for suspicion of her role in the Wyatt Rebellion. There is, however, no evidence that they were able to see each other though Dudley and Elizabeth apparently were able to exchange brief notes through a child of someone employed at the Tower. They clearly became close during the reign of Mary I, given that Dudley was immediately summoned to Hatfield and named the Master of the Horse when Elizabeth ascended the throne.

By April 1559, Dudley had clearly emerged as her favorite as he received the Order of the Garter, though the fact he was already married kept him from being a suitor. Dudley and Amy Robsart were only seventeen when they married in June 1550, though once Elizabeth became queen, Amy lived in the countryside eventually at Cumnor Place near Oxford while he was at court, and Dudley had not seen his wife since April 1559. But his wife's mysterious and sudden death on September 8, 1560 changed everything. She was found at the bottom of some stairs with her neck broken but her clothing did not look disturbed. Amy had ordered her servants to the fair at Abingdon but had refused to go herself and was alone at the time of her death, though there were two women in another part of the house.

Dudley was sent away from court until the coroner's inquest ruled her death was misadventure, an accident. Some scholars have thought Amy might have committed suicide. The rumors that Dudley had murdered his wife to marry Elizabeth, however, haunted Dudley and the queen for decades (see Chapter 15). Elizabeth warmly accepted him back at court, and while there were the various foreign marriages being negotiated, there was also much concern that the queen would marry him, causing serious problems for her rule. Clearly Elizabeth cared about him deeply. Elizabeth apparently disguised herself as Katherine Carey's maid in November 1561 to watch Dudley in an archery contest at Windsor. In October 1562, when Elizabeth thought she was dying of smallpox, she declared that she wanted Dudley to rule as protector of the kingdom until a new monarch could be found, but also swore that nothing dishonorable had passed between them. That year he also became a member of the Privy Council. In 1565 she told an ambassador that "I have heard that you will dine with the Earl of Leicester. I beseech you to regard and honor

6 COURTSHIPS AND FAVORITES 83

Fig. 6.2 Robert Dudley, Earl of Leicester private collection

him as my own brother, for thus do I love him and will love and regard him all my lifelong; for he deserves it" (Klarwill, 231).

When in 1564 Elizabeth was concerned about whom her widowed cousin Mary Stuart, Queen of Scotland, might marry, and the potential impact on England, she suggested Dudley, and gave him the title of Earl of Leicester. Mary offered to marry him if she were named heir to the throne, but it is doubtful that this was ever a serious offer. Leicester himself opposed it and Elizabeth did not like him to be absent from court. She had agreed to let him leave court in February 1566 but was so pleased with his return in April that she publicly kissed him three times when she first saw him.

In 1566 or '67, William Cecil drafted a memorandum about whether or not Elizabeth should marry Leicester and listed the many drawbacks: Leicester would bring nothing to the marriage, it would encourage people to believe the slander said about him and the queen, but most important to Cecil was his concern that were Leicester the queen's husband, he would be unkind to her. Though not an ally of Leicester, Thomas Radcliffe, Earl of Sussex, at one point supported the marriage, since he was convinced that Elizabeth's passion for Leicester would allow her to quickly become pregnant.

In the early 1570s, Leicester began an affair with Douglas Howard, widow of John Sheffield, and extraordinary gentlewoman of the privy chamber. They had a son, Robert Dudley, in 1574 but that year Leicester wrote to her that he could not marry her as it would anger Elizabeth and the relationship ended soon after. In 1575, Leicester invited Elizabeth to his Kenilworth estate and made his last unsuccessful attempt to convince her to marry him. He later secretly married Elizabeth's cousin Lettice Knollys, widow of Walter Devereux, Earl of Essex, on September 21, 1578. He told his close friend Roger, Lord North that he wanted to have a son as heir, and they did have a son named Robert, Baron Denbigh, but he died at the age of three. Indeed, Elizabeth was furious when she found out about the marriage and threatened to send him to the Tower. The Earl of Sussex had to convince the queen that someone should not be punished for marrying. On November 28, 1579, Douglas Sheffield secretly married Sir Edward Stafford. Soon after he was sent to France as an envoy as part of the negotiation to marry the Duke of Anjou. When he returned in February 1580, Elizabeth called him in and forced him to admit to his marriage, and then Douglas was asked if she had married Leicester. She insisted that though he had said he would marry her, he never had. In 1604, early in James I's reign, attempting to support her son by Dudley's claims of inheritance, Douglas stated that Leicester had married her, but there is no evidence to support the claim. While the queen forgave Leicester for his marriage to Lettice, she was less forgiving of her cousin.

Leicester served as governor-general in the Netherlands, with uneven results, leaving England in December 1585 and returning in November 1586. The personal tragedy of this time was the death of his nephew and heir, Sir Philip Sidney, as a result of battle wounds. Leicester returned to the Netherlands the following summer but returned to England in December 1587.

As a reward for his work, he was named Lord Steward of the Household. He then became very involved in the military preparations for the coming Spanish invasion, and it was he who convinced Elizabeth to come to Tilbury on August 9, where she gave her famous speech (see Chapter 10). He and Elizabeth celebrated the defeat of the Spanish Armada, and, on August 27, he left court, possibly to take the waters, as his health was quite problematic. He wrote to the queen on the 29th and a few days later became very ill, dying on September 4. Elizabeth was devastated, locking herself in her room and marking his final communication from him "his last letter" (Doran, *Elizabeth I & Her Circle*, 141). She kept the letter in a jewel box for the rest of her life. Perhaps his importance to her is evident in a letter Leicester sent to Walsingham after she had approved of his going to the Netherlands. Leicester confided that she did not want him to go as she did not want to be apart from him. She said she was not well, and greatly feared she would die without him with her. She finally let him go, and in the end, it was Leicester who died without her being at his side.

SIR CHRISTOPHER HATTON (1540–1591), FAVORITE

There were some who said that Christopher Hatton danced his way into Elizabeth's favor. But though Hatton was an excellent dancer, he had many qualities that served him well as one of Elizabeth's favorites and courtiers; he was very loyal and hardworking. We know little about his background. At the age of fifteen or sixteen, Christopher Hatton attended St. Mary Hall, Oxford as a gentleman commoner, but left Oxford without his degree and in 1560 enrolled in the Inner Temple. He performed in and wrote several entertainments there, which was probably how he first came to the attention of Queen Elizabeth. In 1564 he became one of her gentlemen pensioners, effectively one of the Gentlemen of Arms who protected the queen, and a gentleman of the Privy Chamber. Hatton was known to be an attractive person, but Elizabeth's biographer William Camden also explained his appeal in that he had a "modest sweetness of condition" (Nicolas, 5). He was far less ambitious than Robert Dudley, and his relationship with Elizabeth was thus more private. Hatton never married and expressed himself as a loving suitor who knew his place. He said that he wished to everlastingly serve the queen because of his pure love for her. Hatton served in Parliament and filled the role as spokesman for his queen.

In 1577, Hatton was appointed to the Privy Council, received a knighthood, and was named Vice-Chamberlain of the household (see Chapter 3). He took his position on the Council very seriously. Walsingham valued Hatton, who often helped him smooth over relationships with Elizabeth. He was also good friends rather than rivals with Leicester. Hatton was with the queen and two others in 1579 when someone fired on her barge (see Chapter 9). In 1587, he became Lord Chancellor. During the trials of Anthony Babington and the other conspirators, Hatton was important in pushing the prisoners to make full confessions and he also served on the commission that tried Mary Stuart.

During his time at court, there were frequent allegations that Hatton was secretly a Catholic. There was no evidence whatsoever to support this, though he was an Anglican who was an active opponent of Puritans, and a strong ally of John Whitgift, Archbishop of Canterbury. In 1573, Peter Burchet, a radical Puritan who was also a madman, attempted to assassinate Hatton for his supposed Catholicism. But he mistook Sir John Hawkins for Hatton. Hawkins was wounded but managed to fight Burchet off and he was arrested. Elizabeth was so furious she wanted Burchet immediately executed but her Privy Council convinced her there had to be a regular trial. While in the Tower, Burchet managed to murder a jailor and was then found guilty and executed.

Hatton served the queen to almost the end of his life. In November 1591, he became very ill. Elizabeth visited him and brought him broth. He died on November 20. Though he never married, he had a natural daughter Elizabeth, who was involved with Sir John Perrot and with him had a daughter also called Elizabeth. His heir was his nephew William Newport, who adopted the name Hatton.

Sir Walter Raleigh [or Ralegh] (1554–1618), Favorite 1581–1591, Restored at Court 1597–1603

Walter Raleigh was a courtier, an explorer, author, and a man of exceptional learning. He studied at Oxford and was admitted to the Middle Temple in 1575. His older half-brother was the explorer and soldier Sir Humphrey Gilbert, who served in Elizabeth's household before she became queen. Raleigh commanded a ship in 1578 when Gilbert led a fleet looking for plunder and adventure. Upon his return a year later, he spent some time in Ireland. Raleigh, clearly charming, attracted Elizabeth's attention in 1581, and she made him an esquire of the body. In the following years, he rose in her favor, composing elegant love poetry for her. The queen granted him a beautiful London house, Durham Place, and he received other funds and honors as well, including being knighted in 1585. After Hatton's death, Raleigh was named captain of the guard. After his half-brother's death in 1583 when his ship went down, Raleigh secured a patent to allow him to develop a colony in 1584 in Virginia—named for the Virgin Queen. The first colony was established in 1585 at Roanoke, but plagued with hunger and disease, colonists returned to England the following year. It was re-established in 1587, but, because of the Spanish Armada, help was not able to reach it until 1591 and no one was there, causing it to be known as the lost colony. Raleigh was also known for popularizing tobacco with smoking at court and among the elites. He did not, however, introduce tobacco, which was first smoked in England by 1573.

Unlike Hatton, who managed to work well with everyone, Raleigh made many enemies at court, and was quick to denigrate others publicly and cleverly.

From the late 1580s, he and Robert Devereux, Earl of Essex, were sometimes allies and friends, but over time they became bitter enemies, fueled by their mutual distrust and rivalry for the queen's favor. In 1591, Raleigh secretly married the pregnant Bess Throckmorton, a lady-in-waiting to Elizabeth. They had a strong and enduring affection for each other but knew that if Elizabeth were to learn of their marriage, she would be very displeased. Raleigh lied about it and Bess left court to have her son, returning in April to take up her position with Elizabeth. But, by May, the secret was out. Raleigh's defiance and lack of remorse infuriated the queen and he and Bess were sent to the Tower in August. By the end of the year, they had both been released, possibly because Elizabeth had heard their baby son had died. Raleigh and Bess were banished from court until 1597. He used this time to lead explorations, hoping to find cities of gold. While his 1595 trip was a failure in terms of finding such cities, his pamphlet about it, *The Discoverie of the Large, Rich and Bewtiful Empire of Guiana* (1596) was impressive. He was also part of the attack on Cadiz in 1596, and his success there propelled Elizabeth's forgiveness. He returned to court and to his position of captain of the guard. By 1599 Essex considered Raleigh and Robert Cecil his most dangerous enemies, and soon accused Raleigh of treason, claiming that Raleigh intended to divert the succession to a princess of Spain. The day Essex staged his rebellion, Sir Christopher Blount tried to shoot Raleigh, but his aim was bad. Unfortunately, after Essex's execution, Raleigh fell out with Robert Cecil; Raleigh was angry that he had never been made a privy councilor and blamed Cecil. This was unfortunate for Raleigh, as James VI, in part from Essex's correspondence with him, already had a bad opinion of Raleigh. The death of the queen was most unfortunate for Raleigh, who spent most of James' reign in the Tower before his execution in 1618 (see Chapter 11).

ROBERT DEVEREUX, EARL OF ESSEX (1565–1601) FAVORITE

Through his mother Lettice, Robert Devereux was a cousin of Queen Elizabeth. After his father's death in 1576, he became the ward of Burghley. After his mother married Leicester, Essex was often with the earl, and accompanied him to fight in the Netherlands in 1585 where he was knighted for his bravery. He was there with Sir Philip Sidney, Leicester's nephew, and, as Sidney lay dying, he gave Essex one of his best swords. Returning to court, he caught the interest of the queen, and Leicester worked to advance Essex. Elizabeth spent much of her leisure time with Essex playing cards and agreed that Essex could succeed Leicester as Master of the Horse. The rivalry with Raleigh was so intense that Essex harangued the queen about him, and when she defended Raleigh, Essex in a huff left court and Robert Carey had to go after him and bring him back. Despite his defiance of the queen, there were no serious consequences for Essex, a lesson he learned early. In April 1588 he became a Knight of the Garter. After Leicester's death in early September 1588 Essex tried to establish his favor with the queen at the expense of his rival. Essex was also eager to be seen as a military hero and tried to persuade the queen to allow him to pursue England's enemies, often with poor results. In 1589, even though Elizabeth had refused him permission to participate in an attack on Portugal, Essex secretly joined the ship and though he demonstrated his bravery, the expedition was a failure. Elizabeth again forgave him. Though there were romantic trappings to the relationship, in many ways Elizabeth acted as an indulgent mother in her treatment of the young Essex. Some scholars consider that Essex may have been bi-polar, as at times he would just take to his room for days, and Elizabeth would try to cheer him up. At other times his plans were grandiose.

In 1590, Essex secretly married Sidney's widow, Frances Walsingham, who was pregnant. But though the queen was at first very angry, unlike with Raleigh's marriage, she soon forgave Essex, though his wife lived away from court. One result was that Essex had affairs with other women at court, though he visited his wife frequently enough that she was pregnant throughout the 1590s. They had six children and two stillbirths, though only two of the children, Robert and Frances, lived to adulthood. In the early 1590s, Essex was on good terms with Burghley, who convinced Elizabeth to allow Essex to lead an army as lieutenant-general in support of Henri IV of France in 1591. Again, though Essex showed bravery—and was anguished by the death of his young brother Walter in combat—the Normandy campaign was a failure and Essex returned to court in January 1592. Essex was convinced that Burghley had not supported his cause sufficiently while he was away and was upset that Robert Cecil was now a privy councilor while he was not. He was, however, named as a privy councilor in 1593 (see Chapter 3). As Burghley was becoming frail and in ill health, Essex wanted to replace him as Elizabeth's chief advisor. This put him in a direct rivalry with Burghley's son. There was more tension with Burghley, especially when, in 1594, Essex accused Roderigo Lopez of attempting to murder Elizabeth. Burghley thought the attack had no merit, though eventually Essex succeeded in having Lopez put on trial and executed (see Chapter 9), which led to great popularity with Londoners that Essex continued to cultivate. Essex's success with the 1596 attack on Cadiz also greatly added to his popular acclaim. But a further attempt with an attack on the Azores in 1597 was a disaster and his military reputation was hard hit. Convinced that he had never been recognized for his success in Cadiz, Essex left court. Elizabeth then gave him the office of Earl Marshall in December 1597.

The severe conflict over policy and leadership was in evidence on July 1, 1598 regarding who would be sent to Ireland to repress the rebel Hugh O'Neill, Earl of Tyrone; strong leadership there was essential. Essex, angry at the queen's choice, turned his back on her, a great insult. Elizabeth responded by boxing his ears and he then reached for his sword, only to be subdued by Lord Admiral Howard. Essex left court in anger and refused to make a submission to the queen. Burghley died on August 4, and then days later the situation in Ireland became even more distraught, looking as if any control of

Ireland might be lost. Members of the Council believed they needed Essex's guidance and hoped for a rapprochement with Elizabeth. When he became ill, Elizabeth showed her concern and Essex returned to court. At Council, Essex criticized anyone that council members suggested for Irish command as not good enough and Essex himself was finally appointed and he promised quick success. He was sent as Lord Lieutenant instead of Lord Deputy with a large force in 1599. But the situation in Ireland was far more difficult than Essex had believed, and Essex never was able to engage in battle with Tyrone. Essex wanted to return to court, convinced his enemies were out to destroy him. The time in Ireland had cost a fortune and Essex had achieved nothing. Essex and Tyrone agreed to a truce and Essex began to disperse his troops. Elizabeth was furious, especially as Essex had been commanded not to leave Ireland without the queen's express consent. Instead, he left for England and burst in on his queen the morning of September 28, before Elizabeth was even fully dressed. Later he and the queen talked but then she had him confined under house arrest and it was the last time they saw each other. The Council examined his actions and Essex's health collapsed. There were plans to try Essex in Star Chamber in February 1600, but the queen canceled the trial when the earl sent her a submissive letter. He was released in August but prohibited from court. His political career was in ashes, and she stopped funds to him as well. Essex was again unable to recognize his own failings and blamed for others. His attempted rebellion in February 1601 led to his execution (see Chapter 9).

CHAPTER 7

Potential Heirs to Elizabeth's Throne

According to Henry VIII's will, if his son Edward died without heirs of his body, the throne would pass to his older daughter Mary and if she were to die without heirs of her body, to his younger daughter Elizabeth. This was ratified by the 3rd Act of Succession of 1543. The 2nd Act of Succession of 1536 had declared both Mary and Elizabeth as illegitimate and made it treason to advocate their succession. The third act put them back in the succession but did not remove their status as illegitimate. The will and the third act also stated that if Elizabeth died without heirs the throne would pass to the descendants of his younger sister Mary. This excluded the descendants of Henry's older sister Margaret, and went against the concept of primogeniture, that descent went to the older before the younger. When Elizabeth became queen, the great hope was that she would marry and have sons of her own. But until she did, there was great pressure on her to name an heir. While Elizabeth refused to do so, there were many alternatives. As the Privy Councilor Thomas Wilson stated, "The crown is not likely to fall to the ground for wants of heads that can wear it" (Wilson, *The State of England*, 5). In 1601 he identified twelve different potential heirs who were no doubt waiting for the death of the queen, and this was true throughout the reign. But there were problematic issues with every potential heir. There were many descendants of the first Tudor king Henry VII. There was even a descendant of Edward III's younger son, John of Gaunt. In 1562, when she thought she was dying of smallpox, Elizabeth asked her Privy Council if she were to die that they make Robert Dudley Protector of the Realm, until an appropriate ruler could be found. No doubt the Council was deeply relieved when they did not have to deal with that possibility.

As the reign progressed, some members of Parliament angered the queen for insisting Parliament should have a say in the succession. One was the Puritan Peter Wentworth, who served in many Parliaments, and also spent some time in the Tower as a result. During one of his sojourns, he wrote *A pithie exhortation to her Maiestie for establishing her successor to the crowne*, though it was not published until 1598, the year after his death (see Chapter 4).

Despite all the pressures, Elizabeth never named an heir. She said she knew what it was to be the rising sun in the reign of her sister Mary, with Mary as the setting sun, and never wanted to put herself in that position. Given that experience, it is hardly surprising that she was wary of how any potential heir could be manipulated against her. She was concerned about this even if this heir was a child of her own. "Think you that I could love my winding-sheet? Princes cannot like their own children, those that should succeed unto them" (Elizabeth I, *Collected Works*, 65). Throughout her reign she kept assuring her people they did not have to worry, that God would take care of England. It was stated in the new reign that Elizabeth had on her death bed specifically named Mary Stuart's son James, the king of Scotland, as heir. She certainly assumed at the end of the reign that her Scottish cousin would be her successor, but it is probable that until the very end, she never explicitly named an heir.

Plantagenet Descendants from Richard, Duke of York

Though many of the descendants of the previous dynasty, the Plantagenets, had been executed or imprisoned under the first Tudor kings, Henry Hastings, third Earl of Huntingdon was still thought of as a potential heir in the early reign of Elizabeth. Huntingdon's mother was Katherine Pole, the eldest child of Henry Pole, first Baron Montagu, and he was the eldest son of Sir Richard Pole and Margaret Plantagenet, the daughter of Edward IV's executed brother, George, Duke of Clarence, son of Richard, Duke of York. She married the second earl in 1531. In 1538 Henry VIII, because they had claims to the throne, had many members of the Pole family arrested, and a number were executed, including Henry, Baron Montagu. Young Henry Hastings married Katherine Dudley in May 1553; her father was consolidating his power as Edward VI was dying. Katherine, Countess of Huntingdon, Henry's mother, however, had close ties with Mary, who soon became queen despite the attempts to replace her with Lady Jane Grey. The countess worked hard to reconcile the new queen with her husband and son. Mary had always cared about the Pole family. Margaret Pole, Countess of Salisbury, who was executed in 1541, was Mary's godmother. Mary restored Baron Montagu's lands to his coheirs, Katherine and her younger sister Winifred. The second earl died in 1560, and at the age of twenty-four Henry became the third earl.

In 1562, when the Council worried that Elizabeth would die of smallpox, some members supported Huntingdon as the next monarch. When Elizabeth recovered this made her very wary of him; it took some years for her to trust him, while Huntingdon did everything to reassure her of his complete loyalty and lack of interest in pursuing any claim to the throne. By the time Mary Stuart fled to England in 1568 Elizabeth valued Huntington enough that during the northern rebellion in the fall of 1569, she asked him to share with George Talbot, Earl of Shrewsbury, the guardianship of the Scottish queen, to keep her more securely. During this tense time, Huntingdon was in almost daily contact with William Cecil, who also grew to value him deeply. In April 1570 he was named a Knight of the Garter, and two years later he was named President of the Council of the North. Toward the end of his life, his wife Katherine became close to the queen, and Elizabeth felt she needed to inform Katherine herself when her husband died in 1595, well honored for all his service to the crown (see Chapter 14).

DESCENDANTS OF HENRY VIII'S YOUNGER SISTER MARY (1495–1533)

After Henry VIII's younger sister's brief marriage to Louis XII in 1515, Mary—almost immediately after the death of the French king—married Charles Brandon, Duke of Suffolk. Their son Henry was born in 1516 but was dead by 1522, when Charles and Mary named their next son Henry. Frances was born in July 1517 and Eleanor sometime between 1518 and 1521. The second Henry died in 1534. A year earlier Frances married her father's ward Henry Grey, Marquess of Dorset. Her first two children, a son and a daughter, died in infancy. She then had three surviving daughters, Jane, Katherine, and Mary. In 1552 Frances's half-brothers, from her father's subsequent marriage to Katherine Willoughby, died, and she and her husband became Duke and Duchess of Suffolk. Their decision to agree with John Dudley, Duke of Northumberland's plan to marry their daughter Jane to his youngest son Guildford and have Jane be the next ruler after the death of Edward VI in 1553 led to the death in 1554 of Jane, her husband, and her father in the reign of the triumphant Mary I. Queen Mary and Frances stayed on good terms, however, and both Katherine and Mary were well treated at Mary's court. The year after her husband's execution, Frances married her Master of the Horse, Adrian Stokes, who later served as a Member of Parliament. Frances survived the death of Mary I but died in November 1559.

KATHERINE GREY (C. 1540–1568)

For many Protestants at the beginning of Elizabeth's reign, Katherine Grey was seen as an excellent potential heir. She was the heir presumptive according to Henry VIII's will. But Elizabeth opposed her candidacy. During the plotting to put her older sister Jane on the throne, Katherine was either betrothed or actually married to, Henry Herbert, the eldest son of Northumberland's ally, William Herbert, Earl of Pembroke. But the marriage was not consummated and was dissolved when Mary became queen. When Elizabeth became queen Katherine became a maid of honor. Her position as potential heir to Elizabeth attracted the notice of both foreigners and ambitious members of the court. In August 1559 Sir Thomas Challoner wrote from Spain to William Cecil and the queen that he had heard from an Englishman there, Robert Huggyns, or Hogyns, that there was a plot by a group of Spaniards to control Katherine and marry her off to Philip's son Don Carlos or another Spaniard.

There were other various marriage proposals discussed but they went nowhere, because Katherine had fallen in love with Edward Seymour, Earl of Hertford, who had once been betrothed to her older sister Jane. According to the 1536 Treason Act, it was treason for a person of royal blood to marry without the monarch's consent. Katherine and Hertford, however, fearing such consent would not be forthcoming, decided, with the help of Hertford's sister Jane, to marry secretly late in 1560. Jane secured the clergyman, and he and Jane were the only witnesses. The bride and groom never knew the clergyman's name. The following spring Hertford was sent to France and left their marriage document with Katherine. Unfortunately, Katherine misplaced it, and her sister-in-law Jane had died in March 1561 at the age of twenty. By August Katherine realized that she could not hide her pregnancy and begged Robert Dudley for help. Dudley immediately informed Elizabeth. The queen considered the Grey-Seymour connection a dangerous bid for the succession and was furious. Katherine was sent to the Tower and Hertford, required to return from France, was also sent there. Katherine gave birth to their son Edward in September 1561. Elizabeth appointed Matthew Parker, Archbishop of Canterbury to hold a commission to investigate the marriage. Jane Seymour was dead. The bride and groom did not know the clergyman's name and he never came forward. With no documentary evidence and no witnesses, the commission declared in 1562 that there had been no marriage and the baby was illegitimate. This finding no doubt pleased the queen, and Katherine and Hertford remained in the Tower, theoretically kept separate. But Edward Warner, Lieutenant of the Tower, was sympathetic to the couple and allowed secret conjugal visits. Katherine's second son was born in February 1563. Katherine and her sons were moved from the Tower to be under house arrest with her uncle Lord John Grey. Edward and Katherine never saw each other again though they were allowed to exchange letters. The queen kept Katherine in confinement because there were still many people who supported her claim to the throne and argued that her marriage was legal. One was John Hales who in 1564, very worried after Queen Elizabeth almost died of smallpox in 1562, wrote a tract *A Declaration of the Succession of the Crowne Imperiall of Inglande*, declaring that Katherine's marriage was valid, and were Elizabeth to die with no child of her own, Katherine should be the next queen.

Hales was sent to the Tower in 1565. William Cecil procured his release the next year, but for the next four years he could not leave his home without a license. Katherine was very unhappy, described as refusing to eat and potentially suicidal. After her uncle's death, she and her two sons were put under the control of Sir William Petre. She was then transferred to Sir John Wentworth. After his death in 1567, her final residence for her house arrest was at Cockfield Hall, in the custody of Owen Hopton. The Earl of Hertford paid for her expenses—she had seventeen attendants. Katherine was kept under such close custody because there were still enough people who claimed she was the heir to the throne. Katherine died in January 1568.

Edward Seymour, Viscount Beauchamp (1561–1612)

Though he had been legally declared illegitimate, his father Edward Seymour, Earl of Hertford, did not accept the ecclesiastical court verdict that his marriage to Katherine Grey was invalid, and he gave the older of his two sons the courtesy title of Beauchamp, which would have been his due if he were legitimate. The boys were raised by their grandmother, Anne Seymour, Dowager Duchess of Somerset. Her grandson Edward attended Magdalen College Oxford but left without a degree. At the age of twenty, he married Honora Rogers, a member of his grandmother's household, but his furious father tried to have the marriage discounted, even kidnapping his son. The queen and her Privy Council, however, declared the marriage valid. Burghley wrote strongly to the earl a few years later that he must forgive his son and accept the marriage. Edward and Honora had three sons, Edward, William, and Francis. Beauchamp's lack of interest in any claim to the throne very much pleased Elizabeth. His youngest son Francis, unlike his two older brothers, never caused concern because of being an heir to the throne, as a descendant of Henry VII.

Edward Seymour (1587–1618)

In 1602 Arbella Stuart, already twenty-seven and living with her grandmother Bess of Hardwick, Countess of Shrewsbury, wrote to Edward Seymour, Earl of Hertford, suggesting that she marry his grandson and namesake, who was also her distant cousin. It was a startling idea given that as a young man Seymour had been in the Tower because of his marriage to Katherine Grey. The earl immediately let Queen Elizabeth know but Arbella was seen as very unhappy and was not punished. Seymour at fifteen would have been young to marry; he did not do so until 1609 when he wed Anne Sackville, daughter of Robert, Earl of Dorset. They had no children and he died in 1618. His grandfather, the Earl of Hertford, survived him.

William Seymour (1587–1660)

In the reign of James I, William Seymour became involved with Arbella Stuart, who had earlier suggested she marry his older brother Edward. James, like Elizabeth, refused to arrange a marriage for Arbella, so in 1610 she became acquainted with William Seymour, and they secretly married in her rooms at Greenwich Palace the morning of June 22. Arbella was then thirty-five and William twenty-two. He had apparently been very flattered by her attention. When James learned of the marriage about two weeks later, William was sent to the Tower. Arbella was under house arrest. James decided to send Arbella north to Durham. Two days before she was designated to leave, she disguised herself as a male and escaped. Arbella knew that William had a plan to escape from the Tower at the same time. His younger brother Francis was accused of helping him. The two intended to meet at a port and flee to France. William was not there when Arbella arrived. Though her servants urged her to sail, she wanted to wait and was overtaken by the English and sent to the Tower. William had escaped from the Tower and was able to get to France. He did not return to England until after Arbella's death in 1615. He became Earl of Hertford after his grandfather's death. He married his second wife Frances Devereux, the sister of Robert Devereux, third Earl of Essex, in 1616. During the Civil War Hertford supported Charles I and was one of four men who remained with Charles during his trial and acted as one of his pallbearers. Oliver Cromwell sent William's eldest son, also William, Lord Beauchamp, to the Tower in 1651 for his involvement in royalist circles. Beauchamp remarked that five generations of Seymours had stayed in the Tower. While he was soon released, young William's health failed, and he died in 1654. The earl himself tried to live very quietly, believing the Stuarts would eventually be restored. He was one of the peers who welcomed Charles II when he arrived at Dover in 1660. Under the new king, he became a Knight of the Garter and Duke of Somerset. He died in October 1660. He was succeeded by his youngest son John.

Edward Seymour and Honora Rogers's youngest son Francis never made a claim to the throne or was seen as a serious threat. He served in Parliament, and supported Charles I during the Civil War, leading to Charles II rewarding him after the Restoration in 1660.

Thomas Seymour (1563–1600)

Katherine Grey's younger son had far more interest in his legitimacy and possible claim to the throne than his older brother. In 1589 he attempted to have himself declared legitimate through a notarized statement. Three years later he initiated a legal appeal that the declaration by Archbishop Parker in 1562 that stated his parents had never been legally married was invalid. His father Hertford supported this undertaking. When Elizabeth and the Council learned of this in October 1595, Burghley had Hertford sent to the Tower in November. Hertford wrote to Burghley that his son was obstinate, and he hoped the Lord Treasurer could reason with him. Hertford promised to avoid any interest in the succession and was freed that January. Elizabeth ordered Sir Thomas Heneage, her vice-chamberlain, to compile a document, which was eighty folios, about the illegality of the Hertford-Grey marriage, and had it delivered to Burghley. That spring Thomas Seymour's cousin Sir John Smythe pronounced Thomas as the heir when reviewing troops in Essex, which landed Smythe in the Tower (see Chapter 9). Thomas married Isabel Onley, but the couple had no children. Thomas died in 1600 and Isobel in 1619.

Mary Grey (c. 1545–1578)

There was very little interest in the youngest Grey sister as a potential heir, even though after the death of her sister Katherine—if her two sons were illegitimate and thus lacking in the status of potential heir—Mary, by the will of Henry VIII, would have been the next in line as heir presumptive. Mary was very short, and the Spanish ambassador Guzman de Silva described her to Philip II as "a little crookback," adding that she was very ugly (*CSP, Spain*, I, 468). Yet Mary had the same education as her two older sisters, and there was more to her than those who judged her based on her size and looks might have thought. At the time of her sister Jane's marriage to Guildford Dudley, Mary was betrothed to a much older cousin, Arthur, Lord Grey of Wilton, but the marriage never took place. When Elizabeth became queen, Mary became a maid of honor.

Despite what had happened with her sister's secret marriage, in August 1565 Mary secretly married Elizabeth I's sergeant porter, Thomas Keyes. They clearly cared about each other, and Keyes presented her with a ruby ring among other gifts. He was a widower with half a dozen children and was over twenty years older than she. When the marriage was soon found out, there was much mean-spirited commentary because not only was the marriage of very unequal rank as he was not an aristocrat and she was of royal descent, but Keyes was well over six feet tall, and Mary tiny. Though this marriage did not at all have the same political implications as her sister's had, Elizabeth immediately separated the pair, having Keyes imprisoned at the Fleet prison, and Mary also under close house arrest, being moved several times. She was first kept under the guardianship of Sir William Hawtrey, the high sheriff of Buckingham, at his home at Chequers. Her room referred to as "the prison room," was small. She was allowed one groom and one waiting woman. The queen confiscated her revenues, and her small allowance was not enough to pay for her expenses, making all who kept Mary under house arrest angry at what they had to pay out of their own pocket. Mary was not permitted any visitors and only occasionally allowed to walk in the garden.

In August 1567 she was sent to the household of her step-grandmother, the Dowager Duchess of Suffolk, Katherine Bertie. The Duchess immediately wrote to Cecil that the funding to care for Mary was insufficient. She also reported that Mary was refusing to eat and was very depressed, just as her sister Katherine had been. From 1570 she was under the guard of Sir Thomas Gresham, who wrote frequently to Cecil asking to be relieved of looking after Mary. In 1568 Keyes was released from prison on the condition that he never see Mary again. Mary wrote frequently to Cecil begging for his help in reconciling with the Queen and Keyes also begged the queen that he be allowed to see Mary. He died in 1571 without ever having seen his wife again. When Mary was informed, she was devastated. The following year Mary was freed, and the queen agreed to raise her allowance. She lived first with her stepfather Adrian Stokes, who had married Anne Carew, widow of Sir Nicholas Throckmorton, as his second wife, and later had her own household in London. By 1575 there was further reconciliation with the queen who restored to Mary income from her mother's estate, which allowed her to buy new clothing and some jewelry. In 1577 she was appointed to be a Maid of Honor to the queen, referred to as Grey rather than Keyes, and Mary was part of the Christmas celebrations at Hampton Court.

She spent a great deal of time with her books, owning three different Bibles, books on theology, and Foxe's *Book of Martyrs*. She was kind to her stepchildren, and in the final year of her life occasionally attended court and exchanged new year's gifts with Elizabeth, giving the queen ornately embroidered gloves. She died in April 1578. In her will she referred to herself as a widow and asked that the queen decide her resting place. She left her step-grandmother Katherine bracelets that had belonged to her mother Frances, and jewelry to Katherine's daughter Susan, Countess of Kent. She left Katherine's son Peregrine a gilt cup and silver and gilt saltcellar. She also remembered some of her other women friends in her will. Lady Margaret Neville received a dress of yellow velvet, a petticoat of crimson satin, and what Mary described as her best gown, one of black velvet. Blanche Parry received a small covered gilt bowl. At the queen's request, Mary was buried at Westminster Abbey.

Descendants of Eleanor Brandon (1519–1547)

Eleanor was the third child and second daughter of Henry VIII's younger sister Mary, and Charles Brandon, Duke of Suffolk. As the niece of Henry VIII, Eleanor was an important marriage prospect. Her older sister Frances married Henry Grey in May 1533 and that spring Eleanor was betrothed to Henry Clifford, son and heir of the Earl of Cumberland. Because Eleanor's mother died in June 1533 the marriage did not take place until June 1535. Eleanor was sixteen and her husband eighteen. Eleanor's two sons, Henry and Charles, died in infancy and Margaret, born in 1540, was the only surviving child.

Henry and Eleanor Clifford's marriage was apparently a happy one, but Eleanor died in November 1547 when she was only twenty-eight years old. He was rarely at court after Eleanor's death and was involved in his intensive readings in astrology and magic, an interest he shared with his young daughter Margaret.

Margaret Clifford, Countess of Derby (1540–1596)

As Eleanor, Countess of Cumberland's only child, Margaret Clifford was also mentioned in Edward VI's will. In the spring of 1553 John Dudley, Duke of Northumberland considered marrying his son Guildford to Margaret before he settled on her cousin Jane, but the Earl of Cumberland was not enthusiastic. Northumberland also encouraged his brother Andrew to marry Margaret, but this also did not come to pass, and Margaret was welcome at Mary I's court when she became queen. In February 1555 Margaret married Henry Stanley, Lord Strange, son and heir of Edward, Earl of Derby. They became Earl and Countess of Derby in 1572 upon Edward's death. In Mary's reign, Margaret made it clear that she considered herself an heir to the throne. When Elizabeth became queen Margaret was often at court and several times had the honor of being the queen's trainbearer. Margaret gave the queen thoughtful and expensive New Year's gifts and received some in return from the queen. One of the most impressive gifts from Margaret was a spectacular clock decorated with diamonds and rubies. Margaret and her husband had four sons, two of whom, Ferdinando and William, lived to adulthood. By 1567 there were real problems in their marriage, with Henry angry at Margaret's extravagance and Margaret upset with his unkindness. In 1579 the queen was very upset with Margaret because of her gossip about the Duke of Anjou's private courtship visit, and she was put under house arrest. But the charges became more serious, as that summer Margaret, not in good health, had Dr. Randall living in her household to help cure her. But apparently, he also performed magic to see how long Queen Elizabeth would live. Some of the foreign ambassadors believed that Margaret planned to poison Elizabeth. The only evidence came from Randall, under threat of torture. Randall was executed and Margaret stayed under house arrest until about 1583. She never lived with her husband again but had a house in London. He died in 1593 and she died three years later (see also Chapter 9).

Ferdinando Stanley, Earl of Derby (1559–1594)

Ferdinando Stanley, Lord Strange attended Oxford and was also sometimes at the court of Queen Elizabeth. In 1579, the year his mother got into such trouble, he married Alice Spencer, daughter of Sir John Spencer. They had three daughters. Ferdinando was a patron of the arts, especially of the theater, and he established a theater company, Lord Strange's Men. Some of the Stanleys were Catholic, including two of Ferdinando's uncles, Sir Thomas and Sir

Edward, who had supported Mary Stuart, and his cousin William Stanley, who was part of assassination plots against the queen. Though Ferdinando himself did not express Catholic beliefs, when he became Earl of Derby in 1593 English Catholics abroad hoped that the new earl, descended from Henry VII through his mother, could replace Elizabeth as a Catholic king. Richard Hesketh approached the new earl about a conspiracy to make this happen, but after consulting with his mother, Ferdinando informed Lord Burghley about Hesketh who was subsequently executed. A few months later, in April 1594, Ferdinando became desperately ill and died in great pain. Some thought he might have been poisoned in revenge for turning in Hesketh (see Chapter 9).

Anne Stanley Bridges Touchet, Countess of Castlehaven (1580–1647)

Ferdinando Stanley's eldest daughter, Anne, inherited a considerable fortune from her father. Some considered her an heir to Elizabeth's throne, and she was seen as significant enough to be considered as a potential mate for Fyodor, the son and heir of Tsar Boris Godunov. In the negotiations, Elizabeth referred to Anne as being a cousin who was of the royal blood and spoke of how much she valued her. In the end, Elizabeth shut down the negotiations, claiming she had not realized that Fyodor was only thirteen, five years younger than Anne. Given how often there were such age differences in aristocratic and royal marriages, this was clearly an excuse, and the queen had decided that she did not want to send Anne to Russia. This decision was fortunate, as Fyodor became Tsar in April 1605 at the age of sixteen when his father died. But in June he and his mother were strangled during a coup. In 1607 Anne married Gray Brydges, Baron Chandos and had at least five children. He died in 1621, and in 1624 she married the widowed Mervyn Touchet, Earl of Castlehaven. In 1630 some accusations from Castlehaven's son, who had married Anne's daughter by her first marriage, led to the Privy Council doing an investigation. Anne admitted that her husband had helped his servant to rape her in his presence, which had led Anne to attempt suicide. This charge was confirmed by the alleged rapist; others testified about the earl's sexual behavior, leading to him being formally charged with the complicity of the rape of his wife and sodomy with one of his male servants. The earl denied the charges and called his wife a whore. Castlehaven, found guilty in 1631, was executed. This was an enormous scandal, and beginning with the trial and after, pamphlets were published that called Anne an immoral and evil woman. The most prolific of these authors was Lady Eleanor Davies, the earl's sister. After her husband's execution, Anne lived with her mother Alice, Dowager Countess of Derby and retired from public life. She died in 1647, a decade after her mother.

William Stanley, Earl of Derby (1561–1642)

Unlike his older brother Ferdinando, there was little interest in William as a potential heir when he became Earl of Derby on the death of his older brother in 1594; nor did Stanley himself demonstrate any interest. William Stanley attended Oxford and then traveled widely on the continent. In 1595 he married Elizabeth de Vere and Queen Elizabeth attended the wedding. When he became earl, William was very careful about how he presented himself. He showed himself as loyal to the queen without calling attention to the fact that he was her cousin. He served as one of the jurors at the 1601 treason trial of the Earl of Essex. In April of that year, he became a Knight of the Garter. He did well in James I's reign and, like others in his family, patronized Derby's men, who played both in London and in the provinces. Though some have suggested that William Stanley was the true author of William Shakespeare's plays, no serious scholarship supports this claim.

Descendants of Henry VIII's Older Sister Margaret (1489–1541)

Though the descendants of Margaret would have a better claim to the throne by right of primogeniture than those of Mary, they were excluded from Henry VIII's will. Some people thought it was because all three of her husbands were Scottish, thus foreign.

Margaret was thirteen in 1503 when her father Henry VII dispatched her to Scotland to marry James IV, who was thirty years old. James IV was killed at the battle of Flodden field a decade later in September 1513. Though they had six children, only one son, James V, survived. After her first husband's death, Margaret married Archibald Douglas, Earl of Angus in August 1514. They had one daughter Margaret in October 1515. It was a very unhappy marriage, with Angus using Margaret's money to support his mistress, Lady Jane Stewart, to whom he had been previously betrothed. Eventually, at Margaret's request, Pope Clement VII annulled her marriage in March 1527 because of Angus's pre-contract to Jane Stewart. Margaret's third marriage to Henry Stewart, Lord Methven, was equally problematic, as he too was interested in both his wife's money and in relationships with other women. The last few years of Margaret's life improved as she and her daughter-in-law Mary of Guise, whom James V married in 1538, got along well. Mary worked on a reconciliation for Margaret with her husband and invited her to court often. Margaret died in 1541.

Mary Stuart (1542–1587)

James V was only a year old when he became king of Scotland on the death of his father James IV. By 1529 James had taken control as king. His first marriage to Madeline de Valois in 1537 lasted only six months before her death. Two years later he married another French woman, Mary of Guise. Their first two children were boys who died in infancy. Their third child was Mary, born on December 8, 1542. James V died six days later, ill and in despair after the Scottish defeat by the English at Solway Moss. The English were eager to arrange a marriage between the infant Mary and the young Prince Edward, and when negotiations broke down, they used an army to try to make this happen in what was known as "the rough wooing." To avoid a forced English marriage, when Mary was six her mother sent her to be raised at the French court and eventually marry Francis, eldest son and heir to Henri II and his wife Catherine de Medici. She married Francis in April 1558 at Notre Dame. When Mary I died in November, continental Catholics claimed that Elizabeth was illegitimate and thus no right to rule, and by right of primogeniture, Mary was the rightful queen of England. While in France Mary used the English royal arms, to the anger of the English. Henri II was killed accidentally in a tournament in July 1559, but Mary was queen consort only briefly as Francis died in December 1560. Mary returned to Scotland, where she wanted to be proclaimed Elizabeth's heir to the throne of England. Queen Elizabeth made it very clear to her cousin that she did not want the Scottish queen to marry a prince from Spain or the Austrian Empire, and offered Mary her own favorite, Robert Dudley, promoted to Earl of Leicester. Instead in 1565, Mary married her cousin Henry Stuart, Lord Darnley, a marriage which proved disastrous. They had a son James in June 1566; Darnley was murdered in February 1567. Only three months later Mary married James Hepburn, Earl of Bothwell, a man many believed to be Darnley's murderer. This led to a rebellion against Mary, and she was forced to abdicate and imprisoned. In 1568 Mary escaped and fled to England. Some Catholics believed she had the legal right to be the queen of England. For the next eighteen years, there were conspiracies to have Elizabeth murdered and make Mary queen. Mary was involved in many of these conspiracies, including the final one led by Anthony Babington, and she was executed in February 1587 (see Chapter 9) (Fig. 7.1).

JAMES VI AND I (1566–1625)

James was born on June 19, 1566, the son of Mary Stuart and her second husband and cousin, Henry Stuart, Lord Darnley. When he was only thirteen months old, he became king of Scotland when his mother was forced to abdicate. There was much violence in James' childhood, and a number of those appointed Regent were murdered. In 1582 John Ruthven, Earl of Gowrie managed to convince James to visit Ruthven Castle. This turned out to be a plot against James, and he was imprisoned at the castle. When James was liberated the following year, he began to assume more authority to rule Scotland himself. Though James was upset with his mother's execution in 1587, he did not want it to subvert his relationship with Queen Elizabeth, as he

Fig. 7.1 Mary Stuart private collection

very much wanted to be named her heir. When she wrote to him "I would you knew (though not felt) the extreme dolor that overwhelms my mind, for that miserable accident which (far contrary to my meaning) hath befallen" (*CSP, Scotland*, IX, 285), James accepted her specious excuse that she had not intended the execution of his mother. For the rest of his reign in Scotland, James's goal was to someday become king of England. Though Elizabeth never formally named him, by the end of her reign he was the assumed heir.

In the years before her death a number of men at her court, such as Robert Devereux, Earl of Essex on the one hand, and Robert Cecil on the other, wrote secretly to James. There was a smooth transition. Only hours after Elizabeth's death on March 24, 1603, James was proclaimed the king of England. Though James proved to be the successful heir, there were other potential heirs on the Scottish side (see Chapter 9).

Margaret Douglas, Countess of Lennox (1515–1578)

From her second marriage to Archibald Douglas, Earl of Angus, Margaret Tudor had one daughter, also named Margaret, born in England where Margaret had fled. Mother and daughter returned to Scotland in 1517, where Margaret briefly reconciled with her husband. This reconciliation was short-lived; when Margaret was three Angus grabbed his daughter and took control of her for more than a decade, finally taking her to England when he was forced to leave Scotland. Henry VIII's younger sister Mary finally managed to have Margaret visit her, and then Henry declared Margaret should live with her cousin, his daughter Mary. The two girls, about the same age, became close friends. Margaret also spent a lot of time at Henry's court, becoming a lady-in-waiting for the then queen, Anne Boleyn. Margaret and Queen Anne's uncle, Thomas Howard, second son of the Duke of Norfolk, fell in love and planned to marry in 1536. The king was furious, afraid Howard was attempting to make himself an heir to the throne as Henry had had both his daughters declared illegitimate after the execution of Anne Boleyn. Both Margaret and Thomas were sent to the Tower, though when Margaret became ill, she was allowed to stay at the Abbey of Sion. In October 1537 Thomas Howard died, and Margaret was released. Some years later she was allowed back at court, and in 1543 was a bridesmaid at Katherine Parr's wedding to Henry VIII.

Henry then arranged what he considered an appropriate marriage for Margaret, and she wed the Scottish aristocrat Matthew Stewart, Earl of Lennox in July 1544. On his wedding day, he was naturalized as an Englishman and Henry gave him grants of property. Though it was an arranged marriage, Matthew and Margaret cared deeply for each other, but Matthew had to return to Scotland to work for Henry's interests there and Margaret stayed at court and then in her own household where she gave birth to a son, who died when only about a year old. Soon after his death, she gave birth to another son, Henry Stuart, Lord Darnley in December 1545. Margaret had four sons and four daughters but only Henry and a younger son Charles lived to adulthood.

Margaret's Catholicism distressed Henry VIII at the end of his life, and he apparently also did not want someone Scottish on the throne of England, as his will ignored the claims of his older sister Margaret's descendants, which included her granddaughter Mary Stuart, her daughter Margaret Douglas, and Margaret's baby son Henry. Margaret tried to keep a low profile during

Edward's reign, and many Catholics went to join her household in Yorkshire. After Edward VI's death in 1553, and the accession of Mary, Margaret was welcomed back to court by her old friend, who gave her apartments in Westminster Palace and many expensive gifts. Mary also gave Margaret precedence over her own half-sister Elizabeth. When Mary died, Margaret and her husband were quick to congratulate Elizabeth on her accession, but as a Catholic, she also considered her cousin illegitimate and believed she or her niece Mary Stuart had a better claim.

Margaret's dearest wish was for her son Henry to marry his cousin Mary, and she most likely sent him to the French court to convey his condolences when Mary's first husband, Francis II, died. When Mary returned to Scotland in 1561, Margaret was indiscreet enough to talk about how she hoped the two would marry, and not only rule Scotland but also claim the English throne as well from Elizabeth. When this reached Elizabeth, the Earl of Lennox was sent to the Tower and Margaret was under house arrest with Sir Richard Sackville, a cousin of Elizabeth on her mother's side, and his wife Winifred. Matthew was finally allowed to join his wife in November 1562, and they were released the next February.

Despite what concerns Elizabeth may have had, she allowed Lord Darnley to join his father in Scotland in 1565. But when Mary and Darnley announced their coming marriage, Elizabeth summoned him and his father back to England. When they refused, Elizabeth sent Margaret to the Tower. She was still in the Tower when she learned in February 1567 that her beloved son Darnley was dead. Elizabeth allowed the grieving Margaret to be released. When Lennox failed at his attempt to have James Hepburn, Earl of Bothwell, called to account for Darnley's murder, he returned to his wife. They unsuccessfully begged Queen Elizabeth for justice when Mary Stuart fled to England. When the Scottish regent, James Stewart, Earl of Moray, was assassinated in January 1570, Lennox became the next regent, but Margaret stayed in England with her younger son Charles. Tragically for Margaret, her husband Lennox was murdered in September 1571; she was devastated. Margaret later made peace with her niece/daughter-in-law, Mary Stuart.

When Margaret's son Charles fell in love with Elizabeth Cavendish, daughter of Bess of Hardwick, Countess of Shrewsbury, in 1574, the mothers delightedly collaborated on their instant marriage. Elizabeth was furious, and Margaret was, yet again, sent to the Tower. She was released after a few months, and Charles and his wife lived with her. Their daughter Arbella was born the following year. Margaret was devastated by the death of her last child, Charles, in 1576. She died two years later, on March 7, 1578. Elizabeth paid for her burial in Westminster Abbey. Around 1600 her grandson James VI had a monument created for her. Kneeling on either side of her were the four sons and four daughters who had predeceased her.

Henry Stuart, Lord Darnley (1545–1567)

Henry was the second son of Margaret Douglas and Matthew Stewart. His older brother Henry died very young about a week before Henry's birth, December 7, 1545. Darnley's early life was spent at his parents' estates in Yorkshire. He was educated at home and could converse in Scots, English, and French. He also studied Latin, though his real strengths were as a dancer, singer, and lute player. He was also an excellent horseman who loved to go hunting and hawking. In his early teens, his parents sent him incognito to France in 1559 to congratulate his cousin Mary on her and her husband Francis's accession to the throne. He most likely went back in December 1560 to offer Mary condolences after Francis's death. To show that she had many possible heirs, in 1564 Queen Elizabeth honored Darnley and had him welcome the new Spanish ambassador Diego Guzman de Silva and escort him to meet her. Elizabeth also worked to help Matthew Stewart, Earl of Lennox be restored to his Scottish lands, and in January 1565 she allowed Darnley to join his father in Scotland. There is much discussion as to why Elizabeth did so, as she was clearly aware that his mother, Margaret, Countess of Lennox, was eager for Darnley to marry Mary Stuart. She may not have taken the plan seriously, or more likely, she may well have believed that a marriage with Darnley was less dangerous for England than one with a prince from Spain, the Austrian Empire, or France. As soon as she met him again, Mary was very attracted to her cousin; she was also aware that marriage to him would strengthen her claim to the English throne. Whatever Elizabeth's motives for allowing Darnley to go to Scotland, when she learned that he planned to marry the Scots queen, she sent his mother to the Tower. The marriage took place on July 29, 1565. But very soon there were troubles, as Darnley was both arrogant and unreliable. He wanted all of Mary's attention and was furious that his wife refused him the crown matrimonial, which would have meant that had Mary died Darnley would be king and any children from a subsequent marriage would be the heirs. Observers noted that Darnley drank excessively, was involved with other women, and that Mary was often in tears. Mary, now pregnant, became disillusioned with her husband and she spent more time with her Italian secretary, David Rizzio. Though there is no evidence that there was a sexual relationship between them, Darnley became very jealous. He became involved with some Protestant lords who promised to help him get the crown matrimonial. On March 9, 1566, Darnley and other conspirators hacked Rizzio to death in front of Mary. It is likely some hoped that the shock would cause Mary to miscarry and possibly as a result die herself. Mary, however, rallied, but was deeply unhappy with her husband.

After James was born in June, Darnley's actions continued to be unpredictable and potentially dangerous. He complained of his loss of status and threatened to leave Scotland, in the meantime writing to Pope Pius V, Philip II of Spain, and Charles IX of France to denigrate Mary. He refused to attend his son's christening and left for Glasgow to be with his father. He was soon very ill—some said it was smallpox, but it was apparently more likely syphilis. Mary went to Glasgow, promising a reconciliation, and had Darnley brought back with her in a litter. He was not taken to the Holyrood Palace, but to lodgings at Kirk o'Field. Mary told him that he could recover there and then would join her at court. Darnley wrote to his father about Mary's great kindness and concern for him, and how he was recovering. But the night before he was supposed to move to the palace, there was an explosion at Kirk o'Field, and Darnley and his manservant were found strangled in the garden. More and more people suspected James Hepburn, Earl of Bothwell, a powerful noble who was a close confidant of Mary. The Earl of Lennox agitated for justice for his son and the Privy Council agreed that the Earl of Bothwell would be put on trial. But Lennox, called to be the chief accuser and to provide evidence, was given only two weeks to prepare. Bothwell came to his trial with many armed supporters. Within a few hours, he was acquitted. The year of Darnley's death, the Earl and Countess of Lennox commissioned a painting, The Memorial of Lord Darnley. It shows his parents kneeling before Darnley's effigy. Their last remaining son Charles is behind them, and their infant grandson kneeling in front.

CHARLES STUART, EARL OF LENNOX (C. 1555–1576)

Charles was the last surviving child of Margaret Douglas. In 1574 Charles and his mother visited Mary Stuart at Rufford while she was in the custody of George Talbot, Earl of Shrewsbury and his wife Bess. Charles got to know Bess's daughter Elizabeth Cavendish. They were both about nineteen years old and were very attracted to each other. By the end of the five-day visit, they were in love, and Margaret and Bess conspired together to get them married as soon as possible. By November of the following year, they were parents of a daughter, Arbella. Unfortunately, the following year Charles died of what was probably tuberculosis. His widow Elizabeth also died young in 1582.

ARBELLA STUART (1575–1615)

As the great-great-granddaughter of Henry VII through his older daughter Margaret, Arbella's closeness to the throne made her highly significant. Both her parents died while she was very young and from the age of seven, she lived with her maternal grandmother, Bess of Hardwick, Countess of Shrewsbury. As a child, she was an enthusiastic student who studied Latin, Italian, French, Spanish, Greek, and Hebrew. In 1583 Bess arranged a marriage for Arbella with Robert, Lord Denbigh, the young son of Robert Dudley, Earl of Leicester. But Leicester's son died in 1584 at the age of three. There were also discussions of Arbella possibly marrying her cousin James VI of Scotland. But nothing came of this. In 1588 Arbella went to court to serve as a lady-in-waiting to the queen. Some wondered if she would be the preferred heir to the throne. But her apparent flirting with Robert Devereux, Earl of

Essex, infuriated Elizabeth, and Arbella was sent home. Though she returned to her studies, her life became increasingly unhappy as she fought with her grandmother over her restrictive life. The queen would not arrange a marriage for her. In 1602 she approached Edward Seymour, Earl of Hertford, about marrying his fifteen-year-old grandson and namesake. The earl's own experience as a young man secretly marrying Katherine Grey made him wary of such a match, and he informed Queen Elizabeth. The queen sent Sir Henry Brouncker to Hardwick Hall to interrogate Arbella. Finding her very unhappy, Brouncker informed Elizabeth that Arbella felt herself to be in a very uncomfortable situation and was trying to bring some attention to it; she was not punished for the attempted marriage. Arbella was so distressed by her situation that she ended one letter by saying that the only thing that could make her happy was death.

There was great concern over Arbella's mental state in January of the following year when she declared that she had a secret lover and refused food and drink. She finally named her cousin James, already married to Anna of Denmark, as her lover. Robert Cecil was concerned that Arbella's brain must have strange vapors. Brouncker stated that the only thing Arbella was certain of was her uncertainty. When Elizabeth died, Arbella was invited to court to be her chief mourner at the queen's funeral, but Arbella refused, claiming that since Elizabeth had not wanted to see her during her life, she would not be with her after her death.

At first her life improved when her cousin James became king of England. The king even supported her when a plot was discovered that Henry Brooke, Lord Cobham intended to murder James and make Arbella queen. James understood that Arbella had nothing to do with the plan. Cobham himself was sent to the Tower, finally released in 1618 because of his ill-health. Arbella served the new queen at court and was godmother to Anna's daughter Mary, born in 1605. Arbella hoped James would arrange a marriage for her but when he did not, she decided to find one for herself, and again turned to the Seymour family. In 1610 she got to know the Earl of Hertford's other grandson William. He was over twelve years younger and flattered that she found him of interest. They secretly married but only about two weeks later the king found out and was furious. Her husband was sent to the Tower, and she was put under house arrest in the home of Sir Thomas Parry in Lambeth. She somehow managed to visit William, possibly with the help of some sympathetic servants. In September she was ill with what may well have been a miscarriage. King James ordered her sent to Durham, but her illness delayed the trip. With the help of her aunt Mary Talbot, Countess of Shrewsbury, she escaped by disguising herself as a man, and William escaped the Tower at the same time. But while William escaped to France, Arbella waited too long at the rendezvous and was captured and lodged in the Tower, as was Mary. Arbella's health deteriorated, and as any hope of release faded, she stopped eating. Some scholars argue that she suffered from the hereditary disease of acute intermittent porphyria, which would also explain some of her emotional problems.

She died in September 1615 a few months before her fortieth birthday. The king refused to plan a funeral for his cousin; with no ceremony, her body was placed in the vault of Mary Stuart at Westminster. Her aunt Mary was kept in the Tower until Arbella's death. Mary was very upset about Arbella's death, especially since she had been told that her niece was recovering. The countess said that she could not think about anything but Arbella. After her release, she suffered from melancholy and was convinced she was being poisoned. In 1618 rumors were circulating that Arbella had secretly had a baby, and the countess was called to testify at an inquiry, but she refused, leading to her spending another five years in the Tower.

Isabella Clara Eugenia, the Spanish Infanta, King Phillip II's Daughter (1566–1633)

Isabella was the daughter of Philip II and his third wife, Elisabeth of Valois. After Mary Stuart's execution, she was often mentioned as a possible Catholic heir to the English throne, though her claim went all the way back to Edward III's younger son John of Gaunt's marriage to Constance of Castile. Their daughter Catherine of Lancaster married the King of Castile. By the late sixteenth century, this was a distant claim. When Philip II launched the Armada, he stated that his daughter would be the next queen of England, possibly figuring that England was now used to having a queen. A decade later, some English Catholics, particularly on the continent, still considered that Isabella was a good alternative to other heirs, especially Mary Stuart's son James VI, as they perceived him as anti-Catholic and pro-Puritan.

In 1595 the English Jesuit Roberts Parsons, writing under the pseudonym R. Doleman, published in Antwerp *A Conference About the Next Succession to the Throne of England*, which looked at all potential heirs to the English throne upon the death of Elizabeth, discussing sixteen different possibilities. He was very opposed to James VI and argued that the Infanta's claim was the most appropriate. He described the eldest daughter of King Philip as one who was dearly beloved, and was known for her beauty, wisdom, and piety. This book was officially banned in England.

A number of possible husbands were proposed for Isabella. Finally, in 1597 Philip II arranged a marriage for her with the Hapsburg Archduke Albert and established them as joint sovereigns of the Spanish Netherlands. But Philip died the next year, and his son Philip III was not interested in working to support Isabella's claim to the English throne. Further discussion of the Infanta's claim came from warnings from Robert Devereux, Earl of Essex, in a letter to James VI, warning the Scottish king that Robert Cecil was against him being Elizabeth's heir and that he was supporting the Infanta instead, a complete lie. Essex took it further. Late in the morning of February 8, 1601, the earl left his house with his supporters. He implored Londoners to take up arms and join him, claiming that Robert Cecil and others had offered the crown of England to the Infanta upon the queen's death. People did not join

Essex and he was arrested. At the trial of Essex and Henry Wriothesley, Earl of Southampton, Southampton claimed that he had heard someone say that Cecil had spoken positively about Parson's text. At the trial Cecil proclaimed his innocence, stating that he had had no underhanded dealings with Spain about the succession. At the same time, the Spanish Council of State finally suggested to Philip III that he promote his sister's claim to the English throne. But Isabella's husband, Archduke Albert, thought this a bad idea. He stated that England would not accept Isabella and suggested that Philip support the Scottish king as heir. Isabella and her husband had no children. After her husband's death in 1621, Isabella ruled as regent for her nephew Philip IV until her death in 1633 (see Chapter 9).

CHAPTER 8

Ambassadors at Elizabeth's Court

Much of the important work with other countries—allies and potential enemies—that took place at the court of Elizabeth was accomplished by interactions with the foreign ambassadors. Ambassadors had various aspects to their jobs. As well as negotiating with the English queen and government, ambassadors learned all they could about what was going on at the court and in the country, whether accurate or only rumors and gossip, and wrote letters with great frequency to their monarchs and other important government leaders. Many of them also worked to develop political and diplomatic networks within England to aid them—most often when they were actually working against the queen, especially some of the Spanish ambassadors. While this was the case from the beginning of her reign it became especially so during the nearly two decades that Mary Stuart resided in England. Indeed, while ambassadors were usually following their masters' political agendas, some of them went far beyond that in their efforts to influence events in their country of residence (Fig. 8.1).

During her reign, Elizabeth met with many ambassadors and special envoys to discuss important matters, including trade and marriage negotiations. In some cases, she developed close relationships that worked well in the negotiations. She would invite them to sit with her at banquets, watch entertainments at court with her, listen to music with her, or accompany her when she went hunting. This allowed her the opportunity to have more informal meetings without the scrutiny of her privy councilors. With some other ambassadors, the relationships were more rigid and sometimes even hostile.

As well as their official duties, ambassadors were also high-ranking intelligence officers who could also develop counter-espionage networks. They

Fig. 8.1 Elizabeth receiving the French ambassadors private collection

represented their masters' interests and personal voices on important matters, but they also gathered intelligence, serving as spies for their homeland. They were at the heart of court events—and all the gossip that went with them—and, in that regard, they held a privileged position. Their frequent and lengthy letters are of great value for scholars today, and some ambassadors kept journals or wrote memoirs as well.

This unit focuses specifically on those ambassadors who either had a closer relationship with the queen or who served as true enemies to the Elizabethan state, mostly centering on the ambassadors from France and Spain. For ambassadors from what were seen at the time as more exotic realms, see the section on Others. This section is organized chronologically.

Suárez de Figueroa, Gómez, Count of Feria, Later Duke (c. 1520–1571), Spanish Ambassador to Elizabeth I from 1558 to 1559

Suárez de Figueroa, Gómez, Count of Feria was one of the most trusted advisors of Philip II; in 1567 the king gave him the title of Duke of Feria. The first time he came to England was for Prince Philip's marriage to Mary in July 1554, after which he was often in England over the next few years, playing an important diplomatic role between the two crowns. When Mary's health declined in the autumn of 1558, Philip decided to send Feria back to England, giving him instructions to support Elizabeth's succession and to ensure a good transition—as well as securing good relations with the new young queen. Despite his formal role as the Spanish ambassador, he refused to attend her coronation in January 1559 because of its Protestant nature. Feria represented Spain's interests at the English court until May 1559; he was glad to return to Spain and served as Philip II's royal chamberlain.

Feria met Lady Jane Dormer when he came with Prince Philip in 1554. Jane was one of the queen's ladies in waiting, but also, despite being over twenty years younger than the queen, one of Mary's closest friends. Though Feria was fifteen years older than Dormer, they fell in love, and Mary very much encouraged them to marry. The wedding, however, did not take place until December 29, 1558, more than a month after Queen Mary's death. Jane was a thoroughly committed Catholic. The couple had two sons, but one died in infancy.

Back in Spain, Feria and his wife remained patrons and strong supporters of the English exiled Catholic community, and Feria had a great deal of influence at Philip's court. In 1568 he strongly encouraged the king to appoint Guerau de Spes as ambassador to England. Feria died in 1571. His widow continued to be a force in supporting both Catholics in England and Catholic English exiles for the over forty years of her widowhood.

Alvaro de Quadra, Bishop of Aquila (c. 1516–1564), Spanish Ambassador 1559–1563

Alvaro de Quadra, Bishop of Aquila, replaced Feria as Spanish ambassador. At the beginning of Elizabeth's reign Spain was more concerned about its traditional enemy France than England. Philip II was especially disturbed that Henri II was claiming England for Mary Stuart, wife of the dauphin, and ordered de Quadra to support Elizabeth against France. But de Quadra was also told to offer support and reassurance to the English Catholic community, a directive he took much more seriously. De Quadra was very adept at building connections with Catholics throughout the country. He also worked hard at learning all he could—rumor or fact—from those at court, even though he contemptuously considered these people opportunists and heretics.

As a committed Catholic, de Quadra became increasingly offended by Elizabeth and English Protestants as his ambassadorship continued. After the first year, he wanted to be recalled; in 1562 he described his post as being a prison in a letter to a colleague he was hoping would aid him in gaining a new position. The Elizabethan Settlement horrified him, and the longer he was in England the more he was convinced that the treatment of Catholics was deteriorating. De Quadra believed that most of the English were really Catholic, and he felt he should do all he could to bring England back to the true Church. The Spanish embassy was at Durham Place on the Strand and since there was a back entrance to it from the Thames people could come and go without being noticed.

De Quadra was also appalled by what he believed to be the immoral nature of Elizabeth's private life. He thought her utterly untrustworthy, describing her as possessed with thousands of devils, adding "with her all is falsehood and vanity." He was also convinced that Elizabeth was not "a woman of brains or conscience" (*CSP, Spain*, I, 81, 108). He considered Cecil to be a great heretic and thought that Dudley acted treacherously. Cecil, who did not trust de Quadra at all, worked hard to investigate his activities. In 1561 de Quadra's private secretary, an Italian named Borghese Venturini, who had an extravagant lifestyle and wanted extra funds, agreed to spy on de Quadra. Venturini explained to Cecil how the embassy functioned and the names of those who came to the embassy to attend Sunday Mass, able to come in secretly through the back entrance. He told Cecil who was at the embassy conducting business, and most importantly, what de Quadra was doing to incite English Catholics. Venturini also told Cecil that de Quadra was doing all he could to convince Philip II to make war against England so that the country could be ruled by a Catholic. Cecil came to realize that the embassy was a meeting place for disaffected Catholic plotters, and that de Quadra was no friend to Elizabeth and the English government. Cecil was convinced that de Quadra was not only contemptuous of Elizabeth, but that he also slandered the queen.

But de Quadra also had spies in Cecil's household and learned about his secretary's treachery. De Quadra thought Venturini deserved death but that it would be a scandal if he died in England. He told Venturini he was sending him to Brussels, where he thought he could manage his death more quietly. When Venturini refused to go, de Quadra became furious, and Venturini left the embassy in fear of his life, taking refuge with Cecil. Queen Elizabeth then could have demanded de Quadra's recall, but Cecil thought it made more sense to keep the enemy in place and neutralize him.

In 1563 de Quadra was involved in an incident that led Cecil to take some reprisals. It involved conflicts in France but played out in England. The treaty of Cateau-Cambresis that England and France signed in 1559 had stipulations concerning the city of Calais. France had regained the last English stronghold from the Hundred Years War while England was supporting Spain in a war against France in Mary's reign. The French agreed to either restore Calais in eight years or else pay England 500,000 crowns. As an act of surety in the meantime France sent four nobles to England as hostages. One was Antoine du Prat, Provost of Paris, Seigneur de Nantouillet. He bragged that he had more enemies than any man in Europe, and boasted that when he was in London, he treated Queen Elizabeth with contempt. Despite being a hostage, he clearly had considerable freedom of action. The Catholic nobles were not the only French who had come to London. When the civil war over religion was developing in France, in 1562 the Protestant leader, Louis, Prince of Condé, sent a deputation to ask Queen Elizabeth for aid. Captain Mazine, also a Protestant, was part of this entourage, and someone whom de Nantouillet, for whatever reason, hated.

In January 1563 Mazine was walking by the Spanish embassy which must have been expected, as an Italian man named Andrea shot at the captain with a pistol. Andrea was a servant to the Italian Alfonso la Bononye, who worked at the court as a lute player for Queen Elizabeth. Mazine was wounded, as was an Englishman who was standing close by when a bullet grazed his shoulder. A crowd gathered outside but Andrea was let into the embassy where the provost had been waiting. De Quadra allowed Andrea to leave through the water exit.

Andrea was finally captured, and Cecil and the Privy Council did a full investigation. De Nantouillet claimed that he was justified in hiring someone to murder Mazine; he claimed the captain had formerly tried to murder him in Paris. Andrea confessed that the provost had promised him 100 crowns for doing the captain an evil turn. The provost's servant, Domville, confessed that he had given Andrea the pistol at his master's orders.

Because of de Quadra's role in the attempted assassination, the water gate was locked so that entrance and exit of the embassy was no longer accessible; then Cecil told the ambassador he could no longer keep his embassy at Durham Place since it had become a center for conspirators, and that without the queen's protection, de Quadra might have been murdered by the mob. The embassy was moved to Ely Place, with no access to the river. As for the Provost of Paris, as a highly regarded hostage, the government added restrictions to his movements. Catherine de Medici was upset that Elizabeth had given support to the French Protestants and had Sir Nicholas Throckmorton, the English ambassador, imprisoned in 1563. The following year the English and French signed the Treaty of Troyes and the four French noblemen returned home as did Throckmorton. The French paid the English only 120,000 crowns and it was agreed that France would keep Calais.

Later in 1563 Elizabeth heard that Shane O'Neill had asked de Quadra for help in Ireland against the English. Though de Quadra denied he had given aid, there had been discussions in the embassy about it, and for the queen that was finally enough. She demanded that Philip recall his ambassador, but de Quadra died of the plague in August 1564 before he could return to Spain.

WILLIAM MAITLAND OF LETHINGTON (C. 1525–1573), SCOTTISH AMBASSADOR TO ELIZABETH I DURING VISITS FROM 1559 TO 1563

William Maitland came to England as the Scottish ambassador frequently in the first years of Elizabeth's reign. As royal secretary, he was an important member of the Scottish queen's court, and an ally of his queen, Mary Stuart, especially once she was in England. During the course of his life, he sometimes identified with the Protestant lords, while at other times he lived as a committed Catholic.

He began his career in 1554 when he was appointed assistant secretary to David Panter, Bishop of Ross, the royal secretary to the Regent Mary of Guise, Mary Stuart's mother. Maitland's first embassy to London took place from December 1559 to February 1560, where he worked to preserve good relations between England and Scotland. This was the first of six embassies. When Mary Stuart returned to Scotland, Maitland was an important advisor, as he assured her that he could convince the English that Mary was the rightful heir to Elizabeth, though he was ultimately unsuccessful. Between 1561 and 1565, when he was not in an embassy to England, he attended Mary's council meetings and accompanied her on her progresses. Within weeks of her return to Scotland, Mary sent Maitland back to England. This second visit, in September and October 1561, was particularly important in terms of the relationship of the two queens.

During his audience with Elizabeth, Maitland explained how Mary wanted to increase the good relationship between the Scottish and English realms. But Elizabeth was not satisfied with these platitudes. The 1560 Treaty of Edinburgh had been signed by France and England, but Elizabeth was still waiting for Scotland to ratify it. The treaty stated Mary would recognize Elizabeth as the rightful monarch of England. According to the treaty, Mary also had to give up the use of the English coat of arms she had assumed in Paris when Mary Tudor died. Elizabeth told Maitland "I looked for another message from the queen your sovereign, and marvels that she remembers not better her promise made to me before her departing from France, after many delays of that thing which she in honor is bound to do ... the ratification of the treaty." Maitland attempted to defend Mary's delay by stating that the Scottish queen had other pressing matters, such as the religious situation in Scotland to consider and that she also needed to consult with the Scottish nobility over the treaty. Elizabeth was not impressed. "What consultation needs the queen to fulfill the thing whereunto she is obliged by her seal and handwriting?" Elizabeth felt the need to remind Maitland that Mary was her cousin and kinswoman, and she wanted a positive relationship, but that she had "just cause to be most angry with her," if Mary was still in effect claiming to be the rightful queen by bearing the arms of England (Elizabeth I, *Collected Works*, 60, 62).

During this first audience, Elizabeth dominated the conversation, while Maitland attempted to respond carefully, aware that Mary's refusal to sign the treaty was a problem, but still hoping that he could get a confirmation that Mary would be recognized as an heir if she signed it, which Elizabeth would not confirm. Elizabeth was determined that until Mary stopped using the English arms and renounced her claim that she was the true queen of England, she would not even discuss Mary as a potential heir. Maitland suggested that if the queens could meet, concerns could be resolved. The two women never met, and Mary Stuart also never ratified the Treaty of Edinburgh.

Being the Scottish ambassador at the English court and navigating between the two cousins was no easy task. In May 1562 he was back yet again, and again the following year. In the 1563 embassy Maitland stayed for four months. Maitland again asked that Parliament declare his queen the heir to the throne. But at that point the most pressing issue for Elizabeth was whom Mary Stuart would marry, and again Maitland attempted to be careful in his discussions with the queen and Cecil. The discussion of potential husbands included the Spanish prince Don Carlos, the Austrian Archduke Charles, and Mary's former brother-in-law Charles IX. Very suggestive given what happened within a few years, Robert Dudley's possible candidacy was first raised at this point, as was the possibility that Elizabeth and Mary's cousin, Henry Stuart, Lord Darnley, might be the appropriate match.

In 1565, after the idea of the Dudley match had crumbled and Darnley was in Scotland, Maitland again was sent to England to ask Elizabeth to consent to Mary's marriage with Darnley and to continue to press for her to be named heir. But as he was returning to Scotland, Mary abruptly ordered him back to the English court to announce her marriage to Darnley despite any objections the Elizabeth might have. Maitland refused, and returned to Scottish court, and became increasingly discouraged by Mary's actions and policy. His involvement in the murder of David Rizzio meant that he was formally dismissed as secretary and Mary seized estates of his and gave them to James Hepburn, Earl of Bothwell, who would become her third husband.

But within six months he was reconciled to Mary and Bothwell returned the estates. Maitland attended the baptism of Mary's son James in December 1566, and soon after married one of the queen's ladies, Mary Fleming. She was the queen's cousin and childhood friend and Maitland courted her for three years. His first wife Janet Menteith had died years earlier and he was very much in love with Mary Fleming. He was eighteen years older, but apparently, she felt great affection for him as well. It is most probable he was aware of the plans to murder Darnley. Once Mary was forced to abdicate, Maitland supported Mary's half-brother James, Earl of Moray as regent; however, once Mary had escaped and fled to England Maitland became a strong supporter of hers. Though Moray no longer trusted him, he brought Maitland to England with him in the fall of 1568 for the investigation of Mary's role in Darnley's murder, thinking that Maitland was less dangerous in England at that time than in Scotland with Moray absent. Once both men were back in Scotland, and Maitland was clearly supporting Mary, including the plan to have her marry Thomas Howard, Duke of Norfolk, Moray had him arrested in September 1569 for his part in Darnley's murder. But Moray's assassination on January 23, 1570, led to Maitland's freedom as he continued to support the Scottish queen. In 1573 then regent James Douglas, Earl of Morton, ordered that Maitland and his supporters be arrested again, and Maitland died in prison in June, possibly by suicide so that he could die on his own terms rather than be executed. His wife Mary had been arrested with him. After his death she begged Cecil to intervene to prevent her husband's body being displayed in a posthumous trial for treason. Cecil agreed and Maitland received a decent burial.

Paul de Foix de Carmain (1528–1584), French Ambassador to Elizabeth I from 1562 to 1566

The son of Jean de Foix, Comte de Carmain, Paul de Foix studied Greek and Roman literature in Paris. As a young man de Foix was able to develop connections at the French court, particularly with the queen mother, Catherine de Medici. He also studied jurisprudence at the University in Toulouse, and after completing his studies he lectured there on civil law. This added to his reputation, and Catherine sent de Foix to England in 1561 as a special envoy. The following year began his appointment as the ambassador, a position he held until 1566.

During de Foix's time at the Elizabethan court, one of his most important missions was to ensure a dynastic marriage between the Tudor queen and Charles IX of France. The previous resident French diplomat in London, Gilles de Noailles, had noted in 1559 that on November 1, when Queen Elizabeth had celebrated All Saints Day at Westminster Abbey, there had been candles and a crucifix at the altar, which had been a concern to Protestants, and made de Noailles wonder if she would be willing to marry a Catholic prince. Catherine de Medici very much wanted that Catholic prince to be a French one, especially as she was very worried that Elizabeth might marry the Austrian Archduke Charles. Catherine instructed de Foix to encourage the French match and derail the Austrian marriage. Michel de Castelnau, Seigneur de Mauvissière, who later became resident ambassador to England himself, was with de Foix; Mauvissière's memoirs reveal much of what was said during the negotiations. De Foix told the English queen that Catherine so wanted to see her son "accompanied by a great and virtuous queen such as her" (Paranque, *Elizabeth I of England Through Valois Eyes*, 36).

Elizabeth explained her reluctance to the match by saying her difficulty was "that her good brother the most Christian king was [both] too great and too little" (Mauvissière, 289). She meant he was too great since as king of France, he could never be expected to live in England and her English subjects would want to have their kings and queens reside in their country. And he was too little as he was simply too young. The English queen was seventeen years older than the French king, and she told de Foix she would have to be ten years younger for the marriage to be viable. She added she was afraid that his king would find her old and thus disagreeable. This reason of her age for declining marriage proposals with the French royal house was one that Elizabeth would continue to use during her reign as Charles's brothers. Henri was one year younger and François five years younger than Charles, though the fact that they could reside in England meant that the first objection would have been met. Much later in the reign, despite the age difference the marriage negotiations with the youngest of Catherine's sons, François, were taken very seriously. Despite Elizabeth's objections, de Foix continued to persistently pursue the potential marriage as he knew this was an important goal of Catherine. After months of discussions with the English queen, nothing seemed to change. Elizabeth was adamant. She would not consider marriage with a man so much younger than herself. Catherine de Medici, however, continued to pressure de Foix to keep pursuing the union. As for him, he greatly desired for his ambassadorship to be over. He kept asking to be recalled. Catherine responded, "you will be able to [depart] once we have seen that the marriage of the said queen of England succeeds" (Paranque, *Elizabeth I of England Through Valois Eyes*, 40). De Foix's relationship with Elizabeth was, at times, quite tense as he continued to attempt to gain her agreement to the marriage with the French king, after she had already stated that she was not interested in pursuing the match. The marriage never happened, and de Foix finally left England in 1566, when he was sent to Rome instead—a venue more to his liking. He served there until his death in 1584.

Dom Diego Guzman de Silva (1520–1578), Spanish Ambassador to Elizabeth I from 1564 to 1568

In 1564 Philip II sent Dom Diego de Silva to the English court to replace Alvaro de la Quadra. Like de Quadra, de Silva was a churchman, a canon. When he appointed de Silva in January of that year the Spanish king wrote, "I, being informed that you possess the qualities and abilities which are necessary as well as lineage, prudence, experience of affairs, knowledge of that and other countries, and above all fidelity and a desire to serve me, have chosen you for the office and appoint you as my ordinary Ambassador to the said queen of England" (*CSP, Spain*, I, 342). De Silva arrived in England that summer and Henry Stuart, Lord Darnley, was sent to escort de Silva to his first meeting with Queen Elizabeth. De Silva was especially struck by one of the queen's comments. She took the new ambassador aside and asked him about Philip's sister Juana, the widow of John Manuel, Prince of Portugal, who was two years younger than Elizabeth. Elizabeth told de Silva how much she would like to meet Juana, "and how well so young a widow and a maiden would get on together, and what a pleasant life they could lead." She added that of course, since she was older, she "would be the husband, and her Highness the wife" (*CSP, Spain*, I, 364). This was obviously not something that the queen meant seriously, but it was a fascinating insight into Elizabeth's view of marriage—she should be the husband. De Silva also wrote to Philip that the queen spoke to him both in Latin, which she spoke with easy elegance, and in Italian, which she also spoke remarkably well. De Silva's statement about the queen's facility with Italian demonstrates how differently he responded to Elizabeth from his predecessor. While de Quadra had also stated that Elizabeth's Italian was excellent, he had seen her language skills as yet another example of how duplicitous she was; he was convinced that she had learned the language from Italian heretics. In fact, as a young girl her Italian tutor, Giovanni Battista Castiglione, had been a reformer who had fled to England (see Chapter 16). De Silva's relationship with Elizabeth was very different from de Quadra's. Not only of the Spanish ambassadors, but among her ambassadors more generally throughout her reign, she had the most cordial and comfortable relationship with de Silva. They clearly had a strong mutual respect, and he was something of a confidant of hers. But there were certainly issues between England and Spain during de Silva's tenure as ambassador, such as Elizabeth's volatile relationship with Mary Stuart, Elizabeth's own marriage negotiations, and potential conflicts between England and Spain over trade and Spanish troops in Flanders.

In July 1564 de Silva was asked to visit the queen at Richmond, and he wrote how she received him with great kindness. She insisted that he not only have a meal with her but stay for the entertainment, which was a play and then a masque. Elizabeth made sure he would enjoy it by translating the play, a comedy, to him herself as they sat together, also giving her the opportunity to chat more informally. The queen asked de Silva about Philip's son Don Carlos and added that she understood there were plans to marry Don Carlos to the Scottish queen. De Silva assured her she should not believe it and added that subjects never tire of talking about their princes. Elizabeth's response was a way of turning it around that de Silva would see many times. She agreed that what he said was true, adding that just a few days ago in London she had heard that Philip was planning to offer Don Carlos as a husband to her, a highly unlikely scenario. De Silva enjoyed the play and the masque that followed, where the dancers were all dressed in black and white. The queen told him those were her colors; they were known in the Renaissance as the colors that represented virginity. After the entertainment they all went to a room with a table with preserved and candied fruit, sugared nuts, and pastries. De Silva said he did not leave Richmond to head back to the embassy until two in the morning.

De Silva supported the Imperial ambassador Adam Zwetkovich, Baron of Mitterburg, in the lengthy marriage negotiations with the Archduke Charles, though as de Silva had gotten to know Elizabeth, he doubted that she would ever marry, and she indeed told him that she never had any inclination to do so but added that she was being pressured by her people and might have to marry for their welfare. Zwetkovich also thought that Elizabeth would prefer to be single but would marry because it was in England's best interests. By the summer of 1565, he wrote to Emperor Maximilian II that Elizabeth was growing fonder of Charles by the day, and he was certain of the marriage. De Silva, who had known her longer and better, was more dubious. On August 13 the queen was walking with the two men, and she spoke of her longing for Charles to come and visit and then the marriage could be arranged. De Silva decided to tease the queen and suggested that Charles indeed was in the country in disguise as part of the Imperial envoy. He wrote to Philip that the queen turned white and almost fainted, at which point he burst out laughing, so she knew it had just been a joke. In her usual manner of turning something around, Elizabeth then falsely claimed that many princes had already visited her while in disguise.

In 1566 a Protestant movement was gaining strength in the Low Countries and Philip II decided it must be exterminated, sending Fernando Alvarez de Toledo, Duke of Alva to take care of the matter. The duke was violently successful at the suppression, but thousands of skilled artisans fled Flanders, a number coming to England. Elizabeth and her advisors were very upset with Spanish actions, and Elizabeth questioned de Silva intensely. He went hunting with her so that they could talk, and he encouraged her not to intervene. There were rumors that Alva's army could be used to invade England—and indeed once Mary Stuart was in England this was often discussed. Elizabeth also informed de Silva that she heard that Pope Pius V, France, and Spain were in league together against Protestants. De Silva tried to calm the queen, but by July 1568 he was growing more distressed, concerned that the Flemish exiles were using England as a base so they could return home and battle Alva. De Silva discussed these issues with the queen and then wrote to her about the conversation that they had had. "I spoke to your Majesty on the 11th instant to the effect that, for a long time past, it was stated that many rebels from the Low countries, subjects of my King, who had taken refuge here from those parts by the help of your Majesty's subjects, were returning thither with arms, in order to disturb the peace of the States." He also raised a serious concern, stating: "I am informed that a subsidy is being raised from the clergy of this country in aid of the rebels who are invading my King's dominions" (*CSP, Spain* II, 51).

Also, in the final months of de Silva's tenure as ambassador another crisis in England occurred when in May 1568 the deposed queen Mary Stuart fled to England. In late June Elizabeth told de Silva her concerns. "She would not on any account allow the Queen to go to France... Seeing also the pretensions she had to the English Crown, it would be dangerous, she said, to allow her to be free in this country... She had therefore... determined to bring her to some place in the interior of England." But Elizabeth was also concerned for Mary's safety stating that "She would not allow her to return to Scotland ... to be again endangered" (*CSP, Spain*, II, 47).

In early 1568 de Silva asked to be recalled as he found the climate hard on his health, and he most likely preferred being an ambassador in a place where his religious beliefs were not so frequently challenged, though he was free to hear Mass in the embassy. When he made the request, he stated that he would be leaving with Anglo-Spanish relations in a friendly and harmonious state. But by the time he left that September to take up his new position as ambassador to Venice the Anglo-Spanish problems were getting more serious, and especially without de Silva's tact and skills in working with the English queen, they would only worsen.

In August de Silva went to Hatfield to spend time with the queen and discuss the change in ambassadors. "I was with the queen on the 3rd and 4th instant at Hatfield ... in order to tell her of the coming of Don Guerau de Spes." He revealed "she showed more sorrow that I expected, and, changing color, told me that she was grieved from the bottom of her heart that your Majesty would make any change, as she was so greatly pleased with my mode of procedures in affairs." He continued, affirming, "she dwelt so much upon this that, in order to banish suspicion, I threw the blame upon myself, assuring her that your Majesty had decided to give me leave at my own supplication and importunity, my sole reason being my poor health, which I was sure the climate did not suit" (*CSP, Spain*, II, 63).

During his time in England, De Silva carefully represented Spanish and Catholic interests but did it in a way that also expressed his respect for the queen. He managed to establish a peaceful and productive diplomatic relationship with Elizabeth. In a letter Elizabeth sent to Philip II of Spain on December 20, 1568, she recognized that Guzman de Silva "was always a good minister desirous of preserving harmony between us, which was proved by the calm and quiet which reigned whilst he was here" (*CSP, Spain*, II, 220). De Silva spent the rest of his life as ambassador to Venice, dying there in 1577.

SIR JAMES MELVILLE, OF HALHILL (1535/1536–1617) SCOTTISH AMBASSADOR TO ELIZABETH I IN 1564

James Melville came from a prominent family in Scotland and in 1550 at the age of fourteen he was sent to France where the Scottish queen Mary Stuart was being raised to be queen consort of France. He learned French, and such arts as dancing, fencing, and lute playing. He also learned about European affairs. When he was older, he spent time at the court of the Elector Palatine, Frederick II, and learned German. He returned to Paris to give his condolences to Mary after the death of Francis II in December 1560.

Toward the end of Melville's life, in 1603, the year of Elizabeth's death, he wrote his memoirs which provide us with many fascinating details about the court of Elizabeth. They were first published in 1683. Scholars value the memoirs as an important source for the reigns of Mary Stuart, her son James, and Queen Elizabeth, and they illuminate the human qualities of these monarchs. We cannot, however, verify everything in these accounts, written many years after the events.

Mary returned to Scotland in August 1561 and in 1564 Mary asked Melville to return to Scotland as well. He did so via England and met with Elizabeth, bringing with him a proposal from Count John Casimir Palatine (see Chapter 6). Elizabeth was far more interested in whom Mary Stuart would marry. Two possibilities that she discussed with Melville were Robert Dudley and Henry Stuart, Lord Darnley, whom Elizabeth described as a lusty young prince. Both Dudley and Darnley had previously been mentioned as possible suitors for Mary when Maitland had been at the English court.

Melville presented himself to the Scottish Queen Mary in May 1564. She appointed him to her Council and named him a Gentleman of the Bedchamber; he also received a yearly pension. Mary sent him back to England in September to consult further with Elizabeth about Mary's future husband and to convince Elizabeth to name Mary as her heir, as Maitland had unsuccessfully attempted to do earlier. Mary instructed Melville to get along well with Elizabeth and to amuse her but also discuss serious issues. Melville worked to engage Elizabeth, but he privately admitted that he did not trust her. Melville's descriptions of some of their conversations and her questions about the Scottish queen provide a fascinating insight into Elizabeth's character. As they discussed Mary's potential marriages, they also discussed Elizabeth's own views of marriage. Elizabeth told Melville that she was resolved not to marry. Melville replied, "I know the Truth of that, Madam, said I, you need not tell it me. Your Majesty thinks, if you were married, you would be but Queen of England; and now you are both King and Queen. I know your Spirit cannot endure a Commander" (Melville, 96).

Elizabeth and Mary had exchanged miniatures, but Elizabeth was eager to learn more about her cousin and how they compared. Elizabeth wanted Melville to tell her which queen was the fairest. Being diplomatic, Melville stated Elizabeth was the fairest queen of England and Mary of Scotland. When Elizabeth pressured Melville, he said that Elizabeth had the fairer complexion, but his queen was very lovely. Elizabeth then wanted to know who was taller, and when Melville said Mary was, Elizabeth responded that meant Mary was too tall as she was the perfect height. Melville also confirmed that Elizabeth was a better dancer. When Melville told the queen that Mary played the lute and virginals—a small keyboard instrument—reasonably well for a queen, Elizabeth wanted Melville to hear her play, but she wanted it to seem he happened upon her accidentally. Elizabeth professed herself surprised to have someone listen to her, but then asked Melville who was the better musician and Melville admitted that Elizabeth was (see Chapter 16). He also told that in lieu of comparisons, he could arrange an actual meeting with Mary. "I offered to convey her secretly to Scotland... clothed like a Page, that under this disguise she might see the Queen... Telling her that her Chamber might be kept in her absence as though she were sick" (Melville, 51). Elizabeth responded with a sigh, saying if only she could do this.

Elizabeth spoke frequently to Melville about how much she valued Robert Dudley and what a great opportunity for Mary to marry him. She told Melville that she esteemed Dudley "as her brother, her best friend, whom she would have herself married, if she ever minded to have taken a husband" (Melville, 46). To make him an appropriate consort she decided to give him the titles Earl of Leicester and Baron Denbigh and insisted that Melville stay for the ceremony at Westminster. He said there was great solemnity—until, as the new earl was still kneeling in front of the queen, she tickled his neck. After the ceremony, the queen turned to Melville to ask what he thought of the new earl. After Melville's compliments, Elizabeth sharply turned the tables on Melville and told him, yet "you like better of yonder long Lad," and she pointed out Darnley. Melville at the time was secretly negotiating with Darnley's mother Margaret Douglas, Countess of Lennox, to convince Elizabeth to allow her young cousin to go to Scotland (Melville, 48).

Darnley did go to Scotland and wed Mary Stuart, with disastrous results. When their son James was born in June 1566 Melville returned to England to inform the English queen. He claimed that Elizabeth was very upset, that she said that "the Queen of Scots is lighter of a fair son; and I am but barren stock" (Melville, 131). When he conveyed Mary's request that Elizabeth be James's godmother, the queen agreed. This was the final time Melville saw Elizabeth. Melville continued to play an important role at the Scottish court throughout the minority of James VI. In his last years, he retired to his estates and wrote his very revealing memoirs.

Adam Zwetkovich, Baron of Mitterburg, Imperial Ambassador to Elizabeth I from May to August 1565

Adam Zwetkovich, Baron of Mitterburg, was highly regarded at the Imperial Court. In one of his last letters to his son and heir Maximilian II, the previous Emperor Ferdinand I had spoken of Zwetkovich's worth. He was sent to Russia twice to negotiate a treaty against the Turks. He was a councilor to Emperor Maximilian and also his chamberlain. In 1565 Maximilian sent Zwetkovich to the English court to negotiate a marriage between his brother the Archduke Charles and Queen Elizabeth. Zwetkovich arrived on May 6, 1565. He was also bringing back the insignia of the Garter that Ferdinand I, the Emperor's father, had once worn. By the next month the ambassador reported that he had great hopes regarding a marriage between the two parties. While the queen had pretended to Melville that she played music only for herself, she openly demonstrated her attractiveness as queen with her musical skills. Soon after he arrived, Zwetkovich wrote to the emperor that he had seen Elizabeth dance and play both the lute and the virginals.

But as his time progressed in England, Zwetkovich became convinced that Elizabeth was procrastinating and would never actually agree to the marriage. The issue regarding the archduke's religion remained one of the greatest obstacles as the queen informed Zwetkovich she would not marry anyone who did not share her religious persuasion, and Zwetkovich, thinking the situation hopeless, planned his departure. As it turned out, the negotiations went on for several more years (see Chapter 6), but Zwetkovich's role in these negotiations had ended. Despite this, he had made a very good impression on the queen. On Zwetkovich's departure in August 1565, she wrote a letter to Maximilian, asking him "to reward him [Zwetkovich] for his zeal" (Bajetta, *Elizabeth's Italian Letters*, 26).

Guerau de Spes (1524–1572), Spanish Ambassador to Elizabeth I from 1568 to 1571

Though it was true that de Silva had asked for a new assignment, Philip may have agreed because of his anger over Elizabeth's involvement in the Netherlands, and his anger with the current English ambassador in Spain, Dr. John Man, who had arrived in Madrid in 1566. The Spanish king was contemptuous of Man, an academic instead of a man of noble status, which the Spanish felt was important for any ambassador. Philip considered that by sending Man, Elizabeth had deliberately offended him. The situation deteriorated so badly that by 1568 the king refused to allow Man to have Protestant services at the embassy and insisted that all his servants must attend Catholic services. Philip accused Man of distributing Protestant literature and banned Man from Madrid, insisting that he live in a small village outside the city. This made it impossible to Man to do his job. Philip insisted that Man be recalled, and Elizabeth did so but was unhappy that Man had been ill-treated. Though Philip hoped for a more impressive ambassador, Elizabeth did not agree to another resident ambassador, though she did send special ambassadors about specific issues. Philip may well have felt insulted enough about the situation that he wanted a more aggressive ambassador in England, considering de Silva too tolerant of heretics, including the queen herself. In terms of Anglo-Spanish relations, it turned out to be a very unfortunate decision.

Guerau de Spes, whom the Duke of Feria had strongly recommended to become the ambassador to England, was very different from de Silva. The Catalan de Spes was a knight of the Order of Calatrava. He was a haughty man who despised those he considered heretics. He also lacked any sense of discretion. Philip hoped that with de Spes he could control Elizabeth more through using fear than de Silva's methods of sympathetic engagement. De Spes, though not at the instruction of Philip, came to England to foster a Catholic conspiracy to murder Elizabeth or push her off the throne and destroy the English Protestants. He operated more as a spy than as a diplomat, viewing Elizabeth as a heretic queen. When de Spes arrived at Elizabeth's court he described Cecil as "a man of mean sort, but very astute, false, lying, and full of artifice," adding that the "great heretic," was a "such a clownish Englishman." He was equally contemptuous of Cecil's brother-in-law Sir Nicholas Bacon, calling him "an obstinate and most malignant heretic," who always agreed with Cecil. As for Francis Russell, Earl of Bedford, de Spes stated, "In person and manners he is a monstrosity and a great heretic" (*CSP, Spain*, II, 354–369).

The Duke of Alva several times complained that de Spes's zeal drew him into dangerous situations that went beyond his instructions from Philip. As soon as de Spes arrived in England Mary Stuart's friends and allies communicated with him, and from then on, he was in constant contact with Mary. He was soon involved in conspiracies to overthrow Elizabeth. When de Silva was ambassador, he had also been approached by various conspirators but had wisely refused any involvement.

In late November 1568 something happened that infuriated de Spes and the Spanish. Pirates chased several Genoese ships, carrying treasure that the King of Spain was borrowing to pay the Duke of Alva's troops in the Netherlands, into the English Channel. The merchant Benedetto Spinola, born in Genoa but living in London, informed Elizabeth that the funds were not the property of the king of Spain until the ships arrived in Netherlands. The Genoese bankers considered Elizabeth a more responsible borrower and were delighted to transfer the loan to her; she eventually repaid them according to their terms. This was great news for the Dutch Protestants, as it made Alva's job suppressing them that much more difficult, and the unpaid soldiers eventually rebelled. De Spes was so enraged that he wrote to the Duke of Alva telling him he ought to seize all the English people who were in the Netherlands as well as all their valuables, which Alva did. Elizabeth condemned this illegal action, and the English responded by seizing Spanish ships. This led to an embargo of all English imports to the Netherlands, and this bitter standoff continued for years until there was finally an agreement in 1573 that restored trade and meant that Alva had to leave the Netherlands.

As he continued as ambassador, de Spes became even more committed to the deposition of Elizabeth so that she could be replaced by Mary Stuart. He was willing to meet with any possible conspirators, something of which Cecil, because of his own informers, was aware. De Spes was actively involved in the Ridolfi Plot (see Chapter 9). At first De Spes thought the discovery of the plot would not have harsh consequences for him personally but he soon learned how wrong he was. The queen refused any longer to recognize him as the ambassador. She sent Henry Cobham to Spain to present a formal complaint about de Spes's actions to Philip. De Spes felt angry, bitter, and mortified, wanting revenge on the queen and Burghley. In July 1571 he wrote that he would attempt "to bring punishment on the heads of these people for their insolence" (*CSP, Spain*, II, 321). On December 11 de Spes was told that he must leave England in three days. He claimed that his privileges as an ambassador and the grandeur of his monarch were being ignored and that he needed more time. But Burghley had had enough, and de Spes left England on December 14. As the Spanish ambassador to England, de Spes caused terrible dissension and damaged the relationship between England and Spain. He died the year following his expulsion.

Bertrand de Salignac de la Mothe Fénélon (1523–1589), French Ambassador to Elizabeth I from 1568 to 1575

Bertrand de Salignac, La Mothe Fénelon was born in Périgord, South-West France, in 1523. He was raised by his cousin, Jean de Gontaut. This proved advantageous for La Mothe Fénélon as the de Gontauts were an influential noble family. Jean was a diplomat who, from 1547 to 1548, served the French royal family at the court of Charles V. During that time, La Mothe Fénélon was with his cousin and guardian, learning the art of diplomacy. He also gained experience as a diplomat when he assisted Michel de Seure, the French ambassador sent to the English court in 1560, to negotiate the withdrawal of English and French forces from Scotland. La Mothe Fénélon returned to Elizabeth's court as ambassador in November 1568. By this point, tensions were increasing between the English and French courts. Elizabeth was supporting the Huguenots during the French religious wars. La Mothe Fénélon's mission, therefore, was to maintain goodwill between the two countries. He was also involved in attempting to arrange a marriage between Elizabeth and Henri, Duke of Anjou.

About the same time La Mothe Fénélon arrived in England as ambassador, Mary Stuart had fled to England upon her escape from Scotland and complicated the Anglo-French relationship. In the years following, La Mothe Fénélon advised Charles that Elizabeth was concerned about Mary's plans to marry the Duke of Norfolk and about the Ridolfi Plot, which would not only have supported the marriage but Elizabeth's assassination (see Chapter 9). Though Mary had strong ties to the French court, the Spanish ambassador de Spes did more to support Mary's plots and conspiracies than the French ambassador, who informed Charles that because of the Ridolfi plot, Parliament was pressuring Elizabeth to to have Mary executed. La Mothe Fénélon explained that he thought Mary was being treated with great severity, and he was sure that Charles would feel compassion for the Scottish queen.

The first time La Mothe Fénélon saw Elizabeth, he described her as "being herself well dressed and looking a wonder" (Paranque, "Queen Elizabeth I and the Elizabethan Court in the French Ambassador's Eyes," 270). He was often invited to important events at court, and when, on January 23, 1571, the Royal Exchange opened—something that was highly celebrated in London—La Mothe Fénélon reported that he had been invited to accompany Elizabeth. He described how she "did not forget to make me notice the affection and devotion that was seen in this great people... and confessed to me freely that it gave her great joy in her heart to see herself so loved" (Paranque, "Queen Elizabeth I and the Elizabethan Court in the French Ambassador's Eyes," 281) (Fig. 8.2).

Elizabeth and her court were horrified when they learned about the St. Bartholomew's Day Massacre in Paris on August 24, 1572, and that created grave difficulty for La Mothe Fénélon. Elizabeth and some members of her court were at Woodstock hunting when she was told of the massacre and immediately told her people to stop the hunt and return to the residence. As soon as La Mothe Fénélon heard from his king, he headed to Woodstock so that he could present Charles IX's version as soon as possible. When La Mothe Fénélon arrived at Woodstock Elizabeth immediately ordered that he be placed under house arrest. She worried about her French ambassador, Sir Francis Walsingham, in Paris, and hoped that this would protect him. Eleven days later La Mothe Fénélon finally got to meet with the queen. He found her and her entire court in full mourning attire, and, when he entered, they were all completely silent. One courtier then told him the massacre was the worst crime since the crucifixion. The ambassador explained to Elizabeth that there had been a plot to murder the king, and the massacre had been a response to that, but Elizabeth did not find that at all convincing. She was horrified "that women, children, maids, young infants, and sucking babes were at the same time murdered and cast into the river" (Elizabeth I, *Collected Works*, 216). The situation was extremely tense between England and France, and Sir Francis Walsingham begged to return to England.

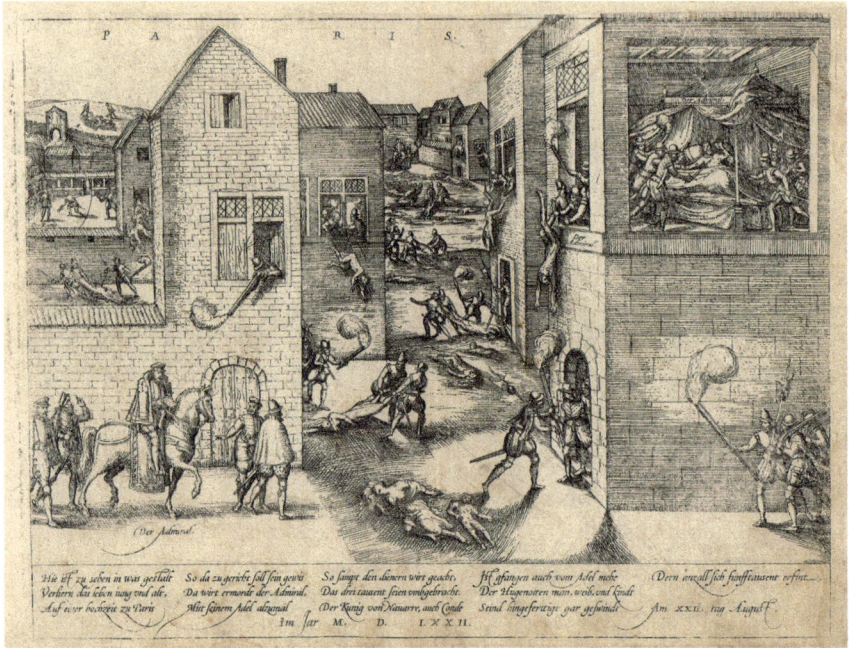

Fig. 8.2 St. Bartholomew's Day Massacre

After Charles IX's death she sent Roger, Lord North to Paris to negotiate with the new king, Henri III and his mother Catherine for a trade treaty that would also offer some support for the French Protestants. This led in February 1575 to a situation that La Mothe Fénélon had to discuss with Queen Elizabeth, though far less tragic was still upsetting to her. Lord North had heard that the queen mother, Catherine de Medici, privately had her dwarfs make fun of Elizabeth. The French ambassador attempted to convince her that Lord North had misunderstood what had been said. Elizabeth responded that it must have been the case as his French was so poor, but she knew how fluent in the language he truly was. She also told La Mothe Fénélon that if she ever insulted Catherine, it was because her French, which was excellent, was also so poor.

Later in 1575 La Mothe Fénélon was recalled as the queen mother thought another ambassador might be more effective at attempting again to arrange a French marriage for the English queen. In his final interview with Elizabeth, after having spent seven years of his life at the English court, he wrote that Elizabeth "took me in one corner of the room where I told her that I had come to testify of your [King Henri III's] true testimonies of the undeniable affection that Your Majesty had to live as a good brother and a perfect ally with her" (Paranque, "Queen Elizabeth I and the Elizabethan Court in the French Ambassador's Eyes," 283). We do not know what the queen thought of the statement. It appears that Catherine and Henri III believed that La Mothe Fénélon had been an effective ambassador, as he was briefly sent back in 1582 to help with the negotiations of the marriage between Elizabeth and François, Duke of Anjou.

Michel de Castelnau, Seigneur de Mauvissière (c. 1520–1592), French Ambassador to Elizabeth I from 1575 to 1584

Michel de Castelnau, Seigneur de Mauvissière, was a highly intelligent man who received an excellent education, which he clearly appreciated, as throughout his life Mauvissière was devoted to cultural activities; he read literature for pleasure, translated Latin works into French, listened to music, and went often to the theatre. The French royal family valued his diplomatic skills, and he was often sent as a special envoy to Elizabeth before his ten years as resident ambassador. From early in his career, he was a close ally of the Guise family.

Mauvissière was sent to England in 1559 to negotiate with Elizabeth over her claim to Calais and was one of the negotiators for the Treaty of Cateau-Cambrésis between France and England. Francis II died in December 1560, and Mauvissière accompanied the widowed Mary Stuart back to Scotland and stayed for a year. He also visited England hoping to help mend the relationship between the two queens. In 1562 he returned to France and was involved in the wars of religion. He was sent to England in May 1565 to again discuss with Elizabeth whether she might reconsider marrying Charles IX, but she declined any negotiation about this. Mauvissière went on to Scotland, where he "found the Queen of Scots in the Flower of her Age, beloved and adored by her Subjects, and admired by all the neighboring Princes" in part because she "was the next Successor to the Crown of England, and one of the greatest Beauties of the Age" (Mauvissière, 290, 297). Soon after this visit, Mary married her cousin Henry Stuart.

At another visit Catherine instructed Mauvissière to again offer Charles IX as well as Henri, Duke of Anjou. If, however, Elizabeth was not willing to make a French marriage, Catherine told him to promote a marriage with Robert Dudley, whom, when she offered him as a suitor to Mary Stuart, she had recently created Earl of Leicester. "Some people gave out, that her affection lay that way, as the Queen of Scots did to Lord Darnley." No doubt the queen mother considered this would be much better for France than a marriage of Elizabeth to the Archduke Charles. But Elizabeth told Mauvissière that she not only was not interested in the French suitors, but if Leicester "were a prince by birth, or descended from the royal family, that she would make a choice of him [but] she was resolved never to marry, or make a subject her companion." Mauvissière told Queen Elizabeth that when he left England he was going on to Scotland. "But I found her much colder towards that queen than before." Elizabeth complained to Mauvissière that Mary had married one of her own subjects against her consent. But with a fascinating insight, he was convinced that actually Elizabeth had "exerted all her art, and spared no pains to promote this marriage" (Mauvissière, 298, 299). He added that he saw how Elizabeth grew much more anxious when Mary Stuart became pregnant. Mauvissière stopped in England on his way to Scotland after the murder of David Rizzio, something he found appalling, and believed that the tragedy came from the passion that had begun the marriage of Mary and Darnley. "And so this Marriage and great amour (which everybody expected would settle the peace of Scotland, and be of such importance to us) immediately turned to ... a private War," which was a war between "the new-married Couple, which was occasioned by some Jealousies; and went so far, that the young king (forgetting the extraordinary honor which this beautiful princess had done him, in taking him to her bed after so great a Monarch) at the Instigation of the Earl of Morton ... and other Scots, had one David [Rizzio] ... shamefully murdered in her Presence" (Mauvissière, 300). A few months later he again met with Elizabeth on his way to Scotland to congratulate Mary on the birth of her son.

Charles IX was very concerned with restoring the damaged relationship between France and England following the English horror over the St. Bartholomew's Day Massacre. In November 1572 the king sent Mauvissière to England to ask Elizabeth if she would agree to become the godmother to Charles's new daughter at her baptism in February 1573. At Hampton Court La Mothe Fénelon presented Mauvissière to the queen and she received him graciously. Though most of the queen's Council was opposed, Elizabeth told Mauvissière that she was greatly honored to be asked, and she was astute enough to send the Catholic William Somerset, Earl of Worcester to represent her at the baptism. Her gift to her goddaughter Maria Elisabeth was a font of pure gold.

In 1575 Henri III sent Mauvissière to England to be the resident ambassador, replacing La Mothe Fénélon. One of his main functions was to negotiate a marriage between Elizabeth and Henri's younger brother François, Duke of Alençon, who became Duke of Anjou in 1576. Another was to support Mary Stuart; as a close ally to the Guise family, he took this responsibility very seriously. Henri III told his ambassador to do everything to convince the English queen to release her cousin, and to be aware of any plots that might replace Elizabeth with Mary, who would restore Catholicism to England. Mauvissière was aware of how difficult the situation was; he had a special agent at the embassy, named Courcelles, whose function was to arrange secret communication between Mary Stuart and her supporters in France. Courcelles later became the French ambassador to James VI.

Though in 1575 Elizabeth was not interested in the French match, years later she had a change of heart. The negotiations went on from late 1578 to 1582 and the Duke of Anjou visited England twice. While Mauvissière worked hard to encourage the negotiations he was also aware of how much hostility there was to the French marriage both in the court and throughout the country. He noted that with wooing Elizabeth looked younger and more beautiful. While Lord Burghley assured him that Elizabeth was still capable of having a child, many feared that if she did, she might die in childbirth, and the French prince would take over. John Stubbes's 1579 pamphlet *The Discovery of a Gaping Gulf* made this point forcefully. If Elizabeth made this marriage "our dear Queen Elizabeth (I shake to speak it) [would be] led blindfold as a poor lamb to the slaughter." The queen was so susceptible because "how much more forcibly shall the stronger vessel pull weak woman." Such a sentiment would have infuriated the queen, and even more was his comment about "how exceedingly dangerous ... for Her Majesty at these years to have her first child, yea, how fearful the expectation of death is to mother and child" (Stubbes, 4, 11, 51). In September 1579 the queen issued a proclamation that prohibited the book's circulation. But she did not feel that the proclamation was enough, and her response to the pamphlet was brutal; after being found guilty of seditious libel, Stubbes lost his right hand; he then cried out "God save the queen!" The crowd remained ominously silent, and Stubbes fainted. Mauvissière had to report the turbulence occurring in England, but he also reassured the French rulers that Elizabeth "denounced the malice and treacherous intentions" of those speaking up against the match (Paranque, *Elizabeth I of England through Valois Eyes*, 137).

But Mauvissière did not trust Elizabeth when she expressed interest in the marriage. Anjou came for a second visit in 1581 and while he and the queen were together, Mauvissière entered and stated that the king his master wanted to know exactly what Elizabeth's intentions toward his brother were. He was shocked by her answer, as were everyone else, though Anjou's shock was mixed with jubilation. "You may write this to the king," she told Mauvissière. "The duke of Alençon shall be my husband." She then gave the duke a ring and the astonished and delighted Anjou gave her one in return. This was not the first ring Anjou had given Elizabeth, but this exchange of rings had a very different and more formal meaning; however, Mauvissière was right to doubt Elizabeth. The queen grew reluctant, stating she must remain a spinster until she could "overcome her natural hatred of marriage," and the ring, she claimed, "was only a pledge of perpetual friendship" (*CSP, Spain*, III, 226, 243, 348).

During his time as ambassador to England Mauvissière demonstrated how much he cared about his family. In 1583 he hired John Florio, an Anglo-Italian linguist and author, and had him live in the embassy. Florio did translations and served as language tutor for his daughter, Catherine Marie. Mauvissière's wife Marie was much younger than he was; he was fifty-five when he became resident ambassador. During the decade they were in England she was often pregnant. Several of these pregnancies ended in stillbirths. At least two of the babies survived, a son in 1577 and a daughter in 1585. Queen Elizabeth was the godmother for both. Also, during his years in England Mauvissière wrote his memoirs to give moral instruction to his son. They covered the years 1559–1570 and were published posthumously in 1621 and translated into English in 1724.

Jean de Simier, Baron de Saint-Marc, Special Envoy to Negotiate Marriage 1579, 1581

To help in the marriage negotiations François, Duke of Anjou, sent his close friend and the master of his wardrobe, Jean de Simier, to England. He arrived January 5, 1579, and initially stayed with Mauvissière. Several envoys had been sent in previous months but had not stayed long or been effective. Simier was very different; he arrived to woo Elizabeth for the duke with gifts and calculated charm. He first met the queen on January 11 at Richmond and he and Elizabeth immediately established a strong rapport. Elizabeth enjoyed giving nicknames, and for him she played on his name, calling him her monkey. For the next two months, they spent much time together, sometimes meeting three times in a day; there was a lot of flirtation and banter. Simier was entertained at feasts, jousts, plays and masques, and dances. Elizabeth asked Christopher Hatton to also entertain him. Ambassadors' reports in February and March continued to speak about the time the queen clearly enjoyed spending with Simier and the entertainments he attended. On April 12 he was with the queen at Whitehall and the two of them walked together in the gardens. On Maundy Thursday each year Elizabeth would wash the feet of poor women—each year the number of women was equal to the age of the queen. She invited Simier to attend the ceremony on April 16 when she washed the feet of forty-five women and gave each woman a purse of money. Simier wrote that he found Elizabeth to be most virtuous, honorable, and witty.

Sometime around then Simier was in Elizabeth's bedchamber one morning when the queen was absent and he pocketed Elizabeth's nightcap, which he sent to the duke. Anjou wrote to Elizabeth in May, assuring her that he would treasure both that and her handkerchief, which Simier had also sent. When Simier's action became known at the English court people were shocked by his temerity and added to their opposition to the duke's visit. The Earl of Leicester had secretly married Lettice, widow of Walter, Earl of Essex, on September 21, 1578. Though some people learned about it fairly soon, he managed for a while to keep it from the queen. The Earl of Sussex told Mauvissière about it in November. It is not entirely clear when Elizabeth learned about it, but she was not only infuriated by the marriage, but that Leicester did not tell her about it himself. Apparently Simier told her in June that he could not understand how Leicester could be opposed to her marriage when he was married himself. Though there were rumors that Leicester tried to have Simier murdered in revenge, there is no evidence to support that.

Anjou spent two weeks in August 1579 at court and Elizabeth expressed herself delighted with him. After he left on August 27, Simier wrote to the queen that the duke could not sleep because he was so sad at leaving. Simier himself left three months later. Back in France in 1580, there was a falling out between Simier and Anjou. By the end of August Walsingham wrote to Burghley "that Simier seems to be altogether in disgrace with his master" (*CSP, Foreign*, XIV, 388–406). Henri III and Catherine de Medici, who thought highly of Simier, attempted to promote a reconciliation, but to no avail. When Anjou visited Elizabeth again in 1581, Simier went also, but at the request of Henri III, and Anjou was angry. He pressed the queen to expel Simier, but Elizabeth refused. Eventually, the marriage plan fell apart and both Anjou and Simier left England. During the rest of the 1580s, Simier was supportive of the English ambassador to France.

Don Bernardino de Mendoza (c. 1540–1604), Spanish Ambassador to Elizabeth I from 1578 to 1584

Don Bernardino de Mendoza was well born. His father was Don Alonso Suarez de Mendoza, third Count of Coruña and Vicecount of Torija. Mendoza studied at the University of Alcala de Henares and was able to read Latin, Greek, French, Italian, and some English. In 1560 he joined the Spanish army and for many years he served under Fernando Alvarez de Toledo, Duke of Alva. In 1576 he was honored for his service, and the same year his diplomatic career began. His first posting was as ambassador to Venice, but in 1578 he was sent to England (Fig. 8.3).

De Spes had been expelled in 1571. Phillip sent Mendoza in 1578 to reopen the embassy. Philip decided this was necessary because of his problems in the Low Countries which worsened with the English intervention. For Philip, it was important that ambassadors be men of high rank and dignity, and Mendoza was certainly that, but he turned out to be a very problematic diplomat, whose time in England greatly worsened Anglo-Spanish relations.

Philip directed Mendoza to be conciliatory, maintain civil relations, and convince the queen to stop intervention in the Low Countries. Mendoza was immediately concerned with figuring out how he could help Mary Stuart. Though Mary was a Catholic, she was so allied with the French that Philip thought it might be problematic if she became queen of England. Mendoza, however, was supportive of her. Exceeding his king's instruction, Mendoza saw his role as helping to replace the heretical Queen Elizabeth with Mary. Mendoza, filled with a sense of superiority, did not even attempt to hide his contempt for the English and his disgust in their heretical religion.

The conflicts between England and Spain were also developing in the Americas and Ireland. Philip sent support to Ireland in 1579 and 1580. In 1577 Sir Francis Drake, with surreptitious support from Sir Francis Walsingham and the queen, had left on his voyage that would circumnavigate the globe. He returned in 1580 in triumph with a fortune by taking treasure from the Spanish all over the world. Elizabeth allowed Drake to do an inaccurate accounting so Mendoza would not know just how much Drake had taken.

Fig. 8.3 Spanish ambassador expelled from England private collection

Drake and the queen were able to keep the considerable unaccounted-for treasure.

Elizabeth celebrated Drake and refused to take Mendoza's complaints seriously, saying that she first needed an explanation of Spanish involvement in Ireland. Mendoza lodged formal complaints about Drake's thievery and cruelty, claiming "that Drake has spoiled his Majesty's subjects," adding that he was "so sure that it cannot be denied... a great quantity of bullion and pearls taken in Mar del Sur, appertaining partly to the King, partly to his subjects." Mendoza also claimed that "in a fight Drake has cut off the hands of some of his Majesty's subjects" (*CSP Foreign*, XIV, 463).

The queen asked Edmund Tremayne, one of the clerks of the Privy Council, to investigate Mendoza's claims. Tremayne was Drake's cousin, so it is hardly surprising that Drake was cleared of all charges (see Chapter 3). Mendoza expressed his anger when Elizabeth refused him an audience in June 1581. When Mendoza finally met with the queen in October 1581, he began his long list of complaints until the queen told him she had heard enough. The meeting was so acrimonious that he wrote to her afterward. "I have been so much grieved to hear that your Majesty said I need not think of frightening and threatening you" (*CSP, Foreign*, XV, 337). Mendoza also worked with his king to take revenge on some English merchants. Thomas Wilford, the president of the Company of Merchants who traded with Spain and Portugal, wrote to Lord Burghley on August 11, 1582, that Mendoza's "malice and revenging mind they [the merchants] have just occasion to fear" (State Papers Online). As Mendoza spent less time at court, he paid Lord Henry Howard, brother of the executed Duke of Norfolk, for any information and gossip that he could learn.

Though Philip had told Mendoza not to become involved in any plots against Elizabeth, Mendoza ignored these instructions. Especially in the last years of his ambassadorship these conspiracies occupied most of his attention. Mendoza was involved in many potential plots and was getting intelligence from disaffected Catholics. He was the special confidant to Mary Stuart. In the early 1580s, Francis Throckmorton became centrally involved in a plot to free Mary and bring England back to Roman Catholicism. The assassination of Elizabeth would trigger a French invasion. Mendoza was deeply involved in the conspiracy. Throckmorton, after being racked, confessed to Mendoza's involvement. In the meantime, Mendoza refused to turn over any papers that Throckmorton had entrusted to him. Throckmorton was executed in July 1584 (see Chapter 9).

The Privy Council invited the legal experts Alberico Gentili and John Hotman to advise if the government could prosecute Mendoza for his involvement in the plot to murder Elizabeth. The experts concluded that as ambassador, Mendoza enjoyed diplomatic immunity. As reluctant as the members of the Council were, all they could do to Mendoza was expel him from England rather than have him executed. After Mendoza's expulsion there were no more ambassadors from Spain to England in the reign of Elizabeth.

Elizabeth sent William Waad in 1584 to explain to Philip why his ambassador had been forced to leave England (see Chapter 3). Not only was Waad treated poorly in Madrid, but Philip refused to even give him an audience. Philip's secretary, Juan de Idiaquez, asked Waad for the letters he carried from Elizabeth to Philip, but Waad explained he had been instructed to present them in person. Philip's response was to have Waad thrown out of Spain. Elizabeth had written that she wanted to preserve amity with Spain, but Philip was not interested.

Philip appointed Mendoza to be ambassador to France and he arrived in Paris in November 1584. He spent much of his time in this new role continuing to support plots to free Mary Stuart and assassinate Elizabeth. This included the final conspiracy, led by Anthony Babington (see Chapter 9). Between Mary's sentence of death on November 19, 1586, and her execution on February 8, 1587, Mary wrote ten letters that she managed to smuggle out. Her letter of November 23 demonstrated the closeness Mary felt for Mendoza. Mary declared her complete innocence—that those of her people who testified against her were all lying, and she was a martyr for her faith. She also wanted to assure Mendoza that she was leaving her claim to the throne to his master Philip II, as she considered her son James a heretic. "Having ever found you ...desirous of my welfare and deliverance from captivity.... I now write to bid you a last adieu ... I die in a just cause, and am happy in having made over my rights to the King your master." It was also important to Mary to send

Mendoza a remembrance. "You will receive from me as a token of my remembrance a diamond which I have held very dear, having been given to me by the late Duke of Norfolk as a pledge of his troth, and I have always worn it as such; keep it for my sake" (Cowan, 108–110).

In 1588 Mendoza first heard in Paris that the Armada had vanquished England and he publicly celebrated, to his great chagrin later. In 1591, the Catholic League was in disarray and Mendoza was in poor health with his eyesight deteriorating. He resigned his ambassadorship and returned to Spain, eventually going completely blind. During his retirement, he wrote a study of war published in 1595 in Madrid. Two years later Sir Edward Hoby published his translation, *Theorique and Practise of Warr*. Mendoza died in August 1604.

André Hurault, seigneur de Maisse (1539–1607), French Ambassador to Elizabeth I in December 1597

Henri IV needed a skillful ambassador to send to England in 1597 as he wanted to inform Elizabeth that he was considering peace with Spain. When Elizabeth had earlier helped France, he had agreed not to make peace without her knowledge and hoped he could involve England in his negotiations. He decided on André Hurault, seigneur de Maisse, as his most adroit diplomat. De Maisse was at the time about sixty-five years old. Henri wrote to Elizabeth that the Spanish were willing to agree to peace and asked her whether her country wanted to be involved. "It is for this reason that I now send to you Monsieur de Maisse, my Councillor of State, in whom I have great faith for his probity and fidelity." Henri was truly eager to make peace. "I can well tire of the calamities and miseries which my people endure because of this war" (De Maisse, xii, xiii). Though the English saw some benefits with peace, Burghley and Elizabeth did not trust the Spanish, and there were still Anglo-Spanish problems both in the Netherlands and in Ireland. De Maisse was not impressed with what he considered the English attitudes toward the French making peace. "As for the peace, the English fear making it all the more because they dislike seeing our realm in tranquility or recovering itself, and they will always be well content to see us at odds" (De Maisse, 15).

In his private journal, de Maisse was contemptuous of Elizabeth both in terms of her nature and her ability to rule. "In her own nature she is very avaricious, and when some expense is necessary her Councillors must deceive her before embarking her on it little by little. She thinks highly of herself and has little regard for servants and Council, being of the opinion she is far wiser than they; she mocks them and often cries out upon them" (De Maisse, 3). But in another comment, he thought better of Elizabeth, though he also concluded that she was powerless. "The queen by nature loves justice and is very tender-hearted, but her officers do as they think fit and as they please" (De Maisse, 12). He was also attentive to the tensions between the Cecils and the Earl of Essex, and he had more admiration for the earl.

De Maisse was originally supposed to see the queen on December 6, but her teeth hurt so she had to cancel but he saw her at Whitehall two days later. Though first brought into the Presence Chamber, where there were several English courtiers, the queen did not see him there. Instead, he was taken to the smaller Privy Chamber and he saw the queen seated in a low chair. She had a stool brought so he could sit with her. "She was strangely attired in a dress of sliver cloth, white and crimson, or silver gauze, as they call it. The dress had slashed sleeves lined with red taffeta.... She kept the front of her dress open, and one could see the whole of her bosom." He also noted her "great reddish-colored wig... Her bosom is somewhat wrinkled ... but lower down her flesh is exceeding white and delicate, so far as one could see." When de Maisse looked at the queen's face he found she appeared very aged, but "her figure is fair and tall and graceful in whatever she does; so far as may be she keeps her dignity" (De Maisse, 25, 26).

De Maisse kept a careful record of how Elizabeth was dressed at every meeting with her. Later he went to Greenwich; she was wearing a low-cut dress in cloth of silver with peach. They had a long conversation, during which she told him that Philip II had wanted her murdered. De Maisse spoke about how his king desired peace, but he noted Elizabeth in their discussion often made digressions. He also pointed out how how learned she was. "She knows all ancient histories, and it is impossible to make allusion to any of them upon which she does not offer some apropos observation." De Maisse was very impressed by his meeting with Elizabeth. "It is a strange thing how lively she is in body and mind, and how clever in all she attempts to do. That day she was in very good humour, and very gay, and when I took my leave, treated me very favourably, and saluted all the gentlemen who were with me. She is, in truth, a great princess, who is ignorant of nothing" (De Maisse, 59, 61).

While the first two meetings were in private rooms, de Maisse also saw the queen in the Presence Chamber. Her dressing that day was especially impressive. "This day she was habited, as is her custom, in silver tissue... She wore innumerable jewels on her person, not only on her head, but also within her collar, about her arms and on her hands, with a very great quantity of pearls, around her neck and on her bracelets" (De Maisse, 83). They discussed the political interests of various European powers. De Maisse saw the queen several times, and also met with Lord Burghley, his son Robert Cecil, and the Earl of Essex. Nothing had really been settled when de Maisse returned to France in January 1598. For us centuries later, the most important aspect of de Maisse's embassy was the detailed journal he kept, and what it tells us about Elizabeth toward the end of her life.

CHAPTER 9

Assassination Attempts, Plots, and Rebellions

Even before Elizabeth became queen some of her sister Mary's supporters thought the best solution to the "Elizabeth problem" was her assassination. Fortunately, this never happened. But for the rest of her life there were numerous plots. At the end of her life, she reflected on this. In 1597 when André Hurault, seigneur de Maisse was on a special embassy from France she told him that she had been queen for forty years and she had reigned because of God's goodness, especially because, he said, "she related to me the attempts that had been made as much against her life as against her state holding it marvelous strange that the King of Spain should treat her in a fashion that would never have believed to proceed from the will of a Prince." Philip, she told the ambassador, had sent fifteen different people to murder her, "who had all confessed" (De Maisse, 38).

From the time that Elizabeth became queen at the age of twenty-five in 1558, her advisors were very concerned about her safety, especially as she often showed a lack of concern about her wellbeing. While she had the protection of three sets of guards, she refused to take precautions that her Principal Secretary, William Cecil, thought necessary, such as having a taster for all that she ate and drank. There was also worry that Elizabeth might be poisoned through contact with some item of clothing. Fear of assassination was also another reason Cecil was so eager to see Elizabeth married and the mother of heirs to the throne. He thought if potential murderers saw a whole succession of potential rulers behind her they would have less cause to do her harm. Sir Francis Walsingham agreed; in a letter he sent Burghley in April 1571 he stated his concern that Elizabeth was in great danger both at home and abroad unless she married. Elizabeth was aware of the dangers and plots. As she told

Fénelon de la Mothe, the French Ambassador in 1571, "Princes have big ears which hear far and near" *(The Sayings of Queen Elizabeth,* 163).

These concerns increased as the reign progressed, especially after Mary Stuart fled Scotland for England in 1568 and became the focal point for Catholic conspirators' attempts to murder Elizabeth and place Mary on the throne. In 1569, when she had only been under the guardianship of George Talbot, Earl of Shrewsbury, for about a month, William Cecil sent Nicholas White to visit her and report back. White learned that Mary was furious that she was forced to leave Bolton Castle and thought of Cecil as her enemy. White added that because of his great loyalty and love of Queen Elizabeth he wanted to give some advice. "There should be very few subjects in this land have access or conference with this lady.... Yet in truth not comparable to our sovereign, she hath an alluring grace, a pretty Scottish accent, and a searching wit, clouded with mildness. Fame might move some to relieve her, and glory joined to gain might stir others to adventure much for her sake" (Strickland, 389). White was right: there were several dangerous and desperate attempts. One response was that in 1571 Parliament passed the Treasons Act which declared it high treason to intend to harm the queen, wage war against her, or say that she was not the legal queen, to call her a heretic, tyrant, or usurper. It was also treason to claim a right to the Crown and to attempt to usurp it during the queen's lifetime, or to assert someone's right of succession (see Chapter 4).

Balthasar Gerard's successful assassination of William the Silent, Prince of Orange, in the Netherlands in 1584 terrified English people loyal to their queen. Philip II had promised a reward of 25,000 crowns for the murder. Gerard shot William in the chest at close range. While he fled, he was caught and executed. When the English heard of it, they were extremely worried this might also happen to their queen. That year Parliament passed the Queen's Safety Act which called for the trial and execution of anyone involved in a plot to injure the Queen (see Chapter 4). The Privy Council also signed the Bond of Association, authored by Burghley and Walsingham, against any who worked against Elizabeth or knew of such a plot. Any who would gain from the plot—clearly meaning Mary Stuart—would also be prosecuted. There were also concerns about plots to poison either William Cecil, now Lord Burghley, or Robert Dudley, Earl of Leicester. Walsingham worked very hard to keep those who were dangerous from establishing ways to communicate with those on the continent unless he was sure he could control the flow of information. After his expulsion from England in 1584, the Spanish ambassador Bernadino de Mendoza wrote to his king about how he had attempted through every possible means to open a line for correspondence with those in England whom he could trust but found "there is no assured way of conveying the intelligence either verbally or by letter" (*CSP, Spain,* III, 549).

Though many assassination plots were centered around making Mary Stuart queen of England, even after her death in 1587, attempts continued. Just how serious some of these attempts were, is another question altogether.

Walsingham and Burghley found that publicizing attempts was effective propaganda, while Catholics claimed that many of these plots were invented just for that reason. As a result, it is often difficult to find a clear, unbiased account of these events. Burghley's 1594 *A true report of sundry horrible conspiracies* detailed the cases of the Roderigo Lopez plot and of William Stanley and others who attempted to destroy Elizabeth, but also blamed these and more plots on Philip II. He talked about "how unjust and dishonorable the King of Spain and his ministers Actions are against the Queene of England." Philip had attempted to take Elizabeth's life by arms and war—by sending the Armada, and he also attempted "secretely sundrie waies by secret murder" (G. B. Harrison, *An Elizabethan Journal*, I, 349).

Walsingham's network of spies was effective at finding out and infiltrating plots and at protecting the queen. Yet in some cases Walsingham appears to have embellished and exaggerated plots. Certainly, he and his network could forge additional materials or documents if they thought this was in England's and Elizabeth's best interests. And some plots appear to have been simply invented.

Some of the plots that were perceived as the most frightening were those which would use magic to harm the queen. Writing after her death, Thomas Heywood stated that even though the queen was greatly loved, just as magic and witchcraft were attempted upon the monarchs of old, they were also tried on Elizabeth in this current age. The early history of Scotland especially included many attacks on monarchs by witches and the use of magic. But Elizabeth was not the only one at her court that some hoped to destroy through witchcraft and magic. For example, in 1588 Edward Croft was furious at Robert Dudley, Earl of Leicester, for the disgrace of his father James, and paid a conjuror to secure the earl's death through magic. This attempt failed, and though the Privy Council examined Croft, he was not brought to trial (see Chapter 3).

Yet the danger to Elizabeth was often real and of desperate concern. Though many English people believed torture to be wrong, Walsingham told Burghley that it was sometimes necessary to gain the information needed to thwart plots against the queen. Prisoners could be placed on the rack, which pulled their limbs and caused much pain. There was great relief and joy that none of these assassination attempts were successful. The Swiss traveler Thomas Platter wrote in 1599 when he saw the queen that she "has up till now successfully confronted her opponents with God's help and support, . . . and although her life has often been threatened by poison, and many ill designs, God has preserved her wonderfully at all times" (*Thomas Platter's Travels in England*, 192).

The plots below are in chronological order.

1558–1562 Anthony Fortescue and the Pole Brothers

When Elizabeth became queen in 1558 Catholics Sir Anthony Fortescue and his two brothers-in-law, Arthur and Edmund Pole, sought out astrologer John Prestall, asking him and another man named Kele, to cast the queen's horoscope and determine how long Elizabeth's reign would last. When the Privy Council found out, Fortescue and the Poles were arrested. They were soon after released with warnings, but the warnings were ineffective. In September 1562, led by Arthur Pole, they again consulted Prestall and Edward Cosyn to find out how much longer Elizabeth would live. Believing her death imminent, they thought to help that along. The men planned to leave the country, have Arthur declare himself Duke of Clarence, beg Catherine de Medici, the Guise family, and the Pope for help, get Mary Stuart to marry Edmund Pole and proclaim her queen of England. With an army, they could overthrow Elizabeth, and with Mary as queen England would again be a Catholic country. But the plot was discovered, and before they could leave England, Fortescue and the Pole brothers were arrested in October 1562 and tried for high treason the following February. While the Poles pleaded not guilty, Fortescue confessed his guilt. All were found guilty and condemned to death, but though they were confined to the Tower they were not executed. The Poles stayed there until their deaths, sometime around 1570. Fortescue was eventually released and left England, but we know nothing of him further, though his death was not before 1611. Prestall had also fled and continued to be involved in dubious activity, including bragging that by magic he could poison someone far away, and he was the only one with the art to do it. He died around 1598.

Worries About Plots in the 1560s

Concerned letters to William Cecil throughout the decade mentioned potential plots against Elizabeth. Sir Nicholas Throckmorton served as ambassador to France from May 1559 to April 1564. In 1560 he wrote to Elizabeth that he had learned that an Italian had been hired to poison her. Threats of Italian poisoners—often unnamed—appear throughout the reign. But Italians were also ones who warned the queen of danger. A year later Throckmorton wrote that he had heard from an unnamed Italian that a Greek, Maniola de Corfeu, had been hired by a great personage—again named—to go to England and murder the queen. Throckmorton hoped that he and his poisons could be apprehended but there is no evidence that he came to England. Another version of the story was reported by de Quadra to Philip II in November 1561. He told his king that Elizabeth had asked him many questions about what he knew about Juan Battista Beltran, a native of Venice, who had been in France and had recently visited Elizabeth's court. De Quadra insisted that Beltran was a man he "knew well as being unworthy of credit" (*CSP Spain*, I, 217). Elizabeth responded that Beltran had told her that Philip II was trying to have her poisoned by a Greek named Vergecio. He added that this was also supposed to have been ordered by Pope Pius IV, and the target was not only the queen but Robert Dudley as well. De Quadra assured Philip that Sir William Cecil had thoroughly investigated the matter, and concluded that Beltran was a swindler, who had hoped to be paid for his intelligence. But the idea that Philip would have wanted to have Elizabeth assassinated continued. In 1568 the Italian Franciotto informed Walsingham that there were plots to poison Elizabeth that involved Philip of Spain. Franciotto warned that the queen needed to be very careful in terms of her food, utensils, bedding, and other furniture, as secret enemies might use them to poison her.

The Northern Rebellion November 1569–January 1570

The delicate balance Elizabeth was able to sustain for the first decade of her reign was destroyed when Mary Stuart, imprisoned and forced to abdicate in Scotland, escaped to England in May 1568. The North had, since the break with Rome, been the most religiously conservative part of England, and the most hierarchical. The rebellion's leaders were Charles Neville, Earl of Westmorland and Thomas Percy, Earl of Northumberland. Northumberland considered the various ways he might free Mary, and consulted with Guerau de Spes, the Spanish Ambassador, and Mary's agent, John Leslie, Bishop of Ross. When Mary's escape became impossible, they moved to the rebellion.

The plan was to depose Elizabeth and her non-aristocratic councilors, such as William Cecil. They would be replaced by Mary with the restoration of Catholicism and noble advisors. The earls wrote to Pope Pius V asking him to excommunicate Elizabeth, though the bull of excommunication did not arrive in England until months after the rebellion was subdued. In November the rebels occupied Durham and Mass was celebrated in Durham Cathedral. The rebels were met by the forces of Thomas Radcliffe, Earl of Sussex. Many of the men who led soldiers to protect Elizabeth later became members of her Privy Council (see Chapter 3). The rebel earls could not sustain the uprising. Their forces dispersed and the two of them fled into Scotland. Northumberland was captured, turned over to Elizabeth, and beheaded at York in 1572. His wife, Anne Somerset, was equally involved in the rebellion, riding out with the rebel forces, and was said to have egged him on; many saw her as the more forceful one in the marriage. She managed to escape to Antwerp in 1570. Her home in Mechelen became a center for English Catholic exiles; she became involved in more Catholic plots and stayed in contact with Mary Stuart. Westmorland also managed to escape to the Spanish Netherlands in 1570 and spent the rest of his life in exile plotting against Elizabeth. He died in 1601. Around 600 of their followers were executed. De Spes wrote to Philip that "the people are hanged in the north daily" (*CSP, Spain*, II, 233).

The Pope issued his bull of excommunication of Elizabeth in February 1570, calling Elizabeth a pretended Queen of England, and a servant of wickedness. He released all Catholics of their allegiance to her. On May 25 John Felton, who had received the bull from the chaplain of de Spes, nailed a copy of it to the garden gate of the palace of the Bishop of London near St. Paul's Cathedral. Felton was arrested and lodged in the Tower. He was executed for treason on August 8, 1570.

Plot to free Mary Stuart 1570

Edward Stanley, 3rd Earl of Derby, though he grudgingly attended Church of England services, and was loyal to the queen, was very sympathetic to Catholicism, and his two younger sons, Sir Thomas and Sir Edward, even more so. In 1570 both were involved in a plot with several people including John Hall, a former gentleman servant of George Talbot, Earl of Shrewsbury. Hall had about four years earlier left his position after six years' employment because he disliked the earl's wife, Bess of Hardwick. The plan was to free Mary Stuart from Chatsworth while she was out riding and take her to the Isle of Man. Hall was in contact with Mary's agent, John Leslie, and had some letters in cypher. Mary was in Shrewsbury's charge so for Hall this was a betrayal on a number of levels. But the carelessness of the Stanley brothers allowed informants to inform William Cecil, and in November both were summoned to court, where Cecil was able to expose their part in the scheme. They were sent to the Tower, but neither was executed. Their father and their older brother Henry were not involved, though some plotters had hoped that the earl would support a Spanish invasion. Hall escaped; he hoped to get to France, but bad weather caused his boat to land in Scotland instead and he was captured at Dumbarton. The Regent Matthew, Earl of Lennox, returned Hall to England, where he was also lodged in the Tower and thoroughly examined, though we do not know his ultimate fate.

Ridolfi Plot (1571)

The Ridolfi Plot was the first major conspiracy against Queen Elizabeth in her reign. The Florentine merchant-banker Roberto Ridolfi was a passionate Catholic who traveled through Europe and was often in England. Pope Pius V had made Ridolfi his papal agent in England in 1567. Once Mary Stuart had fled to England the following year, Ridolfi saw her as a way to restore Catholicism and rid England of a heretic queen. He was suspected of being involved in the planning of the 1569 Northern Rebellion, or at least funding it. For a time he was under house arrest and interrogated by Sir Francis Walsingham. But there was no clear evidence of Ridofi's involvement in the Northern Rebellion and Elizabeth insisted on clemency. Ridolfi became convinced that outside aid was essential for Mary Stuart to become queen, and he looked for colleagues to help him, which included the Spanish ambassador Guerau de Spes, and Mary's steadfast supporter John Leslie.

They conspired with Thomas Howard, Duke of Norfolk and Fernando Alvarez de Toledo, Duke of Alva, to organize an uprising against Elizabeth that would coincide with a Spanish invasion. Alva was stationed in the Netherlands with many troops. Norfolk and Mary Stuart would become King and Queen of England and Scotland, bringing Catholicism back into power. Elizabeth would be deposed and beheaded. Alva's words about Ridolfi being a "windbag and a fool" (Plowden, *The Elizabethan Secret Service*, 34) might have been true as Ridolfi's communications between the conspirators and Mary were the plot's downfall. Ridolfi apparently was too loquacious about his plans. Walsingham and Cecil had agents who infiltrated the conspiracy and broke the codes of the cyphered letters between Mary, Norfolk, and the other conspirators. Some people, however, were convinced that Ridolfi was a double agent who informed on his fellow plotters.

The English intercepted many damning letters and were able to foil the plot. The letters made Mary's involvement alarmingly obvious and demonstrated just how much Mary was a threat to Elizabeth's life and reign. Evidence of Mary's involvement as well as Norfolk's was so compelling that both the House of Commons and Walsingham wanted her executed. A letter to Leicester argued how he had to convince Elizabeth to execute Mary Stuart, that without her Catholics would have no motive to conspire against the queen. The unknown writer begged that Elizabeth be made to understand the danger to the people if an adulteress, a traitress, an irritated tyrant became queen. But Elizabeth refused. While she regarded Mary as dangerous, she did not want the blood of an anointed queen and her cousin on her hands. It took the queen six months after Norfolk, who was also her cousin, had been found guilty of treason for her to agree to his execution in June 1572. After Norfolk was arrested, Keneln Berney confessed that one of his confederates, Edmund Mather, who served Norfolk, had intended to murder Elizabeth, for "if she were not killed, or made away, there was no way but death for the Duke." He claimed that Mather considered Elizabeth such a vile woman as she "desireth nothing but to feed her own lewd fantasy, and to cut off such of her nobility as were not perfumed and courtly-like to please her delicate eye," and that the queen ignored worthwhile noblemen in favor of dancers such as Robert Dudley and Christopher Hatton (Murdin and Haynes, II, 208). Mather was executed soon after Norfolk. The previous year, in 1571, de Spes was expelled from England ((see Chapter 8). Fortunately for Ridolfi he was in France at the time the plot was discovered and escaped punishment. He later returned to Florence to serve the Grand Duke Francesco de Medici, living on until 1612. The Ridolfi Plot meant that Elizabeth agreed that Mary, who could never be trusted, would stay under house arrest in England and needed to be watched carefully.

Queen's Illness March 1572—possibly Poison

In March of 1572 while she was at Richmond, Elizabeth became very ill with a stomachache that caused her great pain. The French ambassador wrote that he had heard that she had been poisoned. Her illness continued for five days. Lord Burghley and the Earl of Leicester stayed at her bedside as did her women. While it is possible it was caused by the stress of the queen's worry over what to do about Norfolk's fate, or perhaps simply bad food, La Mothe Fénélon's letter reveals the fear that it had been an unsuccessful assassination plot. Burghley was frequently concerned about Elizabeth's health, whatever caused the illness. A few months earlier in October, he had written to Walsingham that Elizabeth had become suddenly sick and then vomited. He added that such events could drive men to the end of their wits.

Possible Attempt at Kenilworth 1575

The Earl of Leicester invited Elizabeth to Kenilworth in July 1575 for elaborate entertainments. She also did some hunting while she was there. According to Antonio de Guaras, the resident Spanish agent, while she was hunting, someone, whom he named as a traitor, shot a crossbow at her. He was immediately apprehended, but people at the scene said that he was just hunting deer and shot wide. Though the bolt passed near the queen, she was not harmed.

Plot Against the Queen, 1577

For many years the Englishman, William Phayre, was part of the English community in Madrid but was also during that time on good terms with the English government. In 1561 he helped the new English ambassador to Spain, Thomas Challoner, to find housing and then wrote to him often with any gossip he had heard. When Challoner became ill in 1564 and returned to England, Phayre was *chargé d'affaires* until Dr. John Man arrived in 1566 as the new ambassador. This background makes it perhaps surprising that when Phayre returned to England in 1577 he became involved in a plot against Elizabeth. He was convicted of treason. From the Tower, he wrote to Burghley begging for mercy and offering to become a spy for the English, but Burghley did not trust him and Phayre was executed.

Image Magic 1578

There was a strong belief in witchcraft and magic in Elizabethan England; one way that people believed one could harm someone was through image magic. This was done by creating a picture or a wax doll (also known as a poppet) and then attacking the image or doll, possibly by stabbing it in the heart, attaching bristles, or harming it by other means, such as holding the doll over a fire, as was done in an attempt to murder the Scottish King Duff many centuries earlier. While Elizabeth was away on progress in Norwich a man discovered three wax images, each about 12 inches high, in a dung heap in Lincoln's Inn Fields. One appeared clearly to be the queen as it had the name Elizabeth on the forehead; the other two were assumed to be her close advisors. The Elizabeth poppet had a large pin stuck into it at her breast. Her advisors were especially concerned as Elizabeth had been feeling ill and wondered if it was the result of the wax image. Actually, her illness was dental problems, but the concern was so great that the Privy Council asked the magus and astrologer John Dee to go to Norwich to perform counter magic. There were a number of such events during her reign. In 1571 Richard Lugge, a Mr. Read, and John Adeane were found in possession of a book that had an illustration of the queen. Someone had drawn an arrow in her mouth.

First Thought to Be Attempted Assassination 1579

On the evening of Friday, July 17, 1579, the queen was on her barge on the Thames near Greenwich. With her was the French envoy Jean de Simier, there to discuss the potential marriage of Elizabeth with François, Duke of Anjou. Also on board were Edward Fiennes de Clinton, Earl of Lincoln, and Sir Christopher Hatton. Suddenly a bullet whizzed by the queen's head and one of the oars' men was hit in the arm. It caused him such pain he screamed and started bleeding profusely. Elizabeth tossed her scarf to him to help stop the bleeding, telling him to be of good cheer, for the bullet was meant for her though it had hit him, and she would be sure he was taken care of.

But the bullet was not meant for Elizabeth. Thomas Appletree [in some accounts Applegate], a young servant of Elizabeth's cousin Henry Carey, had been given a gun, and with some friends went out on a boat on the Thames. Appletree took some random shots—one of which almost hit the queen. Appleby was arrested, found guilty, and sentenced to be hanged. A public scaffold was set up. Hatton addressed the crowd, stating that had Elizabeth been killed, "our religion, and true faith in Jesus Christ, which we enjoy with unspeakable comfort of free conscience, might hereby have suffered confusion, and persecution of blood." After two decades of happy rule, there would have been "bloody wars" (Stow, *Chronicle*, 1201). Hatton stated that Appletree deserved to die for putting the queen in such danger. But then Hatton announced that there was a royal reprieve and Appletree was pardoned, a sign of the queen's mercy. The incident immediately became very well known with the publications of a broadside and ballad, and soon after Elizabeth's death, Henry Chettle used it as an example of both her bravery and mercy in his tract, *England's Mourning Garment*.

Margaret Clifford 1579

There were yet more accusations of magic and witchcraft. Margaret Clifford, Countess of Derby, was a potential heir to the throne as a descendant of Mary Tudor the French Queen and Charles Brandon through their younger daughter Eleanor. Margaret was the only surviving child of Eleanor and her husband Henry Clifford, Earl of Cumberland. Since two of Eleanor's older sister Frances' daughters, Jane and Mary, did not have children, and Katherine's two sons had been declared illegitimate, Margaret's claim became more important, at least in her eyes. In 1555 she had married Henry Stanley, the future Earl of Derby.

Margaret was accused of trying to kill Elizabeth by witchcraft on potentially questionable evidence, though rumors about it circulated in the letters from the Spanish Ambassador Bernardino De Mendoza and Hieronomo Lippomano, the Venetian ambassador to France, who was later the Venetian ambassador to Spain. Mendoza wrote to Philip and to Gabriel de Zayas, the secretary of state to Philip II in charge of France and England. Elizabeth was initially upset that the countess was gossiping against the potential marriage with François, Duke of Anjou, with one of the daughters of Francis Russell, Earl of Bedford, and had both women placed under house arrest. But a few days later, on August 25, he sent further letters claiming the countess's most confidential servant had informed against her that she had tried to discover through witchcraft how much longer the queen would live. The next month, on September 10, Lippomano wrote that the queen had discovered a conspiracy where the Countess of Derby had agreed to poison Elizabeth. The countess was kept under house arrest for several years.

This plot to poison the queen appears highly unlikely. Margaret, however, employed a doctor, William Randall, to help her deal with her various illnesses. He was also skilled in astrology and questionable practices, and he may well have attempted to use magic to find out how soon Elizabeth would die, and if Margaret would be her heir. Indeed, the prime evidence against Margaret was from the doctor she employed, which allegedly was given with the threat of torture. Margaret wrote to Walsingham and Sir Christopher Hatton to plead her case. She was released in 1583 and died in 1596 (see Chapter 7).

THROCKMORTON PLOT 1583

Francis Throckmorton was a young Catholic gentleman who became involved in a plot to kill Elizabeth. Mary Stuart's Catholic supporters on the Continent recruited him. He was the nephew of the ambassador to France Sir Nicholas Throckmorton, but his side of the family was Catholic as opposed to Protestant. Throckmorton was educated at Oxford and the Inner Temple. In 1578 he got into trouble for attending Catholic services, but his Protestant relations petitioned on his behalf. But within a year he was abroad and discussing with other English expatriates plans to return England to Catholicism. This group had the support of Philip II and Pope Gregory XIII, with the promise of an invasion led by Mary's uncle, Henri, Duke of Guise. In the early 1580s, he returned to England determined to promote Mary Stuart and the Catholic cause. Berardino de Mendoza, the Spanish ambassador, was deeply involved. There were also some meetings at the French embassy. The plan was that Elizabeth's murder would trigger the French invasion.

Sir Francis Walsingham had a spy in the French embassy, a man calling himself Henry Fagot, who served as a chaplain to the ambassador's household. The historian John Bossy intriguingly suggests that Fagot was actually

Giordano Bruno, though many scholars refute that. Bruno had been an Italian friar. He was a poet, philosopher, and mathematician who believed the universe was infinite and had an interest in the occult; he was in England during this time. In 1600 he was burned as a heretic in Rome. But we do not know if he was Fagot. In 1583 Fagot wrote to Walsingham about Throckmorton's visits and how he had sent funds to Mary. He later added that Throckmorton was a chief agent for the Scottish queen who only showed up at the embassy at night, and had long, suspicious meetings with others. In November 1583 Walsingham had Throckmorton arrested. He refused to confess, and Walsingham ordered that Throckmorton be racked. Throckmorton managed to smuggle a note out to Mendoza, promising that he would die a thousand deaths rather than betray his friends. But after being racked a second time, he confessed everything he knew, and Walsingham learned the Spanish ambassador as well as the French, ambassador, Michel de Castelnau, Seigneur de Mauvissière were involved in the plot. Throckmorton was tried in May 1584 and executed on July 10. In January 1584 Mendoza, the last Spanish ambassador to serve in England during Elizabeth's reign, was expelled. Walsingham did not move against Mauvissière as his spy in the embassy meant it was more useful to leave the embassy intact (see Chapter 8).

The same month Henry Percy, Earl of Northumberland was sent to the Tower for his role in the plot. The government considered putting him on trial for treason. The earl was found dead in his bed the night of June 21, 1585. He was shot through the heart. His own pistol was still in his hand, and the investigation by Privy Councilor Thomas Bromley and others determined his death was suicide. Some Catholics, however, claimed that Sir Christopher Hatton had had the earl murdered.

John Somerville, or Somerfield 1583

John Somerville was a young Catholic gentleman who apparently assumed he was the only one who could save Catholics from the evil Protestant Queen Elizabeth. He headed to London and bragged about his intentions to kill Elizabeth and was soon arrested and executed. While not part of a grandly organized plot, Somerville proved that there were people definitely primed and ready to kill Elizabeth if they got the chance. John Somerville came from a Catholic family. He had studied at Oxford and in his teens married Margaret Arden, the daughter of Edward Arden, distantly related to William Shakespeare through Shakespeare's mother Mary Arden. Arden was prominent in local politics in Warwickshire. In the autumn of 1583 Somerville was under investigation because of an acquaintance associated with Mary Stuart. In October he was ill and staying at his father-in-law's house, but he rose early the morning of October 25 to ride to London, where he planned to shoot Elizabeth with his pistol. Somerville carried with him a small wax lamb of God that had been blessed by the pope. On his way he stopped at an inn Oxfordshire and started chatting, explaining that he not only planned to kill the queen but hoped to see her head upon a pole since she was both a serpent and a viper. Since he said this in front of five witnesses, he was soon arrested. Somerville also spoke of his troubled mind, and some officials wondered if Somerville was right in his wits. Upon his interrogation, Somerville admitted he planned to kill the queen, but also implicated his wife, her parents, and a priest named Hugh Hall, who was part of Arden's household in the guise of a gardener. They were also arrested, and though they claimed innocence they were all found guilty. Somerville and Arden were moved from the Tower to Newgate to prepare for their execution. Somerville killed himself in his cell, and Arden was executed the following day. Both their heads were placed on the London bridge. Though the women had also been sentenced to death, they were pardoned. Hall was not executed at that time in the hope he would testify again others. There seems little doubt that Somerville was not right in his wits (Fig. 9.1).

Fig. 9.1 Somerville attempted assassination private collection

Parry Plot 1584

William Parry was known as either a spy or a traitor and he was most likely both. Though well educated, he had serious financial problems. He tried hard to have Burghley be his patron and get him an appointment. When Parry had fled to Paris in 1580 to avoid creditors, he wrote to Burghley offering intelligence about the Catholics who were plotting against the queen in favor of Mary Stuart. In late 1583 he met with Thomas Morgan, who, as an agent for Mary Stuart, was involved in many plots against Elizabeth. Parry first told Morgan he would murder Burghley, but Morgan said the queen was the more important target. Parry agreed to the murder if the pope gave remission of his sins; he then returned to London. But Parry also continued to hope that he could convince Burghley and Walsingham to help him receive a position that would help him resolve his financial problems. By the summer of 1584, he became disillusioned, convinced that these efforts would never yield results. Parry suggested to Edmund Neville, who had for a time left England because of his Catholicism and had served in the Spanish army in Flanders before returning to England in 1584, that they murder Elizabeth near St. James Palace. They and some servants could surround her coach and shoot her. Then Parry thought they should murder the queen in her private garden at Whitehall. Though at first agreeing, Neville denounced Parry in February 1585, and Walsingham became convinced that Parry's plan had been serious. Indeed, Parry had gotten within the Palace Gardens and was well within killing range of Elizabeth, but he lost his resolve or never actually intended to kill her. Some people suggested that Elizabeth had stared Parry down. Parry, then serving as a Member of Parliament, was arrested, tried for treason, and executed in March 1585. Neville was lodged in the Tower and finally released in 1598. The scene in the gardens where Parry was close enough to murder Elizabeth was obviously frightening to the queen's councilors. Scholars are still unclear about Parry's intentions. Perhaps he was unsure himself.

Pedro De Zubiaur 1584

The evidence about this plot is so brief and tantalizing we can hardly know if it was real. When Mendoza was expelled from the country, he asked Pedro de Zubiaur to stay in England and through secret means send what intelligence he could about events there. Zubiaur, a Spanish merchant and ship captain, had come to England after Drake had returned to England with captured Spanish gold and goods, attempting to get restitution. Around March 16, 1584, Henry Fagot, who had written to Walsingham about the Throckmorton conspiracy, wrote directly to Elizabeth about Zubiaur. He claimed that Zubiaur had visited him several times since the beginning of Lent, and then had asked him as the chaplain to take his confession. Fagot stated that he was so shocked by what he had heard, despite the seal of the confessional, he felt he must communicate with the queen. According to Fagot, Mendoza had charged Zubiaur and several others to assassinate Elizabeth by whatever means they could, perhaps poisoning her undergarments, bouquets of flowers, or her smelling water. Fagot stated that Zubiaur claimed that though one of the ten commandments was "thou shalt not kill," the murder of Elizabeth would save an infinite number of souls, and as a result, God would welcome him into heaven. While John Bossy argues that Zubiaur had come to make his confession, the story of the plot itself was "quite extraordinarily unlikely" (Bossy, 36), and suggests it was all an invention, lacking any credibility. It appears that Walsingham did not believe that the Spaniard would talk of such a plot to an unreliable priest right in the French embassy, and though addressed to Elizabeth we have no indication she received the letter, or that Walsingham further investigated Zubiaur. He apparently felt it was a way for Fagot to make himself seem important. Zubiaur was arrested, but not until June of 1585, and it was because some secret letters from the Prince of Parma had been seized and the courier confessed that they had been given to him by Zubiaur. In several more letters that year Mendoza complained to Philip that since Zubiaur's arrest he was not able to get any more information from England. In October 1586, Zubiaur was taken to Holland and exchanged for some English prisoners held by the Spanish. Zubiaur continued to be of value. In August 1588 Mendoza wrote that Zubiaur had sent him news from Dunkirk. While Zubiaur had an interesting career aiding the Spanish cause, Fagot's tale of sensational ways to poison Elizabeth was most likely fiction.

Friar in Dunkirk 1585

All we know about this plan, such as it was, was an anonymous report. An official who read the report described it as "The speeches of a friar in Dunkirk" (Alford, 135). The friar talked to an English agent about the need to kill that wicked woman, the queen. He stated that once this had happened then all of Christendom would know peace. In his room, the friar showed the agent his picture of the assassination of the Prince of Orange, and stated that Gerards was a Burgundian, and no doubt another Burgundian would be glad to kill such a wicked woman as Elizabeth.

Jeremy Vanhill 1585

The laborer Jeremy Vanhill publicly called for the queen's death in a vividly brutal manner. "Shyte uppon your Queene; I woulde to god shee were dead that I might shytt on her face" (Levin, *The Heart and Stomach of a King*, 116–117). He added that he wished that Elizabeth was as ill as a man he knew, Peter Aveger. Given that Aveger died that very night, this was also seen as a direct threat to the queen. Vanhill was executed.

Babington Plot 1586

Anthony Babington's fascination and loyalty to Mary Stuart began when he was about eighteen years old in 1579 and served as a page in George Talbot, Earl of Shrewsbury's household at Sheffield, where Mary Stuart was lodged. The following year he went to Paris and met with Thomas Morgan, who had already been involved in various plots to free Mary and replace the murdered Elizabeth. Around 1583 he was able to smuggle letters from Morgan to Mary, but for the next few years was not involved in any active plotting. That changed in May 1586 when the Catholic priest John Ballard visited him (Fig. 9.2).

Ballard had apparently visited Rome in 1584 with another priest Anthony Tyrell, to gain consent from Pope Gregory XIII for the assassination of the queen. Ballard had recently communicated with Bernardino de Mendoza, who supported the plan to murder Elizabeth. Ballard told Babington that the pope had appointed Henri, Duke of Guise to lead an invasion. He also told Babington that John Savage had already agreed to be the assassin. Savage had served in the Spanish army in the Netherlands. On his way back to England, he stopped at Rheims and met with Ballard and William Gifford, who taught theology there. Gifford was a protégé of Cardinal William Allen and would become the Archbishop of Rheims in 1587. After the meeting, Savage, who had already some years earlier discussed assassinating the queen, agreed that he would be honored to murder Elizabeth. Babington found other young

Fig. 9.2 Babington plot private collection

men, mostly in their twenties, willing to commit, including Thomas Salisbury, Edward Abington, Chidiock Tichborne, Charles Tilney, Edward Winter, and Robert Barnewell. Later Edward Jones, Henry Donne, Robert Gage, John Travers, and John Carnock also joined with Babington in the plot. Except for Savage, the conspirators were for the most part young Catholic courtiers. But there was one other man deeply involved with a very different perspective.

Gilbert Gifford, a relative of William, studied abroad with Cardinal Allen at Douai while he was still in his teens, though he had been quite a problematic student. In September 1582 he left to return to England but by October 1583 he was at Rheims, and Allen decided to give him another chance. There he met John Savage, and the two discussed how they would eventually assassinate Elizabeth, so it was not surprising when Savage later agreed to do so. In October 1585 Gifford went to Paris to meet with the ubiquitous Thomas Morgan. He crossed into England in December and Morgan gave him a strong recommendation to Mary, stating she could trust him. In January 1585 Mary Stuart had been moved to Chartley Castle, where Sir Amyas Paulet guarded her very strictly, which made secret outside communication with Mary seem impossible. Gifford managed to open a secret means of communication by putting messages in leather sacks in the bottom of beer barrels sent weekly back and forth from Chartley Castle. But what the other conspirators did not know was that when Gifford returned to England, he was in Sir Francis Walsingham's employment, and it was Walsingham who had set up this method of communication. Gifford collected Mary's correspondence from the French embassy, where it had accumulated for the past two years and passed it on to Walsingham. Once Walsingham's code breakers led by Thomas Phelippes were able to decipher them, they were sent on to Mary. Soon Walsingham was reading all letters in and out.

In July 1586 Babington wrote a coded letter to Mary pledging his allegiance and promising to deliver her from her imprisonment and to accomplish their design—the murder of Elizabeth—and then free Mary. Walsingham was reading the correspondence before either of them and had Phelippes add a postscript asking for the names of all the conspirators. When the plot became close to being carried out, Gifford fled the country. In August 1586, he got in touch with Mendoza and told him about the Babington plot and requested Mendoza's approval for the murder of Elizabeth. But he was also keeping in touch with Walsingham, who had granted him a pension of £100. By March 1587 Gifford had been ordained a priest. But by December he was arrested in a brothel and as a priest sent to a church prison where he died in 1590 at the age of thirty.

In part thanks to Gifford, Walsingham had enough evidence to condemn Babington and his conspirators, but even more important, enough evidence to condemn Mary Stuart. The conspirators were arrested and rigorously interrogated. Eventually they simply all pled guilty, implicating each other, and were all condemned to die as traitors. As interesting as the plot was, its significance was that this was finally the case that led to the trial of Mary Stuart herself, and her own execution in February 1587 (see Chapter 7).

Stafford Plot 1586–1587

As a young man William Stafford had numerous connections to Elizabeth's court. His mother Dorothy, a widow, was a gentlewoman of Elizabeth's privy chamber (see Chapter 14), and his older brother Edward served as ambassador to France, though there were some serious concerns about Edward's gambling and his relations with supporters of Mary Stuart, including Mendoza and Henri, Duke of Guise.

On December 26, 1586, William Stafford visited the new French ambassador in London, Guillaume de L'Aubespine, Baron de Chateauneuf, asking for help to go to France. Both the Stafford brothers were at odds with Robert Dudley, and William claimed he could no longer bear to be around him. According to William, Chateauneuf suggested that they plan to murder Elizabeth and save Mary Stuart, who had been condemned to death for her role in the Babington Conspiracy, though Elizabeth had yet to sign the death warrant. Also involved in the plot were Chateauneuf's secretary Leonard des Trappes, and a servant of William's brother Edward named Michael Moody. One idea, foreshadowing Guy Fawkes, was to plant barrels of gunpowder in the room beneath the queen's bedchamber so they could blow her up. Another suggestion was to poison her shoes.

Soon after, in January 1587, William Stafford told Walsingham about the plot. De Trappes was arrested at Dover when he attempted to leave the country for France, and Chateauneuf was called before the Privy Council. Chateauneuf agreed he had known about the plot but stated it was Stafford who had suggested the plan and he had argued against it. His reason for not informing Elizabeth's government, he said, was to avoid causing trouble for William's mother and brother. Stafford was then sent to the Tower, but no charges were brought. Chateauneuf and De Trappe were kept under house arrest for a few months but later forgiven. It is important to note that during that time Elizabeth did sign the death warrant, though she had told her secretary William Davison, not to send it on. Of course, he did so, and Mary was executed on the 8th of February at Fotheringhay Castle.

This is a very strange story. Some scholars think it was a plan by Stafford to get into Walsingham's good graces by revealing a plot, but it may be more likely that it was masterminded by Walsingham and Burghley. One reason might have been to put more pressure on Elizabeth to sign the death warrant because of how dangerous it was to let Mary live and allow more conspiracies. Or they may have come up with the scheme to make it more difficult for the French to protest Mary's execution. Chateauneuf might well have been aware that all was not what it seemed. By the way they responded to the plot, clearly Burghley and Walsingham had not taken it too seriously. By May 1587

Chateauneuf was back in Elizabeth's favor. And by the end of 1588, Stafford was out of the Tower.

1586–1588

In December 1586 the Scottish diplomat and soldier Sir William Stewart became involved in a plot for a Catholic uprising in Scotland that would convince James VI to convert. Stewart met with the former Spanish ambassador to England Bernardino de Mendoza in Paris. The plan was that once Scotland was re-established as a Catholic nation, with an alliance with Spain, they could collaborate to destroy Elizabeth and restore England to Catholicism. But once Stewart had returned to Scotland in the spring of 1588, he realized this plan was very problematic. The Catholic Scottish nobles were fighting with each other, and James had no interest in an alliance with Spain. Stewart quickly abandoned the idea.

Cecily Burche 1589

In September 1589 Cecily Burche was sentenced to stand in the pillory because she publicly told people that "she trusted in god to see the blood run through the streets as water runneth in the Thames. And she trusted to see a new prince to reign over us" (*Levin, The Heart and Stomach of a King*, 117).

Supposed Plot to Assassinate Elizabeth Revealed by Edward Kelley 1589

Edward Kelley was something of a conman, convincing the astrologer John Dee that he could communicate with angels for Dee. Dee and Kelley left England in 1583 and by 1587 they were established in Prague under the patronage of the Holy Roman Emperor Rudolph II. While Dee returned to England in 1589, Kelley stayed in Prague, and in June 1589 wrote to Burghley to warn him that the Englishman Christopher Parkyns (or Perkins), now a Jesuit, had come from Rome to Prague and was a danger to the queen. Kelly claimed that Parkyns stopped at an inn in Prague where Kelley happened to be, and that he heard Parkyns talk about a horrible conspiracy to murder Elizabeth. Kelley stated that Parkyns had bragged that the pope and his people had seven ways to do that, and if even the first to the fifth failed, they were sure the sixth or the seventh would be effective. Sir Francis Walsingham had Parkyns apprehended when he returned to England in October.

Parkyns received his B.A. from Oxford University in 1565 and left England soon after; in 1566, at the age of twenty-four, he began studying to be a Jesuit. He was ordained as a priest in 1575. Five years later Father Robert Parsons and Cardinal Allen decided that Parkyns would be an excellent choice for the Jesuit mission to England. He agreed that he would go but stated that he had to be able to attend Protestant services and take the Oath of Supremacy. But problems developed for Parkyns with the Jesuits, and he was expelled for bad conduct in 1581; Parkyns, however, living in Rome, did not abandon his priesthood. When Burghley's grandson William was about twenty years old and traveling in Rome, he got into trouble because of his grandfather's enemies; Parkyns was able to intervene to rescue him.

By the late fall of 1588, Parkyns was in touch with Walsingham and served as his informant. While still a committed Catholic, Parkyns was appalled by the behavior of the Spanish faction among English Catholics in exile. What Parkyns had been doing made Kelley's accusations even more questionable. By May 1590 Burghley and Walsingham let Parkyns know he had been exonerated, and he returned to England. In the 1590s he served on a variety of diplomatic missions. He became one of the queen's Latin secretaries in 1601, and his service to the crown continued in the reign of James. As for Kelley, in 1591 the emperor had him imprisoned because of his problematic behavior and he was in and out of prison for the next few years, dying there at the end of 1597.

BOOK PUBLISHED IN PARIS ABOUT PROPHESY 1590

F. P. Crespit's book, *Prieur des Celestine de Paris—Prior of the Celestine of Paris*—described a prophesy that Queen Elizabeth would be beheaded.

NICHOLAS HASELWOOD 1591

In May Nicholas Haselwood, a yeoman told people that he wished that Queen Elizabeth was dead. His punishment was to be put in the pillory.

WILLIAM HACKET 1591

On July 16, 1591, two gentlemen of Puritan sympathies, Edmund Copinger and Henry Arthington, proclaimed William Hacket to be the new messiah, Jesus Christ, and the King or Emperor of Europe. Before Hacket had come to London he had proclaimed himself a second John the Baptist and had been whipped. Hacket could pray so loudly and extravagantly it seemed to people he was addressing God face to face. What made Hacket so dangerous was Copinger proclaiming to the London crowds that Elizabeth had forfeited her crown and would be replaced by Hacket. Arthington addressed Hacket as king of the earth, stating Elizabeth was no longer queen. The three were arrested and one of the most damning bits of evidence at the trial was the testimony that Hacket had taken a picture of Elizabeth and destroyed her breast, another example of using magic to annihilate the queen. Hacket was executed, Copinger starved himself to death in prison, and Arthington was freed in a year after confessing Hacket had bewitched him.

Sir Brian O'Rourke 1591

Brian O'Rourke was the younger son of the Irish chieftain Brian Ballagh O'Rourke, and during the 1580s was involved in several rebellions against the English in Ireland. As the decade progressed Elizabeth became increasingly concerned about Spain and how the Irish might help Philip in his attempt to conquer England. After the Spanish Armada was defeated in the summer of 1588, some of the Spanish fleets ended up wrecked on the coast of Ireland. O'Rourke helped some of the surviving Spanish and continued to fight the English in Ireland. The Lord Deputy Sir William Fitzwilliam reported in 1590 that O'Rourke had created an effigy of the queen, who then had his soldiers hack at it, finally tying it to a horse's tail and dragging it around. He claimed O'Rourke felt such contempt for Queen Elizabeth because she was a nurse of heretics. This was not seen as simply insulting, but rather could be image magic, where harming the effigy could also harm the actual queen. Fitzwilliam also claimed that his predecessor, Sir John Perrot, colluded with O'Rourke, and that Perrot planned to murder the queen for the benefit of Philip (see Chapter 3) . While Fitzwilliam attempted to capture O'Rourke, the Irishman fled to Scotland in 1591. But he was captured in Glasgow, returned to England, and sent to the Tower, accused of trying to depose Elizabeth and abusing the effigy of her. Found guilty, he was executed in November 1591.

Henry Collins and Gratian Brownell 1592

Henry Collins, a servant of Sir John Gage, was sent to prison in Marshalsea in 1592 for stating that he planned to kill the queen. One of the other prisoners there, Gratian Brownell, stated that there were many prisoners who wanted the queen dead, that someday they would be fortunate as someone would eventually destroy the queen and after that, all would be well. The same year another prisoner named Harris told Brownell that he had heard Cardinal William Allen was in a merry mood, and soon they would have their liberty. Harris, Collins, and Brownell were all Catholics. Clearly, Allen's alleged merriment did not help the men. Instead, Brownell in an undated letter to Lord Burghley begged for his freedom. We do not know how long any of them were imprisoned, or if they were ever released.

Gilbert Laton (or Layton) 1592

Gilbert Laton was a recusant who left England in June 1590 with John Rosceter and they eventually traveled to Spain. At first, they were imprisoned but with the help of the English Catholics in Spain, especially Jane Dormer, Dowager Duchess of Feria and assisted by Father Robert Parsons, they were released. They then met with Parsons, who asked them to return to England and "take way the life of a heretical usurping Princess . . . and persuaded

Laton and Rosceter to undertake to kill her Majesty" (*CSPD*, 1591–1594, 55). Rosceter, however, soon died, leaving Laton on his own. Parsons, along with Don Juan de Idiaques, an advisor to Philip II, and Sir Francis Englefield, who had left England at the time of Elizabeth's accession, told Laton to do the deed as soon as he returned to England and that the best way was to kill the queen when she was traveling on progress. Idiaques assured him this was not only for the good of England but for all of Christendom. Laton returned to England around Easter 1592 but was arrested before he could carry out his plans. Elizabeth and her government were merciful in Laton's case; he was kept in the Tower for some years, finally released in 1597, under warning to not only behave as a good subject but to avoid the court as well as any of the places the queen might be.

JOHN DANIEL, HUE CAHILL, PATRICK COLLEN, WILLIAM RANDALL 1593

John Daniel, an Irishman, confessed to Burghley that he and others had been paid by Philip to murder Elizabeth by poisoning her. Hue Cahill had provided the poison. The murderer was to be the Irishman Patrick Collen, who was tried for treason and executed. Daniel named several potential conspirators. He also explained that William Randall would create balls of poison. Cahill and some others apparently escaped to Scotland, but Randall was arrested and turned over to Richard Topcliffe, infamous for his use of torture, for further examination. Randall named more potential conspirators, some of whom were arrested, and also spoke of these balls being used to poison wildfire to burn the queen's ships at Dieppe, Rouen, or Chatham. Later Topcliffe wrote that Randall's wife had also been arrested when she came from Dartmouth to petition for her husband's release. Topcliffe was afraid that the petitions might be on poisoned paper, and worried that she had been lodging with "Garrat, the Queen's shoemaker; it is fearful for such a person to have opportunity to touch anything that comes near Her Majesty's person" (*CSPD*, 1595–1597, 25) Topcliffe claimed to find it strange that Randall was not arraigned and hanged for treason. We do not know what eventually happened to Randall and his wife.

WILLIAM STANLEY, RICHARD HESKETH, AND FERDINANDO, EARL OF DERBY 1593

In the 1580s William Stanley was acclaimed as one of England's most skilled military captains. This made his betrayal even more shocking. In 1585 Stanley accompanied the Earl of Leicester to the Netherlands, but two years later he surrendered Deventer to the Spanish and announced his support of the Catholic cause against the queen. In the early 1590s, he was involved in several plots against Elizabeth but fortunately, they were poorly planned. An unnamed

Italian was supposed to make the attempt on her life while she was in progress. Once Elizabeth was dead, the Spanish would send another invasion. Fortunately, the attempt was easily suppressed. In both May of 1590 and May of 1591 Henry Stanley, Earl of Derby—a cousin of William's—was told by the Privy Council to prepare the defenses of North Wales and Cheshire against the possible landing of Sir William's army in Anglesey.

Though the landing did not happen, Stanley was conspiring with the Jesuit Robert Parsons and Cardinal William Allen. Another conspirator was Richard Hesketh. In 1589 Hesketh was involved in a riot where someone was killed, and he was exiled for three years. By 1592 he was a retainer of Stanley's. They intended to involve the Earl of Derby's son, Ferdinando, Lord Strange, thus a cousin of Stanley's, in a plan to make him king, as he was the great-grandson of Henry VIII's younger sister Mary through his mother Margaret Clifford, who had already been into trouble because of her closeness to the throne. Henry, Earl of Derby died in November 1593. William Stanley sent Richard Hesketh to propose to the new earl that they kill Elizabeth and make Ferdinando a new Catholic king. Ferdinando refused and informed the Privy Council. Hesketh was soon arrested and executed for treason. While Stanley, who stayed out of England, lived until 1630, the young new Earl of Derby died horribly in April 1594. Some were convinced he had been bewitched to death or that he was poisoned by Catholics, furious he had betrayed their cause. William Camden suggested that a wax image, with pins in its belly, was found in his chamber. The earl's Master of the Horse fled as soon as the earl became ill. We do not know what caused the earl's death.

Roderigo Lopez 1594

Roderigo Lopez, a highly skilled Portuguese physician of Jewish background came to London at the beginning of Elizabeth's reign. He was soon admitted as a fellow of the College of Physicians and was a physician at St. Bartholomew's Hospital. Around 1563 he married Sarah Anes, daughter of a wealthy Jewish merchant. The Lopez family attended Anglican services but apparently secretly continued their practice as Jews. Lopez became physician for the Earl of Leicester, and in 1581 for Elizabeth and her household. Lopez was highly thought of as a talented physician. We know in 1588 he gave the queen both perfumed gloves and white silk stockings for New Year's. But Lopez's success made him notable and vulnerable. The scurrilous anonymous tract, *Leicester's Commonwealth*, accused Lopez of using poison and practicing abortion. Lopez was also Walsingham's physician, and quite possibly Walsingham had Lopez work for him in intelligence. Lopez's sister was married to Alvoro Mendez (see Chapter 11) and the two exchanged letters as Mendez was trying to strengthen relations between England and the Ottoman Empire and stop good relations between Spain and the empire. But Walsingham died in 1591, and whatever Lopez continued to do was without the knowledge of the English government. Lopez also served as a physician for the Earl of Essex, and Essex became furious when Lopez was indiscreet about his treatment. Essex became convinced from what may have been problematic evidence that Lopez was part of a Spanish plot to poison Elizabeth. Essex wanted to show Elizabeth that he was saving her from a dangerous plot. Lopez proclaimed innocence, stating he had worked for Walsingham and that he was deceiving the Spanish. Put on trial in February 1594, he was found guilty and sentenced to a traitor's death. Elizabeth delayed the execution until June, suggesting she may have had doubts about Lopez's guilt, but by then London was filled with so much anti-Jewish sentiment that she finally agreed. She did return most of Lopez's confiscated estate to his widow Sarah and their children. Writing in the mid-seventeenth century, Godfrey Goodman, Bishop of Gloucester, stated that since Essex was so instrumental in the fall of Lopez, he asked Sir Henry Savile, provost of Eton, who had been close to Essex, what he thought, and Savile confessed to Goodman that he thought the earl had been at fault about Lopez (see Chapter 11).

Sir John Smythe 1596

John Smythe was a soldier, diplomat, and author. He had a difficult temper and apparently was also a problem drinker, which led to serious consequences in June 1596. Through his mother Dorothy, he was the cousin of Thomas Seymour, younger son of Katherine Grey and Edward Seymour, Earl of Hertford, whose marriage had been declared invalid (see Chapter 7). Smythe and Seymour were friends, and Smythe invited him in early June to come and make merry with him at his house. On June 11, Seymour accompanied Smythe when he went to Colchester to observe the training of the county militia. Sir Thomas Lucas, who was involved in the training, invited them to a dinner party at his home. Many people at the party were later examined by the Privy Council. There was a lot of drinking and conversation that night and, at one point, Smythe was upset enough to leave the table for a while. He also drank a great deal the next day before he and Seymour rode off again to see the county militia who were in their final days of training. In his later confession, he claimed so much drinking was not typical behavior. When he and Seymour arrived, Smythe asked the men if they would accept him as their captain. He then told them that they did not need to fight in foreign wars and terrible events were happening at Greenwich, that so many had been slain anyone going there would slip in the blood. This was all the fault of the traitor William Cecil, Lord Burghley. He then promised them a leader better than himself—a nobleman of the blood royal, Thomas Seymour. The soldiers did not, however, follow Sir John Smythe, who was soon arrested and lodged in the Tower, accused of treason. Smythe, Seymour, and many witnesses were examined. Seymour was not arrested, and Smythe explained that he had consumed a great deal of alcohol. While in the Tower he wrote often to Lord Burghley; sometimes his tone was angry, at other times apologetic. He also made his written submission to the queen, who in 1598 freed him from the Tower on the condition that he return to his house in Essex and not go a mile from it.

Edward Ewer 1596

In November of 1596, Edward Ewer told people that the world would never be a merry place until Queen Elizabeth was dead or killed. Ewer was also a horse thief, so we do not know for which crime he was executed.

Edward Squires 1598

Known as the pathetic assassin, we might question just how serious Edward Squire's assassination attempt was in 1598. Squires worked in the queen's stables but wanting more adventure he sailed with Francis Drake's final voyage to the Indies in 1595. The ship he was on was separated from the fleet and was captured by the Spanish. In Seville, the English Jesuit Richard Walpole apparently convinced Squires that he should return to England to assassinate Elizabeth as well as the Earl of Essex and paid him in advance. As a result of his agreement to poison the queen, Squires returned to England and returned to his job in the stables. His assassination attempt was to rub poison on Elizabeth's saddle and pommel, but this caused no harm to the queen. To avoid detection, and also perhaps to attempt to fulfill the other part of his assignment, Squires set sail with Essex and while at sea rubbed poison on the earl's chair, but this attempt was also unsuccessful. The Spanish were unhappy with the lack of results and concluded, rather than that Squires was just a failure, he might be a double agent, so they informed the English government about Squires's attempts against the queen and he was arrested in November 1598 and indicted for high treason. After numerous examinations, and perhaps under torture or the threat of it, he confessed. At his trial, the government went on at great length about the evils of Spain and the Jesuits, which was useful propaganda, and then he was executed.

Valentine Thomas and James VI 1598

The English Catholic Valentine Thomas visited Scotland in the winter of 1597–1598 and had an audience with James VI. A few months after returning to England he was arrested for theft. While under arrest he made a confession in which he claimed that James VI had paid him to murder Queen Elizabeth. Thomas was subjected to a thorough examination. There was a great deal of concern about Thomas's confession. William Knollys wrote about the debate over it in the Privy Council. Elizabeth wrote to James to assure him that she knew he was incapable of so terrible a crime. She did not, however, want Thomas to be executed; rather, he was kept in prison. She suggested that this punishment should demonstrate how little credit she gave to what Thomas claimed.

James was very upset both by her leniency with Thomas and that she did not make a stronger statement of his innocence. He was apparently worried that Thomas's accusations might be used to prevent him from being Elizabeth's successor. For the next several years he kept making demands to her ambassadors in Scotland, sending his emissaries to England, and peppering Elizabeth with letters.

There appears to be no evidence that Valentine Thomas was telling the truth, but James from a safe distance was watching and considering what he might do to become king. John Petit, an English agent in Scotland, wrote to his friend Peter Hallins in 1598 about his concern that James would "not wait till the fruit be ready to fall" (*CSPD*, 1598–1601, 128). Elizabeth was concerned that he wanted to hurry her into her grave. "Though a king you be, yet hath my funeral been prepared, as I hear, long ere I suppose their labor shalbe needful" (*Salisbury Papers*, 10, 288), she wrote him in August 1600.

A year later, at the time of the Essex rebellion, Elizabeth was even more concerned. Essex was secretly corresponding with James, and at the time of his revolt, two of his friends, Sir William Eure and Sir Edmund Ashfield, wrote to James hoping for his help. When Elizabeth learned of the correspondence, the two men were sent to the Tower for communicating with the Scottish king about the succession. In April 1601, two months after Essex's execution, Elizabeth wrote a stern letter to James making clear that she would no longer discuss the matter of Valentine Thomas, and that James had no right to criticize her actions about Eure and Ashfield. The same month Robert Cecil wrote to the Scotsman Patrick, Master of Gray, mentioning how pleased he was by the quiet at court since Essex's death, but that James VI still kept insisting that he be exculpated from the accusations of Valentine Thomas. James only calmed down when Robert Cecil assured him all was well through his own secret correspondence with the Scottish king. After Elizabeth's death, James arrived in London on May 7, 1603. One of the first things he did as king was to order the execution of Valentine Thomas.

Thomas Farryngton 1598

In October 1598 Thomas Farryngton told people that Queen Elizabeth was really the Anti-Christ and would be thrown down to hell. Not only was he placed in a pillory, but his ears were cropped.

Supposed Attempt Against the Queen 1599

On August 23, 1599, John Chamberlain wrote to Dudley Carleton that Richard Fowler—a man they knew well enough for Chamberlain to refer to him as Dick—was in the Tower on suspicion of some practices against the queen. Chamberlain added, "I always thought him foolish, but hope he is not devilish" (*CSPD*, 1598–1601, 305). Fowler had been arrested because a letter was found in a portmanteau, he received that concerned a plan to murder Elizabeth. But when the case was investigated it turned out the plot was against Fowler not the queen—the plan being to frame Fowler as a traitor, and Fowler was released. It is not clear if those who conspired against him were found.

Potential Poison Attempt 1600

Three well-born Austrians who had been in Orleans visited England and went into one of Elizabeth's palaces; they reached the kitchens, and then bolted from the palace as quickly as possible. Though nothing happened, there was great worry over poison and Elizabeth then notified officials, especially those at the ports, that no one, especially those of noble or illustrious birth, would be allowed to enter England unless their names had first been submitted to the government.

Image Magic 1601

At the end of Elizabeth's reign there was another example of image magic. William Waad, a diplomat who also served in a range of positions at Elizabeth's court (see Chapter 3) wrote to Robert Cecil about a chest in France that was given to a servant of Charles Howard, Lord Admiral, and brought into England. The Lord Admiral had asked Waad to search a box from the chest when it arrived at Westminster. There was concern about opening it as those who handled it had become ill. What Waad found was very concerning: a portrait of Elizabeth in metal, where mercury had eaten into the metal. Waad sent it on to an apothecary, who found that it was a poison so strong it had destroyed the metal and caused one of the apothecary's assistants to become ill. Waad concluded it was an ill omen to have Elizabeth's image placed in such poison.

Essex Rebellion 1601

In August 1600, though he was freed from house arrest, Robert Devereux, Earl of Essex, was forbidden to go to court, thus effectively ending his political career. But he was also in enormous debt, making a retirement from public life perilous. Moreover, with no evidence whatsoever, he became convinced that his political enemies were selling out England by supporting a Spanish heir to the throne. To avoid financial ruin, he needed his monopoly on sweet wines, which was up for renewal in October 1600. But Elizabeth refused to do so, and the earl, living at Essex House, was surrounded by supporters who encouraged his feelings of persecution and conspiracy. When Essex was summoned to appear before the Privy Council on February 7, 1601, Essex and his followers became convinced that he must seize control of the court with aid of the people of London. The following day Essex and 300 followers marched through London expecting supportive crowds to join him. He claimed that Robert Cecil and his colleagues were selling out English interests with underhanded dealings with Spain to make Philip III's sister, Isabella Clara Eugenia, the Spanish Infanta, the heir to the throne. People did not join Essex and many of his own followers drifted away. Essex and those who stayed with him rushed back to Essex House, which was then besieged. Essex decided to surrender. Taken to the Tower of London with some of his followers, he was put on trial for treason. Found guilty, he was executed on February 25, 1601, at the age of thirty-five (see Chapter 6).

1601 Attempt to Seize the Queen

Captain Thomas Lee was with the Earl of Essex in Ireland and accompanied him back to court in 1599 when Essex returned without permission. Lee was well known for violence and his irascible temper. Lee was not one of the conspirators with Essex in 1601, but he decided he wanted to seize the queen and force her to sign a release warrant for the earl. He tried to convince Sir Henry Neville and Sir Robert Crosse to help him, but they turned him in instead, and on February 12 he was arrested while lurking outside the presence chamber. William Poynes, who found him, said he was acting very suspiciously, pale, and covered with sweat. On February 13 he was arraigned, tried, and found guilty of treason. He was executed the very next day.

1603

According to the manuscript Elizabeth Southwell wrote in 1607, after she had eloped to Rome with Sir Robert Dudley and converted to Catholicism (see Chapter 15), as the queen was on her deathbed in March, two of her ladies found a queen of hearts playing card nailed to the bottom of the queen's chair. The nail went through the forehead of the queen on the card. If this happened—we only have Southwell's word for it—the nail through the card was the last example of the use of image magic to damage or kill the queen.

CHAPTER 10

The Spanish Armada

As war loomed between England and Spain in 1587 there was growing anxiety about it. People knew about numerous prophecies that 1588 would be an amazing year. It could be a year of wonders, or perhaps a very woeful year, or maybe even the end of the world. In 1553 Kasper Brusch prophesized catastrophe in 1588 and claimed that the prophecy was originally from the fifteenth century astrologer Regiomontanus. One solar eclipse and two lunar eclipses were expected in 1588. The prophecies were talked about so frequently by so many people that the Privy Council asked Dr. John Harvey to publish a book explaining there was no cause for alarm. His book was titled *A Discoversive Probleme concerning Prophesies*. Harvey explained that he wrote the book to stop people from feeling so threatened and menaced. Harvey argued that those who claimed that the dangerous planet Mars would dominate the heavens in 1588 were misinformed. But this did not calm the anxiety; the prophecies played into the fear of a Spanish invasion (Fig. 10.1).

From the beginning of Elizabeth's reign there were tensions between England and Spain due to conflicts between Protestants and Catholics. Some of the Spanish ambassadors, Alvaro de Quadra, Guerau de Spes, and finally Don Bernardino de Mendoza, were involved in plots against Elizabeth. After Mendoza was expelled in 1584 there was no resident Spanish ambassador for the rest of Elizabeth's reign (see Chapter 8).

From very early in her reign the slave trading of John Hawkins and Francis Drake led to conflicts with the Spanish government. Hawkins made several voyages to the Canary Islands where he learned of the possibility of financial gain through the slave trade. Clearly Hawkins was thinking of this when he left Plymouth in 1562. In Sierra Leone he captured as many as 300 Africans

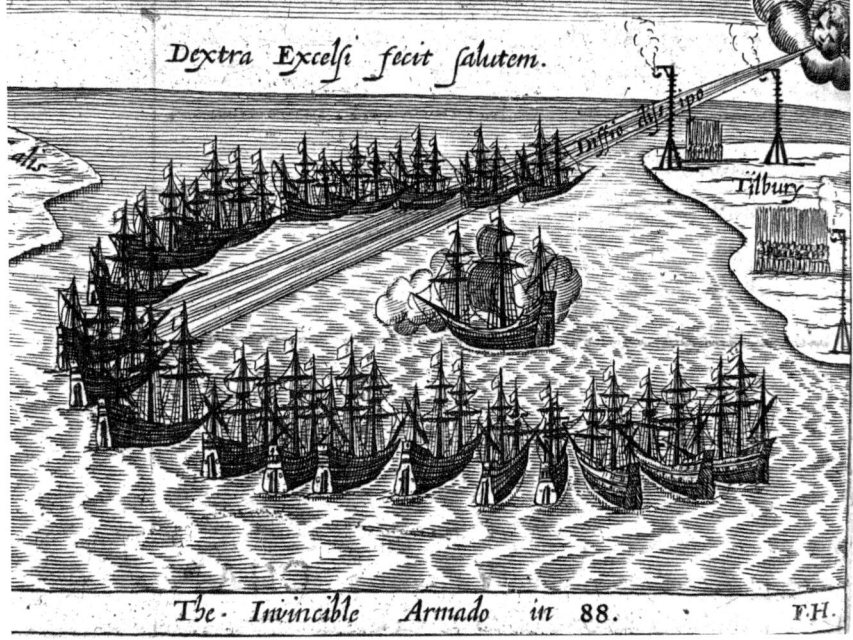

Fig. 10.1 Spanish Armada Private Collection

and took by force a number of Portuguese ships. When he reached the West Indies, he was able to sell his goods and slaves. Philip II was angry about the English interlopers into the Iberian slave trade.

In 1564 there was a second voyage to capture slaves with Drake accompanying Hawkins. It had more government sanction and support. Three privy councilors—Robert Dudley, William Herbert, Earl of Pembroke, and the Lord Admiral Edward Lord Clinton—joined the syndicate supporting it; the queen was also a sponsor. The Spanish ambassador Guzman de Silva told the queen that his king was opposed to the voyage, but Elizabeth ignored him. Hawkins captured over 400 slaves in Sierra Leone, obtained goods to trade as well, and sailed to the West Indies and the coast of South America. There he sold the slaves and goods, making a substantial profit. Elizabeth celebrated by granting Hawkins a coat of arms; one of the images on it showed a Moor who was bound, a clear reference to his activities as a slaver. There were further voyages in the next few years that involved capturing slaves, trading, and stealing Spanish treasure, leading to more fury from Philip and disapproval expressed by Spanish ambassadors (see Chapter 11).

By the early 1570s Drake was sailing as captain and raiding Spanish outposts. In what was clearly piratical behavior, Drake attacked Spanish ships loaded with an array of goods. The 1577 voyage, which lasted three years, was especially significant. Drake went around the world, raiding Spanish ports.

When he returned to Plymouth in September 1580, he carried enormous treasure stolen from the Spanish. In 1581 the notorious pirate was knighted.

In the meantime, the English were worried about Spanish involvement in Ireland and the Spanish were increasingly upset over English involvement in the Netherlands. One great fear during Elizabeth's reign, certainly from the 1570s onward, was that the Spanish were in an alliance with the Irish and that the Spanish would use Ireland as a base for war with England. Philip was further enraged when in 1585 Elizabeth signed the Treaty of Nonesuch with the Dutch and sent the Earl of Leicester with 7000 English troops. He saw it as an act of war.

English worries about Spanish animosity became even more intense after the 1584 assassination of William the Silent by Balthasar Gérard. Three years earlier Philip II had declared William the Silent, Prince of Orange, a traitor and outlaw, and promised a reward to any who assassinated him. The complicity of some Spanish ambassadors, especially Mendoza, in plots against Elizabeth made the English greatly fear that the Spanish would encourage the assassination of the English queen.

Mary Stuart's execution in February 1587 in some ways made the invasion more appealing to Philip. The Spanish king was concerned about making Mary Stuart the new queen of England and allying England with France. But before her death Mary wrote to Philip that she left her claim to the English throne to him, not her son James VI, the king of Scotland, as she considered him to be a heretic. And without Mary Stuart, Philip stated that after he conquered England his own daughter, Isabella Clara Eugenia, would be the next queen. Indeed, Philip wanted to send his Armada in 1587. That year Drake captured a small boat in the outer bay of Lisbon and learned of the creation of a great fleet in the harbor at Cadiz. Walsingham helped Drake's plan to protect England, by spreading misinformation about the purpose of Drake's voyage. At the port of Cadiz Drake burned many of the Spanish ships. After this successful attack, he continued up the coastline destroying more ships and looting. Drake said that what he was doing was "singeing the beard" of the king of Spain. This was a huge loss for Spain and Drake had found a way to delay the Spanish Armada for a year. Though Elizabeth apologized to Philip, Spanish officials were utterly unimpressed, and rightly so. The Spanish began to describe Drake as the "captain General" of the English navy. In some of their texts Drake's name is given as "Drago," a play on his name that suggested his dragon-like aggressiveness and savagery. Because Drake was able to demonstrate that the Spanish were seriously at work on their plans to invade England, the English efforts to prepare its defense intensified. Lord Charles Howard, Baron Howard of Effingham was named commander of the English fleet with Drake his second in command. Howard discussed naval war strategies thoroughly with Drake and Hawkins.

The Armada comprised 130 ships that sailed from Corunna in late May 1588. The command had originally been under Álvaro de Bazán, 1st Marquess of Santa Cruz, but he died on February 9, 1588. Philip replaced him with

Alonso Pérez de Guzmán y de Zúñiga-Sotomayor, 7th Duke of Medina Sidonia. The duke was extremely reluctant. He wrote to Philip that he lacked military experience both on land and on sea, and that he knew nothing about either the English enemy or the Spanish war plans. He also pointed out that he was in ill health, tended to suffer from seasickness, and had no command experience. None of this deterred Philip, who appreciated Medina Sidonia's loyalty and his staunch Catholicism. When the fleet left Corunna Medina Sidonia was hardly confident. He stated that they were sailing in hope of a miracle. Fortunately for the English, the miracle did not happen for the Spanish; the victory was explained by stating that God was an Englishman.

The Spanish fleet was sighted off the coast of Cornwall in late July. The English ships set out from Plymouth to confront the Armada with Howard as commander, Drake as vice admiral and Hawkins as rear admiral. For Howard what was most important was preventing the Spanish from landing on English soil, and he was successful in making sure this did not happen.

The English ships were smaller and more maneuverable than the large Spanish galleons. The English fleets divided into two squadrons. Drake captured the ship Rosario, one of the Spanish pay ships carrying as much 50,000 gold ducats. The English used fire ships to scatter the Spanish fleet very effectively. The Armada was further disrupted by heavy storms. The battle of Gravelines destroyed a number of Spanish ships. On their return to Spain there was more severe weather, and many ships were wrecked on the coasts of Ireland and Scotland. More than a third of the Armada ships were lost and did not return to Spain.

Because of the threat of invasion, Leicester gathered a force of 4000 men at Tilbury in Essex to defend England if necessary. Leicester invited Elizabeth to come and address the troops, stating that her courage would comfort not only the soldiers but all who would hear of her visit and speech. Burghley and Walsingham told Elizabeth that a trip to Tilbury would be too dangerous, and she should stay safely in London, but Leicester promised to protect her; Elizabeth went to Tilbury, though descriptions of her wearing armor are much after the fact. There are several versions of her speech, but many scholars accept as accurate the one later reported by Lionel Sharpe, who was at Tilbury as Leicester's chaplain. Decades later he sent the speech to George Villiers, Duke of Buckingham in a letter of comfort, when the duke was feeling distressed.

Elizabeth started her speech with "My loving people. . . . I have always so behaved myself that, under God, I have placed my chiefest strength and safe guard in the loyal hearts and good will of my subjects." For Elizabeth, the love of her people had always been important. "Therefore I am come amongst you, as you see, at time . . . being resolved, in the midst and heat of battle, to lay down for my God, and my kingdom, and for my people, my honor and my blood, even in the dust." Her description of herself is fascinating in its play with gender. "I know I have the body of a weak and feeble woman, but I have the heart and stomach of a king, and of a king of England too, and think foul scorn that Parma or Spain, or any prince of Europe should dare invade the borders of my realm." She ended with the promise, "to which, rather than any Dishonor shall grow by me, I myself will take up Arms, I myself will be your General" (Levin, *The Heart and Stomach of a* King, 144). Her early biographer William Camden stated that "incredible it is how much she encouraged the Hearts of her Captains and Soldiers by her Presence and Speech to them" (Camden, 416). James Aske described Elizabeth at Tilbury as "our sacred Queen" who showed "courage wonderful" and was an "Amazonian queen" (Aske, 24).

Soon after the victory, Elizabeth gave a public prayer acknowledging her own weakness and demonstrated her faith and thanksgiving for the saving of her country and her people. She stated that "I must humbly, with bowed heart and bended knees, do render by humblest acknowledgements and lowliest thanks." Elizabeth expressed how much danger there was in the world as Satan was doing all he could to bring trouble to the queen and England, but she was so grateful for God's protection. "Such hath been Thy unwonted grace in my days, although Satan hath never made holiday in busy practices both for my life and state, yet that Thy mighty hand hath overspread both with shade of Thy blessed wings" (Elizabeth I, *Collected Works*, 424) (Fig. 10.2).

There was an elaborate ceremony of thanksgiving for the great victory on Sunday November 24. Queen Elizabeth departed from Somerset House on her way to St. Paul's in what was called a chariot-throne, drawn with white horses. She was dressed in silver and white and was accompanied by members of the Privy Council, many of her ladies-in-waiting, and much of the nobility—at least four hundred in all. As they proceeded through London the crowds cheered the queen. There were musicians playing and the Lord Mayor greeted the queen and gave her the sword of the city, which she gave back when she returned from St. Paul's that evening. Henry Lyte, who had been at Tilbury and heard her speech had written a book, *The Light of Britayne*, about the legends of ancient Britain, and as she traveled through the city, he presented her with a manuscript copy.

When the queen arrived at St. Paul's she left her chariot and was welcomed by John Aylmer, Bishop of London and fifty clergies. Elizabeth knelt for a private prayer, and then walked into the church to her special seat. Dr. John Piers, Bishop of Salisbury preached the thanksgiving sermon. As well being a bishop, he had been the queen's almoner for more than a decade and preached regularly at court which may have been the reason he was chosen. The year following the sermon he was created Archbishop of York. He used Exodus 15:10 for his text—"Thou didst blow with Thy wind, the sea covered them: they sank as lead in the mighty waters" (White, 201). Afterwards Elizabeth spoke to the people, and she thanked God for the triumphant victory and said the Lord's prayer. She dined at the Bishop of London's palace with Aylmer as her host. Though problems with Spain continued for the rest of the reign, the victory over the Spanish Armada was the high point of Queen Elizabeth's reign (Fig. 10.3).

Fig. 10.2 Elizabeth in procession to St. Paul's private collection

10 THE SPANISH ARMADA 173

Fig. 10.3 Elizabeth surrounded by her people private collection

PART II

Society and Culture

CHAPTER 11

Elizabeth's England and Others

We might assume that Elizabeth's England was mostly homogeneous, but in fact England, and especially London and even Elizabeth's court, was fairly heterogeneous. During Elizabeth's reign, London became increasingly cosmopolitan, and the arrival of different groups of people both enriched the diversity of the English populace and caused concern among those whose nationalistic pride and xenophobia resisted the presence of anyone perceived as different.

In the early modern period, three terms were used interchangeably to describe otherness: foreigner, alien, and stranger, and while the definitions overlapped, they typically designated someone from beyond England's borders or even from outside a local community. While these terms were not always used pejoratively, they often conveyed a deep antagonism and fear of those who were unknown or unfamiliar. As Emanuel van Meteren, a Dutch merchant who lived in England during Elizabeth's reign put it, the English were "very suspicious, especially of foreigners, whom they despise" (Rye, 70).

Especially at times of cultural, economic, religious, or social crisis the English would often turn on those they perceived as different or other, though that perception of "other" was wide-ranging. Many of those who arrived in England came willingly, but others came forcibly. Those who came from outside of England included French and Spanish, people as far away as Russia, Jews especially from the Iberian Peninsula but other places as well, some called Indians, which could mean either those from India or from the Americas, and Moors, which was a broad term with some further described as tawny Moors or black Moors. These were people from not only Africa but the Middle East as well. Elizabeth invited ambassadors and envoys from far away to her court.

She also had entertainers and servants from a range of distant places. Just as wealthy and aristocratic young Englishmen toured the continent, so too did their continental counterparts come to England.

Legally slavery did not exist in Elizabethan England, but there was certainly interest and awareness of it and several de facto cases and some mention of slaves. When Catherine of Aragon came to England in 1501 two women slaves were listed among their entourage. From the 1560s onward Sir John Hawkins and Sir Francis Drake established the English slave trade from Africa to the Americas (see Chapter 10); even if it was not called slavery, some people were kidnapped from far parts of the world, brought to England, inhumanely designated and given as "gifts." They were only able to learn rudiments of the English language, and even if they could leave their household, they had nowhere to go, and no way to return home. Some of the people were taught English and returned to their homes to act as translators, but most of them were never able to see their home again. One of the greatest tragedies for many who came from far away, especially if they were brought against their will, was that they often did not long survive. Many of their lives went largely unrecorded, so it is difficult to find out what happened to them.

This section includes a sample of those who came to England, especially if they had the opportunity to see or interact with the queen, and we have records about them. These commentaries also inform us about the nature of the English, or at least as it was perceived by others.

Wealthy European Visitors

Foreigners who came from the continent came for a range of reasons. Some came for visits with the clear plan to return home, while others were immigrants who came for economic or religious reasons. Some of the young continental aristocrats kept records of the places in England they visited, which provide us with some fascinating information. They particularly wanted to see the court and other royal and aristocratic great houses, and many were eager to see the queen.

A visitor early in the reign was Levinus Lemnius, a Dutch physician and author born in 1505. He came to visit England in 1560 as he not only wanted to see the country, but because his son William had migrated to London where, like his father, he was a skillful doctor. Lemnius expressed how delighted he was by the courtesies he was he shown. He described people's houses as clean and neat with beautiful furniture and the dinners he was served were sumptuous but was relieved that the diners did not drink too much. As someone who was most likely entertained by his son's friends, he may well have thought more highly of the English, whom he found friendly and affable, than he would have had he only met strangers. The Antwerp merchant Emanuel van Meteren, though he lived in England for much of Elizabeth's reign, also commented on the nature of the English people but not as positively as Lemnius. "The people are bold, courageous, ardent, and cruel in war, fiery in attack and having little fear of death; … very inconstant, rash, vainglorious, light, and deceiving, and very suspicious, especially of foreigners, whom they despise" (Rye, 70).

Cecilia Vasa

Princess Cecilia Vasa, daughter of King Gustav and sister to King Erik XIV of Sweden, was a spirited young woman who often made unwise decisions. Soon after the wedding of her sister Catherine to Edzard, Count of East Frisia, in the fall of 1559, Cecilia, then nineteen, and her brother-in-law John were traveling with them, when John was discovered in Cecilia's bed chamber. There was an enormous scandal. Cecilia claimed her father physically punished her. In 1563 when her brother was king there was further scandal; he became upset that she was entertaining people in her rooms and greatly restricted her movements. The following year she married Christopher, Margrave of Baden-Rodemachern. For years Cecilia had been fascinated with Queen Elizabeth. In fall, 1565 the pregnant Cecilia and her new husband and entourage traveled to England for a state visit with the queen, though the visit was non-political.

When she arrived in Dover several courtiers led by William Parr, Marquis of Northampton met her with a royal reception. Soon after her arrival in London Queen Elizabeth received her. When Cecilia gave birth to a son named Edward Fortunatus, Elizabeth served as his godmother and presented Cecilia with a salary. The Swedish princess also received many gifts from others at court. Cecilia worked hard to be fluent in English, dressed in English fashion, and attended many social functions. But the friendship the queen and the English people had with the princess when she first arrived badly shifted within a few months, mostly due to Cecilia's extreme extravagance. The princess was deeply in debt and complained of harassment by creditors. Cecilia begged Elizabeth for help, but Elizabeth believed she had already done enough for Cecilia. Creditors begged the Privy Council for help in getting paid. In April 1566 Elizabeth gave permission for the princess and her husband to leave England, debts unpaid. For years after creditors continued to press for payment but to no avail.

Helena Snakenborg

For Elizabeth, what was best about Princess Cecilia's visit was one of the six Maids of Honor who accompanied her, Helena Snakenborg, the daughter of a Swedish nobleman. Helena admired the queen so much she copied her clothing which Elizabeth saw as a great compliment. Elizabeth developed a strong affection for Helena, another redhead, and convinced Cecilia when she left to release Helena from her service. Helena stayed in England first as a maid of honor, and then as a gentlewoman of the Privy Chamber. The Marquis of Northampton, who had met Helena when she first arrived, fell in love with her. Helena was thirty-five years younger. After the death of his long-estranged wife Lady Anne Bourchier early in 1571, Northampton married Helena that May. Elizabeth enthusiastically approved of the marriage. She arranged for the wedding ceremony to take place in the royal chapel. Unfortunately, Helen was widowed only a few months later, and the queen paid for Northampton's funeral and burial.

Helena returned to court after her husband's death and became acquainted with Thomas Gorges, a Groom of the Queen's Chamber; they fell in love. While Gorges was the second cousin of Anne Boleyn and thus remotely related to the queen, he was not an aristocrat and Elizabeth did not think that he was of high enough status to marry the Marchioness of Northampton. The two married secretly in 1576, which greatly angered Elizabeth who expelled Helena from court; Gorges was briefly in the Tower. But the queen was very fond of Helena, and Helena's friend Thomas Radcliffe, Earl of Sussex and Lord Chamberlain, also intervened for her. Helena and Gorges were forgiven and resumed their places at court and Elizabeth gifted her with two more manors. The queen was the godmother for their first child, a daughter named Elizabeth. They had seven more children. Gorges served as special ambassador to Sweden in 1582 and was knighted in 1586. In 1591 the poet Edmund Spenser dedicated a poem to Helena. Helena and the queen remained close; in the last decade of the reign Helena represented the queen at the baptisms of many of Elizabeth's godchildren. When the queen died Helena served as the chief mourner at her funeral.

In the latter part of Elizabeth's reign several young continental aristocrats visited England, as seeing the queen became important for the status seekers. Sir Francis Walsingham, for example, was besieged with letters begging to be allowed into England and to court. These travelers often had a member of their entourage keep careful notes of their adventures. These travel narratives allow us to know the places that attracted tourists, which were often the queen's various palaces—Whitehall, Greenwich, Windsor, and Hampton Court, as well as Woodstock, where Elizabeth was under house arrest in her sister's reign. This was a very popular place to visit. Elizabeth had used a diamond to carve into a window a statement of her innocence. The visitors went to the Tower of London where they saw the collections of jewels and armor; they also saw the zoo there and many spoke of the lions and other animals. They often visited the mint to see coins being produced. They provide detailed descriptions of the rooms in the various palaces and what were in them. Some of them went to the theatre and many loved the lavish gardens. There were descriptions of Bridewell, where women were imprisoned and punished. These accounts often provide fascinating information about England but there is also much inaccurate information presented. *The Diary of the Duke of Stettin's Journey*, for example, states that the Tower of London was a castle built by Julius Caesar. Thomas Platter was told that Woodstock Palace was also built in Caesar's time. These wealthy tourists visited many palaces and when they tipped the guards, they were given tours. Often the visitors were told fascinating historical tidbits that were exaggerations or possibly invented for the occasion. Another problem was that a number of these visitors did not speak English and were dependent on interpreters. The Duke of Stettin's party were shown the bed at Windsor where Prince Edward had been cut alive out of his mother's womb—except of course Jane Seymour did not have a caesarian birth.

John Casimir

After the death of Frederick III, Elector Palatine in 1576, his son Louis inherited the main part of the Palatinate, but his younger son John Casimir received part of it as well, which became independent, making John the Count Palatine of Lautern. He was in contact with Sir Philip Sidney and the Earl of Leicester about supporting the Protestants in the Netherlands. Elizabeth granted him funds so he could bring an army to the Netherlands, but he was not too successful. He visited London early in 1579 to explain his failure but confirm his continued support for the Dutch. Fifteen years previously he had expressed his desire to marry the queen. While she had not had any interest in the proposal, she treated him very well during his three-week visit. His first two days he stayed at Thomas Gresham's beautiful mansion, and then went to Whitehall, and visited Hampton Court. Leicester was very glad to see him and took him to visit Oxford. He went hunting, watched a tournament, and the Lord Mayor of London hosted a banquet for him. Elizabeth decided to honor the count by inducting him in full ceremony to the Order of the Garter. The queen herself buckled the garter on his leg for him (see Chapter 6).

Lupold von Wedel

Lupold von Wedel, born in 1544, came from a German noble family. As a younger son, his family intended that he would be trained for a legal career. But von Wedel had no interest in the law; instead, he wanted to travel. Soon after his mother died in 1573, he left home and traveled through Europe, Egypt, and the Holy Land for the next two decades. He was in England and Scotland in 1584 and 1585. He traveled through England, was able to receive permission to also go to Scotland, and then returned to England.

While in Scotland he went to Kirk o' Field, to see where James VI's father Henry Stuart, Lord Darnley had been strangled. He wrote as well about the building that had been blown up to try to hide the murder. Von Wedel also explained in his travel journal how Mary Stuart, whom he described as a very beautiful woman, had planned the murder, getting her lover to do the deed. He also described her escape to England, the intrigue with the Duke of Norfolk, and how Mary was still imprisoned.

When he returned to England, he visited Hampton Court and saw the queen. In some ways he was quite aware of current gossip and beliefs, and in other ways mistaken about the politics of Britain. He claimed that though

Elizabeth had ruled for twenty-six years, she had never called a Parliament, and the reason one was now being called was to keep James VI from being her heir. He saw Elizabeth interact with some of her courtiers, including the Earls of Leicester and Hertford as well as Christopher Hatton. He talked about how she had for a long time had an involvement with Leicester but then Hatton was the one she loved most recently. He detailed the various reasons that Hertford had been in disgrace but was now back in favor.

Samuel Kiechel

Samuel Kiechel was a merchant in the Germany city of Ulm. In 1584, when he was in his early twenties, he traveled for three years through Europe and Asia. One of the first places he visited was England. He arrived in London on September 11 and was there until October 29, when he had the opportunity to witness the inauguration ceremony for the new Lord Mayor, Sir Wolstan Dixie. He then visited Scotland, returned to London on November 14. After a visit to Canterbury, he left England to continue his travels one week later. He was impressed by how charming and pretty he found the English women and was able to see Queen Elizabeth at Richmond. What impressed him most was how beautifully dressed the yeomen of the guard were who surrounded her and how even nobles would go down on one knee when they spoke to her.

Count Frederick of Mompelgard, Future Duke of Württemberg

Count Frederick of Mompelgard, future Duke of Württemberg, decided in 1592, when he was thirty-five, that he longed for a tour of England. To facilitate the visit he first went to see the Landgrave William of Hesse, who had already been corresponding with the English queen, and the Landgrave gave him a letter of introduction to Elizabeth. One of the goals of the visit was to receive from Elizabeth an invitation to be inducted into the Order of the Garter, with all celebration and ceremony possible. This was his goal until finally in the early part of James I's reign he received his wish for his garter and his magnificent formal ceremony that he then devised for himself. The count traveled with other nobles and servants, including his secretary, Jacob Rathgeb, who wrote about the time in England. The count and his entourage arrived at Dover on August 9 and then went on to London. But the queen was at the time holding court in Reading, and as soon as she learned the count had arrived, she invited him to join her. He stayed with the Lord Mayor and the Earl of Essex came to welcome him, the next day taking him to meet Elizabeth. He had a second audience with her in Reading, and Elizabeth played the lute for him, with strings of gold and silver. Essex hosted a banquet for him there. The count then accompanied the queen to Windsor, where she allowed him to hunt in the royal parks and he enjoyed other amusements designed for him. He visited Hampton Court and then went back to London, where he also went to the theatre. By October the count was back in Germany. Sometime after the count returned home, he claimed that when he was with the queen at Windsor, she promised to confer on him the Order of the Garter. From 1594 onward he sent various messengers and embassies to England to request that Elizabeth fulfill what he claimed she had agreed to. He was installed in his absence in 1597, but it was not until James I was king that he was sent his garter. When he received it he gave himself an extravagant celebration.

Paul Hentzner

Paul Hentzner, born in 1558, was a lawyer in Brandenburg. In 1596 he became the tutor for a young aristocrat. The next year they began a three-year journey through Europe including England. In 1612 he published a book on his travels. Hentzer was especially impressed with Whitehall, spending time in the Royal Library, with its books beautifully bound in velvet with clasps of gold and silver. He noted particularly a small manuscript book in Elizabeth's handwriting, created for her father Henry VIII for New Year's 1546, a translation of her stepmother Katherine Parr's prayers into Latin, French, and Italian (see Chapter 16). Hentzner was impressed by the number of languages she could speak. Hentzner also noted where Elizabeth kept her jewel boxes, which themselves were set with pearls. Her bed frame was made of wood of many different colors intertwined and was covered with quilts of silk, velvet, gold, silver, and embroidery. He also noted her musical instruments but was really struck by a clock that when wound up had an Ethiopian riding on a rhinoceros, with four attendants who would bow when the hour struck.

Hentzner was able to see the queen at Greenwich one Sunday. He found her very majestic with a stately air. She wore white silk trimmed with pearls and a black silk cloak shot with silver. Her necklace was long with beautiful jewels, and her hands sparkled with the rings on her long fingers. Hentzner found her not only magnificent but very gracious. Most of her ladies were also dressed in white. Elizabeth went to evensong service, where Hentzner found the music beautiful. After attending church the queen dined. Hentzner noted that she preferred to dine with very few people. The opportunity to observe the queen was clearly something Hentzner appreciated.

Thomas Platter

Like some of the other travelers who kept a travel journal, Thomas Platter, from Basel, Switzerland, was a physician. After he completed his training but before he established his practice, he traveled through France, Spain, Flanders, and England. When he was about twenty-five, he came to visit England for two months in the fall of 1599. He was traveling with his older half-brother Felix. One reason that scholars have been fascinated with Platter's time in London is that he went to the Globe theatre, and on September 21, 1599 he saw the play *Julius Caesar*. But we can learn much more from what Patter recorded.

Like others, he toured Elizabeth's palaces, saw the queen, and left detailed comments about these adventures.

Elizabeth was a devoted musician and loved to play the virginal (see Chapter 16). When Platter toured Hampton Court he noted all of the jewels and the many musical instruments the queen had, including one small virginal made completely of glass. When Count Frederick had met the queen at Reading, he mentioned her playing a lute with strings of gold and silver. Years later Platter mentioned seeing the instrument at Hampton Court. He saw a large plate with a cover in gold and silver showing the queen being driven in a carriage. A Latin phrase at the top stated that Elizabeth should be celebrated for virtue rather than guile—though there were many who thought guile was one of Elizabeth's strongest characteristics. He also saw many clocks and was struck that the queen had a piece of a unicorn's horn, thought to keep her from illness. From Hampton Court he went on to Windsor. When he visited the church, he played the organ there briefly, and then was delighted with the music during the service. The overseers at Windsor Castle must have loved showing visitors the royal beds as Platter wrote about them in great detail as well.

Platter had clearly studied the history of Queen Elizabeth and he and his party were determined to see Woodstock, where Elizabeth had been kept under house arrest in the reign of her sister. When Platter visited places, he would tip the overseer well and so was given a lot of information. As a prisoner, Elizabeth was allowed to be in three rooms, and there were guards at each end. The overseer told Platter that it was seven years since the queen had visited Woodstock. The overseer remembered that when she walked into the rooms where she had been prisoner, she had tears in her eyes as she recalled how strictly she was kept and her fears regarding her fate. Since Woodstock had such bad memories for Elizabeth she did not want to visit often or reside there. Platter was also fascinated by the old-ruined building across from the palace, where Henry II's mistress Rosamund Clifford stayed. He was told all the legends about how Henry secretly visited, how Queen Eleanor learned of it, and then forced Rosamund to drink poison. That evening, as they were drinking beer in the village, the locals told Platter's company that the palace of Woodstock had been built originally in the time of Julius Caesar. It is unclear whether the locals actually believed that or thought it fun to fool the foreigners, but in fact Henry I built the hunting lodge at Woodstock, which Henry II rebuilt into a palace.

The most thrilling moment of his visit was when Platter saw the queen. "She was most lavishly attired in a gown of pure white satin, gold-embroidered, with a whole bird of paradise for panache, set forward on her head studded with costly jewels, wore a string of huge round pearls about her neck and elegant gloves over which were drawn costly rings." (*Thomas Platter's Travels in England*, 192) He also described how youthful she looked, and how dignified she was. He noted as well how very much her people esteemed her.

Virginio Orsini, Duke of Bracciano

In January 1601 Virginio Orsini, Duke of Bracciano, visited Elizabeth's court, the highest-ranking Italian to ever to do so. His mother was Isabella de Medici and thus he was the nephew of Grand Duke Ferdinando of Tuscany. Orsini had a tragic background. When he was only four his mother died, most likely murdered by his father Paolo when he learned she was having an affair with his cousin. Some years later Paolo married his lover Vittoria Accoramboni after her husband had been murdered. When Virginio was thirteen he became duke upon the death of his father, who may have been poisoned.

Bracciano married Flavia Peretti, the niece of Pope Sixtus V, in 1589, when he was seventeen. In 1600 he met William Cecil, the grandson of Lord Burghley, when Cecil was visiting the Duke Ferdinando's court in Florence, and Cecil would have encouraged the visit, given Bracciano's connections. Since they were children, Bracciano and his cousin Marie de Medici had been very close, and he chose to accompany her to France when her marriage to Henri IV had been arranged. From there he went on to a brief visit to England. He was encouraged to make the visit from powerful continental Catholics, who wanted to know if Elizabeth was close to death and what would happen in England as a result. This was not a diplomatic visit, but he was treated with great honor. He was in England from January 3 to 13, 1601. He visited court at the same time as the Russian ambassador.

Elizabeth was well-aware of international concerns about her health, and she wanted to show Bracciano the splendor and power of her court and her own vitality. The English learned on Christmas Day that Bracciano wanted to visit. Filippo Corsini, who was a wealthy and significant Italian merchant and the agent of the Duke of Tuscany, coordinated the visit and served as host. As soon as the duke arrived, he asked Corsini to go to the court and inform the queen of his arrival and his hope to see her and "privately kiss her hands" ("The Elizabethan Court Day by Day - 1601," Folgerpedia).

Bracciano was dazzled by his visit. On Sunday January 4 he went to the French embassy so that he could hear Mass. Afterwards he received several aristocratic guests. His visit to the queen was set for Tuesday January 6 the Feast of the Epiphany. The queen sent a splendid coach to bring him to court at Whitehall that day and he was then met by Roger Manners, Earl of Rutland, accompanied by Francis, Lord Darcy and Miles, Lord Sandys. Rutland greeted him in the name of the queen and brought him to the rooms of Edward Somerset, Earl of Worcester, that had been set aside for him. But Bracciano wrote to his wife that he spent little time there as so much entertainment had been arranged. He was taken to a sumptuous hall where he saw many ladies and gentlemen, some Knights of the Garter, dressed all in white as was everyone at court that day. He noted that they also wore "so much gold and so many jewels, that it was a marvelous thing" (Wyatt, 130). The people all greeted him, mostly in Italian, and some others in French or Spanish. He wrote that "I found only two gentlemen who spoke nothing but

English and with these I used others as interpreters" (Wyatt, 130). He became even more impressed when he met the queen, whose Italian he found perfect. "Her Majesty was dressed all in white, with so many pearls, broaderies, and diamonds that I was amazed how she could carry them" ("The Elizabethan Court Day by Day - 1601," Folgerpedia).

From a small balcony, he observed the celebration of the Epiphany service. He loved the high quality of the music that he heard that day. After the service he was brought to the queen's dining room and observed the elaborate ceremony preparing for the queen's arrival. There was even more ceremony when she arrived, elaborately washing her hands with Edward Somerset, Earl of Worcester holding the basin, George Clifford, Earl of Cumberland with the water, and Thomas Sackville, Lord Treasurer received the towel from George Carey, 2nd Baron Hunsdon, the Lord Chamberlain. William Stanley, Earl of Derby brought in the queen's cup. Music was played during the luncheon. The duke dined in the Council Chamber.

Also at the meal was the Russian ambassador Grigori Ivanovic Mikulin. After the splendid lunch the queen asked the duke to accompany her to her private rooms. They were entertained with music, which he greatly enjoyed. There was also entertainment by the Children of the Chapel, with an Epiphany carol. Later there was a grand banquet, and afterwards he was brought to his room so that he could rest. But then Worcester and Cumberland visited and then there was more entertainment, where he also met the Principal Secretary, Robert Cecil, who suggested to the duke that he salute the various ladies of quality, which he did in Italian and French, and Cecil interpreted for those who needed it. After this Queen Elizabeth entered and asked him to accompany her for the evening entertainment. There was more music, and then "was acted a mingled comedy, with pieces of music and dances," as he wrote to his wife, assuring her he would describe it in much more detail when he returned. The duke also mentioned that the queen "conversed continually with me" ("The Elizabethan Court Day by Day - 1601," Folgerpedia). He was then brought to yet another grand room with a variety of sweet confections to eat. Before the queen left him, she told him she would see him again before he departed England. The duke stayed until two in the morning, again conveyed back to the merchant's house in a grand coach.

More entertainment was planned for Bracciano during his visit. On January 8 Thomas Cecil, Lord Burghley had a banquet in his honor. He saw again many of the lords and ladies he had met at court. The duke described the banquet as being sumptuous, and after the dinner there was dancing. The following day Henry Brooke, Lord Cobham, and Sir Walter Raleigh took the duke to tour Hampton Court. Then one of the Lord High Admiral Charles Howard's sons had a banquet for him, after which they went hunting. The next day he visited the Tower of London.

On January 11 the queen again invited the duke to court. He first went to Mass at the French embassy and then had a meal with the ambassador. The queen again sent a gorgeous coach. As soon as he arrived at Whitehall "her Majesty received me with so gracious a countenance that I could not ask more." She had a ball in his honor, and what delighted the duke most was that the queen herself danced, "which is the greatest honour that she could do me." The queen kept the duke close by her, and he found the evening wonderful. Bracciano was leaving on January 13 and the day before Elizabeth "dispatched two of her most confidential gentlemen to fetch me and convey me in a close carriage; and by way of a back garden gate they brought me in to her Majesty." Unfortunately, we do not know what exactly passed between them, as the duke wrote to his wife that "what the Queen did I am saving for you at my return," but added that "it seemed to me I had become one of the paladins who used to go into those enchanted palaces" ("The Elizabethan Court Day by Day - 1601," Folgerpedia). We do know that she gave him a valuable piece of jewelry with emeralds, rubies, diamonds, and pearls. Given the duke's name and the time of his visit, it is thought that perhaps Shakespeare named his duke in the play *Twelfth Night* Orsino.

Philip Julius, Duke of Stettin-Pomerania

The final traveler who kept a record of his visit in Elizabeth's reign was Philip Julius, Duke of Stettin-Pomerania who visited England September 10–October 3, 1602, less than six months before Elizabeth's death. The young duke was only eighteen years old, and he traveled with sixteen gentlemen and several servants, having first been to several other countries on the continent. The duke ordered his secretary Frederic Gerschow to keep the diary as a thorough record of what they saw and heard every day at all the places they visited. Unfortunately, part of the diary was lost but Gerschow redid it from memory. Unlike other fairly recent visitors the duke did not comment that the queen looked young, but noted that though she was old, at least from a distance she was not ugly. He was also a great admirer of the Earl of Essex, noting where Essex, whom he considered a brave hero, was executed, when he toured the Tower. He asserted that Essex was loved and admired throughout the country. The group had found a German tailor, Master Leinvert, who served as a tour guide. Gerschow found that Leinvert knew much about England, but he also was unsure that the information was entirely accurate. Like Platter, the duke went to Woodstock, where he also saw the three rooms, and was glad to see her bedstead, and he told the story that was often repeated in the seventeenth century that there was smoke in Elizabeth's bedroom leading her to fear she would be murdered by being burned to death in her bed.

Embassies from Russia, the Ottoman Empire, Morocco, and Poland

Russia

As well as the tourists there were embassies from other parts of the world bringing people to London who were perceived as strange and exotic. From the time of Edward VI the English had been exploring Russia to develop trading routes. In early 1553 a group of merchants and courtiers decided to finance a voyage to discover a northern route to Asia to develop new trade markets. Those on two of the three ships ended up in Lapland, with all of them freezing to death, and their ships and bodies found in the summer of 1554 by Russians. The third ship, captained by Richard Chancellor, reached Russia, and he met with Tsar Ivan IV. Upon his return to England the Muscovy Company was established, and this began the trade and diplomatic relations between England and Russia.

Anthony Jenkinson, Eliseus Bomelius, and Tsar Ivan IV

Anthony Jenkinson continued the connections between England and Russia. From the time he was about seventeen he traveled extensively, leaving England in 1546. As well as his travels in Europe, in 1553 he entered the Ottoman Empire, managing to receive a special license to trade. In 1557 the Muscovy Company appointed him captain-general of a convoy of four ships and he left for Russia. Arriving in Moscow in December, Ivan IV offered Jenkinson great hospitality. He left Moscow in April 1558 continuing to do more traveling. He returned to Moscow in September 1559, again feted by the Tsar, and returned to England in 1560. He created a map of Russia that was published in 1562, the earliest known map of Russia engraved by an Englishman. Almost immediately after his return, the Muscovy Company had him prepare for another expedition through Russia to Persia. Ivan gave Jenkinson a secret commission, asking Jenkinson to purchase gems and silks for him in Persia. In the area of Shivan, though within the domains of Persia, the local power was with the ruler Abdullah Khan, whom Jenkinson referred to as king. He then went to the Shah's court at Kazvin, but was turned away, as the Persians did not want to establish trade with England at the time. Jenkinson returned to Shivan, and Abdullah agreed for the Muscovy Company to have customs-free trade in his domain, allowing access to the silk produced there, as well as trade in spices. Jenkinson returned to Moscow, bringing beautiful silk and jewels to Ivan, which pleased the Tsar so much he agreed to more privileges for English trade. Jenkinson continued to make diplomatic missions to Moscow but not to Persia. Ivan often preferred to have Jenkinson bring his messages to Elizabeth rather than have his own ambassadors do it more officially. While Russian ambassadors occasionally came to England for a variety of reasons, Ivan often did not trust them and preferred to use Jenkinson or other English representatives for particularly significant messages. Perhaps the strangest message that Jenkinson brought from Ivan was in 1567. Jenkinson brought a formal letter from Ivan that was general in tone, but he also brought a secret letter. Ivan wanted Elizabeth to send him some masters who could help his development of Russia. Elizabeth sent Humphrey Locke, who was a fortifications and building expert as well as Thomas Green, a goldsmith. But Ivan also wanted an offensive and defensive alliance with England, and this caused some conflicts between England and Russia for the rest of Ivan's reign. When Elizabeth sent Thomas Randolph in 1568 to further discuss trade, Ivan had other issues in mind.

He asked if he and his family could find asylum in England if he ever had to flee Muscovy and offered if she ever needed to flee England, she was welcome to Russia. Even more, he wanted England and Russia to be joined so that Elizabeth would be the friend to Ivan's friends, and she would be the enemy of his enemies. While Elizabeth temporized, in 1569 the Russian ambassador Andrei Savin arrived with a treaty for Elizabeth to sign. Instead of returning to Russia with a signed treaty Savin brought the offer from Elizabeth that he was promised refuge if necessary and would be given a residence, but it would be at his own expense, and she knew she would never need refuge in Russia. Angry, Ivan revoked the Muscovy Company's privileges. He sent the English queen a furious letter claiming she was queen only in name, and the country was ruled by boors who were only seeking their own profit. Since Ivan trusted Jenkinson, Elizabeth sent him to Russia to deal with the situation. Ivan agreed to restore most of the concessions for the Muscovy Company and to postpone considering the alliance.

In 1570 Eliseus Bomelius, a physician and astrologer, with his wife Jane left England for Russia to serve Ivan. Bomelius was born in Wesel, Westphalia, the son of a Lutheran minister, who was friendly with the English reformer John Bale. It was probably on Bale's suggestion that Bomelius left Germany for England and trained at Cambridge. Bomelius married Jane Richards in 1564. Many in London consulted him, including William Cecil, who asked for astrological predictions about Elizabeth's potential marriage. In April 1570 Archbishop Matthew Parker wrote to Cecil that many people had great confidence in Bomelius's magic, and Parker was alarmed that Bomelius had told him about a dangerous conspiracy against the queen. When Cecil questioned Bomelius, however, he learned Bomelius knew about the conspiracy from an astrological forecast, which Cecil did not take seriously. Bomelius then wrote to Cecil that he should be the queen's physician and that he was in high demand: claiming the Russian ambassador was sending him daily messages asking him to go to Russia. When Cecil was not forthcoming with the appointment, Bomelius decided to serve Ivan instead. For some years he was very successful, as Ivan thought him skilled in magic, and Bomelius became wealthy. But finding favor with Ivan was an uncertain business, and in 1579 Bomelius was charged with intriguing with the Polish and Swedish kings against Ivan. He was extensively tortured and died in prison. It was not until 1583 that his widow was allowed to return to England, where she remarried three years later.

Perhaps allowing Jane Bomelius to return to England was part of Ivan's diplomatic efforts. In August 1582 Ivan sent Fyodor Andreievitch Pissemsky as ambassador to attempt to again negotiate a close relationship between England and Russia. He also had another idea. Though he was now married to his seventh wife, he wanted to negotiate a marriage with a cousin of Queen Elizabeth, Lady Mary Hastings, a sister of Henry, Earl of Huntingdon. We do not know where Ivan got the idea of marrying Lady Mary, or how he had even heard of her. It is possible the idea had come from Bomelius.

Ivan instructed Pissemsky to discuss this marriage with Elizabeth only in a private audience. Ivan explained he needed a portrait of Mary; Pissemsky had to meet Mary himself so that he could describe her accurately. He also needed to make sure he knew how she was related to the queen, her father's rank, and how many siblings she had. If Elizabeth mentioned the fact that he was currently married Pissemsky should explain that he would get rid of his wife so he would be free to marry Mary, who of course would have to convert to Orthodox Christianity. Pissemsky and Elizabeth finally had this meeting in January 1583. Elizabeth was not very enthusiastic about the possible marriage alliance. She informed Pissemsky that Mary had recently recovered from smallpox so it would not appropriate at that time to either meet him or sit for a portrait. The queen also warned that Lady Mary was not beautiful enough for Ivan. But Pissemsky was persistent, and eventually he did meet Lady Mary as she was in a group of gentlewomen and some courtiers, including her sister-in-law Catherine, Countess of Huntingdon, and the Earl of Leicester's sister. Though Pissemsky had been given an interpreter when he met Lady Mary, they did not actually speak. Apparently after looking at her thoroughly, he said that it was enough and wrote to the Tsar that Mary was tall, slightly built, with white skin, fair hair, light eyes, and a straight nose. He added her fingers were long and tapered. He did receive a miniature of her to take back to Russia. He left in June 1583 with a new English ambassador, Sir Jerome Bowes, whom Elizabeth instructed to dissuade the Tsar from marrying Lady Mary, claiming she had poor health, and did not want to leave her family. This was certainly true. The rumors at Elizabeth's court about Ivan's cruelty and serial marriages led Lady Mary to beg Elizabeth to end any marital negotiations. Her friends, however, teased her for several years by referring to her as the Empress of Muscovia until Ivan died in 1584. Lady Mary, still unmarried, died five years later.

Boris Godunov

After Ivan's death Russia was in a chaotic period that remained unsettled until Boris Godunov had control as regent for Ivan's mentally challenged son Feodor around 1585 and eventually as Tsar himself in 1598. Godunov encouraged Anglo-Russian trade to flourish again. In 1586 Elizabeth sent Robert Jacob to Russia, traveling with Jerome Horsey, and a midwife only known in the records as Anna, as Godunov had requested medical help for his wife Maria Skuratova-Belskaya.

In the summer of 1600 the new Tsar ordered Gregory Ivanovitch Mikulim, accompanied by Ivan Sinovjeff, his secretary, to visit Elizabeth and cement these friendly relations. Mikulim landed at Gravesend September 18. Mikulim was invited to an audience with Queen Elizabeth at Richmond on October 14. When he was brought in to meet her, she arose from her throne to talk with him through his interpreter. She responded to his good wishes by asking for news of the health of the Tsar and his family. She spoke warmly of her friendship with Russia and allowed both Mikulim and his secretary Ivan Zinovief to have the honor of kissing her hand. She then sent them to talk about commercial affairs with Robert Cecil. Elizabeth invited Mikulim to join her for a state dinner at Whitehall on January 6, Twelfth Night. He ate with her in the Great Chamber after attending services with her in the chapel. While in London Mikulim had his portrait painted.

Mikepher Alphery

In 1601 Boris Godunov decided that it would be worthwhile to send four youths of good families to England, where they could be educated in English and Latin, go to university, and then return to Russia. He entrusted Mikifor Olferevich Grigorev, Theoder Semenove, Sophone Michalove, and Nazarey Davidove to the English ambassador John Merrick. They arrived that November. John Chamberlain, the brother-in-law to Merrick's niece, wrote to Dudley Carleton to let him know that the young men were in London, and were going to be educated at Winchester, Eaton, Cambridge, and Oxford. Mikifor stayed with the merchant John Biddell, who had connections with Russian trade, and we know that he did eventually indeed study at Cambridge and took the name Mikepher Alphery. We do not have records about the three others at the other institutions. It appears they needed some years to learn English and Latin before they were ready for university training. Mikepher did not go to Cambridge until 1609.

Though many saw Godunov as a good ruler, he also faced considerable hostility that intensified when an impostor claimed to be the younger son of Ivan IV and led an army against Godunov in the fall of 1604. When the Tsar died suddenly the following year, the country devolved into a chaotic time known as the Time of Troubles, and the boys in England were forgotten. The situation in Russia did not calm down until Michael Romanov was elected tsar in 1613.

The new Tsar sent Aleksey Ivanovich Zyuzin to argue for the four students' return. The only one they could locate was Mikepher Alphery. He spent three days with the ambassador and asked for more time to study. He had received his B.A. in 1612 but in 1613 he was in the midst of studying for M.A. This was agreed to and Alphery received his M.A. in 1615. But he was also that year ordained deacon and priest in the Church of England. In 1615 Ivan Gryazev was even more emphatic about the students being returned to

Russia. He was deeply upset about Alphery's conversion, and Alphery was aware of how Moscow would respond as well. His conversion was a matter of conscience, and he had turned against believing as an Eastern Orthodox Christian. Zyuzin's attempt to kidnap him as well as trying more conventional diplomatic methods failed. When Tsar Michael's ambassadors Sepan Volynsky and Mark Pozdeyev asked to have the students identified for him in 1617 so they could be returned to Russia, they were told that two were in India with the East India Company, one had married an Irishwoman and lived in Ireland, and the one left in England, Mikepher Alphery, was not available. The Tsar had his ambassador, Isaak Pogozhev make a more emphatic request in 1622, suggesting returning at least one of them was important for good relations. The Russians also pressured the former ambassador Merrick, and he finally arranged a meeting with Alphery and Pogozhev. Alphery was even more vehement that he did not want to leave England. Since 1618 he had been rector of Woolley in Huntingdonshire and had married an English woman named Joanna Bett.

Merrick intervened with King James arguing that it was important that Alphery be allowed to stay. He said that he wrote to the king as someone knowledgeable about Russia, that if Alphery desired to return to Russia he should certainly do so, but it would be doing a grave wrong to force him, now a member of the Church of England, to leave against his will. Alphery and his wife had several children and, except for when he was deprived of his living by Puritans, he stayed in his position until his retirement, dying in 1668.

The Ottoman Empire

Murad III

In September 1579 a Turkish envoy from the Ottoman Emperor Sultan Murad III arrived in London with a letter from the Sultan, who offered the queen security by land and by sea for all the English merchants trading with the Ottoman Empire. He requested the queen's friendship in return. The letter from the Sultan was itself a gift to the queen: beautiful and elaborate calligraphy, the traditional Ottoman elegant rhetoric, and the sultan's official signature. A translation had been made in Latin, and then all was placed in a satin bag and taken to England to be presented. Elizabeth acknowledged this as a great honor. A trade agreement was successfully negotiated in 1581.

This was the first Turkish official to visit Elizabeth's court, and the trade developed well. The following year in 1582 the Sultan liked English products so much he sent a merchant/envoy to London to make purchases. In 1583 the first Turkish ambassador arrived, and Elizabeth sent William Harborne as the first ambassador to the Ottoman Empire. Elizabeth sent the Sultan an elaborate bejeweled mechanical clock, cloth, gilt plate, and some dogs. She insisted the merchants help pay for the gifts. The ambassador from Turkey brought many gifts for the queen, including lions for her zoo, Turkish scimitars, and what were said to be unicorn horns, which were especially treasured not only for their rarity, but because they were believed to possess magical healing powers.

In 1592 Elizabeth granted a charter to fifty-five English merchants. These merchants now had exclusive rights of trade with both Venice and Turkey, and this began the Levant Company. The following year Elizabeth also, on the advice of her ambassador, now Edward Barton, sent gifts to the Sultana Safiye, including a miniature of Queen Elizabeth set in jewels, gilt plate, garments of cloth of gold, and glass bottles with silver and gilt. Murad's mother Nurbanu asked for advice from Barton about a gift that Elizabeth would treasure. After this consultation, she sent the English queen a Turkish gold dress of princely attire.

Mehmet III

Sultan Murad died in 1595, and was succeeded by Mehmet III, who strangled all his brothers to assure his accession. In 1599 the English sent most impressive gifts to celebrate the new Sultan. For the Sultan Mehmet III was the organ clock, a spectacular achievement. It was sixteen feet high, and the base had five bronze lions. Above the keyboard was a large clock. The columns were carved gilded oak. There was an image of Queen Elizabeth and carvings of pyramids and crescents. The organ took over a year to create, and then was dismantled and packed in separate crates. For the Sultana there was a beautiful coach valued at £600. Thomas Dallam the organ-maker was also on board to ensure that these amazing gifts were delivered in perfect working order. When they arrived in Constantinople Dallam had to not only reassemble the organ, but repair it, as parts of it had been damaged on route. The coach and especially the organ were extremely complicated items to transport long distances. They both incorporated elaborate technology. Mehmet was entranced with his gift, and gave Dallam, who presented it to him, forty-five pieces of gold as a reward. The Sultan's mother herself dictated a personal letter of thanks to Elizabeth. She sent a beautiful gift (see Chapter 16) and asked if the queen might help her in acquiring some cosmetics. Unfortunately, Ahmed I, Mehmet's successor, had the organ destroyed.

Morocco

Morocco also sent envoys to England in 1589 and 1595. There was certainly awareness of Morocco in late Elizabethan London. In Shakespeare's *The Merchant of Venice* one of the characters is the Prince of Morocco. The most important ambassadorial visit took place over six months in 1600. The Moroccan Sultan Mulai Ahmad al-Mansur was interested in a secret negotiation against Spain and possibly the Ottoman Empire. Its public face was to be a discussion of trade. In March 1600 the queen wrote to the Sultan requesting that he release nine Dutch captives who had been enslaved. The Sultan responded that he was sending a diplomatic mission that was outwardly a trade delegation on its way to Aleppo—clearly not a direct route. The leader of the delegation of sixteen was Abd al-Wahid bin Masoud bin Muhammad al-Annuri, al-Mansur's advisor. In England he was known as Hamet Xarife.

The delegation also had two prominent merchants. Abdullah Dudar, an Andalusian, was the interpreter. His original language was Spanish, but he was also fluent in Italian. In late June the delegation set sail, and their ship arrived in Dover August 8. The delegation comprised sixteen men as well as the Dutch captives. Representatives from the Barbary Company met them and brought them to London. Robert Cecil asked Thomas Gerard to be the diplomatic escort and take care of the embassy. It was an honor but also an expense, as whatever expenses the queen did not cover, he had to meet himself. Gerard met them at Gravesend, found a place for them to rest overnight, and then brought them to London. The housing he had found for them was Anthony Radcliffe's house on the Strand, near the Royal Exchange. Gerard thought Radcliffe, a former London sheriff and the master of the Guild of Merchant Taylors, would be a good host as he could connect the embassy with London merchants. Some in the neighborhood were unhappy with the visitors as they were perceived as being attired very outlandishly and behaving strangely. As observant Muslims, they wanted their meat slaughtered in a certain way, so they did it themselves. When they were at court, they refused to drink wine and instead drank water with spices that they had brought with them.

After they had been in London for five days, they went to Nonesuch Palace for an audience with Queen Elizabeth. They wore their turbans. While they may well have looked dramatic, one English observer suggested that they looked like old country women. Abdullah Dudar translated what the Moroccans said in Arabic into Spanish, and though the Queen knew some Spanish, Sir Lewes Lewknor then translated for her and her courtiers. Then Dudar spoke in Italian to Elizabeth and asked that they speak to her privately. Finally, Elizabeth had Noel de Caron, the Dutch ambassador, brought in and in great ceremony turned over to him the nine Dutch prisoners whose release she had secured. Here the complexities of communication were especially marked, as Queen Elizabeth spoke to the Dutch prisoners in French and Caron then translated that into Dutch.

There was a second meeting three weeks later at Oatlands Palace. The secret offer to Elizabeth explained by Al-Annuri was a formal military alliance aimed at invading Spain and attacking Spain's colonies in the Americas and the Far East. Al-Mansur wanted to eliminate Catholic Spain. In the end this was too much for Elizabeth. She was not at all sure she could trust Al-Mansur and such an alliance would also be problematic with Anglo-Ottoman relations given that the Moroccans and Ottomans were enemies. She wrote to al-Mansur to thank him for all his kindnesses with the embassy but was carefully noncommittal about any alliance.

As the negotiations were breaking down, in October the Moroccan embassy began to think of departing. But neither merchants nor mariners had any interest in helping them go anywhere. They thought them too dangerous and scandalous. The embassy was back at court to take their leave. Then Dudar died. Some English were convinced that the other Moroccans had murdered him because he was too positive about the English. Yet the Moroccan embassy did not leave. They were still in London and attended the Accession Day festivities at Whitehall on November 17, Al-Annuri in his long dark robes, his white turban, and his decorated scimitar. Around this time he also, as the Russian ambassador Mikulin had done, had his portrait painted in his formal robes. Elizabeth and her ladies watched from the windows inside the palace gallery. The French ambassador, Monsieur de Boissie and the Russian ambassador Gregorii Mikulin were honored with seats next to her. Al-Annuri and the rest of his entourage were outside as part of the crowd of Elizabeth's subjects.

The very same day John Pory's translation of *A Geographical Historie of Africa, written in Arabicke and Italian by John Leo, a More* was published. This was the work of Leo Africanus, his Christian name in his captivity. He was the highly educated Muslim al-Hasan ibn Muhammad ibn Ahmad al-Wazzan. Born in Granda, and raised in Fed, he had been captured and given as a "gift" to the Pope Leo X. His description of his life had been published first in Latin, then French and Italian before it was published in English and the English edition was dedicated to Robert Cecil, with Pory suggesting the publication was especially timely given the Moroccan embassy. The text was not only important to Elizabeth's government but provided more information to the English people about those who were different.

As the embassy prolonged its stay, people began to suspect that it was more than a trade delegation. As well as the secret negotiations, members of the embassy were also very interested in obtaining rare and valuable jewelry and astronomical devices as the Sultan was very interested in both astronomy and astrology as well as navigational devices such as compasses. They also had many questions about English technological advances. Some of the English began to think that the entourage were spies or even magicians. As London merchants became increasingly suspicious, and there was no diplomatic or military agreement to be had, the embassy finally left early in 1601.

Poland

Polish embassy to England 1597.

The son and heir of John III of Sweden, Sigismund, was elected King of Poland in 1587. Though he continued as King of Poland for the rest of his life, after he succeeded his father as King of Sweden in 1592, he ruled only seven years before he was deposed in 1599. One reason for the deposition was his intense Catholicism and his broken promises to the Lutherans in Sweden; another was his close relationship with Spain and the Holy Roman Empire. He married Anne of Austria, granddaughter of Holy Roman Emperor Ferdinand I, in 1592. These religious and political values meant problems with the Protestant Elizabeth of England. As England supported the Dutch against the Spanish in the Low countries, English as well as Dutch sailors and privateers seized Spanish ships, including ones sailing with goods to the Polish port city of Gdańsk.

But the English were pleased in July 1597 when they learned that Sigismund was sending a special ambassador and saw it an excellent sign that there would be better relations, especially as they thought this was a sign of peace. In December 1559 Sigismund's father, then John Duke of Finland and brother of Erik XIV, had come to visit Elizabeth, and she now wanted to honor his son. Paul de Jaline, or Pawel Dzialynski/Dzialin, was a royal secretary to the Polish king; he was highly educated and known for his urbanity. The Privy Council told the Lord Mayor of London that the house of Sir John Spencer was to be made ready for the guest and his entourage. Robert Cecil in a letter to Robert Devereux, Earl of Essex, described de Jaline as "a gentleman of excellent fashion, wit, discourse, language and person." Since the queen so wanted to honor Sigismund and the report she had of de Jaline was so positive, the queen "did resolve to receive him publicly in the Chamber of Presence, where most of the earls and noblemen about the court attended, and made it a great day." On July 25, in the room filled with the nobles she had invited, de Jaline came in beautifully dressed in a long-embroidered robe of black velvet. He kissed the queen's hand but then surprised everyone by stepping back about ten feet and "then began his oration aloud in Latin with such countenance as in my life I never beheld," Robert Cecil wrote to Essex. His oration, loud and furious, was filled with insults because of the troubles between England and Spain, how important the relationship was between Poland and Spain, and the king's anger at how the English actions were sabotaging it. De Jaline lectured the queen on what he called her bad behavior toward Polish merchants which was "mere injustice." He accused her of "assuming thereby to herself a superiority not tolerable over other princes" (Elizabeth I, *Collected Works*, 334, 335). Elizabeth and all her court were shocked. The Lord Chancellor Sir Thomas Egerton started to rise to respond but before he could the queen "Lionlike rising" (Speed, 899) responded herself in Latin, with a brilliantly quick-witted rebuke. "Oh, how was I deceived! I expected an ambassage, and you have brought a complaint," she told him, and was quick to put him in his place. "I marvel, I marvel indeed at so great and so insolent boldness in open presence, and I cannot believe that if your king had been in place he would have uttered such speeches." But if this was from the king, "if by hap he gave you commandment to utter them … [he is] a young man … not so perfectly the course of the handling of such business with other princes as his ancestors have observed with us." She had more to say to him as well. "And concerning our self, you seem unto me to have read many books, but books of princes' affairs you have not attained unto, and are further ignorant what is convenient between princes." Robert Cecil was so impressed by what he described as her wise and eloquent answer. "To this I swear by the living God, that her Majesty made one of the best answers, ex temper, in Latin, that ever I heard" (Janet Green, 989, 1005). Essex wrote back to Cecil "what a princely triumph she had of him by her magnanimous, wise, and eloquent answer! It was happy for her majesty that she was stirred and had so worthy an occasion to show herself" (Elizabeth I, *Collected Works*, 335). But it was not only the court that was celebrating their queen. Janet Green suggests that "probably all London, was ringing with her praise" (Green, 992), and argues that in Elizabeth's reign this speech was as celebrated as the one at Tilbury.

De Jalin realized that his behavior had been completely inappropriate. The Privy Council told the London merchants to shun him. There were no more visits, no presents. Elizabeth asked Burghley, his son Robert, Lord William Howard, and Sir John Fortescue to deal with "all the barking of his ambassador," as Robert Cecil put it (Green, 991). Burghley had an answer ready for the ambassador, which impressed Elizabeth, in two days. De Jaline was invited to appear before this commission. So that he fully understood the queen's displeasure, Burghley kept the ambassador standing. De Jaline made his apology, but did so by attempting to shift the blame, stating that he had only delivered an oration that had been written for him. By August 15 he had left England. In Poland he wept when he explained his disgrace to the Council.

Jewish Refugees

Edward I expelled all Jews from England in 1290. Though there were few if any Jews left in England in the Middle Ages, the view of them as inhuman and monstrous became ever more intense. Described as those who caused Jesus's crucifixion, Jews were associated with sorcery, mass poisonings, and the ritual murder of Christian children. Elizabeth's own attitude toward Jews is explicit in a letter she wrote to her sister Mary condoling her about rebels, and how appalled she was "to see the rebellious hearts and devilish intents of Christians in names, but Jews in deed" (Elizabeth I, *Collected Works*, 43). Jews were formally readmitted under Oliver Cromwell in 1656. But Jews began to return to England in the sixteenth century, though they needed to live as unnoticed as possible and officially present themselves as Christians.

In Henry VIII's reign in the 1530s, to make the court more glamourous, Thomas Cromwell invited Italian musicians to immigrate. At least nineteen who came were of Jewish background. The most significant were the members of the Bassano family and the Lupo family. The next generation of both families were musicians at Elizabeth's court (see Chapter 16). Emilia, or Aemilia, Bassano was the daughter of the court musician Baptiste Bassano, who died when she was seven. She lost her mother, the English woman Margaret Johnson who may have been an aunt to the court composer Robert Johnson, when she was eighteen. Soon after she became the mistress of Elizabeth's cousin Henry Carey, Baron Hunsdon. In 1592, when she became pregnant, Hunsdon settled some funds on her, and she married her cousin Alphonso Lanier, another court musician, though this marriage was unhappy. Lanier was pursued by the astrologer Simon Forman. In the Jacobean period she became a renowned poet. The Bassanos assimilated fairly well. Within a generation or two most of their descendants were at least publicly practicing Christians, but some scholars argue that many, including Lanier, secretly kept their Jewish identities.

There was a small organized Jewish community in London who practiced their religion in secret. There was also such a community in Bristol. Many of these Jews had fled the Iberian Peninsula and were merchants and some doctors. A number of these Jews left England as Henry VIII became more intolerant after Cromwell's 1540 execution and even more when Mary I ascended the throne and restored Catholicism.

When Elizabeth became queen however, if Jews maintained themselves outwardly as Christians, they could continue to live their lives quietly. Many more foreigners were in England under Elizabeth than earlier in the century. The Inquisitors in Spain were aware that many Jews had fled to England. The 1588 Spanish Inquisition records stated that "it is public and notorious in London, that by race they are all Jews, and it is notorious that in their own homes they live as such observing their Jewish rites" (Seton-Rogers, 7). Certainly, if it were known about in Spain, Elizabeth and her government knew as well. But if these people on the one hand kept quiet about their private activities but on the other brought their economic and professional skills to bear, they were not in danger. It appears that it was an open secret that there were Jews in Elizabethan England.

Dr. Hector Nuñez

Nuñez, both a doctor and a merchant, had connections with the court. He was from Portugal, where he had gotten his medical training, but decided he would be safer in England, settling in London in 1549. He was elected a fellow of the Society of Physicians in 1554. Nuñez combined a medical practice with international trade. His wife Leonor was also a Portuguese Jew. Among those who used Dr. Hector, as they called him, as a medical consultant were many people at court including William Cecil and his wife Mildred, and Lord Henry Howard. Nuñez and Sir Thomas Heneage, Treasurer of the Queen's Privy Chamber, were friends. He also helped with treaty negotiations with Portugal in 1572, and Walsingham asked for his aid in working on negotiations with Spain in the 1580s. He also used his Iberian connections to inform Walsingham about plans for the Armada as the negotiations broke down. Nuñez died in 1591.

Joachim Gaunse

Another man who fortunately enough ended up with ties to Lord Burghley and especially Walsingham was Joachim Gaunse. Walsingham was the governor of the Royal Mining Company. Around 1581, Walsingham's agent George Nedham invited Gaunse, a Jew who was from Prague who had a great knowledge of chemistry and metallurgy, to come to England to improve the work of the copper mines at Keswick in Cumberland and later also in Neath, Wales and probably Cornwall. Gaunse brought great innovations. Traditionally it took English smelters months to purify a batch of copper but with Gaunse's new process it took only a few days. Copper was critical for producing bronze, and bronze was needed in the 1580s as the English government wanted to strengthen their military preparedness as war with Spain was looming. Bronze allowed for the manufacturing of accurate cannons for warships.

In 1585 Sir Walter Raleigh was so impressed with Gaunse that he asked him to join the Roanake expedition as metallurgist and mining supervisor. Gaunse was the first Jewish person to set foot on North American soil. The first effort at colonization was a failure and colonizers were happy to return to England when Sir Francis Drake stopped there the following year. For the next three years Gaunse continued his work with mining, traveling to different mines. He found housing in Blackfriars in London, but he also spent time in Bristol, possibly because of the Jewish community there.

In September 1589 Gaunse was in Bristol. A Bristol minister, Richard Curteyes, who knew some Hebrew, heard from a man named Jeremy Pierce about Gaunse's beliefs. Curteyes told Gaunse that he wanted the opportunity to speak in Hebrew and Gaunse agreed to meet him at Richard Meyes's inn. But since Curteyes believed that Gaunse was an infidel, Curteyes invited several more men to be witnesses to the conversation. So instead of a chance to practice his Hebrew, Curteyes decided to interrogate Gaunse as they spoke Hebrew, asking what he thought about Christ's divinity. Gaunse replied he did not believe that Christ was the son of God. This was, as Curteyes called it, so odious, that he switched to English so more could witness what Gaunse had to say. Despite the dangers, Gaunse made the decision to stay true to himself, stating that since God was almighty, he had no need for a son. Curteyes took his witnesses with him and reported Gaunse to Robert Hitchen, Mayor of Bristol, which led to Gaunse being brought in to be examined before the mayor and aldermen of the city. At this time Gaunse said he was not a heretic but was proudly a Jew who was circumcised and had never been baptized. Hitchen declared Gaunse to be "a most wicked Infidel," and "his ungodly and most heathenish opinions and demeanor" should not "be suffered among Christians" (Abrahams, 99).

Hitchen and the aldermen were very concerned and decided, especially given Gaunse's connections, that they would write to the Privy Council and ask the members how they should deal with Gaunse. Unfortunately, Gaunse's records end with this letter. Though we have many Privy Council meeting minutes it is possible that the one dealing with him is missing. What is more likely, however, was that Walsingham and Burghley, given what Gaunse had done for the government, made the choice to either connive "at his quietly remaining in England," as Israel Abrahams suggests (92), or he was smuggled out of England for his safety.

Solomon Cormano

In 1592 Solomon Cormano arrived in London with messages for Elizabeth from the wealthy Jew Solomon Ben Ya'esh, born in Portugal as Alvoro Mendez. Mendez had been a goldsmith who made a fortune in India. As the Inquisition had become more intense on the Iberian Peninsula, Mendez had traveled in Europe, including England, before he settled in the Ottoman Empire in 1585 and publicly reclaimed his Jewish faith. He was a close confidant of Ottoman Emperor Murad, and one reason he sent Cormano and his entourage was to encourage close relations between England and the Ottoman Empire. While in London, Cormano held Jewish services where he was staying. Edward Barton, the English ambassador in Istanbul wrote to Burghley after Cormano had returned, and they had a meeting. Barton told Burghley that Cormano had stated that he and his entourage had not only themselves practiced their religious services but did so with some of secret residents in London.

The Jew of Malta and Roderigo Lopez

But this open secret only worked until a spotlight was turned on any of them. Certainly, the public perception of Jews was negative, with people often referring to someone who acted cruelly as acting very "Jewishly." Popular ballads often referred to Jews as dangerous villains. Christopher Marlowe's popular play *The Famous Tragedy of the Rich Jew of Malta*, was first performed in February 1592. The main character Barabas is such a monster that his revenge on his daughter Abigail, who leaves him because of his horrific actions, is to not only murder her but all the sisters in the nunnery where she sheltered (Fig. 11.1).

The negative feelings Londoners had about Jews became intense in 1594 when Roderigo Lopez, brother-in-law of Alvoro Mendez and physician to Queen Elizabeth and other members at court, was charged with planning to murder the queen (see Chapter 9). Though publicly an Anglican, Lopez was part of the small community in London who secretly practiced their Jewish faith, and friend and foe alike publicly referred to Lopez as "the Jew." At the time of the trial there was a revival of Marlowe's play, with twice as many performances as the original one, and Londoners clearly made the connections between Barabas and Lopez. Thomas Edgerton, lead prosecutor at the Lopez trial, described him as "Lopez, a perjured murdering traitor, and Jewish doctor, worse than Judas himself, undertook to poison" the queen (State Papers Online). Lopez was found guilty, and Sir Robert Cecil declared that this verdict had the applause of the entire world. In June 1594, when Lopez was taken to his execution at Tyburn, there were massive jeering crowds. That August his widow Sarah wrote to the queen beseeching her for help for her and her five children as they were in such misery and dire straits. Elizabeth helped the widow and her children.

Fig. 11.1 Lopez private collection

Those Brought to England Without Their Consent
Ippolyta and the Dark-Skinned Page Boy

During Anthony Jenkinson's travels after he left Moscow in September 1558 one of the places that he went was the war-destroyed ruins of Astrakhan in Central Asia, an area Ivan had conquered in 1556. The native people of the area were the Nogai tribe, who practiced Islam. Thousands of them had become enslaved, and Jenkinson himself purchased several, remarking how inexpensive they were, one of whom was a young girl he called Aura Soltana, whom he dismissively referred to as a "wench" in a letter. This could mean a young girl but could also be a woman of low status or loose morals.

We will never know her name at the time of purchase. He returned to Moscow, again feted by the Tsar, and returned to England in 1560. He gave the girl to Queen Elizabeth as a "gift" to show his loyalty. At Elizabeth's court she was given yet another name, Ippolyta, probably at the time she was baptized, and the little we know of her, from some scarce court records, is with that name, Ippolyta the Tartarian. She was no doubt quite young as one of the early gifts she was given was a doll, a baby made of pewter. Every year she had a clothing allowance and some years there were also warrants for new clothes for her in the records. The money allotted for her garments suggest she was as fancily dressed as other court ladies. In the 1564 warrant for elegant new clothes for her, the queen referred to her as someone dear and well-beloved. She had two pairs of Spanish leather shoes made for her. The last record for her is from 1569 when a black cloak was made for her out of rabbit fur lined with a rich silk fabric that was woven with beautiful and elaborate designs. There are no records describing her service, suggesting that she may have simply been a companion to the queen. While she may well have had beautiful clothing and no onerous duties, we also need to note that she was brought to a strange land with no choice whatsoever, seen as someone exotic, with her own history erased.

Also, in the wardrobe records is a reference in 1574 of a small, black-skinned boy, who was a page boy who attended the Queen. Elizabeth had made for him a white silk coat striped with gold and silver, knitted stockings, a pair of garters, a pair of white shoes, and another pair of white pantofles, which were indoor shoes with high-heeled cork soles. There was record of more clothes made for him in 1575. Unfortunately, these are the only records of him that exist.

Calichough, Ignorth, and Nutioc

Martin Frobisher also kidnapped people to present to the queen, but the Inuit people, forced to be in England, died before they could be brought to court. In 1576 Frobisher brought back one man, wanting to show the English people, but especially his queen, about the strange lands and even more the strange people he had encountered. But the poor man only survived for a few weeks after his arrival. The following year he brought back to Bristol what appeared to be a family: a man, a woman, and a child of about fourteen months. The man was called Calichough, the woman Ignorth, and her son, whom she was breast feeding, named Nutioc. In fact, the man was captured at a different time from the woman and her child. There were a number of descriptions of them from the people of Bristol, and John White, who a decade later would go to Roanoke, made sketches of them. The Cathay Company sent the Flemish artist Cornelis Ketel to Bristol to paint their portraits, and he did five paintings of Calichough. Three were of him in his native dress, in one he was dressed as an English gentleman, and one of him naked. It was as if Calichough was a scientific specimen instead of a human being. Ketel also made four paintings of Ignorth. A number of these paintings were intended as gifts for the queen, and Jacob Rathgeb, the Duke of Wurtemburg's secretary, described the lifelike portraits when they toured Hampton Court. Unfortunately, the paintings are now lost, though we do still have White's drawings.

Though Calichough had been hurt when captured or onboard ship to England, for an audience of people of Bristol he rowed a little boat and used a dart to kill two ducks. People remarked on how strange they thought both Callichough and Ignorth were—instead of linen and wool they were wearing animal skins and they ate raw fish. While they were in Bristol they were in the care of Dr. Edward Dodding, but by early November Calichough was dead, and soon after so was Ignorth. The child Nutioc was sent to London in the care of a nurse so that Elizabeth could see him, but in London he too became ill and died before he could be presented to the queen.

Manteo and Wanchese

Walter Raleigh also had Amerindians brought to England in the 1580s. But instead of considering them exotic or subjects to be examined or to entertain, Raleigh wanted them trained as interpreters and guides. In 1585 two men, Manteo and Wanchese, were brought to London and Raleigh lodged them at Durham House. Thomas Hariot stayed there also. He not only tutored them in English but also learned their language and devised an alphabet of 36 symbols to express what he called the Virginian language. The two were in England for about eight months but they clearly felt very differently about their experience. Manteo was loyal to the English for the rest of what we know about his life. Wanchese very strongly was not. They were both returned to North America as part of the 1585 expedition under Richard Grenville, the first attempt to establish a colony at Ronaoke. The first group was virtually all men, adventurers instead of families. John White and Thomas Hariot were among those at Roanoke. Manteo tried to establish positive relationships with the local people, while Wanchese rejoined his people. Grenville returned to England for more supplies, leaving Ralph Lane in charge. Manteo saved Lane and a large scouting party when he warned Lane that the Amerindian singing that he heard in the distance was not a welcome—rather they were preparing to attack. Francis Drake stopped at Roanoke and the colonists returned to England with them. Manteo also went with them, along with another Amerindian, Towaye, possibly a kinsman of Manteo. They again stayed at Durham House and were extremely helpful in the plan for the next attempt at colonization. Londoners noted them as they were paraded through London. Grenville returned to Roanoke about two weeks after Drake had taken the colonists away, and Grenville had fifteen men stay at Roanoke to maintain the English claim. The 1587 group of colonists had a number of families. John White was the governor. When they arrived, Manteo found out that the English Grenville had left behind had been slaughtered by Wanchese and others of his tribe. White left after some months to bring back more supplies from England, but because of events beyond his control, especially the Spanish Armada, he was not able to return until 1590. Manteo had stayed with the colonists, and we do not know the fate of the colonists or his fate either. In the 1590s Raleigh also had some natives of Guiana brought to England for language training and information in the geography of the region.

Though not as light skinned as the English, Ippolyta, Callichough, Ignorth and Nutioc, Manteo, Wanchese, and Towaye were not dark skinned like Africans. Bernadette Andrea suggests that Tartars and Inuits did not appear "other" in the way Africans would (301). We have a brief reference to another

Russian slave in 1569. We are not sure of the nationality of the slave, and the case had to do with the illegality of slavery in sixteenth-century England. The slave in question could have been a Tartar, or Russian, Finnish, or Polish. A man named Cartwright was a merchant who was seen savagely beating a man. When he was stopped, he claimed he had the right to beat him as he was a slave he had bought while he was in Russia. The resultant case stated that Cartwright did not have the right to beat the man, and he could not in England own a slave. The man was freed from his service.

The issue came up again in 1587. Hector Nuñez, the Jewish doctor and merchant discussed earlier, wrote to the queen to complain about a slave he had purchased a year earlier. Sir Francis Drake and his men had ransacked some Spanish settlements including Santo Domingo, which is now a city in the Dominican Republic, and had taken with them some slaves that had most likely been brought there from West Africa. Many of these Africans, as well as many of the English onboard, died in a terrible storm. A sailor named John Lax convinced one of the survivors to come with him to London after they had landed in Portsmouth in 1586, and in London sold him to Hector Nuñez for 4£, 10 s. Nuñez had two African women servants, called Grace and Mary, who were in household at the time, though called servants we do not know if they received wages. Unfortunately, we do not have any name for the man Nuñez purchased, but he clearly had courage given his situation in a place so foreign to him, as he refused to serve as a slave. Nuñez begged the queen to either recover his money from Lax or force the man to serve him. We do not have the queen's answer but given the earlier case it is likely that Nuñez lost both his money and the man he would enslave, though we do not know what life the man was able to create for himself in Elizabeth's England.

In 1577 William Harrison wrote that "As for slaves and bondmen, we have none; nay such is the privilege of our country by the especial grace of God and bounty of our princes, that if any come hither from other realms, so soon as they set foot on land they become as free in condition as their masters" (*Chronicle and Romance*, 239). However, for those who were brought into Elizabethan England without their consent and were either kept or given as gifts they often found they had little choice about their lives, de facto slaves. Lives like Ippolyta might at least seem luxurious; others did not even have that.

Polonia

A case with certain parallels with Ippolyta is that of Polonia, who we also unfortunately do not know much about, or what her ultimate fate was. In 1597 Mrs. Peirs consulted the medical practitioner and astrologer Simon Forman about the illness of her twelve-year-old African live-in maid Polonia. Forman noted that she had much pain on the side of her stomach and a "faint heart, full of melancholy" (Ungerer, 24). The cure he prescribed was to "purge her of Neptune," apparently choosing a propitious time astrologically for her to be purged. We have no information about how Polonia came to be a part of the Piers household, though Imtiaz H. Habib argues that Piers was a merchant who had either acquired her himself or she was a "gift" (105). It is possible that Polonia was suffering from menstrual problems though more likely it was depression caused by being taken away from her home and forced to work in a completely different culture, given that in the sixteenth century the average age for a girl to begin menstruation was eighteen.

African Servants—Or Slaves?

Many associated with Elizabeth's court also had Africans working in their households. It is not entirely clear if they were paid servants or de facto slaves. Edward Stanley, Earl of Derby referred to some of his domestic staff in 1568 as slaves. Arthur Throckmorton, son of the ambassador Sir Nicholas Throckmorton, mentioned that he had acquired Anthony, a black man from Guinea, sometime between 1587 and 1591. In 1592 the Privy Council approved commercial expeditions to Sierra Leone, which would have allowed more Africans brought forcibly to England. Anthony was probably a "gift" from his brother-in-law Sir Walter Raleigh, who had kidnapped the man on one of his voyages. In 1597 Raleigh had his page, a boy of about ten whom he had brought back to England from what is now Guyana, baptized as a Christian named Charles. Robert Cecil's African servant Fortunatus was buried at St. Clements Danes in 1602.

There was also a black community in Edinburgh that had been established at the end of the fifteenth century when the Portuguese took a Scottish ship and claimed all the possessions. James IV ordered his navy to take over a Portuguese ship, which happened to be a slave ship. The Africans in Edinburgh were often seen as exotic and used for ceremonial purposes. At the baptism of James VI's son Henry in 1594, the original intention was to have the royal carriage pulled by a lion, but the organizers became afraid that the lion might be too difficult to control. They substituted a black man who was given rich, exotic apparel and chains of pure gold.

Diego

Francis Drake had a black manservant called Diego. In 1571 he escaped from his Spanish masters when Drake raided the town of Nombre de Dios in what is now Panama. Diego spoke both English and Spanish and was very valuable to Drake as he was seeking Spanish treasure and Diego also helped him negotiate provisions for his men. He was again with Drake as he explored the Pacific Ocean. But in 1578 when Drake stopped at Mocha Isle off the coast of Chile for water and provisions Diego was killed by some islanders.

Maria

The other example of Drake's dealings with Africans is extremely disturbing, and comes from the account Francis Fletcher, the chaplain aboard Sir Francis Drake's 1587–1590 circumnavigation of the globe, kept on the voyage. He described how soon after stopping at Ternate on what is now known as the Maluku Islands in Indonesia Drake stopped at an island with many forests for wood supplies. But Drake also left behind three Africans, two men and a woman. Drake named the island Francisca, saying he was naming it after one of the male Africans, but of course that name and Maria, the way the African woman was referred, were names given them by Drake as opposed to what they called themselves. They were left because Maria "being gotten with childe in the ship, and now being very great" (Fletcher, 184), they did not want her to give birth on the ship. Fletcher added that he did not know who fathered the child, as she had been used by the captain and his men. It appears obvious that she had been repeatedly raped. Abandoning the three was most probably the equivalent of a death sentence.

Expelling Africans

The 1590s was a difficult period in England with inflation and poor harvests. This most likely contributed to Elizabeth's proclamation in 1601 declaring that she was expelling Africans from England. But there were other reasons as well, and it appears that in the end the expulsion never happened. Elizabeth's proclamation states that she is very concerned for the welfare of her subjects "distressed in these hard times of dearth." She stated that her people were annoyed and discontented about how the "Blackamoors which (as she is informed) are crept into this realm since the troubles between Her Highness and the king of Spain," and that they were consuming resources necessary for the native-born English. Another reason for explusion was that "most of them are infidels." In fact, many of the Africans in England had been baptized. The proclamation ends by stating that the Queen had "Caspar van Zenden, merchant of Lubeck for their speedy transportation" (Bartels, 316). There are many issues with this proclamation. The small number of Africans in England made little difference to the ability of native-born English people to work or to have food and lodging. Moreover, the Africans in England did not creep in— overwhelmingly they were brought in against their will. But van Zenden had already been involved in a prisoner exchange with Africans between Spain and Portugal. Other correspondence with Robert Cecil reveals that he saw this as a money-making venture for him—he would not return the people to Africa, but rather would sell them as slaves in the Iberian Peninsula. One problem with the fulfillment of the proclamation was that most people who had Africans in their households refused to give them up. Van Zelden wanted to claim them anyway, but this made Robert Cecil very uncomfortable, possibly because he had at least one African in his own household. Despite Elizabeth's decree we have no evidence that any Africans were taken away, and as the seventeenth century continued more Africans were forcibly brought to England.

CHAPTER 12

Mirrors

In John Speed's 1632 *History of Great Britain*, he wrote that on September 7, 1533 Anne Boleyn "bare into the world that excellent Princess, which afterwards proved the mirror of the world, even Lady Elizabeth, our late and most famous Queen" (771). Elizabeth herself must have thought of the symbolic meaning of mirrors when she was very young. Her father married her last stepmother, Katherine Parr, when she was nine, and the two became very close. Elizabeth wanted to give Katherine a special gift. When she was eleven, she did a prose translation into English of one of Katherine's favorite texts, Marguerite of Navarre's French poem, *The Mirror of the Sinful Soul*. In the poem the female narrator is a sinful soul who offers the readers a mirror in which they can see their own souls. Elizabeth gave Katherine the translation with the pages bound together and a cover she embroidered herself. The dedication, which stated that she wished the queen everlasting joy, was written on the last day of the year of 1544 at her residence at Ashridge (see Chapter 16).

In Tudor times mirrors were important in actuality and as metaphor, especially in relation to Queen Elizabeth. There have been many stories told and retold about Elizabeth's hatred of mirrors in the later years of her reign. But Elizabeth's own history with mirrors is more complex and given the mirrors in her palaces, she was not as hostile to seeing her reflection as has been often stated.

The use of mirrors goes back to the ancient world. High quality glass mirrors were a luxury in Elizabethan England. They were also referred to as looking glasses or simply as a glass. Venice was the center for the creation of mirrors. They were created out of blown glass that was then flattened, polished, beveled, and silvered. The image in these mirrors was often very clear and sharp and they were shipped out to places all over Europe. Less high quality, but much less expensive glass mirrors, were created in the Holy Roman Empire and Antwerp. Mirrors created out of tin were inexpensive and available but not of great value. Mirrors came in all sizes, often decorated in the frame with jewelry or art. Some would be very large and placed on a wall in a palace, while pocket mirrors, used by both women and men, were sometimes worn as necklaces. They were also hung from a jeweled belt, or in the base of a fan, or on a tobacco container. Large mirrors could lighten a room or simulate a window if they were hung opposite one. Mirrors were also sometimes perceived as a way to see a person's soul, which may be one of the reasons that going back to the ancient world breaking a mirror was associated with bad luck and ill fortune.

The gift of a fine mirror was extravagant enough to merit being noted. Sir Francis Walsingham was looking for a gorgeous mirror and William Brooke, Baron Cobham wrote to him describing a small mirror that a woman could wear hanging from a belt that was set in gold with many small diamonds and rubies and on the back an engraving of a palace, but it would cost 200 crowns. A mirror that was sent to the Ottoman Emperor was as big as a man and its frame was adorned with many jewels. Elizabeth gave Thomasina de Paris, a female dwarf for whom she cared very much, many gifts including looking glasses (see Chapter 16).

In 1564 Thomas Randolph noted to William Cecil that Mary Stuart had received a looking glass whose frame had many gemstones. Mary was greatly upset in 1586 when many of her belongings were confiscated, including a mirror. It was described as having covers on each side that were portraits—one was of Elizabeth and the other of Mary. These covers were also enameled, and the designs contained diamonds, rubies, and emeralds. While Mary and Elizabeth never met, their images were side by side covering a mirror, which could be conceived as a window into their souls. It is interesting to think that the images of the two queens were so close together, while the queens themselves were never in the same room.

Some mirrors of the time were made to be deliberately distorting, particularly convex mirrors which reflected objects either larger or smaller, sometimes causing the image to be grotesque. Some duplicated everything, and there are a few mirrors mentioned that had many images of the same thing. Some mirrors were thought to be magic.

Mirrors were considered so interesting they were often described metaphorically as a means to greater perception and truth. In Elizabeth's reign dozens of texts were published that included the title mirror, using it as a way for someone to learn about a subject, such as *A mirror for mathematiques a golden gem for geometricians, The mariners mirror* or *the mirror of alchemy*. Others were concerned with health, such as *The mirrour or glasse of health Necessary and needefull for every person to looke in* or *The Mirror of Madness*. There were many mirror texts that discussed religion or politics, while others discussed the value of friendship. Many were manuals for proper behavior and provided advice on being a better person, such as *A glasse for all disobedient sonnes to looke* or *A myrrour for virtuous maydes*. The term "mirror of modesty" occurred in several titles, the most famous by Thomas Salter. One mirror text was violently opposed to theatre: William Rankins' *A mirrour of monsters wherein is plainely described the manifold vices, &c spotted enormities, that are caused by the infectious sight of playes*. One of the most famous was *The Mirror for Magistrates*, which examined the tragic lives of many important historical figures. Richard Robinson's 1589 *A golden mirrour conteining certaine pithie and figuratiue visions prognosticating good fortune to England* is a celebration of the victory of the Armada and the queen through a dream vision. After seeing Drake's victory, he describes the crowds

> With singing, ringing· and clapping handes they sayd,
> God save our Noble Quéene, our mother and a mayd
> And all with chearefull voyce did sing and pray,
> God save our Noble Quéene *Elizabeth* alway. (Robinson, 10)

The crowd made such a joyous noise that the dreamer awoke and decided he must write down seeing the vision as a mirror.

Elizabeth herself used mirrors as metaphors, for example, writing to the Duke of Anjou in December 1579, she stated, "My dearest, I give you now a fair mirror to see there very clearly the foolishness of my understanding, which I found so suited to hoping for a good conclusion," when there was such a strong negative response by the English to her marrying him (Elizabeth I, *Collected Works*, 238–239). She also used the idea of a mirror when she wrote to James VI in 1593 when there had been some trouble between them: "I would you could behold as in a glass the inside of my inward heart unto you, and there you should view no hate to any no bloody desire, no revenging mind, but all fraught with thoughts how safely to preserve you from domestic and foreign guiles" (*Salisbury Papers*, IV, 334).

Many people wrote to Queen Elizabeth begging for help or mercy and in their addresses often called the queen a mirror of fine qualities. In 1571, Edmund Mather was found guilty of planning to murder Elizabeth and sentenced to be executed; he wrote to the queen suggesting that she should give him mercy because she was a mirror of clemency. In this case Elizabeth did not choose to be such a mirror; he was executed in 1572. When William Eure was in the Tower because of his communications about the succession with James VI, he wrote to the queen begging for his freedom and called her the sole mirror of justice. He did much better when James I became king. In June 1603 the new king awarded him an annuity of £100 for life (see Chapter 9). Sir Richard Hawkins, the son of John Hawkins, was also an explorer, who was captured by the Spanish during a trip to South America about 1594. After being kept in Lima for three years he was transferred to a prison in Seville. After he escaped and was recaptured, he was imprisoned more strictly in Madrid. In 1602 he wrote to both Robert Cecil and the queen, addressing

Elizabeth as the mirror of princes and his dread sovereign. That year Cecil was finally able to secure Hawkins' release.

That some mirrors could have potentially magical elements was a source of pleasure or of fear. Elizabeth sometimes visited the famous astrologer and magician John Dee. In March 1575 she asked him if he would show her his famous looking glass, and "and to show unto her some of the properties of it." Dee wrote in his diary that when he showed her the range of things she could see in it, she was delighted. Apparently, the mirror was convex or concave and provided optical illusions. Sir William Pickering (see Chapter 6) gave the mirror to Dee, and it was a prized possession. He eventually gave it to Edward Kelley, who worked as a conduit to Dee's angelic conversations, and Kelley then presented it to the Holy Roman Emperor Rudolf II.

Burghley, however, was very concerned about a magic mirror as potentially being used to harm Elizabeth. He described in the Privy Council meeting of March 11, 1591 how a lewd man of very dubious reputation had been showing a mirror that possessed many reflections of the queen. The man had been examined by his own secretary Vincent Skynner, and Burghley asked Sir Gilbert Gerard, Master of the Rolls, and Sir William Fleetwood, Recorder of London, to investigate further as he feared that in some way the queen could be harmed through this manipulation of her image. But the man had either escaped or Skynner had allowed him to leave. Fleetwood later explained that they searched in vain for him.

Elizabeth's palaces had many mirrors in them. One way we know about the places is that well-to-do young foreign aristocrats would travel to England (see Chapter 11). Baron Waldstein was in England at the end of Elizabeth's reign in 1600 and was presented to the queen. He found the palace of Whitehall to be a truly majestic place and noted a large mirror there. In 1613 the Duke of Saxe-Weimar also noted the mirror at Whitehall, adding that at the top of it was a portrait of Queen Elizabeth. When Philip Julius, Duke of Stettin-Pomerania, visited England in 1602, he was able to go into Queen Elizabeth's cabinet, a small private room. There he saw some beautiful books and a looking glass set with costly pearls. The place that most impressed Baron Waldstein was Hampton Court. After describing the Paradise Chamber, filled with gems and art, he then went into a gallery where he saw a splendid looking glass in gold and alabaster. The Duke of Stettin-Pomerania also noted seeing it, as did Paul Hentzner, who visited in the 1590s as a tutor to a Silesian nobleman. He also noted that it was very clear, as did the young Swiss physician Thomas Platter when he visited. At Hampton Court Baron Waldstein also saw in another gallery a very large mirror with the inscription "Salvator Mundi," Savior of the World. Hentzer also saw when he visited Windsor that there were two rooms for bathing whose walls were lined with mirrors.

Commentary about Elizabeth at the end of her reign, or after her death, often referred to her hatred of mirrors. These stories most likely had a kernel of truth to them, in that she probably did not enjoy looking at herself in small hand mirrors. Godfrey Goodman, Bishop of Gloucester, had another theory about how her ladies-in-waiting solved this problem. He reported he had heard that they had somehow obtained looking glasses that did not show Elizabeth's wrinkles. Magic mirrors indeed!

In 1603, shortly before the queen died, Sir John Manningham wrote in his diary a story he had heard that also involved a mirror. Sir Christopher Hatton and an unnamed knight had a challenge for who could present Elizabeth the truest picture of herself. One brought a flattering portrait, while the other a mirror, so that queen could look at herself and truly know what she looked like. Hatton had died in 1591 and the story is probably apocryphal. But Manningham did not record whether Hatton brought the portrait or the mirror or how Elizabeth was said to have responded, and which she preferred, flattery or truth.

But some of the stories were far nastier, whether for political reasons, or to emphasize her vanity and foolishness. In what appeared to have been a drunken conversation between the playwright Ben Jonson and William Drummond at the latter's home in 1618, Jonson made a variety of comments on Elizabeth's body and sexual behavior (see Chapter 15) but also stated that Elizabeth would never look at herself in mirrors and as a result her ladies could paint her nose vermillion and she would never know.

Elizabeth Southwell was one of Elizabeth's ladies-in-waiting at the time of her death and wrote about it later after she had eloped to Italy with Sir Robert Dudley in 1605 and converted to Catholicism (see Chapter 15). Southwell maintained that when the queen was dying, she had a vision of herself with her body in a light of fire, and the next day the queen asked for a true looking glass. This was the first time, asserted Southwell, that Elizabeth had been willing to look at herself in a real mirror for twenty years, as her ladies had shown her to herself with mirrors "made to deceive her sight" (Loomis, 485). Looking at herself, the queen realized that all who had commended her beauty were lying to her, and as a result they dared to not come before her now that she had seen what she truly looked like. John Clapham also stated that Elizabeth at the end of her life wanted to see herself in a mirror, and then perceived "how often she had been abused by flatterers whom she held in great estimation" (Clapham, 96).

In 1603, soon after Elizabeth's death, Henry Chettle published *England's Mourning Garment*, and he included a discussion of Elizabeth and mirrors. He wrote that he had heard it credibly reported, and accepted as true, that Elizabeth did not want to gaze into a mirror and trusted her ladies to have her look her best. He added he himself had seen some of her ladies hide away their looking glass if the queen was coming—suggesting that some of the young ladies-in-waiting enjoyed looking at themselves. But he also argued that while it was true Elizabeth never wanted to look at herself in a mirror, she avoided them not out of vanity or self-delusion, but rather because of modesty and humility. As Anna Riehl Bertolet argues, "in Chettle's interpretation, Elizabeth's refusal to see herself in the mirror offers an occasion for a compliment to her virtuous modesty" (Riehl, 61).

Elizabeth, especially when she was older, may well have preferred to avoid hand mirrors that showed her age and wrinkles. But the large wall mirrors in her palaces belie the statements that in the last decades of her reign she absolutely refused to ever look in a mirror. While Chettle agreed, but for very different reasons, that Elizabeth avoided mirrors, in *England's Mourning Garment*, he described Queen Elizabeth as the maiden mirror of the age.

CHAPTER 13

Dreaming Elizabeth

In the sixteenth century many people took their dreams seriously. In 1564 T. Hedley wrote to Thomas Randolph, saying that "Men fear the events of things they would not have come to pass, and dream nightly of their day's thoughts" (State Papers Online). Some dreams were thought to be just the fragments of the day, while others were haunting dreams of guilt. Many also believed that some dreams could be prophetic and significant. People wrote that they learned of the death of a loved one far away in dreams. Some were so moved by a dream that they immediately reacted when awake. One vivid example is from the French king, Henri III which we know about from a January 1583 letter Sir Henry Cobham, the English ambassador in France, sent to Sir Francis Walsingham. The king ordered his guards "to slay all the lions and other wild beasts which were kept for his pleasure," because of a dream he had just had in which he heard that the lions were planning to murder him (State Papers Online). There are many examples of dreams by French royalty, including Catherine de Medici, who in 1559, it is said, tried to warn her husband Henri II not to joust because of a dream she had. The king ignored her and died as a result of being harmed during the joust. Her son Charles IX had nightmares after the 1572 St. Bartholomew's Day Massacre, where he would mumble in his sleep about blood. People knew about these dreams during the reign of Elizabeth as they were written and gossiped about.

While the English royal dreams were perhaps not as dramatic as those in France, we know of several dreams that Elizabeth had that she mentioned. We also know about dreams that others had about Elizabeth both in England and beyond her shores, of dreams that may well have been invented, and dreams that were presented on stage. A number of dreams reveal the importance of Elizabeth's mother Anne Boleyn. Another important topic included anxieties that Elizabeth herself had about courtship and marriage, as well as others had about the queen, her sexuality, and the fear about lack of an heir. There were several dreams described about the crisis involving the execution of Mary Stuart. For her subjects, times of crisis appear to be when they especially dreamed about their queen—and wanted to let her know.

Early Dream About Anne Boleyn

A dream that was not about Elizabeth but was told to her was one Alexander Alesius relayed when she became queen. Alesius was born in Scotland in 1500 but had to flee when he was about thirty years old because of his reformed religious beliefs. He settled in Wittenburg, where he and Philip Melanchthon became close friends. In 1535 Alesius came to England, bringing Melanchthon's writings to Henry VIII and Archbishop Thomas Cranmer. Alesius settled in London, where he developed a close friendship with Cranmer. In 1539, when the political climate in England had become very hard on reformers, Alesius left. Twenty years later he wrote to the new queen. He wanted to tell her about a dream he had at the time of her mother's death that he thought might be significant to the new queen (Fig. 13.1).

Alesius first wanted the new queen to know that "I take to witness Christ, Who shall judge the quick and dead, that I am about to speak the truth." He explained that on the day that Anne Boleyn was to be executed, something happened. "There was revealed to me (whether I was asleep or awake I know not) the Queen's neck, after her head had been cut off, and this so plainly that I could count the nerves, the veins, and the arteries." He explained that he had been so "terrified by this dream," that he got up and left his lodgings and traveled to Lambeth, Archbishop Cranmer's residence. As Alesius went into the garden he saw the archbishop pacing. Cranmer asked Alesius why he had come so early, given it was not yet four in the morning. Alesius told Cranmer about the dream, and how horrified he had been. Cranmer was so stunned he stood "in silent wonder." Then he asked Alesius if he knew what would happen that day. Alesius said no. He had been staying in his lodgings since Anne Boleyn had been taken into the Tower. Cranmer explained that "the Queen of England upon earth will today become a Queen in heaven" (Levin, *Dreaming the English Renaissance*, 112). Then Cranmer burst into tears. Alesius wrote to Elizabeth so she would know about his dream and Cranmer's feelings. Elizabeth in quiet ways showed how much she valued her mother. One example is the ring the queen wore with a large E on it. But when the top of the ring opened, inside were two miniatures—one of her and one of her mother Anne Boleyn.

Fig. 13.1 Anne Boleyn private collection

Elizabeth's Dreams

In 1578 Queen Elizabeth was feeling great sadness, especially since Robert Dudley, Earl of Leicester, was not at court. Another of her favorites, Sir Christopher Hatton, wrote to Leicester that "the Queen is found in continual great melancholy," which he found difficult, and he could only guess at the reason. But then he offered an important clue in describing a dream she had told him. "She dreams of marriage that might seem injurious to her, making myself to be either the man or a pattern of him" (Levin, *Dreaming the English Renaissance*, 141). While Hatton was not the man, as one of the queen's favorites he might well have been the pattern, since the most important favorite was Leicester. And there were a few possible marriages that might have been troubling Elizabeth. She was in the midst of fraught marriage negotiations with François, Duke of Anjou, and Leicester had recently secretly married Lettice Knollys, the Earl of Essex's widow. Though theoretically Elizabeth did not yet know about it, she may have suspected. If only we could know if the queen herself had suggested that Hatton write to Leicester about her dream.

When Elizabeth officially learned of Leicester's marriage, she was furious, especially as he had not told her himself. This may be one reason she agreed to Anjou's visit in 1579, the only foreign suitor she allowed to come to England. She at least for a time took the courtship quite seriously (see Chapter 6), and after he left, they wrote often to each other. In January 1580 she called him "my dearest," and was writing to him in the middle of the night. "But at this hour I muse as do those on night watch, dreaming, not having slept well" (Elizabeth I, *Collected Works*, 245).

If worry about Leicester and Anjou caused Elizabeth to dream and have problems sleeping, how much more anxiety the queen would have had after Mary Stuart was found guilty at Fotheringay in October 1586. Though she had been condemned to die, Elizabeth did not want to sign her death warrant. Though by this time, after Mary's involvement in so many plots to have her murdered, she may well have wanted her cousin dead, Elizabeth feared how other monarchs would respond, and it greatly troubled her to think of executing an anointed queen. Neither Burghley nor Walsingham were well, but their illnesses might also have been strategic. It was up to Sir William Davison, her new Secretary, to obtain Elizabeth's signature. On February 1, 1587, after many attempts, Davison was again urging the queen to sign the warrant. She told him that she "had been troubled that night upon a dream she [had] that the Scottish Queen was executed." Davison later relayed the dream and that she claimed in it to "have been so greatly moved with the news against my self as in that passion she could have done I know not what." This was clearly a warning from the queen to Davison, but Davison did not take it too seriously as they had this conversation "in a pleasant and smiling manner" (Levin, *Dreaming the English Renaissance*, 142). She signed the warrant but also told Davison not to send it on without her express permission. Once he had secured her signature, however, he immediately informed Burghley, who convened a Council meeting in his room, and they agreed to dispatch it. Though Elizabeth must have known this would happen, she was furious with Davison, as she had warned him when she spoke of her dream, which Davison described after he was sent to the Tower. He was released in September 1588.

Propaganda Describing Dreams of Elizabeth

While Elizabeth may well have had dreams about Mary Stuart, they would not have been either of the dreams that Adam Blackwood described in the book he published in 1587, *Martyre de la rayne d'Escosse*. This piece of propaganda referred to Elizabeth as a bastard, who had "cruel and barbarous designs" in seeking the death of the Scottish queen. Blackwood was Scottish, but lived in France, and was an ardent supporter of Mary Stuart. Blackwood explained that as soon as Elizabeth had ordered Mary's execution, she began to doubt her decision. "The Harpy could not sleep the entire night having another demoness within in her soul who tormented her strangely and vengefully about the execution of her cousin, to such an extent that she repented of having ordered it." In Blackwood's account, Elizabeth is a Harpy whose soul is possessed with a demon who tormented her sleep. She was so upset that Sir Walter Mildmay got the Earl of Leicester out of bed; he went to see the queen, trying to convince her to rescind the execution order because, he said, he was sure there would be a bloody tragedy if the Scottish queen were to die. It is hard to imagine that the actual Leicester would have made that argument. According to Blackwood, Elizabeth listened, but then decided to reaffirm the death sentence despite her ill dreams. But this version was not the only one that Blackwood related. For good measure he added that "there are those who tell it differently." His second version has one of Elizabeth's ladies-in-waiting sleeping in the same room as the Queen. The lady-in-waiting, Madame de Stratford, cried out in a terrible voice that awakened the Queen; the lady then began weeping. Elizabeth asked Madame why she wept, and "she declared that she had seen the Queen of Scotland being beheaded and Immediately after this Elizabeth's head was cut off as well." Elizabeth responded, "that the same vision had appeared to her in her sleep leaving her greatly terrified" (Blackwood, 345–349). Such a dream could presumably terrify Elizabeth, though given its source it is highly doubtful she ever had it. The Madame de Stratford no doubt refers to Dorothy, Lady Stafford who was one of the women Elizabeth most wanted to sleep in her bed chamber with her. It is important to note that to the readers of Blackwood's text Elizabeth's comments to Madame reduced Elizabeth's strength and autonomy, and by being related second, it showed the "Harpy" and "demoness" as both terrified and weak, and much more deserving of execution than the martyr Mary (Fig. 13.2).

Sermon That Mentioned a Dream

The dean of Peterborough Richard Fletcher, one of Elizabeth's favorite pastors, preached before the queen at Greenwich right after the execution while the queen was still consumed with guilt and rage. Fletcher began his sermon with the text that stated, "The Angel of the Lord appeared to Joseph in Egypt in a dream, saying arise, and take up the child and his mother and return into the Land of Israel for they are dead that sought the child's life."

Fig. 13.2 Elizabeth signing death warrant private collection

Fletcher then told the queen that "the Angel of the Lord delivered you as miraculously as ever he did St. Peter." Fletcher was referring first to all the dangers Elizabeth faced when she was a prisoner during the reign of her Catholic half-sister Mary, where the queen's Catholic advisors wanted Elizabeth dead. Fletcher assured the queen and others at court that God's angels got great pleasure from smiting Elizabeth's enemies. Fletcher then discussed how angels protected the princess while she slept—and that Elizabeth may have experienced what the angels did as a dream that she had. God's angels first got the pleasure of smiting Elizabeth's enemies. One of the angels then struck the sleeping prisoner-princess "on the side with his right hand." This caused her chains to fall off. The angel then led the princess through the "iron gate that your enemies would have rampered," Fletcher told the queen, "against your most just and natural succession." But Fletcher also reminded the queen that God's angels not only protected her in her sister's reign but also against the many plots against her in which Mary Stuart was involved. Elizabeth's life had been saved, Fletcher asserted, because she had been "warned and informed of our enemies' secret maliciousness by the Angel of God, by divine and miraculous intelligence, the many detections of their manifest designment have sealed it unto you" (McCullough, 125, 129, 130). Fletcher was implying that in some sense Walsingham and his spy network were now Elizabeth's angels. Fletcher thought it important for the queen to recognize that for the good of her realm she had to accept the death of someone who had so severely threatened not only her but all of England.

English Dreams About Elizabeth

Thomas Chaloner

While Thomas Chaloner's 1562 dream did not specifically mention the queen, it was about one of the ladies of her bedchamber, Elizabeth Sandys. Though he was at the time ambassador to Spain, and very unhappy about his position there, he was thinking of whom he might marry when he returned to England and asked his youngest brother Francis to sound out Sandys. Unfortunately, she chose to marry Sir Maurice Berkeley instead. He wrote that he had a dream that predicted her refusal. He saw her leaving the privy chamber to head to the chapel beautifully dressed; a great number of ladies followed her. Even though in the dream he was beautifully dressed all in tawny, and friends told him he had never looked better, Sandys ignored him.

Mary Cocker

Mary Stuart's death did not end the anxiety in England over the war with Spain looming. In April 1587 Mary Cocker's nighttime experience was so intense that she felt the need to inform the authorities. Mary was the wife of the laborer Robert Cocker of Braughling in Hertford, and she testified before two justices of peace that late one night she was lying in bed, and she saw a presence that she thought must be a ghost. It was "a bright thing of long proportion without shape, clothed as it were in white silk." The creature kept circling her bed until she finally found the courage to speak to it. "In the name of God, what art thou and why troublest thou me?" The spirit or ghost had an important message for her to pass on to Queen Elizabeth. "Go to thy Queen and tell her that she receive nothing ... of any stranger, for there is a jewel in making for her which the party, if he could, would deliver to her own hands... which if she receive, will be her destruction. And if thou dost not tell her this much ... thou shall die the cruelest death that ever died any" (State Papers Online). As soon as the spirit completed its speech, it vanished. Though Cocker was married it is not clear if her husband was asleep and saw nothing or was not in bed at the time. Today it would appear that Mary Cocker had an unusually vivid dream that suggested her concern for the queen's safety. As people feared the Armada, and potential tragedy for England, this experience which was arguably a dream could represent great fear of what could happen. Keith Thomas argues that Mary's unconscious was "making explicit a great deal which could not be said directly" (Thomas, 600).

Many were very worried about the coming **Armada** (see Chapter 10) but through a combination of English naval skill and favorable weather conditions, the English triumphed. Robert Greene explained why God had allowed Philip II to send the Armada against England. God "brought in these Spaniards to waken us out of our dreams, to teach the brave men of this realm that after peace comes wars" (Greene, B4).

Simon Forman

In 1597 the astrologer Simon Forman recorded in his diary two different dreams that he had about the queen. Forman was a doctor and astrologer to many of the fashionable people in London, thought he had no formal medical training. He kept a very complete diary.

The first dream was particularly elaborate. He stated that he "dreamt that I was with the Queen, and that she was a little elderly woman in a coarse white petticoat all unready." All unready in the sixteenth century meant being in a state of partial undress, suggesting a sexual component to the dream. "She and I walked up and down through lanes and closes, talking and reasoning." Though Forman says the two had a conversation he did not relate what it was about—possibly he did not remember that part of the dream. "At last we came over a great close where were many people, and there were two men at hard words. One of them was a weaver, a tall man with a reddish beard, distract of his wits. She talked to him and he spoke very merrily to her, and at last did take her and kiss her" (Rowse, 20). A. L. Rowse argues that the weaver represented Essex, another tall man with a reddish beard who was known for his flirtations with the queen, though he was decades younger than she. It is an especially persuasive identification as the weaver was "distract of his wits" and "frantic." By 1597 many in London may well have realized how problematic Essex's behavior was. John Harington visited Essex in 1600 after he had returned from Ireland without the queen's consent (see Chapter 9). He found Essex "shifts from sorrow and repentance to rage and rebellion so suddenly as will prove him devoid of good reason or right mind ... he uttered strange words bordering on such strange designs, that made me hasten for and leave his presence" (Harington, I, 178–179).

The dream continued with Forman pulling the queen away from the weaver and then they walked down a dirty lane. In the way of dreams her clothing changed. "She had a long white smock very clean and fair, and it trailed in the dirt and her coat behind." At first Forman in the dream was polite. "I took her coat and did carry it up a good way, and then it hung too low before. I told her she should do me a favour to let me wait on her, and she said I should." But then he pushed for more intimacy. "Then said I, 'I mean to wait upon you and not under you, that I might make this belly a little bigger to carry up this smock and coat out of the dirt.' And so we talked merrily; then she began to lean upon me, when we were past the dirt and to be very familiar with me, and methought she began to love me. When we were alone, out of sight, methought she would have kissed me" (Rowse, 20). His comments suggest that he wanted to impregnate the queen, though of course the queen was far too old to bear a child. This need for a pregnant queen certainly implies great worry about what would happen to England when the queen was aged and childless. Elizabeth in the dream is not presented as traditionally sexually attractive—rather her attraction comes from her power. There are fascinating contradictions in the dream—queen more powerful than subject but male more powerful than female.

A month after this first dream, Forman recorded a second dream about the queen. In this one, she came to Forman dressed all in black, and she wore a French hood. In the first dream Elizabeth wore white; in the second she was completely in black. In the Renaissance black and white were the colors that represented virginity and purity. Elizabeth often liked to dress in black and white, and referred to them as her colors. The second dream, with the queen in black, may have been Forman's unconscious recognition that the reign was coming to an end. The French hood is especially interesting as while it was a headdress that English women wore in this period, there are also cases in the late sixteenth century where some women were forced to wear the French hood as punishment for charges of lasciviousness. Forman's dream could again be at some level discomfort with an unmarried female monarch, and again the intersections of sexuality and power with Elizabeth as queen of England.

Joan Notte

The weaver in Simon Forman's dream might have represented Essex. While Essex is not in Joan Notte's dream, the danger to the queen from Essex was the impetus for what invaded Notte's sleep. On March 20, 1601 John Garnons, who had previously been a justice of the peace, wrote to Robert Cecil about some disturbing dreams that his goddaughter had. Her husband related them to Garnons. Notte had two dreams she thought important enough to share with the government. In each of the dreams there were a variety of beasts that threatened both Elizabeth and her Robert Cecil. In one of the dreams

Anne Boleyn was also a character. Although she had been dead for nearly seventy years Notte described how "Queen Anne Boleyn... appeared warning Queen Elizabeth not to go further from London than St. James" (State Papers Online). It is interesting that in Joan Notte's dream it was Elizabeth's mother who came back from the dead to deliver the warning. Was Anne Boleyn's own spectacular and horrific death such a matter of public memory that those who felt anxious about Elizabeth's safety would connect the daughter to the mother? Notte's unconscious may have connected Anne Boleyn, a queen consort whose vulnerability was expressed by attacks on her sexual reputation and who had been unable to produce a living son, and Elizabeth, queen regnant, also called a whore by her enemies and also childless? Anne Boleyn was killed by her husband, the man who had so desired her that he had worked for almost seven years to make her his queen. Though over thirty years younger than Elizabeth, Essex approached the queen using romantic gestures; the rumors of sexual misconduct that had circulated throughout the reign about Leicester and Hatton had their last appearance in whispers about the queen and the young earl. Henry VIII had his wife Anne executed. Would Essex kill Elizabeth to become the king? At the beginning of her reign, Elizabeth learned about a dream about her mother from someone who had greatly admired her. At the end of the reign Anne Boleyn was in another dream, there to protect her daughter.

Spanish Dreams About Elizabeth

But it was not only Elizabeth's own subjects who dreamed about the queen. The story of Mary Stuart's execution, and Elizabeth's role in it, spread throughout Europe and influenced the dreams of those far from England reflecting a range of religious and political anxieties. In 1590 Philip II ordered the arrest of a twenty-one-year-old woman, Lucrecia de Leon, daughter of a legal clerk in Madrid. Lucrecia had vivid dreams that received widespread publicity and she was brought before the Spanish Inquisition.

Lucrecia's dreams reflected the anxieties of many people as Spain was at war with England. In her dreams she had guides she called the Ordinary man, the Lion Man, and the Old Man. They took her to visit foreign countries; England was a frequent destination. Her most vivid and horrifying dream about Elizabeth occurred on December 18, 1587. Lucrecia dreamed that she and her guide "flew across the seas and came to a seaport, where there were many ships, medium-sized and large, being made ready." Drake had been a character in her dreams previously and she saw him in this dream as well, about to pay the sailors who would fight against Spain. Drake went to his house, and "we saw how he took out from a safe place a hoard of treasure that he had hidden – this was something I had seen in another dream." Drake was well known in Spain for the treasure he had stolen from the Spanish. In the way of dreams, Drake's house then became the queen's palace. "From there we came into another room, where I saw a woman who looked a little more than fifty years old. The Ordinary Man said to me, 'Look, there is Elizabeth, queen of England.'" Though we would expect a queen to be on a throne, instead Elizabeth was sitting on a low stool. In her lap was a dead lamb, cut open. Lucrecia saw her "taking up with both hands the blood that was held inside the lamb and was drinking it with great relish." Sitting beside Elizabeth "was a very beautiful woman, though very pale and dressed in the black of a widow." Elizabeth ordered the beautiful widow to also drink of the lamb's blood, but she refused. The queen became very angry, "and stood up and, taking a sword from her side, she struck suddenly at the woman, cutting off her head." But the dream did not end there. Elizabeth then washed the lamb's blood off her hands and gave the lamb to Drake, who ordered that the remaining meat and skin be given to his soldiers. Drake ordered his men "that they should hang the flesh of the lamb from their banners," which Lucrecia interpreted as intended as an insult to Philip II. "Then the Ordinary Man took me back across the sea to the Old Man. As he did so I heard the sound of war drums" (Osborne, *Dreamer*, 61). The imagery in Lucrecia's dreams is shocking and horrifying. Lucrecia's dream guide does not explain the symbolism of the grisly scene of the queen and the dead lamb, but the lamb, a particularly potent religious image that often-represented Christ himself, may suggest persecuted Catholics, whom Elizabeth was devouring. The widow was clearly Mary Stuart. Elizabeth, instead of ordering Mary's execution, in the dream murders the Scottish queen herself, who by then had been dead ten months. Lucrecia's contemporaries also found this dream powerful and disturbing, demonstrating Elizabeth's ruthlessness as an enemy of Spain.

A week later on December 23, Lucrecia had another dream, this time about Elizabeth's older sister. Lucrecia saw "the English Queen Mary who appeared with a rope in her hands and about her throat. The Old Fisherman asked her, 'Why do you appear like that?'" Mary's answer in the dream was one that the historical Mary might have given at that moment had she had the opportunity. "Does it not seem to you that I deserve it since all of the sins committed by my sister fall upon me? There was a time when I could have remedied the situation and I did not" (Osborne, 87). One wonders too if Lucrecia was aware that it was in part Philip's influence when he was Mary's consort that saved Elizabeth's life. The dream reflected some guilt that Catholics had not taken care of Elizabeth years earlier when they had had the opportunity, and also suggests how strongly the Spanish feared Elizabeth.

James VI

In 1598 the King of Scotland had a dream that deeply disturbed him. He dreamed that though she was so much older than he was, Queen Elizabeth would outlive him, and he would never get to become king of England.

Literary Representations of Dreams

Dreams about Elizabeth also appeared in literature. Helen Hackett discusses the 1593 George Peele poem, "The Honour of the Garter," describing it as an "illustration of what a panegyrist could do in the genre of dream-vision" (46). The poem's narrator falls asleep outside of Windsor Castle. In his dream he noted armed men on horses emerging from clouds, and then saw a range of classical and biblical heroes. After that

> Under the glorious spreading wings of Fame,
> I sawe a Virgin Queen, attyrde in white ...
> Elizabeth on a compartment
> Of gold ...
> ...
> She was the Soveraigne of the Knights she led. (46)

There are several sixteenth century meanings for compartment, but it could mean the divisions of a shield, and Elizabeth appearing on a golden shield would show her as the powerful and beautiful ruler.

Only two years after the queen's death, Thomas Heywood dramatized the dangers Elizabeth faced in the reign of her older sister Mary in his play, *If I Know Not You, I Know Nobody*. This was clearly the point, as the subtitle was "The Troubles of Queen Elizabeth." At the beginning of the play Mary and her advisors discuss how Elizabeth must have been involved in Thomas Wyatt's rebellion, and Mary's Chancellor, Stephen Gardiner, Bishop of Winchester advises Mary that Elizabeth ought to be executed. These threats caused Elizabeth severe difficulties sleeping. One of her gentleman ushers tells a servant woman that "Her sleeps are all unquiet" (line 151). Elizabeth is then forcibly brought to court, and afterwards sent to the Tower, where she acts bravely despite her terror. Later in the play she is held at Woodstock guarded by Sir Henry Beningfield, as his name is spelled in the play. At Woodstock there are attempts to assassinate her. In a pivotal scene Elizabeth has been writing and then reading her English Bible. She then puts the Bible aside and tells her servant Clarentia

> My heart is heavy and my heart doth close,
> I am wearing of writing, sleepy on the sudden,
> Clarentia ... command some music
> In the with-drawing chamber. (lines 1042–1045)

As Elizabeth sleeps, she dreams of angels protecting her. What Fletcher has described in his sermon before her was now presented on stage. The stage directions have the Bishop of Winchester and several others including some friars appear from one side of the stage and two angels appear from the other.

The friars go to the sleeping princess beginning an attempt to murder her that the angels thwart. They drive Elizabeth's enemies off the stage. The angels open the English Bible that Elizabeth had been reading previously and put it in her hands as she sleeps. As Elizabeth awakens, the angels exit. The princess is not sure if she has had a dream or if it was something that had truly happened, asking Clarentia "saw'st thou nothing?" (line 1054) Clarentia tells Elizabeth that she did not see or hear anything. Elizabeth then realizes that she is now holding the Bible she had previously put aside and becomes convinced that she had a miraculous dream: "twas by inspiration" (line 1062). She is even more convinced when she sees where the Bible is opened to.

> Whoso putteth his trust in Lord
> Shall not be confounded. (lines 1064–1065)

Though the dream very much comforted Elizabeth, she was still not out of danger. But the audience would know that she would triumph as she does at the end of the play when she becomes queen. Dreams about and by Elizabeth demonstrated much anxiety, but Heywood's staging of the dream Fletcher spoke of demonstrates the love the people had for Elizabeth and their appreciation of her as a Protestant queen.

CHAPTER 14

Women Friends of Queen Elizabeth

When many people think about Queen Elizabeth and her relationships with others they think about her relationships with the men at her court, her favorites, and advisors. But she was also close to some women, and these relationships were clearly important. But it is also true that since Elizabeth was the daughter of a king—though one he declared illegitimate before she turned three—and then she eventually became queen, these friendships were never equal. She may well have felt most comfortable when she was with her women, but Elizabeth could never fully relax, nor could she fully trust and confide in any of the women she cared about. She learned early that to keep safe she had to keep her own counsel. The women around her, too, knew that the queen could get angry with them with impunity and also had to deal with her moods and moments of selfishness. When she cared about a woman the queen wanted her with her despite what else was going on in the woman's personal life, as her cousin Katherine Carey Knollys and her husband Francis learned to their dismay. The queen, however, cared deeply about some of the women at her court, and she mourned with them when they lost husbands and children, and deeply mourned herself when they died. Elizabeth held her court at several different palaces, so a number of these women who were appointed to her bedchamber or privy chamber would travel with her. Some of the women she was close to were in salaried positions, some in non-salaried positions, and some had no appointment at all. Below are descriptions of some of the women she most valued from the beginning of her reign or even before she ascended the throne to the end of her life (Fig. 14.1).

© The Author(s), under exclusive license to Springer Nature
Switzerland AG 2022
C. Levin, *The Reign and Life of Queen Elizabeth I*,
Queenship and Power, https://doi.org/10.1007/978-3-030-93009-7_14

Fig. 14.1 Elizabethan women private collection

KAT ASHLEY (D. 1565)

Two who were very close to Elizabeth as they knew her from when she was a small child, were Katherine Champernowne Ashley and Blanche Parry. Kat—as she was always known—Champernowne was born into a gentry family in Devon. While we know very little about her early life nor the date of her birth, she clearly received a good education—better than most women of her class at the time. By October 1536 Kat had become a member of Elizabeth's household when she was probably still in her teens. Sir Anthony Denny, who was a member of the king's privy chamber as early as 1533, had married her older sister Joan in 1538, and that connection led Thomas Cromwell to approve Kat's appointment. Kat served as Elizabeth's governess from about 1537. Thomas Wriothesley visited Hertford Castle in December 1539 where both of Henry's daughters were staying at the time to talk with Mary about a potential suitor. But while there he went to see the six-year-old Elizabeth and bring greetings from her father. He let Cromwell know that she "replied to the King's message with as great gravity as she had been 40 years old. If she be no worse educated than she appears she will be an honor to womanhood" (*L&P, Henry VIII*, XIV, Part II, 257).

In 1545 Kat married another member of the household, John Ashley, a senior gentleman attendant, who was a cousin of Elizabeth through her Boleyn relatives. In 1547 when the thirteen-year-old Elizabeth went to live in Chelsea, in the household of her stepmother Katherine Parr, who soon married Thomas Seymour, Katherine Ashley was with her. The scandalous behavior of Seymour convinced Parr, once she became pregnant, to advise Elizabeth to live elsewhere, and she and her household, including Ashley, went to live in the Denny household. After Katherine Parr's death in September 1548, Thomas Seymour pursued marriage with Elizabeth as well other illegal and dangerous activities (see Chapter 15). Not only was Seymour sent to the Tower, so too in January 1549 was Ashley, and her husband John was sent to Fleet prison. Kat Ashley, in a panic, confessed all she knew about what had happened at Chelsea. Elizabeth did everything she could to get Thomas's brother, Edward Seymour, Duke of Somerset, and Lord Protector, to release Ashley. She explained that Ashley "hath been with me a long time and many years, and hath taken great labor and pain in bringing me up in learning and honesty. And therefore I ought of very duty to speak for her, for Saint Gregory sayeth that we are more bound to them that bringeth us up well than to our parents," since parents simply carry people into the world while "our bringers-up are a cause to make us live well in it" (Elizabeth I, *Collected Works*, 34).

Elizabeth was able to get both the Ashleys back into her service in 1551. This would have been a great relief and joy as Kat Ashley gave her more continuity than anyone else in her life at that point. Ashley continued in Elizabeth's service when Mary became queen in 1553. But in 1556 Mary's Council suspected Ashley of being involved in a conspiracy against the queen, and Ashley again spent some time in the Tower, and after her release she was not allowed back into Elizabeth's service. As soon as Mary died, Elizabeth brought Ashley back and made her the Chief Gentlewoman of the Privy Chamber. Her husband John was named Master of the Jewel House. Kat Ashley was closer to the queen and had more influence than most of those at court. She even felt that she could tell Elizabeth that her reputation was suffering from her closeness to Robert Dudley, and Elizabeth should make a marriage with an appropriate foreign prince, advice Elizabeth had no intention of taking.

But Elizabeth did become angry with Kat for her involvement in encouraging the courtship of Erik XIV of Sweden in 1562. Kat soon, however, recovered her position at court and the confidence of the queen. Unfortunately, early in 1565 Ashley became ill. She appeared to have recovered, but in July suddenly relapsed. On July 17, Elizabeth sat at Kat's bedside with her. The next morning, servants had to inform the queen that Kat Ashley had died. Elizabeth felt great grief. She was supposed to meet with the Imperial ambassador, Adam Zwetkowich, Baron Mitterburg, but sent word that could not meet with him until July 22 as she was in mourning. The Spanish ambassador

Guzman de Silva wrote to the King of Spain about how greatly grieved Elizabeth was over the death of her old friend. Though during the rest of her reign Elizabeth was close to some other women, none mattered to her as much as Ashley.

BLANCHE PARRY (1508–1590)

Elizabeth also knew Blanche Parry throughout her life. Parry came into Elizabeth's household when she was just a baby and rocked her cradle. By 1536 Parry was one of Elizabeth's ladies-in-waiting. Her aunt and namesake Blanche Herbert, Lady Herbert of Troy, was a significant member of the household which is most likely what facilitated Parry's position. Parry was twenty-five years old when she rocked the princess's cradle; she would spend the rest of her long life in service to Elizabeth and had a fierce loyalty to her. Once Elizabeth grew up the two women found they had much in common. They both had Welsh ancestry and interest in Welsh culture. They both enjoyed horseback riding, and both loved to read. They both loved jewels. Perhaps most important, they shared a religious viewpoint of moderate Protestantism.

As soon as Elizabeth became queen, she appointed Parry as a Gentlewoman of the Privy Chamber. This was a salaried position: £33 6s. 8d. After Kat Ashley died in 1565 Parry became the chief gentlewoman. Elizabeth asked her to take care of her personal jewelry and she also took charge of the books given to the queen, and, like her queen, had real interest in history and literature. Knowing what her queen preferred, Blanche's New Year's gifts were often jewelry and clothing. As well as her salary, Elizabeth rewarded her loyal service with leases of crown lands. Parry used her influence with the queen to help some friends and relatives, but she was careful not to get involved in any political matters. The astrologer John Dee was a friend of Parry's, and she was the godmother for one of his sons.

In the last years of her life, Blanche lost her sight. In 1587, as a result, she could no longer tend the queen's jewels, and that job was taken up by Mary Scudamore, but she continued to serve the queen until the very last weeks of her life. In 1589 she asked Lord Burghley to write her will and serve as her executor. To Elizabeth's great grief, Parry died on February 12, 1590, after fifty-seven years of dedicated service. She was buried at St. Margaret's chapel at Westminster. The queen paid for her funeral and, showing how much she valued Parry, insisted that the funeral ceremony be one fit for a baroness, rather than the gentlewoman that she was.

In her will Parry set up an annual bequest of £28 to the parishioners of Bacton and Newton which continued to be paid for centuries. Blanche owned several diamonds and left her best one to the queen. She left Cecil her second-best diamond, and also gave a diamond to Sir Christopher Hatton. She remembered other ladies at court who had long been her friends and the queen's too, including Frances, Lady Cobham, and Lady Dorothy Stafford, with diamonds and gold chains. She had arranged to have a monument made of stone and alabaster at the Bacton Church in Hertfordshire. It shows her with a seated Elizabeth, while Blanche is kneeling beside her and holding a book. In a sense it is a Protestant version of the worshiper with the Virgin Mary. With the monument is Blanche Parry's epitaph, which she wrote herself, stating that "I lived always as handmaid to a queen." She also later added

> So that my time I thus did pass away
> A maid in Court and never no man's wife
> Sworn of the Queen Elizabeth's Bedchamber always
> With maiden queen a maiden did end my life. (Whitelock, 271)

For Blanche Parry it was highly significant that throughout her life, like her queen, that she was "never no man's wife."

Marjorie Williams Norris (or Norreys) (d. 1599)

Henry Norris's marriage to Marjorie Williams was important to him both personally and professionally. The first Baron Norris was orphaned early in his life. His mother died when he was a small child and his father, also Henry, was one of the men executed in 1536 with Anne Boleyn on the charge of adultery when his son was only about eleven. Henry and his sister were raised by his childless uncle and Henry was given some minor positions at Henry VIII's court. In 1539 the king had restored some of Henry's family estates. By 1544 Henry had married Margery Williams, the co-heir of her wealthy father. It was a very strong marriage, and between 1547 and about 1557 the couple had seven children, six sons—John, William, Edward, Henry, Thomas, and Maximilian—and one daughter, Catherine.

Norris had further offices in the reign of Edward VI and had supported Lady Jane Grey. He was fortunate that Margery's father Sir John was a strong supporter of Mary, and this protected Norris. Mary named Williams as an extra guardian, along with Sir Henry Bedingfield, of Elizabeth when she was under house arrest at Woodstock. On several occasions Williams broke the isolating anxiety and monotony for Elizabeth at Woodstock by inviting her to dinner at Rycote, and thus Elizabeth was introduced to Henry and Marjorie Norris, and she clearly valued them once she became queen. She granted back to Norris all lands confiscated when his father had been executed. It is possible that Elizabeth felt a strong connection since Norris's father had died with her mother, and to his death, he had absolutely denied that he had been her lover. The queen and Margery also established an enduring friendship, which proved essential to the success of Margery's husband and sons' careers.

With Margery's father's death in 1559 the Norrises inherited Rycote, in Oxfordshire. This was always referred to as both Henry's and Margery's home, instead of the usual practice of referring to it as Henry's, and this became their main home for the rest of their lives. Though Margery was not appointed to be a member of the privy chamber, Elizabeth considered her a close friend. Elizabeth called Margery her "crow," as an endearing nickname because she had black hair and a dark complexion. In 1560, in clearly a role that showed Elizabeth's trust, Margery was the chief mourner at the funeral of Amy Robsart, the queen's favorite Robert Dudley's wife who had died under mysterious circumstances. Margery Norris would also have been the woman of appropriate rank in the country of Oxfordshire, where Rycote was located, and the county where Amy's death occurred.

Elizabeth often visited the Norrises at Rycote, and in September 1566 while visiting she knighted Henry, thus making his wife Lady Margery. There were also extended visits in 1568, and 1570 and possibly other years as well. When the queen visited in 1570, she took great pleasure in hunting, and invited the French ambassador La Mothe Fénélon to join her.

The Norrises were upset when Elizabeth did not visit them in 1582 and the Earl of Leicester came to explain that decision. In a letter he wrote to Sir Christopher Hatton, on the one hand Leicester described what a strong supportive couple the Norrises were, and how committed to the queen, while on the other hand he admitted that he wished he could have stayed elsewhere as Margery especially was so vocal about their disappointment.

Norris spent much of his career as a member of Parliament and at times served as a special envoy to France, named as ambassador there in 1566. Being ambassador was difficult as the French disliked the Norrises' strong Protestantism and efforts to help the Huguenots. While Margery was in France, she took part in state business and was in touch with the queen herself about activities there. From 1569 onward Henry Norris asked to be recalled, or at least to be able to send Margery and their children back to England, but he remained as ambassador until 1570 when Sir Francis Walsingham came to relieve him. In 1572 Norris was named a baron.

Margery raised her sons to be patriotic and have a strong sense of service. From the 1570s her six sons were all in the military fighting in the Netherlands, France, and Ireland. The Norrises deeply supported their sons, selling some of their manors and incurring debt to finance their sons' martial careers. Margery's friendship with the queen continued. In 1590 her second eldest son Sir John, one of the most impressive soldiers of his age, arrived at court. He served at different times in France, the Netherlands, and Ireland. He immediately wrote to his mother about how much the queen valued her, "Right honorable my very good Lady and Mother, her Majesty the same night that I arrived here entertained me very kindly, and the next morning likewise; asked often for your Ladyship and wished herself at Rycote" (Kolkovich, 85).

Sir William, Margery's oldest son, was in Ireland from 1573 until 1576 as a Captain of the Horse. He went back to Ireland again in 1579 where he died of fever. When Elizabeth visited Rycote in 1592 Margery was desperately worried about the rest of her sons, especially as there were rumors about the death of another son. When Queen Elizabeth arrived, and Henry greeted the queen, he used her nickname for his wife to talk about their joy in the visit but also the deep worry Margery was feeling. Rumors about a son's death "hath so often affrighted the Crow my wife, that her heart, hath been as black as her feathers ... And although, nothing be more unfit to lodge your Majesty, than a crow's nest, yet shall it be most happy to us, that it is by your rightness, made a Phoenix nest" (Kolkovich, 83–84). Sir Henry devised an entertainment for Elizabeth that he hoped would lead her to think of his sons more highly. There was a message and gift for the queen theoretically from each son, with the gift designed to remind Elizabeth of each of their individual service. Tragically, five of six boys died in service. Maximillian was killed in Brittany in 1593 while serving with his brother John. In the 1590s John and his brothers Henry and Thomas were serving in Ireland and Margery and her husband frequently wrote to unsuccessfully beg that their sons be allowed to return home. Sir John, called "Black Jack," became known as one of the great military leaders of the period. He was recognized not only for his ability but also for his chivalry and courage. John died in 1597. Elizabeth wrote a letter of condolence addressed to "mine own Crow," and spoke of both Margery's sorrow and how proud the queen was of John's service (Elizabeth I, *Collected Works*, 389). The pain became even worse for Margery and her husband two years later when Henry and Thomas died within a week of each other in Ireland. Elizabeth wrote not only of the sorrow Margery and Henry would be feeling, but also promised to recall their last surviving son Edward, so he could be with them. Edward then stayed in England and lived until 1603. Margery Norris, however, died in 1599, devastated by the loss of so many sons. Her death was a great sorrow to the queen.

KATHERINE CAREY KNOLLYS, LADY KNOLLYS (C.1523–1569)

Elizabeth felt deep fondness and loyalty for most of her maternal relatives, which was very different from the distrust and wariness she felt toward her relatives through her father. This intense affection was especially the case in terms of her two first cousins, Henry and Katherine Carey, the children of her aunt Mary Boleyn. Mary Boleyn was Henry VIII's mistress though William Carey, her first husband, recognized both children as his own. While some people have speculated that one or both may have been Elizabeth's half-siblings as well as her cousins, a number of scholars argue persuasively that they were most likely simply her cousins, and that was always how Elizabeth treated them. Katherine was probably born around 1523. She was appointed as a maid of honor to Anne of Cleves in 1539 and the following year she married Francis Knollys. Despite the sixteen children Katherine bore, of which thirteen grew to adulthood, she also maintained a close friendship with Elizabeth, which probably began when Elizabeth was a child. In 1556 when the Protestant Knollys family fled England, Elizabeth wrote a letter of farewell to Katherine in which she said that her heart was broken.

Once the Knollys family heard of the death of Mary I, they joyfully returned to England and were there for Elizabeth's coronation. The queen appointed Katherine to be one of the four Ladies of the Bedchamber along with Kat Ashley and Blanche Parry. These were salaried positions. As well as Katherine's appointment, Sir Francis received appointments as well, including being named to the Privy Council. Despite the responsibilities Katherine had to her husband and children, Elizabeth wanted Katherine to be at court with her, which was sometimes very difficult for Katherine and Francis. Katherine had her last child, Dudley, in May 1562. The baby died in July, so Katherine was away from court at that time. Though sometimes the queen was short-tempered and very demanding of Katherine, she deeply cared for her. When Katherine became very ill in the summer of 1565, Elizabeth immediately had one of her own physicians, Dr. Robert Huick, treat her. The queen especially wanted Katherine to recover quickly as her son Henry was getting married on July 16. Dr. Huick apparently did the trick as Katherine recovered quickly and very much enjoyed her son's lavish wedding, as did the queen. Tragically, when Katherine became very ill a few years later, there was not such a happy outcome.

In May 1568 when Elizabeth sent Sir Francis Knollys north to guard and examine Mary Stuart, he requested that his wife might accompany him. Elizabeth refused, as she did not want to be without Katherine's company. As Knollys had to stay longer and longer in the north of England he became more discouraged, especially as he learned that Katherine was not well. He wrote to Katherine around New Year's in concern, that despite "the outward love that her majesty bears you, she makes you often weep for unkindness to the great danger of your health" (Doran, *Elizabeth & Her Circle*, 213). Knollys suggested perhaps they should both retire to their country house and leave their court positions, but he said he was leaving the decision to her. Though William Cecil has written to Knollys around Christmas that Katherine was improving, she had relapsed in early January and never answered her husband's letter. Elizabeth was deeply concerned and had Katherine taken care of in a chamber near her own room and so she could make regular visits and was devastated when Katherine died on January 15. So was Knollys, who was also distraught that he did not get to see his wife before her death. Elizabeth, as she had done with Katherine Ashley, put the Bedchamber into deep mourning. Nicholas White, a close confidant of William Cecil, wrote that for the queen "all her felicities gave place to some natural passions of grief ... and how by that occasion her highness fell for a while, from a prince wanting nothing in this world to private mourning, in which solitary estate, being forgetful of her own health, she took cold, wherewith she was much troubled" (Strickland, 386). The French ambassador La Mothe-Fénelon went to see the queen at Hampton Court five days after Lady Knollys's death and found her very sad about the death of the woman whom she had "loved better than all the women in the world." Elizabeth insisted on a lavish funeral for which she paid £640. Katherine was buried in St. Edmund's Chapel at Westminster. The epitaph on the tomb described her as a "mirror pure of womanhood" who had been "in favor with our noble queen, above the common sort" (Whitelock, 125).

KATHERINE CAREY HOWARD, COUNTESS OF NOTTINGHAM (C.1545–1603)

Elizabeth's beloved cousin Katherine Carey Knollys had a namesake niece, her brother Henry's daughter. The Careys were dear enough relatives to the queen that though only about fifteen years old, Katherine became a Gentlewoman of the Privy Chamber in January 1560. Elizabeth's closeness to her from the beginning of the reign is suggested in an odd incident that Henry Killigrew wrote about in November 1561. He explained that that afternoon, Robert Dudley was "shooting a match in the park" at Windsor. "The Queen stole out upon them only accompanied with Kate Carey and two others, whom she followed as a maid" ('Elizabeth: November 1561, 21–30', in *Calendar of State Papers Foreign: Elizabeth, Volume 4, 1561–1562*, ed. Joseph Stevenson [London, 1866], pp. 410–423. *British History Online*). That Elizabeth would disguise herself as a maid to go watch Dudley was rather scandalous, but it also suggests how comfortable the queen felt with her young cousin that she asked Katherine to help her in this disguise. After Katherine married Charles Howard in 1563, she continued her place in the Privy Chamber. She and her husband had at least two sons and three daughters, and the queen was the godmother to their daughter Elizabeth, who became a maid of honor in 1579. That Elizabeth married Sir Robert Southwell in April 1583, and their daughter Elizabeth, Katherine's granddaughter, became a maid of honor in 1599, and was at the queen's deathbed in 1603 (see Chapter 15). Another of Katherine's daughters, Frances, Countess of Kildare, also joined her mother in the Privy Chamber. Katherine oversaw some of the queen's jewels. She was eventually put in charge of presiding over the table where the ladies dined; when the queen dined with them, Katherine was responsible for receiving Elizabeth's food and plating it for her. Katherine became ill in late 1601 and her health continued to decline. She died on February 24, 1603. Elizabeth was terribly upset; some of her contemporaries claimed that the queen was more distressed about Katherine's death than her own husband was. Her melancholy over her friend Katherine's death might have contributed to Elizabeth's death exactly one month later.

DOROTHY STAFFORD (1526–1604)

Dorothy Stafford was one of the daughters of Henry, Baron Stafford, and was a distant cousin of Queen Elizabeth. In 1545 Dorothy married her cousin, Sir William Stafford, which brought about another indirect connection with Elizabeth, as he had been the second husband of her aunt Mary Boleyn, who had died the previous year. Sir William and Dorothy were confirmed Protestants. Another of Dorothy's cousins was Elizabeth Sandys, who was a member of Princess Elizabeth's household until in 1554. Mary I ordered her removed because she thought Sandys was too committed to Protestantism. The following year Sandys accompanied Dorothy and her husband William who, with two of their children, left England for Geneva. There Dorothy had her last child, a son John. Sir William died a few months later. Dorothy then got into a dispute with John Calvin and she, Sandys, and her children moved to Basel, where they lived until January 1559. While in Basel they spent time with another Marian exile John Foxe, and Sandys was most likely Foxe's source for what he wrote about Elizabeth during Mary's reign in his *Book of Martyrs*. In the summer of 1559, they went to France and met Mary Stuart. Mary was claiming that she was the legitimate queen of England and apparently used "disdainful speech" about Queen Elizabeth to Stafford and Sandys and to others who were allied with Elizabeth (August 1559, 26–31, in *Calendar of State Papers Foreign: Elizabeth, Volume 1, 1558–1559*, ed. Joseph Stevenson [London, 1863], pp. 502–524. *British History Online*).

In the fall the two women returned to England and were both appointed to the Privy Chamber. Sandys married Sir Maurice Berkeley in 1562, and Elizabeth was the godmother to her son Robert the following year. When James Melville visited Elizabeth's court in 1564, he was happy to renew his acquaintance with Lady Stafford, whom he had met when they were both in France five years before. He considered her to be an honorable and godly lady and perceived that the Queen thought very highly of her. He called Lady Stafford Elizabeth's "Dame of Honor," and was pleased that he had the opportunity to dine with Dorothy, considering "that she might confer with me." He added that he got "good intelligence from her" (Melville, 49).

There may have been some tension later in the reign because of the questionable political behavior of Dorothy's two sons Edward and William. In January 1578 Henry Killigrew wrote to William Davison to let him know that "Lady Stafford had slandered many Ladies in Court," and was under the charge of the Knight Marshall (State Papers Online). Whatever happened, it was apparently resolved soon, and Elizabeth clearly cared very much for Lady Stafford. Indeed, Elizabeth valued Dorothy so much that she was the woman she most wanted to sleep in her bedchamber. It was well known enough that Lady Stafford did so that when Adam Blackwood wrote his tract against the English queen after the execution of Mary Stuart, he described an apocryphal scene where Elizabeth and Dorothy had identical nightmares (see Chapter 13). Dorothy died a year after her queen, and she was buried in St. Margaret's Chapel at Westminster. Her funeral monument was in the nave below that of Blanche Parry and recorded that she had served the queen for forty years, "lying in the bed chamber" (Dorothy Stafford, ODNB Online).

Ann Russell Dudley, Countess of Warwick (1548–1604)

Ann, the eldest of three daughters of Francis Russell, Earl of Bedford, joined Elizabeth's household as a maid of honor when she became queen, or even before her accession, though Ann was only about eleven years old. Many years later, her niece, Lady Anne Clifford, explained that virtually her whole life, Ann had served the queen, first as maid, then as wife, and finally as widow. When she was sixteen, Ann became the third—and dearly loved—wife of Ambrose Dudley, Earl of Warwick. Ambrose's brother Robert arranged the marriage with the Earl of Bedford, and Robert was very careful to ask Elizabeth's permission before he did the negotiations. Though the queen was furious if her maids indulged in extramarital affairs or secret marriages, she enthusiastically supported the marriage of Ann and Ambrose. The two were married on November 11, 1565. Ann wore a dress of purple velvet embroidered with silver with an outer skirt of silver with a golden headdress. The queen's maids of honor wore yellow satin with green velvet and silver lace. Ambrose Dudley was dressed in purple velvet embroidered in gold with sables. His brother Robert wore purple satin embroidered with gold. When everyone was in place Elizabeth was escorted to the ceremony. After they were married there was a grand banquet and then a tournament with the celebration continuing for two days.

The marriage meant two politically important families sympathetic to Puritans were now in alliance. Ambrose was nearly twenty years older than his sixteen-year-old bride. His only child, from his first marriage, had died, and both Ambrose and his brother Robert were eager for him to have another child and heir. Unfortunately, there were no children in the marriage. But Ann's empathy and strong maternal feelings were demonstrated in other ways. Since her mother had died young, Ann was a second mother to her younger brother William, and her sister Elizabeth, who eventually married John Bourchier and became Countess of Bath, and her sister Margaret, who eventually married George Clifford and became Countess of Cumberland. They were seven, ten, and twelve years younger than she respectively. She also played an important role in their children's lives as well. This was especially true for Margaret's daughter Anne—Ann's namesake—as she was also her godmother.

In the 1570s and 1580s Ann and her husband were mostly at court or living nearby and Ann was able to continually attend the queen. Though Ann was usually at court, she was delighted to host the queen at Warwick Castle several times, with especially elaborate entertainments there in 1572, where the Elizabeth went back and forth several times between Warwick Castle and Kenilworth Castle, which the queen had granted to Ambrose's brother Robert.

According to her niece Anne Clifford, the countess was committed to helping people who were in distress, and we can see that in her correspondence. She wrote to Robert Cecil to thank him and his father Lord Burghley for their help to her neighbor and good friend Sir Henry Cook. She wrote to the Masters of Requests for help for the distressed gentlewoman Elinor Sampson. She informed her uncle Roger Manners that she had remembered him to the queen and promised her his humble duty and service. She assured Manner that the queen had told her how aware she was that he was an old and faithful servant. She also wrote to Walsingham asking for support for her husband's nephew Sir Robert Sidney. She worked to support religious separatists and was also a patron to writers. George Turberville wrote a series of poems dedicated to her and Henry Constable wrote a poem about both Ann and her sister Margaret, saying that both sisters were of such excellent virtue one could not stay that one was better than the other.

The marriage of the Countess and Earl of Warwick was loving and supportive, and Ann was devastated by her husband's death. Sir Edward Stafford went to visit Warwick as he was dying in February 1590. He found Ann "sitting by the fire so full of tears that she could not speak." In his will her brother-in-law Robert wrote about her as he made his bequest "my noble and worthy sister ... at whose hands I have found great love and kindness," and that he held her in such honor and esteem as any brother ever held his sister ("Dudley [née Russell], countess of Warwick, ODNB). In her widowhood the countess spent a lot of time with her sister-in-law Katherine Dudley Hastings, Countess of Huntingdon, and the queen, and they were known at court to be among her closest intimates. Since Henry Hastings, Earl of Huntingdon had been named Lord President of the Council of the North in 1572, Katherine only attended court occasionally as she was so often in York with her husband. But when Robert Dudley died in 1588, she returned to court as soon as she could to mourn with the queen, and two became much closer. The Earl of Huntingdon died in December 1595, and Elizabeth decided she needed to break the news to Katherine personally and did everything she could to comfort her. In her last years the queen was grateful for the close friendship of both women.

In 1603 when Elizabeth was ill and at Richmond at the end of her life, Lady Warwick would often visit and Anne Clifford, who was about thirteen years old, remembered that sometimes she would accompany her in aunt in her coach, and then would wait in the outer chamber while Lady Warwick sat with the queen. Anne Clifford wrote that Ann was "more beloved and in greater favor with the Queen than any other woman in the kingdom, and no less in the whole Court and the Queen's dominions which she deserved. She was a great friend to virtue" (Williamson, 37).

CHAPTER 15

Slander Gossip Rumors

From the time she was a young girl, Elizabeth had to deal with slander, gossip, and rumors about her, most of them dealing with her sexual behavior, and this only intensified once she became queen. Elizabeth's government was so concerned about the dangers of rumors that in 1581 Parliament passed an Act against Seditious Words and Rumors uttered against the Queen's Most Excellent Majesty. But though there were so many problematic stories collected about the queen, other women, especially royal or at court, also suffered from slander, scandal, gossip, and rumors. And, as it was with Elizabeth, most of the rumors had to do with women's sexuality. Looking at some of these other examples puts the strange stories about Elizabeth into context.

During Elizabeth's older sister's reign, Mary too was a subject of scandal and rumors. In the first year of her reign, before her marriage to Philip of Spain, rumors began circulating in Norfolk that May was pregnant by Stephen Gardiner, Bishop of Winchester and her Lord Chancellor. There was enough talk that Henry Radcliffe, Earl of Sussex and the Queen's Lieutenant, went to Norfolk to investigate. The description of this investigation sounded like the telephone game. The first one found who passed on the rumor was Laurence Hunt, but he explained he had heard it from his wife, who had heard it from Sheldrake's wife, who had heard it from her husband, who had it from a man named Wilby, who learned of it from John Smith, who had been told of it by the widow Miles. She claimed that two men told her, but she did not know their names.

In 1567 Bess of Hardwick, then having been widowed by her third husband Sir William St Loe, was very upset by the stories spread by Henry Jackson, a university-trained cleric who had been her sons' tutor, and she asked Elizabeth for help. On behalf of the Privy Council William Cecil wrote to Matthew Parker, Archbishop of Canterbury, about how disturbed the widow was over the scandalous reports Jackson had spread about her. He asked that the case be brought up before the Ecclesiastical Commissioners so her good name could be restored. A few days later Elizabeth wrote to the archbishop to also encourage him, stating if Jackson had unjustly defamed Bess, the punishment should be extreme. We do not know what exactly had been said, but many years later, when her 1568 marriage to George Talbot, Earl of Shrewsbury had irretrievably broken down, Shrewsbury stated that when he was courting Bess, her name had been a "byword" at Court, and that ought to have been a warning.

In 1583 rumors were circulating at court and in the countryside about the same Earl of Shrewsbury, who was guarding Mary Stuart. People whispered that the two had had an affair and there were one or two children as a result. We do not know who started the rumor. When Mary heard she was furious, especially as she was trying to convince Philip II of Spain to marry her and feared this rumor would dissuade him. But Mary herself started another rumor, whether she believed it or not, that the aforesaid Bess, Countess of Shrewsbury and her two sons William and Charles Cavendish, had originated these stories about her and Shrewsbury. Mary was furious at Bess, since Bess's daughter had married Mary's cousin Charles, and Mary thought Bess was scheming to have their daughter Arbella Stuart replace Mary as heir to the throne. Thus, Mary wanted to thoroughly discredit Bess.

Clearly sexual commentary was a strong way to diminish potentially powerful women, though rumors of other sorts also spread through England and the continent. People often spread or objected to rumors depending on the political or religious standpoint. For example, French ambassador Michel de Castelnau stated that the stories about Mary Stuart and Shrewsbury were all malicious inventions. If the sexual rumors about other women were disturbing, there was so much more concern about what was said about Queen Elizabeth. In 1566 William Cecil wrote to his friend Thomas Smith who was at that time in Paris: "I affirm that the Queen's Majesty may be by malicious tongues not well reported; but in truth she herself is blameless, and hath no spot of evil intent" (Wright, I, 225).

Rumors About Elizabeth and Thomas Seymour

After her father's death in January 1547 when she was thirteen, Elizabeth lived with her last stepmother Katherine Parr in her household at Chelsea. But within a few months Katherine had married Thomas Seymour and he joined their household. He had keys to every room in Chelsea. Her governess Kat Ashley later testified that many mornings he would come into Elizabeth's bedchamber, sometimes before she was out of bed. If she were already up and dressed, he would ask about her but also slap her on her buttocks. Seymour would be wearing only his night shirt and if she were still in bed Seymour would pull open the bed curtain and pretend to climb into bed with Elizabeth. She would move as far from him as she could and got up earlier so that she would be up and dressed when he came. Though this clearly upset Elizabeth, she may also have found it exciting.

Once Katherine became pregnant for the first time, she became uncomfortable with what might happen between her husband and step-daughter—especially as she may have found them in an embrace—and suggested to Elizabeth she leave. In May 1548 she went to live with Sir Anthony Denny and his wife Joan, who was Katherine Ashley's sister, at Chesthunt, Hertfordshire. Elizabeth and her stepmother stayed on good terms, however, writing to each other. Elizabeth was greatly saddened when Katherine died after giving birth to a daughter, who probably died young, in September 1548. After Katherine's death there were rumors that Seymour would marry her. Of course, Elizabeth and Seymour could not marry without the consent of the Privy Council, or she could lose her place in the succession or possibly even her life. According to the Treason Act of 1536, it was treason for anyone of royal blood to marry without the king's consent. Seymour became involved in other doubtful and illegal ventures, and then, after attempting to kidnap his nephew Edward VI, Seymour was arrested and lodged in the Tower (see Chapter 6). But because of the possible connections with Elizabeth, so were her governess, Kat Ashley and the cofferer, or treasurer, of her household, Thomas Parry. In terror, they confessed about all the activities at Chelsea. The Council sent Sir Robert Tyrwhitt to Hatfield to examine Elizabeth and force her to confess. She was fifteen years old. Elizabeth was informed there were rumors that she was pregnant. Rather than being shamed and humiliated, Elizabeth responded with dignity and eloquence. She wrote to Thomas's brother, Edward Seymour, Duke of Somerset and Lord Protector. "Master Tyrwhitt and others have told me that there goeth rumours abroad, which be greatly both against my honour and honesty (which above all other things I esteem) which be these; that I am in the Tower; and with child by my lord admiral. My lord, these are shameful slanders for the which ... I shall most heartily desire your lordship that I may come to the court ... that I may show myself as I am" (Elizabeth, *Collected Works*, 24). When Somerset refused, Elizabeth did not back down, and demanded that the Lord Protector send out a proclamation demanding that people restrain their tongues and state that these accusations were lies. While Elizabeth did not receive the proclamation, her careful presentation of herself for the rest of Edward VI's reign did much to restore her reputation from these slanders.

Slander About Elizabeth's Involvement in the Death of Amy Robsart

Robert Dudley's wife, Amy Robsart, died suddenly on 8 September 1560. She was found at the bottom of some stairs with her neck broken. Dudley was at court with Elizabeth when this happened, obviously Elizabeth's favorite. He had not seen his wife for more than a year before her death. Immediately many claimed Dudley had murdered his wife and some claimed that the queen was involved.

The letter the Spanish Ambassador Bishop de Quadra sent to Margaret, Duchess of Parma, the half-sister of Philip II, only a few days after Robsart's death is a strange blend of fact and rumors, and much of what he wrote was doubtful. He narrated several days of events. He began his letter by saying that Cecil was in disgrace and thinking of retiring, since he saw the country would be in ruin because of "Robert's intimacy with the Queen." De Quadra added that Cecil told him that "Robert was thinking of killing his wife," though not by poison. He claimed that Cecil stated that there was a public comment that Robsart was ill but in fact her health was fine. De Quadra's letter then described that the next day, when Elizabeth returned from hunting, she told him "that Robert's wife was dead or nearly so," but asked him not to say anything about it. He finished the letter by saying since he had written it, he heard the queen had announced the death of Robert's wife, that "she broke her neck," (*CSP, Spain*, I, 175) and assumed this means she must have fallen down a flight of stairs. De Quadra knew that Amy was dead by September 11, but whether Cecil or the queen told him what he reported is more problematic; it may well have been the beginning of the slander, gossip, and rumors that developed around Robsart's death.

Less than ten days after Robsart's death Thomas Lever wrote to Sir Francis Knollys and Sir William Cecil about the "dangerous suspicion, and muttering" going on in Coventry. He worried that unless Elizabeth's government could dispel these suspicions, "the displeasure of God, the dishonor of the Quene, and the Danger of the whole Realme is to be feared" (Murdin and Haynes, I, 362). The ambassador in France, Sir Nicholas Throckmorton, was devastated with the rumors that circulated there. Mary Stuart, who had claimed she and her husband Francis II were the true king and queen of England, quipped that the queen's horsekeeper had murdered his wife to make room in his bed for Elizabeth. Throckmorton wrote "One laugheth at us, another threateneth, another revileth the Queen." He added that some people told him, "what religion is this that a subject shall kill his wife, and the Prince not only bear withal but marry with him" (*CSP, Foreign*, III, 352). In January 1561 the Spanish ambassador de Quadra wrote to his king that Dudley's brother-in-law Henry Sidney assured him he had thoroughly inquired, and Robsart's death was accidental. But he also admitted that public opinion held the contrary view, and that many preachers from their pulpit were making comments prejudicial to Elizabeth's honor. Throughout Elizabeth's reign rumors continued about Dudley and the death of Amy Robsart, and his enemies argued that he was a murderer, with Robsart being only the first he committed. Dudley as the murderer of his first wife and then many others is described in the 1584 *Leicester's Commonwealth* and Cardinal William Allen's 1588 *Admonition to the Nobility and People of England*.

Perhaps ironically, after Robert Dudley, Earl of Leicester, died on September 4, 1588, rumors soon spread that his second wife Lettice had had him murdered. Other rumors were that Dudley died because Edward Croft had paid a conjuror to use magic in revenge for his mistreatment of Croft's father Sir James (see Chapter 3).

SLANDER ABOUT ELIZABETH, HER LOVERS, AND AS THE MOTHER OF ILLEGITIMATE CHILDREN

Even before Amy Robsart's death there were many rumors about Elizabeth's relationship with Robert Dudley. The Count de Feria wrote to Philip II in April 1559 that "during the last few days Lord Robert has come so much into favour that he does whatever he likes with affairs and it is even said that her Majesty visits him in his chamber day and night" (*CSP, Spain*, I, 46).

June 1560

The parson Thomas Holland was charged with uttering malicious words against the queen. His defense was that another churchman had told him that someone was in the Tower of London for telling people that Elizabeth was with child.

August 1560

Sir Thomas Mildmay and Richard, Lord Rich did an examination in Essex of Mother Anne Dowe, a sixty-eight-year-old widow, for her comments about Elizabeth and her relationship with Dudley. They interviewed Dowe herself and several other witnesses. Dowe stated that she was in a house near a parsonage and heard her hostess state that Dudley had given the queen a new red petticoat worth 20 nobles. Dowe responded that Elizabeth did not need this gift as she could buy one for herself. Dowe stated that three days later she saw a man she knew, Mr. Coke. She told him about the petticoat, and he responded by asking her why she thought the queen had been given a petticoat—rather, Dudley had given the queen a child. In the Elizabethan period the gift of a red petticoat was a metaphor, some believed, for taking someone's virginity. Mr. Coke had a bottle of wine with him and both he and Dowe then had a drink. Certainly, she had been drinking, testified John King, when she came into his shop. She told him that Dudley and the queen had played legerdemain together, which might mean they were performing conjuring tricks together, but more likely Mother Dowe meant they were having sexual relations, especially as she added that Dudley had given the queen a child—which she had learned from Mr. Coke. King responded that Elizabeth did not have a child, Mother Dowe responded that she soon would, and had heard this from many people. King told her she should hold her peace, and, since she was drunk, she would repent her words when she sobered up.

Mildmay wrote to William Cecil that they sent Mother Dowe to the common jail.

January 1561

The Spanish ambassador de Quadra wrote to Phillip II that most people believed, and it was confirmed by certain physicians—whom he did not name—that Elizabeth was unhealthy and would not be able to have children. He added, however, that there were also many people who believed that Elizabeth had already had children. He added "I have seen no trace and do not believe it" (*CSP, Spain*, I, 180).

February 1561

In February 1561 there was an examination of what happened at John Leche's house when a group of people were there. One of the guests was Thomas Burley, who was well known as a drunk. He told Leche and the others that he knew that Lord Robert did swive the queen. Swive meant for a man to have sex with a woman.

June 1562

De Quadra twice that month claimed that the queen was secretly married to Dudley, which Cecil found disturbing enough that the information was listed in the articles against de Quadra. Another witness claimed that de Quadra had composed a sonnet about the supposed marriage. Unfortunately, we do not have a copy of it but are told that it was "full of dishonour to the Queen and Lord Robert" (*CSP, Foreign*, V, 71).

January 1563

In Suffolk Sir Owen Hopton, who some years later became Lieutenant of the Tower, examined Edmund Baxter and others for comments they made about the queen and Dudley. Baxter had stated that Lord Robert was the queen's lover. He also called Elizabeth a naughty woman, that she was incapable of ruling the country, and worse, there was no justice for anyone. Baxter also claimed that Sir Nicholas Bacon, Lord Keeper of the Privy Seal, was a "wretch." His wife had said that when she saw the queen at Ipswich, Elizabeth had looked very pale, as if she had recently had a child. Baxter was held in Menton jail.

April 1564

A Spaniard in London wrote about a rumor that Elizabeth had left Richmond, and some thought it was to rid herself of an indiscretion—hinting she was terminating a pregnancy.

February 1566

In a letter to King Philip, Guzman de Silva wrote that the French ambassador Paul de Foix de Carman informed him that he had been assured by someone in a position to know that the Earl of Leicester had slept with Elizabeth on New Year's night, though de Silva was doubtful since the information came from a Frenchman. Moreover, de Silva had expressed serious doubts before that there was anything improper in the relationship between Leicester and the queen. In 1564 he had written to the Duchess of Parma, explaining that she "bears herself toward [Dudley] in a way that together with some other things that can be better imagined than described make me doubt sometimes whether Robert's position is so irregular as many think. It is nothing for princes to hear evil, even without giving any cause of it" (*CSP Spain*, I, 381).

1570

A man named Marshame, or Marsham, from Norwich, was brought before the Assizes and had to pay a fine of £100 or have his ears cropped for telling people that Elizabeth had had two children with the Earl of Leicester. He was most likely Robert Marsham, who was a nephew of the late Alderman Thomas Marsham.

1572

1572, in the wake of the Ridolfi Plot (see Chapter 9), was a year awash with rumors and slander. William Fleetwood, the Recorder of London, examined Robert Blosse, the son of a London goldsmith, for telling people that the queen had married Leicester and that they had four children, claiming that he had learned it six years previously from an old priest in Hampshire. Five years later, using the name Mantell, Blosse asserted that Edward VI was still alive and then went so far as to claim that he was Edward, who had returned to claim his throne, and found a few women willing to support him. Elizabeth's government thought that Blosse was insane, the victim of frenzies, and he was sentenced to a year in Colchester jail. But he managed to escape and when recaptured, was executed in 1578.

Also, in 1572 Matthew Parker wrote to Cecil in great concern about the shameful words he had heard about the queen in relation to both Dudley and Christopher Hatton spoken by a man brought before the mayor of Dover. Parker told Cecil that what was said was so horrible he refused to commit it to paper but would tell Cecil when he saw him. The unnamed man also predicted that because of the queen's behavior there would be civil war in England as violent as the St. Bartholomew's Day Massacre in Paris. Catholics would destroy the Protestants, with a Catholic regime which would have Elizabeth murdered and then her bones, along with her father Henry VIII's, burned publicly at Smithfield.

Henry Wriothesley, second Earl of Southampton, was arrested in June 1570 for suspected complicity in the plot to have Thomas Howard, Duke of Norfolk, marry the queen of Scots. There were suspicions that he had been involved with Guerau de Spes, the Spanish ambassador and John Leslie, Bishop of Ross. Southampton denied the allegations, and at first was under house arrest, but the following year was moved to the Tower of London until he was released and returned to favor in May 1573. In September 1572, while in the Tower, Elizabeth Massie testified that she had heard the earl state that "there was a privy stairs where the Queen and my Lord Leicester did meet, and if they had not used sorcery, there should have been young traitors' ere now begotten" (*CSP, Scotland*, IV, 396). It appears that at least some Elizabethans considered that magic was the best form of birth control.

1575

In December of 1575 Nicholas Ormanetto, Bishop of Padua and Nuncio in Spain, wrote to Ptolemy Galli, Cardinal of Como that Sir Henry Cobham had come to attempt to achieve a less hostile relationship between the illegitimate Queen Elizabeth and Philip, but stated that the hope of a close friendship between England and Spain would not be successful. He added that he had also heard from someone, unnamed, that Cobham claimed Elizabeth had a thirteen-year-old daughter, and that she was willing to marry her off to someone of the King of Spain's choosing. He added that he had heard of the daughter before, but the English in Spain claimed they knew nothing about such a person, and there is no evidence that Cobham had actually said anything about the matter.

1580

In 1580 the Essex laborer Thomas Playfere informed people that Elizabeth had had two children by Lord Robert—he had seen them himself when they had been shipped out at Rye in two of the queen's best ships.

1581

In 1581 H. Hawkins was arrested for stating Elizabeth already had five illegitimate children. Hawkins explained Elizabeth's frequent progress throughout the countryside as her excuse to leave court and her illegitimate children by

Leicester, that every progress produced a child. The preacher Thomas Scot wrote to the Earl of Leicester about this so that he would know about such traitorous speeches.

1582

April 1582 was the very end of the Elizabeth's final marriage negotiation with François, Duke of Anjou (see Chapter 6). At the time the Spanish ambassador Bernardino De Mendoza wrote to Philip that he had heard that Elizabeth had had an argument with the French ambassador, Mauvissière, when he told her the most important reason for her to marry Anjou was that people were saying she had slept with the French prince. Elizabeth responded that she could ignore the rumor. The ambassador responded that while the queen might be able to do so in England, it would be very damaging for her abroad, where it had already been publicly stated. Mendoza announced that this made the queen extremely angry, and she stated that a conscience that was innocent feared nothing.

1587

A young Englishman was arrested in Spain under suspicion of being a spy. His story when he was examined was very surprising; he claimed that he was Arthur Dudley, the son of Robert and the queen. He said he was raised in the household of Robert Southern who told him his real identity on his deathbed. He claimed that the queen refused to acknowledge him and a year or two earlier he had fled England to wander the continent. Now he was offering his talents to the King of Spain. At first the Spanish accepted the story, but then began to doubt it, figuring that the so-called Dudley was really an instrument of the queen. He was sent to a Spanish prison and no more is known about him.

1588

William Allen was a passionate English Catholic who became appalled that in Elizabeth's early reign many Catholics were attending Anglican services. In 1565 he left England for the last time, and on the continent was ordained as a priest, and eventually became a Cardinal. He established the English College at Douai and it became a strong force in training missionaries who would fight against Elizabethan Protestantism in every way they could. Allen was fighting for the reconversion of England, which meant the destruction of Elizabeth. As part of the preparation for the Armada in 1588 Allen published his *Admonition to the Nobility and People of England*. The text called on English Catholics to overthrow Elizabeth, whom Allen described as "an incestuous bastard, begotten and born in sin." Not only was Henry still married to Catherine of Aragon, but Allen stated that Anne Boleyn was Henry's own daughter, since

Henry had had affairs not only with her sister Mary but her mother as well. While Dudley was Elizabeth's first lover, Allen assured his readers, the older Elizabeth became, the more lovers she took. She "shamefully has defiled her person," making her notorious throughout the world (Allen, 11, 19).

1590

Dionisia Deryck, a widow, was arrested for saying that the queen had as many children as she had. While two were supposedly still alive, one a boy and the other a girl, all the other children had been burned alive as infants. Leicester was the father, and he was the one who had cast them into the fire. Since we do not know how many children Deryck had had, we cannot know how many babies she thought were dead. It is a horrific story but also very strange, as there is no reason given why most of the babies were killed, but two were spared. The same year Robert Garner told a similar story. Leicester and the queen had had four children. The three daughters were alive, but the son had been burned to death. Given the strong desire for a male heir, it makes the murder of the boy child even more horrifying. Both Deryck and Garner had to stand in the pillory.

1598

Edward Frances (or Francis) of Melbury Osmond, Dorset attempted to seduce Elizabeth Baylie. When she refused his advances, he made the argument that since the most important in England had done so—Elizabeth and Robert Dudley—she should also. He added that, because of the queen's affairs with various noblemen at court, she had two sons and a daughter. But Baylie was still not impressed, so Frances began to denigrate the queen, saying that the queen was herself base born. He added it would have been better for England if Elizabeth had been cut off twenty years ago, so England had a king instead of a queen. He then tried to bribe the witnesses not to testify, offering £40 to men, and £20 to the women; all refused it. Frances fled and forfeited his bond.

1601

William Knyght, who was in Frankfurt, wrote to the English government that he had been with another Englishman Hugh Broughton and heard him make monstrous speeches about the queen. Broughton called her an atheist, and also claimed that Queen Elizabeth had a daughter whom she wanted the Prince of Condé to marry and have her succeed to the throne instead of the rightful heir, James VI. But then the story got even more bizarre and melodramatic. As well as the daughter who supposedly survived, there was another who was murdered as an infant. Broughton claimed that a midwife had been taken into a secret chamber where she was told to save the mother—Elizabeth—at whatever cost to the child. But she was so skilled that she was able to save them both. Afterward, she was told to bring the baby girl into another room, where she was commanded to toss the baby into the fire, and so the baby was completely burned. She was well paid with a handful of gold, but before she left, she was given a glass of wine being told "Thou whore, drink before thou goest from hence" (Levin, *The Heart and Stomach of a King*, 84). She drank the wine, returned to her house, and then, it was said, six days later died of poison—but she revealed this secret before she died.

1609

In 1609 the Latin book *Pruritanus* was smuggled into England from France. The printer had worked with a French Jesuit seminary. The text disputed the legitimacy of the English Reformation and called Henry VIII the Anti-Christ, whose reason for pushing the Reformation was his incestuous lust of Anne Boleyn. There were also attacks on Elizabeth and King James. The ones about Elizabeth were especially scurrilous. The queen was described as an immodest woman who had given births to sons and daughters. She had taken many, many lovers, men of many different backgrounds and nationalities. She had sexual relations even with, as dark-skinned people were called at the time, blackamoors. James I was furious about the book and tried to find out who the author was. He became even more upset when he learned the book was being sold at the Venetian embassy. Marc Antonio Correr, the Venetian ambassador, assured the king he knew nothing about it. He investigated and found out that a priest that he had hired to serve Mass at the Embassy Chapel had concealed many copies of the book at the porter's lodge and was selling them surreptitiously. All the copies were turned over to Robert Cecil, now Earl of Salisbury, and the priest was fired. The king ordered that the book be burned at Paul's Cross.

ELIZABETH IS NOT LIKE OTHER WOMEN
1559

At the beginning of her reign on April 29, 1559 the Spanish ambassador de Feria wrote to Philip II that "If my spies do not lie, which I believe they do not, for a certain reason which they have recently given me, I understand she will not bear children" (Hume, *Calendar of State Papers, Spain*, I, 63). This would be a painful rumor to be spreading, as so many thought it was critical at that time that Elizabeth marry and provide an heir.

1578

At the beginning of the year Bishop Antonio Salviati, the Nuncio in France wrote to Ptolemy Galli, Cardinal of Como, that he had been told by people who had knowledge of the English court that Queen Elizabeth's physicians were afraid that she was dying. The problem was that Elizabeth never had the purgation that all women should have; as a result, she did not menstruate. Instead, in her thigh she was able to have some flow, but it had all dried up, and now the queen was very ill.

1584

By the middle of the 1580s Mary Stuart was not only furious at Queen Elizabeth, but also at the wife of the man she considered her jailer, George Talbot, Earl of Shrewsbury. Bess of Hardwick, the Countess of Shrewsbury, had spent much time with Mary, especially as they gossiped and embroidered together. But they eventually fought bitterly. Mary's revenge was to write a letter to Elizabeth detailing what she claimed Bess had told her, but it was clear this was a different form of embroidery. Mary claimed that Bess told her that there was no doubt the queen was not like other women, and as a result it was ridiculous for Elizabeth to consider marriage with the Duke of Anjou, since it could never be consummated. Yet even though Elizabeth could not have proper relations, Mary stated that she was told of her pleasure in continually gratifying herself with new lovers, including the French envoy Jean de Simier and the duke himself. Mary also claimed that Bess had spoken about how vain the queen was, and that her ladies-in-waiting secretly laughed at her about it.

1619

In the summer of 1618 Ben Jonson set out to walk all the way to Scotland. By this time, he was famous as a poet and playwright and something of a celebrity, and he was pleased to be celebrated as he traveled. Once he got to Scotland he stayed for some time with William Drummond at his home, Hawthornden, a few miles south of Edinburgh. Drummond was considerably younger, also a writer, and quite wealthy. In the evenings Jonson would drink and talk, and then afterward Drummond would record the conversations. He made several negative comments about many of his fellow writers and repeated the gossip he had heard about the late queen. It sounded quite similar to Mary Stuart's comments decades earlier. Jonson claimed that Elizabeth had a membrane which made it impossible for her to have intercourse, but despite that to her delight she had relations with many men.

Rumors at Times of Crisis and War

Late 1586–Early 1587

After the Babington conspiracy was exposed, but before Mary Stuart's execution, England was rife with rumors. Some claimed that Mary Stuart was dead, while others were sure that she had escaped. People heard that the Spanish fleet had arrived, or that the Duke of Guise had landed with an army in Sussex. Others reported that there were new dangerous conspiracies to kill the queen, that the city of London was on fire, or that the queen was already dead. Queen Elizabeth's first biographer William Camden argued that some of the rumors were deliberately started by Protestants to convince the queen that the situation had become so dire that she had to sign the execution order for Mary Stuart.

August 1588

The Spanish ambassador Don Bernadino de Mendoza was expelled from England in January 1584 for his role in conspiracies to have Elizabeth assassinated. He then resided in Paris as an ambassador working against English interests. Some very optimistic reports of the Armada's success reached Paris, as did news that the English had held it off. Mendoza wrote to his king that while the English ambassador had printed a statement to say that the English had been victorious, the French would not allow them to be distributed as it was all lies. Mendoza convinced himself that what he saw as the positive news was true, and sword in hand, rushed into Notre Dame shouting "Victory! Victory!" He was convinced that the Spanish had conquered England, and Elizabeth was a prisoner who had been sent to Rome, where she was forced to walk the streets barefoot. When the truth came out that Spain had lost, Mendoza was "dismayed, obscured himself, not daring to shewe his face" (Levin, *The Heart and Stomach of a King*, 88–89).

Charles Emmanuel I, Duke of Savoy, sent a special courier to Rome with the news of the defeat of the English, leading to great rejoicing.

In Spain since Philip had heard twice from Mendoza about the Spanish victory, Philip declared the victory in Spain and had it printed as a broadside. Once it was distributed there was wild public rejoicing.

Venice voted to convey congratulations to Philip on the great victory.

In Prague, the Spanish Ambassador there, Don Guillen de San Clemente, was sure of the victory and there were celebrations.

In Spain around the time of the Armada Pedro de Ribadeneyra called the queen of England "an abominable monster and idol." Luis de Gongora y Argote described Elizabeth as a "libidinous and ferocious she-wolf" (Izquierdo, 313–314).

1597

The French ambassador André Hurault, seigneur de Maisse was sent to England on a special embassy and had several meetings with Elizabeth. At one, they had a long conversation "of the things that they had said about her and made current in Rome, and that it was nothing but malice and lying." A Cardinal Cosmo had sent one of his servants to London who posed as a merchant and asked that he be taken to see bear baiting, but he did not see what he had been looking for. He finally confessed that his master had sent him to London because the Cardinal had heard that Queen Elizabeth would have Catholics covered in bear skins and then have dogs eat them, that at one time she had ordered 104 women to die in this way altogether. She added to de Maisse, "these were lies that they told of her by malevolence" (De Maisse, 57).

Rumors Involving Mary Stuart

1567

When Mary Stuart's husband Henry Stuart, Lord Darnley was found strangled in the garden at Kirk o' Field on February 10, 1567, the rumors spread rapidly. While most of them claimed that the murderer was James Hepburn, Earl of Bothwell, with or without the collusion of the Scottish queen, there were other candidates for who had arranged the murder as well, including several of the other Scottish lords such as James Stuart, Lord Moray, Mary's illegitimate half-brother. The strangest and most preposterous one was that the murder was engineered by Elizabeth, who had intended to destroy not only Darnley but Mary also.

1587

After the Babington Plot had been discovered, and Mary found guilty of being involved, but before her execution, there were rumors that Mary had escaped, and everyone had to "make diligent search and hue and crye," as Thomas Ward, Constable of Honyton, wrote at the beginning of February 1587. People in the countryside also heard that London was on fire. Right after the execution, Lord Scrope wrote to Sir Francis Walsingham that there were so many "dangerous rumors abroad here," that he had fifty horsemen ready just in case (Wright, II, 333).

Rumors the Queen Was Dead, How She Died, and Her Final Destination

1572

November 1572 Catholics at Antwerp were writing to Pope Gregory XIII that they had heard rumors that they were sure were true that Queen Elizabeth was dead.

1576

In July the Venetian ambassador in Paris wrote to the rulers in Venice that Paris was filled with rumors that Queen Elizabeth was dead. He assured them that the English ambassador was very irritated with the rumors and insisted that Elizabeth was in excellent health. The ambassador thought it was important to inform them as the rumors were intense enough, they would be reaching Venice soon.

1587

Amid other rumors in January of 1587, some thought that the queen was dead.

1594

William Hancock, a tailor, lodged with one of Queen Elizabeth's musicians at Hackney, and Hancock was indiscreet in his chatter, especially about what he had heard about the queen. This was particularly true when he went into the candlemaker John Rogers's shop, telling Hancock that the queen was dead and that her body had been taken to Greenwich, but it was all kept very secret. Hancock denied that he had ever said this; George Bankes, Rogers's servant, however, testified that this is exactly what Hancock had said.

1600

An Englishman in Spain wrote to Robert Cecil that the Spaniards were reporting that Queen Elizabeth was dead.

1603

Up until a few weeks before her death Elizabeth was in good health. But then she had trouble sleeping and lost her appetite. Though doctors hoped she would get better, this did not happen, and she died on March 24 between about two and three in the morning with a number of her ladies around her. Soon there was much discussion—some about whether or not Elizabeth had named James as her heir. But there were other issues, more disturbing, as well. John Clapham wrote that "divers rumors have been spread concerning the manner" of the queen's death (Clapham, 97). John Chamberlain wrote to Dudley Carleton on March 30 that he had heard there was some whispering that in her last days the queen's brain was somewhat distempered, but he assured Carleton that this was simply not true. Elizabeth Southwell claimed that the queen knew that Robert Cecil had told people that she was insane, "and therefore in her sickness, did many times say to him Cecil know I am not mad" (Loomis, 487).

Southwell was related to the queen; her great-granddaughter was Elizabeth's first cousin on the Boleyn side. She was one of the women at the queen's deathbed at Richmond, and also part of the group of women who took turns sitting with her coffin at Whitehall. She was sixteen or seventeen at the time. In 1605 Southwell eloped with Sir Robert Dudley, the natural son of Douglas Sheffield and the Earl of Leicester. He had just lost a lawsuit in front of James I; he had sought to be declared the legitimate heir of his father and thus that he was Earl of Leicester. Dudley was already married to Alice Leigh with five daughters, but he left England with Southwell disguised as his page. At Rome they converted to Catholicism and married, as the Pope did not recognize Dudley's Church of England marriage. In 1607 Elizabeth Southwell Dudley met Father Robert Parsons and told him of her recollections of the death of Elizabeth and he encouraged her to write it down. While it is an eye-witness account, it is also written by someone who had turned her back on her country and had been encouraged by someone who had many times conspired to murder Queen Elizabeth. There are some events in the manuscript that were never told elsewhere. With no corroboration for these stories we cannot know their veracity, especially given the perspective of Southwell and Parsons.

Though Elizabeth had asked that her ladies-in-waiting not share what was private and confidential, Southwell's great aunt Philadelphia Scrope, a Lady of the Bedchamber, gossiped with her about the queen's visions of fire, which may well have been hallucinations caused by fever. But Southwell took it further and described it as the queen having a premonition of her burning in hellfire eternally. Southwell was the only one to describe how Elizabeth Guildford, who was at the dying queen's bedside, took a break and walked about several rooms and then saw the queen walking in a further room—but returning to find the queen still in bed, somehow Elizabeth's ghost was uneasily strolling the palace though her body was not yet dead.

Before Elizabeth died, she had insisted that her body not be "opened," embalmed. Many Elizabethan women made the same request to protect privacy. Her Council apparently followed her instructions, quite possibly because of sixteenth-century medical beliefs that one could tell from a body if a woman was a virgin or had delivered a child; these medical beliefs were quite different from today. Examining Elizabeth's body would have potentially opened James VI's succession to various questions, if those who did it concluded that she was not a virgin or had given birth to a child. A few days after the queen's death her body was moved to Whitehall where it lay in state. Five or six of Elizabeth's ladies stood guard at all times. According to Southwell, one night Elizabeth's head and body burst; it made a terrible sound, split the coffin, and gave off a terrible smell. There is no other mention of this by anyone, but Southwell explained "no man durst speak it publicly for displeasing Secretary Cecil" (Loomis, 487). Though Catherine Loomis insists this is quite possible, she adds that "ultimately, it does not matter whether Elizabeth's corpse burst through its coffin" (509). But given the amount of gossip and rumors about the queen both throughout her reign and at her death, it is doubtful that news of this would not have spread and been discussed with some glee. Lady Anne Clifford's mother, Lady Margaret Russell Clifford, Countess of Cumberland, was one of the women who watched over the queen's body and spoke to her daughter about it, and there was no mention of an exploding body.

1612

After Robert Cecil's death, Henry Howard, Earl of Northampton wrote to James I to disparage the Earl of Salisbury in a way he thought his monarch would especially appreciate, as it also denigrated his predecessor, claiming that Cecil was now kneeling before Queen Elizabeth both in agony as they burned in hell.

QUEEN ELIZABETH WAS REALLY A MAN

Bram Stoker was not only an author. For many years he was the close friend of the actor Henry Irving and was also the business manager of Irving's Lyceum Theatre in London. Late in life Irving was looking to purchase a country home and visited the village of Bisley. Irving heard about the legend of the Bisley boy and thought Stoker would be interested. Stoker was, and included the Bisley boy in his final book, *Impostors*, published in 1910. Thus, it popularized the idea that Queen Elizabeth was really a man.

This was the story told in the village of Bisley: When the young Elizabeth was about ten, with her governess Katherine Ashley and the treasurer of the household Thomas Parry, she was sent to Overcourt, a large manor house in Bisley. There she often played with a boy of her age named John who lived nearby with the Neville family. Just a few days before Henry VIII was to visit, Elizabeth suddenly died. Ashley and Parry were terrified about how angry this would make Henry, so they scoured the countryside for a girl they could substitute as Elizabeth. They could not find one, but the Neville child resembled the dead princess so Ashley and Parry made an arrangement with the Neville family. The boy was dressed in Elizabeth's clothing and Henry never realized this was not his child. One reason for this was the boy's striking resemblance to Elizabeth, since the boy was actually the illegitimate child of

Henry's now dead illegitimate son, Henry Fitzroy, Duke of Richmond. The imposture was never discovered, and John Neville ruled as Elizabeth for the entire reign. It was said that in the mid-nineteenth century a minister in Bisley, the Rev. Thomas Keeble, was involved in a building project at Overcourt and found a coffin; inside was the skeleton of a young girl with the rags of what was once a rich Tudor dress. He secretly reburied the coffin, so no one ever knew where it was.

The story of the substitution of a boy continued to be spread, and there were a variety of publications about it in the mid-twentieth century, which further explained what a great ruler the impostor Elizabeth was. The argument seems to be: Queen Elizabeth was a great ruler. A woman could not be a great ruler. Therefore, Queen Elizabeth must have been a man. More recently in 1995 Chris Hunt published his gay-themed novel *The Bisley Boy*, which explained Elizabeth's relationships with her male favorites in a very different light. Steve Berry, a former trial lawyer, transitioned into being a novelist writing a series about a former U.S. Justice Department operative who owns an antiquarian bookstore in Copenhagen. The eighth book in the series is called the "The King's Deception," and the theme, with many twists and turns including Libyan terrorists, is how the English government is doing everything to keep secret that the famous Queen Elizabeth I was really a man. In his "Writer's Note," Berry discusses what is fact, what he invented, and what is supposition in his novel. Berry certainly appears to believe the imposture is true, citing some historical "facts," such as the statements that Elizabeth refused to allow doctors to examine her, that her unflattering clothing "totally concealed her body." Neither of these statements is true. He also argues how unfeminine her face looks in her portraits. Another of his arguments is how different her energy level was from her siblings, and that while Mary lived into her forties, "All of Henry's other known offspring died before the age of twenty. Yet Elizabeth lived to age 70 … most uncharacteristic for a child of Henry VIII." (Berry) Berry believes strongly in the importance of knowing history. He said in an interview: "History matters at lot. It's a big deal. Where we came from, what happened, what we do is governed by what came before us" (Grossman). History does matter, but perhaps the most important historical question is why both in the sixteenth century and today there is such a need to believe on the one hand that Elizabeth needed to take multiple lovers and had many children that she hid and/or destroyed, or on the other, that the real Elizabeth died as a child and was replaced by a man.

CHAPTER 16

Elizabeth's Pleasures

The letters and documents of Queen Elizabeth I's reign are peppered with the phrase "at the queen's pleasure." But since that meant an indeterminate time of service for an appointed official or a term in prison for an indefinite term there would not necessarily be much pleasure either for the queen herself or the person operating at her pleasure. There were many times that Elizabeth did not find much pleasure in her life. Being queen was hard work and there were many tensions and difficulties. When early in her reign Kat Ashley begged Elizabeth to stop spending time with Robert Dudley, the queen passionately responded that "in this world she had so much sorrow and tribulation and so little joy" (Whitelock, 37), that if she found things that gave her pleasure, she would not give them up. One reason Elizabeth found Dudley so attractive was that he was able to make her laugh. He clearly worked hard to think of ways to keep her amused. Many write about doing something done at the queen's pleasure. In this section, we are talking about what gave Elizabeth pleasure. Some of these pleasures were more physical, while others were more mental or emotional.

TRANSLATIONS

When Elizabeth was young, she had a great passion for her studies and that especially manifested itself in her study of other languages. Kat Ashley was Elizabeth's governess, and she began her young charge's training in foreign languages. Elizabeth studied French with Jean Bellemain, a Calvinist who had to leave France, and Italian with Giovanni Battista Castiglione, an Italian humanist reformer. Elizabeth may have first studied Latin with her brother

Edward's tutor Richard Cox, whom the queen appointed Bishop of Norwich at the beginning of her reign. In late 1546 William Grindal, educated at the University of Cambridge, was appointed as Elizabeth's tutor, and taught her both Latin and Greek. He tragically died of the plague in January 1548. The fourteen-year-old princess successfully fought to get Roger Ascham, educated at Cambridge, as her tutor. Ascham cared deeply about teaching in a way that really engaged his students. Elizabeth truly enjoyed his teaching methods, especially his use of double translation, where she would translate work into English and then back into the original language. Elizabeth was completely fluent in French, Italian, and Latin and her reading and writing skills in these languages were remarkable. She also had fine skills in Greek and in Spanish, though they were not as excellent as the others. Given her joy in working in other languages, the young Elizabeth, even before she started training with Ascham, did several translations as gifts. In 1544, as a gift to her stepmother Katherine Parr she did a French-to-English translation of Marguerite of Navarre's *Mirror of the Sinful Soul*. The following year she translated Katherine Parr's English prayers into French, Italian, and Latin as a gift for her father, Henry VIII. Elizabeth also translated the Italian sermons of Occhines into Latin as a New Year's gift for her brother Edward the first year he was king. All were not only carefully translated but transcribed in her beautiful italic hand.

When Elizabeth became queen, she remembered those who had taught her languages. Castiglione, who Mary had imprisoned in the Tower during her reign, was appointed a Groom of her Privy Chamber and received a manor from her. Roger Ascham became her Latin Secretary. The queen frequently asked Ascham to read with her in the evenings from her favorite passages from classical works. These evenings convinced Ascham to write *The Schoolmaster*, where he discussed the most effective ways to teach Latin but used his work to explore the need to make education engaging and use education to develop ethical values. In the text he also wrote about the young queen. "Beside her perfect readiness in Latin, Italian, French, and Spanish, she readeth here now at Windsor more Greek every day than some prebendary of the church doth read Latin in a whole a week" (*The Schoolmaster*, 54). Ascham died in 1568, and his book was published posthumously two years later.

Throughout Elizabeth's reign she annotated with multilingual marginalia a number of the books she would read. She translated a Seneca letter on how one should accept adversity around 1567 and of a letter by Cicero around 1579. Both were particularly difficult times. In 1567 she was dealing with the aftereffects of the murder of Mary Stuart's husband Lord Darnley and Mary's subsequent marriage to his assumed murderer, Lord Bothwell. In 1579 Elizabeth was seriously considering marriage with François, Duke of Anjou, and dealing with all the controversies this potential match caused. Cicero's letter to Curio is about the possibility of reconciling ideals of friendships and political necessities. These were issues that troubled Elizabeth as she considered, and ultimately rejected, the French marriage. Both translations were gifts to her godson Sir John Harington. Janel Mueller and Joshua Scodel suggest that "the sources that Elizabeth chose to translate engage with issues that go to the heart of her convictions and concerns regarding her rule, her court, and her realm of England" (8).

The last decade and a half of Elizabeth's reign was very difficult. There was the final plot of Mary Stuart and her execution, the constant fears of further Spanish invasions after the Armada, increasing problems with Ireland, and bad harvests and inflation. Even more painful for the queens were the deaths of some of those she cared about and most trusted, such as the Earl of Leicester in 1588 and Sir Francis Walsingham in 1591. Her translations in the 1590s were not done as carefully nor were they given as gifts. Some of them were done rather quickly and some were unfinished or fragmented. These translations were clearly a way for Elizabeth to focus her mind and deal with some of the anxieties with which she was burdened. One example of her translations in this period was Boethius's *The Consolation of Philosophy*, which the queen did when she was at Windsor in October and November of 1593. There was no intention of circulation for the translation; it was done for Elizabeth's own solace.

Hunting

Hunting was very popular with the nobility and especially royalty throughout Europe in the sixteenth century. Ambassadors' letters are filled with references to royalty in the countries in which they were based going off to hunt. But hunting could also be very dangerous. In one hunt Catherine de Medici fell and fractured her thigh. In another in 1567 Sir Henry Norris wrote to William Cecil that "the Queen Mother, riding or hunting her horse, fell, and she bruised her shoulder and brake her face" (State Papers Online). Having a broken face sounds like a strange and painful accident. Hunting was clearly important enough to the French court, that when the young Francis II met with the English ambassador Nicholas Throckmorton in February 1560, the king asked him if his queen liked hawking and hunting. Love of hunting was something that the new English queen and the French royal family shared.

Not only did Francis's mother go hunting, so did his wife Mary Stuart. While she was queen consort, she had "a marvellous chance and escape," as Sir Henry Killigrew wrote to Elizabeth in December 1559. Mary was "riding in hunting and following the hart of force, was in her course cast off her gelding by a bough of a tree, and with the suddenness of the fall was not able to call for help. And albeit there did follow divers gentlemen and ladies of her chamber, yet three or four of them passed over her before she was espied, and some of their horses rode so near her as her hood was trodden off." When Mary got her breath back, she was able to sit up and call for help. She was not hurt but went back to court and stayed in her room. Killigrew added "She feels no incommodity by her fall, and yet has determined to change that kind of exercise" (State Papers Online). Mary Stuart clearly decided not to give up hunting after all, as once she was back in Scotland, she spent a great deal of time going hunting and hawking, a hunting game with a trained hawk. She was so skilled on horseback that once she was under house arrest in England, there was great concern about allowing her to go hunting, as she might easily manage to escape. The Scottish queen frequently begged to be allowed to go hunting for the exercise, and this was sometimes permitted but with the insistence that a number of those loyal to Elizabeth accompanying her. But the government wrote many letters to those in charge of Mary demanding that the times Mary go hunting be severely limited.

If Mary Stuart was fond of hunting, so was Elizabeth, and she was quite skilled at it. As soon as Elizabeth became queen, she named Robert Dudley as her Master of the Horse, and he often went hunting with her, both when she was at court, and even more when she went on progress, bringing her court to visit members of her nobility. Early in her reign, Elizabeth's love of riding and hunting concerned some people, as her close advisors were worried about the kind of accidents that had happened to those in the French royal house, but fortunately Elizabeth did not suffer from such incidents.

Sir Francis Chaloner writing in 1563 to his older brother Thomas, the ambassador in Spain, believed that Elizabeth was not doing the job of ruling, and though he does not mention him, implies that the fault was Robert Dudley's. "The Queen is entirely given over to love, hunting, hawking, and dancing; consuming day and night with trifles; nothing is treated earnestly" (State Papers Online). Given that in 1563 Elizabeth was going hunting and hawking with Dudley, dancing with him, and flirting with him, he might well have been seen as the cause of Chaloner's perception of Elizabeth not taking ruling seriously. In truth, Elizabeth took her position as queen very seriously, but she did enjoy hunting. During the attempts to convince Queen Elizabeth that she should marry the Archduke Charles, brother of the Holy Roman Empire, in July 1566 Thomas Dannett wrote to the queen from Vienna that the archduke "is well beloved among his people, active, and loves the exercise of arms, hunting, and riding" (State Papers Online).

As much as Elizabeth enjoyed hunting, she also used it for political and diplomatic reasons as well. Elizabeth spent a whole day hunting with one of her favorite ambassadors, Guzman de Silva, when there were difficulties with Spain in the Netherlands she needed to discuss. In 1570 the queen was visiting her friends, Margery and Henry Norris (see Chapter 14) and she invited the French ambassador, La Mothe Fénelon, to go hunting with her. It must have been quite an experience, as he wrote that she "took the crossbow and killed six fallow deer"—fallow was a kind of deer common at the time (Paranque, "Queen Elizabeth I and the Elizabethan Court in the French Ambassador's Eyes," 273). Even if Elizabeth had a servant who set up the crossbow for her, it required a lot of upper body strength and agility to use it, and women usually used the easier long bow instead. Showing herself so strong and skilled to the French ambassador would be an effective method of sending a message to the French royal house of her abilities. When the queen was at Eton, she gave the ambassador an audience but told him she was a little fatigued because the day before she had hunted all day and well into the night and had killed a big deer. Le Mothe Fénelon had another much more difficult experience with the queen and hunting, as Elizabeth and members of her court were at Woodstock for a hunting party when she heard about the St. Bartholomew's Day Massacre in August 1572. They immediately stopped hunting. Le Mothe Fénelon headed to Woodstock, where for a time he was placed under house arrest (see Chapter 8).

Elizabeth continued to hunt throughout her reign. When she visited Sir Anthony Browne, Viscount Montagu at Cowdray Castle in West Sussex in 1591 he presented her with a crossbow. She then killed three or four deer at the park at Cowdray. To celebrate the French ambassador in 1599 he was entertained with hunting as well as dancing. When she was sixty-seven years old, she was still hunting. Rowland White wrote to Sir Robert Sidney from the palace at Oatlands in September 1600 that every second day Elizabeth was out hunting. In 1601 Sir John Popham wrote to Robert Cecil that "it is my greatest comfort to understand her Majesty has that strength of body that she is able to undergo such travail in hunting" (State Papers Online). As late as September 1602 Robert Cecil wrote to George Nicolson that "so goes the Queen my mistress, who has had very constant health and has been continually in hunting and hawking this summer" (State Papers Online). Certainly, going hunting was politically valuable for the queen. Elizabeth could use a hunting trip to create a chance to speak informally with her own courtiers and advisors or to ambassadors. She could also show herself as skilled and vigorous. But it was also something that clearly also gave her pleasure, and she did it from the beginning of her reign until the end.

Walking in and Enjoying Gardens

Elizabeth also loved brisk walking, especially in beautiful gardens. During her sister's Mary reign, when she was in the Tower or under house arrest in Woodstock, one of the things that greatly distressed her was that she was not allowed to go walking. Once she was queen she walked regularly in the beautiful gardens at her various palaces, especially Hampton Court. The queen would get up early. She would spend some time on her devotions and then read dispatches and prepare for council meetings. She would dance the galliard on her own and then usually go for a walk in the gardens. If the weather was cold or windy, she would walk in her long galleries. When Melville visited her in 1564, he noted that at eight in the morning she would take an hour's walk in the garden and one morning she invited him to walk with her so that they could talk informally. Several times during her reign that Elizabeth had private discussions in gardens, and the meetings were often noted by others, but they had no idea what was said. It was frequently noted that when Elizabeth went on progress, she very much enjoyed the gardens in the palaces she visited. At Kenilworth, the Earl of Leicester had a beautiful formal garden designed. When Elizabeth visited it was set aside for her exclusive use. Sometimes she would enjoy it on her own; other times she used it for meetings. Also on progress, and especially at Kenilworth, there were elaborate performances in gardens. They were meant to celebrate Elizabeth, demonstrate power and wealth, or attempt to convince the queen to some action, such as, at Kenilworth in 1575, when Leicester made a final attempt to convince her to marry him. These garden extravaganzas happened first in France and were organized by the royal family to demonstrate their magnificence; in England Elizabeth did not produce them; rather they were produced for her.

Dance

The ability to dance was perceived as a necessary court skill and Elizabeth would have been trained to be an expert in a range of dances while in her early teens. Dancing was something the queen very much appreciated, and sometimes used for some political meaning throughout her reign. She also got great pleasure at watching others dance, especially as she got older. Elizabeth also perceived dancing as a pleasurable way to exercise. Most mornings she would perform as many as seven galliards, one of the most demanding and energetic of all the Elizabethan dances, as a correspondent wrote to the Earl of Shrewsbury in 1589. It was done in triple time and was very lively. While there were some traditional English dances, particular the morris dance, at Elizabeth's court the dances were for the most part the latest dances from Italy, France, and Spain. There were so many opportunities to have dances at the Court—many holidays, visits of ambassadors and other distinguished guests, and celebrations such as weddings.

The Italian Jasper Gaffoyne had been appointed as dancing master by Henry VIII in 1542 and he continued in the role for all of Henry's children, before he finally retired from Elizabeth's court in 1584. He was paid £23 a year. His position was taken over by Thomas Cardell, who also played the lute. One of the dances that Elizabeth enjoyed most, along with the galliard, was the volta, which originated in Italy. It was a dance for couples, which she especially liked to dance with Robert Dudley. The dance was full of complex steps, with the man helping the woman leap. The couple also embraced. Elizabeth enjoyed dancing not only the volta with Robert Dudley, but other dances as well. There was also the pavan, which was a slow and stately dance, and the almain, which was based on a German dance, but it was much livelier when done at the queen's court. The gavotte began as a country dance in England but when it became a court dance it was performed in a more stately manner. At the end of the reign Elizabeth told the French ambassador de Maisse that she was so skilled in Italian dances that she was known as the Florentine.

Il Schifanoya, a native of the Italian duchy of Mantua, lived in London. He wrote many letters about happenings at court and the city to the Mantuan ambassador in Brussels and also to the leading officials in Matua. Il Schifanoya wrote in January 1559 about how appalled he was by the new Protestant regime, which in their litany "omit Saint Mary, all the Saints, the Pope, and the Dead." He was also upset by "the statue of St. Thomas stoned and beheaded, which is now thrown down entirely." In the same letter he also talked about on the day of the Epiphany "the unusual licentiousness practiced at the Court in dances and banquets" (State Papers *Online*), which suggested that for at least some Catholics Protestantism and dancing were intimately connected.

Elizabeth herself danced from the beginning of her reign to the end. At the feast after her coronation she danced with Thomas Howard, Duke of Norfolk. Thomas Smith wrote to a friend from Hampton Court in 1572 about the celebration of Christmas there and all the dancing. During Lupold von Wedel's visit to England in 1585 (see Chapter 11), he noted that he saw a dance at Christmas court where slender and beautiful women were dressed magnificently. In 1599 the queen held a great feast and at the age sixty-five danced three or four galliards.

In June 1600 the queen was very upset and sad over the actions of the Earl of Essex. Despite these feelings she planned to be the honored guest at the 1600 wedding of Henry Somerset, Lord Herbert, and future Earl of Worcester and Lady Anne Russell. As part of the celebration eight ladies-in-waiting were part of the entertainment. "They have a strange dance newly invented." They would all wear the same costume: the skirt was silver, the top was embroidered with gold and silver silk and they had cloaks of carnation taffeta, and they each represented different qualities. Lady Mary Fitton was the lead dancer. After the first part of the dance each of the women then asked someone else to join the dance and Fitton asked the queen to dance with her. "Her Majesty asked what she was? 'Affection,' she said. 'Affection', said the Queen, 'is false.' Yet Her Majesty rose and danced" (Nichols, III, 499).

The queen also greatly enjoyed watching others dance throughout her reign. In June 1559 Paulo Tiepolo, Venetian Ambassador explained that "The Queen's daily arrangements are musical performances and other entertainments, and she takes marvelous pleasure in seeing people dance" (Venice: January 1559, 16–31', in *Calendar of State Papers Relating to English Affairs in the Archives of Venice, Volume 7, 1558–1580*, ed. Rawdon Brown and G. Cavendish Bentinck [London, 1890], pp. 10–24. *British History Online*). On January 6, 1594, the court celebrated Twelfth Night with dancing until one in the morning. Elizabeth was seated on a high throne where she could watch all the dancing, and the young Earl of Essex, who would later cause her such grief, sat with her. When the French ambassador de Maisse visited the English court in 1597 he described Elizabeth greatly enjoying her ladies dance, though she would stop them if she did not like a part of the dance. He added that he had an audience with the queen one evening; when he departed, he observed her half dancing her way back to her chamber. The day after Christmas at Whitehall in 1602 Mary Fitton danced two galliards for the queen.

Dancing also had political implications at Elizabeth's court. When James Melville made his diplomatic mission to the English court in 1564, Elizabeth asked how she compared with Mary Stuart in several different ways. The queen was emphatic about knowing which of them was the better dancer, and Melville admitted that the Scottish queen danced "not so high and disposedly" as Elizabeth (Melville, 125). The following year when the Austrian ambassador Adam Zwetkovich came to negotiate with Elizabeth about marriage with the Archduke Charles, the queen deliberately allowed him to see her dance (see Chapter 8).

Dance was also used in the marriage negotiations with François, Duke of Anjou. His negotiator Jean de Simier was entertained at dances. When François, Duke of Anjou himself visited Elizabeth in 1579 and 1581 she danced with him frequently. To honor the Danish ambassador, on Twelfth Night 1599, the queen danced with the Earl of Essex. In 1600 Elizabeth was very pleased with Virginio Orsini, the Duke of Bracciano, when he came to visit (see Chapter 11). Bracciano was the highest status Italian to ever visit Elizabeth's court. His letters to his wife described all the honors and delights he experienced, but he felt that his most splendid moment was on January 9, when the queen consented to dance, which was the greatest honor the English queen could do for him. Some Catholic allies had asked Bracciano to see how fragile and near death the queen was: Elizabeth would have been aware of this, and vigorous dancing would have been the message she wanted to be sent that she was still vital and in control.

This was very much the message she wanted to send her cousin James VI. The Scottish king would often send Sir Roger Aston when he had messages for the English queen. Sir Anthony Weldon wrote that he had heard from Aston that when he arrived at court, "ever he was placed in the Lobby; the Hangings being turned ... where he might see the Queen dancing" (Weldon, 2). With such reports as these, it becomes more understandable that James had a nightmare he would never become king of England (see Chapter 13).

Elizabeth loved to dance so much that many people gossiped that the way to gain prominence at her court was to dance well. Those who disliked the hardworking and talented Sir Christopher Hatton claimed his skill at the galliard and his good looks were what led to his success at court. Elizabeth dancing with attractive men disturbed others. In 1589 the Parson Wylton said in church that the queen was an "arrant whore," and his reason what that "all dancers are whores" (Levin, *Heart and Stomach*, 83).

Elizabeth used dance to demonstrate the glory of court, and to show her vitality and youthful vigor. But Elizabeth also really enjoyed dancing; it was one of her real pleasures.

Music

Elizabeth loved music. While listening to music or playing an instrument is greatly valued today, it had far reaching meanings in the queen's time period. To the English people, music was a way to connect the human on earth to God. Many English people believed that listening to, or participating in, holy music was another way for humans to briefly understand the divine. For the English, the belief that they could truly compose, understand, appreciate, and make beautiful music was part of their sense of self, and through music people were able to reach toward heaven. The anonymous author of the 1586 book, *The Praise of Musicke*, suggested that music brought "sweet harmony" to all living creatures, that the "pleasant harmony of the celestial globes caused" was of great importance. If people "be allured and mitigated with musicke, we may safely conclude that this proceedeth from that hidden vertue, which is between our soules and musicke" (38, 53).

Elizabeth well understood the importance of the pleasure she took from music to dance to, but also listening to music and playing instruments herself. This was something she had in common with her father. Henry VIII was a skilled musician who loved to play a range of instruments, including the organ, lute, and virginals, and he loved to sing. He often had musicians playing at his court. The king oversaw the musical education of Mary, Elizabeth, and Edward, and Elizabeth started learning to play as a young girl. In the reign of her sister Mary, she played for the queen in 1557 when Mary visited her at Hatfield. Her pleasure in music, which worked as a symbol of her ability to create harmony during her reign, continued until the end of her life. In December 1597 she told de Maisse that she had at least sixty musicians at her court, and when she was young, she "composed measures and music, and had played them herself and danced them" (De Maisse, 95). Over the course of her reign she received as gifts many beautiful musical instruments. When Philip Julius, Duke of Stettin-Pomerania traveled in England in 1602 he visited Whitehall and he noted "almost every room there was a musical instrument," again a way to display how she could bring harmony (*Diary of the Journey of Philip Julius, Duke of Stettin-Pomerania*, 27). Her early biographer William Camden suggested that she was not only one who could "play handsomely on the lute," and had the ability to "sing sweetly," but that she did so because she realized she needed to know music "so far as it might beseem a Princess" (Camden, Introduction, n.p.).

She was proud of her skill as a musician and sometimes created situations where foreign ambassadors could "accidentally" hear her play, which she claimed she did privately for her own entertainment, and, most importantly, to relieve her feelings of melancholy. *The Praise of Musicke* explained that playing music or listening "is the cause of the delectation"—which gives great pleasure, enjoyment, and delight—that enters people's nature (54).

When James Melville visited Elizabeth's court in 1564 and the queen asked Melville for the many comparisons between her and Mary Stuart, one involved asking Melville to judge them both as musicians. She mentioned to Melville that to refresh and entertain herself she would play the lute or the virginals, the generic English term for all keyboard instruments, such as harpsichord and spinet. Elizabeth then asked Melville if his queen played well. His response was "reasonably, for a Queen." Elizabeth wanted to have Melville hear her play but keep up the pretense she only did it for herself. So that evening she had her cousin, Henry, Baron Hunsdon take Melville into a quiet gallery where he could hear music being played by the queen. After he had listened for a while, Melville entered the room and found the queen in the room by herself playing. Melville considered that she played "excellently well," though she stopped playing as soon as she saw him and acted surprised that he was there. The queen then explained to Melville that she did not play for men, but she played instead when she was by herself attempting to ward off melancholy.

Music and medicine were very interconnected, and music was one way of overcoming being "Melancholike and dolefull." *The Praise of Musicke* gives an example of a man who had severe feelings of melancholy. "If at any time he perceived himselfe to have beene melancholik, took his *Citterne* in his hand & professed that he tooke ease thereby" (55, 60). A cittern was an instrument similar to a lute, but often with a grotesquely carved head. Thus, Elizabeth explaining she played to deal with her melancholy would have made a great deal of sense to Melville. But that evening she clearly had other motives as well. Before Melville left her presence, the queen "inquired whether my Queen or she played best?" Melville stated that he "found myself obliged to give her the praise" (Melville, 50). Melville's anecdote not only reveals Elizabeth's musical skills but her competitive personality, especially with her cousin. Though she pretended to be playing for herself when she played for Melville, the following year in June 1565 she openly played both for the lute and the virginals for the Austrian ambassador Adam Zwetkovich and the Spanish ambassador Guzman de Silva, who informed Philip II that she played both very well. This was a special gesture of intimacy, with Elizabeth wanting to convince the two ambassadors how eager she was to marry the Archduke Charles. As late as 1592 she played for the Duke of Wirtenberg when he visited England. On August 18, 1592 he had an audience with the queen and after they had chatted in French "he so far prevailed upon her that she played very sweetly and skillfully on her instrument, the strings of which were of gold and silver" (Rye, 12).

More than thirty years after she had played for Melville, she had another interesting conversation about music with another ambassador. André Hurault, seigneur de Maisse was sent to the English court by Henri IV at the end of 1597. On December 24, 1597 the queen sent a coach to fetch him. He wrote that he found her very kindly disposed to him. "She was having the spinet played to her in her chamber, seeming very attentive to it." De Maisse stated that the queen was so involved in the music that she was surprised when he entered "or at least she feigned surprise." Though he had been sent for, he still apologized for interrupting her pleasure. "She told me that she loved music greatly" and they then discussed her love of music and how earlier in her reign she had really enjoyed playing instruments and loved listening to music "and still took great pleasure in it" (De Maisse, 55–56).

Elizabeth loved music and she loved musical instruments, and the queen understood that in the early modern period, musical instruments were devices for controlling unseen aspects of the world and the body politic. Thus, Elizabeth's love of music was also love of what it represented. Wealthy foreign visitors who visited Elizabeth's palaces were impressed by the musical instruments they saw that were owned by the queen both for her own use and for the use of her musicians. They were also a display of her power, particularly the power of harmony.

Thomas Platter was impressed by a virginal made of glass that he saw at Hampton Court. Many instruments were specifically engraved with references to the Queen. Baron Waldstein noted at Hampton Court a "most interesting and ingenious musical instruments." On the case of one it was inscribed "May Elizabeth live for ever" (Waldstein, 154–155). Waldstein also saw ivory flutes on which the queen's musicians played. Thomas Platter also saw beautiful instruments that Elizabeth played. When Philip Julius, Duke of Stettin-Pomerania traveled in England in 1602 he visited Whitehall he noted "almost every room there was a musical instrument" (*Diary of the Journey of Philip Julius, Duke of Stettin-Pomerania*, 27). In the New Year gifts rolls there are a number of examples of musical gifts, including lute strings from Innocent Comy and five song books from Peter Wolfe.

Virginio Orsini, Duke of Bracciano, not only enjoyed the dancing at Elizabeth's court when he visited in 1600, but also the music. He was completely impressed with the music he heard during the Epiphany service. He also wrote to his wife about how a musical entertainment had been prepared for him, with "several instruments as far as I know never heard in Italy, but miraculous" (Wyatt, 131).

There were many impressive musicians employed by Queen Elizabeth. Both the Bassano family and the Lupo family were invited to come from Venice to the court of Henry VIII, and their descendants, a group of close cousins, were professional musicians at Elizabeth's court. Both families were of Jewish background but outwardly were practicing Christians (see Chapter 11). The Bassanos were not only musicians, but also makers of instruments and composers. The Bassanos formed a consort for recorders and apparently played other instruments as well. The consort was supported by the court and younger members of the family were eventually appointed to it. They played in the consort for Elizabeth throughout her reign, beginning with her coronation and wore their mourning livery as they played for her funeral. The musicians included Andrea, Arthur, Augustine, Edward, and Jeronimo Bassano; another musician with the groups was their cousin Alphonso Lanier who was the husband of Emilia Bassano. Robert Baker also played with them. Augustine Bassano was appointed to the consort in Edward VI's reign. His brother Lodovico was officially appointed in 1569 and continued until his death in 1593. The records suggest he died of severe depression, maybe a suicide. Their cousin Jeronimo Bassano was both a wind player and a viol player. He was appointed to the recorder consort in 1579. Ambrose Lupo, who was originally an Iberian Jew who came to England via Italy, was one of the most important viol players at the queen's court and established a string consort. He worked until his death in 1591. His son Joseph became a member of the consort in 1563, and his brother Peter in 1567. Joseph's son Thomas joined the consort in 1588 when he was sixteen, though he did not start receiving payment until 1591. In 1601 the queen gave Joseph a gift of £200 in recompense of his long and faithful service. When Augustine Bassano died, he bequeathed Thomas Lupo his two best lutes and all his music books. Two other string players at Elizabeth's court who were Iberian Jews who came to England from Italy were George and Innocent Comy.

Others were also from Italy. Alfonso Ferrabosco had first left Italy for France and performed as a singer and a musician at the French court before he moved to England early in Elizabeth's reign. He was listed as one of the queen's musicians by 1562. He married an English woman and had at least two sons. In 1578 he and his wife went back to Italy, but his sons Alfonso and Henry were raised in England, and both also performed at court. The younger Alfonso Ferrabosco became known as one of the most distinguished lute players in Elizabethan England. He was employed by Queen Elizabeth, and he played the lute at the queen's funeral in 1603.

As well as Italian musicians, there were also home-grown ones as well. From about 1579 we have records of some lutenists, anywhere between three and six, employed full time at the court. Being appointed to this position was very prestigious and exclusive. In the last decades of her reign, as well as the younger Ferrabosco, there was also Thomas Cardell, John Johnson, Mathias Mason, and Robert Hales. One of them, Mason, was initially paid £30, which was doubled in 1589, and presumably the others were paid about this amount as well. Cardell was also her dancing master. John Johnson was employed as a lutenist for Queen Elizabeth from about 1579. By the age of seven Johnson was an apprentice to a professional lutenist. He might have been introduced to the court by the Earl of Leicester. In 1588 John Case published a list of great English musicians of the time and included Johnson. He was not only a performer but a composer and mixed Italian and English styles in his own work. His music was either for a solo lute player or for lute duets. Elizabeth clearly appreciated his work. Johnson died in 1594, and the following year she made a very generous grant to his widow Alice. His son Robert was also a significant composer in the seventeenth century. Mason, like Ferrabosco, was also given an important role at the queen's funeral. Robert Hales was both a lutenist and a singer and worked at court beginning in 1583. He is recorded as having performed for the queen a song composed by John Dowland in 1590 as part of the Accession Day celebrations. Dowland was also a lutenist as well as a composer. Dowland may have been part of an entertainment that Giles Bridges, Lord Chandos presented to the queen at Sudeley Castle when she visited in September 1592. The queen was also a patron to such composers such as Thomas Morley, Thomas Tallis, and William Byrd.

Games

Queen Elizabeth also enjoyed playing cards and games such as chess with her friends and courtiers. Elizabeth was very fond of playing cards, though she would sometimes lose her temper when she was not doing so well, as Robert Carey once mentioned to his father Lord Hunsdon. She especially enjoyed playing with Roger, Lord North, who would often tactfully lose to her. The queen also very much enjoyed playing chess, and in the early years of her reign she played chess with Roger Ascham until his death in 1568.

Lord Burghley, the Earl of Leicester, and her godson Sir John Harington all kept chess sets available for when the queen wanted to play. Elizabeth was aware of how the game of chess could be a metaphor for the dangerous political games of diplomacy. In 1565, when Lord Darnley had gone to Scotland and Mary Stuart planned to marry him, the French ambassador Paul de Foix came to see Elizabeth while she was playing chess and told her he thought "this game is an image of the words and deeds of men. If, for example, we lose a pawn, it seems but a small matter: nevertheless, the loss often draws after it that of the world of the game." Elizabeth answered, "I understand you: Darnley is but a pawn, but may well checkmate me if I do not take care" (Goodman, I, 76). Elizabeth enjoyed playing cards and playing games—especially if she won—and they allowed her to relax and then to play the far more serious game of ruling her country.

Gifts

From the time Elizabeth was a small child she was strongly involved in the politics of Renaissance royal gift exchange. Gifts were given and received for a range of reasons, few having to do with uncomplicated affection. Particularly for royalty, gifts had great political significance in terms of power and relationships. Elizabeth spent a lot of time creating gifts before she became queen, beginning when she was only six years old, and gave her brother Edward for his second birthday a cambric shirt that she herself had embroidered. When she was eleven, she did a translation from French to English of Marguerite of Navarre's *Mirror of a Sinful Soul* for Katherine Parr. She wrote it all in beautiful italic hand and made a book for her stepmother with beautiful and elaborately embroidered covers that she made. The following year she did a translation of Katherine's prayers for her father Henry VIII, again in a book she had beautifully embroidered.

Elizabeth also made gifts for her sister Mary during her sister's reign. She made the top part of a dress with the "sleeves of cloth of silver, richly embroidered over with Venice silver, and rayed with silver and black silk" (Chambers, I, 32). A beautiful gift that probably brought Elizabeth little pleasure was from her sister Queen Mary, however. Though in July 1553 the new queen had welcomed Elizabeth's presence at court, in the months that followed she pressured Elizabeth to convert and attend Catholic mass. Mary began telling people that Elizabeth was not her sister, but the daughter of Anne Boleyn's lover, her musician Mark Smeaton, and Mary gave her cousins Frances, Duchess of Suffolk and Margaret, Countess of Lennox precedence over her half-sister. In December 1553 Elizabeth asked for permission to leave court to go live at Ashridge, and the Spanish ambassador Simon Renard encouraged Mary to make Elizabeth think all was well by giving her a present. Mary presented Elizabeth with a coif, a short cloak made of sable. Elizabeth thanked her for the gift, but begged Mary to agree to see her personally if she heard anything against her. The queen promised that she would. Only a short time later, however, had Elizabeth brought back to court under guard and kept under house arrest until Mary sent lords to escort her sister to the Tower. Elizabeth wrote to her in panic, reminding the queen of her promise. Despite having given her word, Mary refused to see Elizabeth and she was immediately despatched to the Tower. The coif would have hardly consoled her. One gift that Elizabeth received around the same time that she did treasure was a miniature book of private prayer Lady Elizabeth Tyrwitt gave her when she was in the Tower. As queen Elizabeth wore it in hanging by a gold chain to her girdle, and "at her death left it by will to one of her Women of the Bed-chamber" (Nichols, I, xxxvii).

Once she became queen, she created fewer gifts for other people. Embroidery took great concentration and needed equipment. It would have been very difficult for Elizabeth to take the time and concentration to do embroidery to relax; she was far more likely to do other things, such as reading, to have some quiet times. The queen did give many gifts, but often in fact she "regifted" gifts she had previously been given, as Elizabeth as queen received many, many presents. In England at the time it was customary to give the monarch gifts at New Year's celebrations. Each year she received about 170–200 gifts. Many times, she would give gilt plate in return that was worth much less than the value of the gift given her. Since there were so many gifts, a few she immediately kept for her own use, and the others were given to others to store or care for. One gift Elizabeth kept was from her cousin Lady Margaret Strange, later Countess of Derby (see Chapter 7) in 1562. It was "a little round mount of gold" made to have a pomander in it (Nichols, I, 108). Elizabeth was very sensitive to bad smells, so this would have been a very welcome present. An unusual gift Elizabeth received that year was from John Yonge, who would serve in Parliament during her reign as well as serving as a Sheriff and a Justice of the Peace. When on progress she stayed at his mansion in Bristol. Yonge's gift to Elizabeth was a painting framed in walnut wood;

on the frame were certain verses about money. To accompany the painting he also gave the queen a round piece of silver. She had the painting delivered to George Bredeman, the Keeper of the Palace at Westminster probably to be exhibited there, but she kept the piece of silver herself.

At the beginning of her reign it was more likely that nobles, courtiers, and bishops would give her bags of gold but soon her ladies let people know the queen much preferred to receive gifts of clothing or jewels, and gifts that were homemade were especially welcome. Even the bags of gold, however, were in beautiful and distinctive bags. Some gifts Elizabeth received were representative of the work people did for the queen. Her bakers would give her confections. In 1562 the artist Levina Teerlinc gave the queen a box painted with an image of her and other people at the court. Nicholas Hilliard, one of her favorite artists, gave the queen in 1584 a painting containing the story of the five wise virgins and the five foolish virgins. The same year Dr. Robert Huick, who had attended Elizabeth as her physician for many years before she became queen, gave her two pots, "one of green ginger, the other of orange flowers" (Nichols, I, 117). Another of her physicians, Dr. Richard Master, gave the queen two pots, one of ginger and the other nutmeg. Mr. Morgan, her apothecary, gave her a pot of green ginger and another of orange flowers, while another apothecary, Mr. Hemingway, gave a pot of preserved pears.

Some of those close to Elizabeth were able to get the queen's measurements from her tailor Walter Fish when they wanted to give her gifts of clothing. For others, such gifts had to be loose fitting or fitted over under clothing as most of those who created or procured clothing gifts for the queen would not have her exact measurements. Many of the gifts of clothing would be beautifully embroidered and these would have taken a great deal of time to create and would be very costly to produce. Often the Ladies of the Privy Chamber and Bedchamber would give advice on which colors and motifs would most please Elizabeth. For example, word was gotten to Bess, Countess of Shrewsbury, that Elizabeth had enough red garments but would be glad for something blue.

People would also give her books that were written for her or dedicated to her. The queen also enjoyed highly unusual gifts. Many summers the queen would take many members of her court and leave London to go on progress, sometimes to her own properties but often honoring her courtiers by visiting them—and it was a very costly honor to host the queen and her court. As well as food and entertainment, and occasionally actually rebuilding, at each place she visited her host would give her a gift, usually a jewel. The New Year's gifts were carefully reported each year. A number of these lists—known as gift rolls—still exist though some have been lost. From these, as well as other sources such as letters and journals, we have significant information about the gifts given to Elizabeth, and what this tells us about her tastes.

One person created beautiful intricate embroidered gifts of clothing for Elizabeth that were given whenever she completed them. Elizabeth, however, would have been exceedingly ambivalent about these gifts, as the person who was giving them was her cousin Mary Stuart, her enforced guest from when she fled to England in 1568 until her execution in 1587. At the same time Mary embroidered night caps, what was said to be a very elegant headdress along with a collar and cuff, and later a crimson satin skirt that she embroidered with fine silver thread, and other lovely pieces that she hoped would convince Elizabeth to invite her to court and allow her freedom, she was also conspiring to have Elizabeth murdered so that she could become queen of England. In 1571 there was the Ridolfi plot, a plan to assassinate Elizabeth and make Mary Stuart queen (see Chapter 9). According to the Spanish ambassador Gureau de Spes, one of Robert Dudley, Earl of Leicester's New Year's gifts to the queen soon after demonstrates that Leicester was well-aware how the plot made Elizabeth furious. De Spes described the gift as "a jewel containing a painting in which the Queen was represented on a great throne with the queen of Scotland in chains at her feet, begging for mercy, whilst the neighbouring countries of Spain and France were as if covered by the waves of the sea, and Neptune and the rest of them bowing to this Queen" (*CSP, Spain*, II, 290).

Elizabeth especially loved clocks and watch pieces. In 1562 Thomas Heneage gave Elizabeth an hourglass "garnished with gold, with glass sand, and all in a case of black velvet embroidered with silver" (Nichols, I, 117). While that was lovely, a decade later the queen got an even more impressive gift from the Earl of Leicester. His gifts were not only extravagant but very thoughtful. His 1572 New Year's gift was an armlet made of gold with rubies and diamonds, but what made it really special was it "having in the closing thereof a clocke, and in the fore parte of the same a fayre lozengie dyamonde without a foyle, hanging thereat a rounde juell fully garnished with dyondes and perle pendant" (Nichols, I, xxxvi). Leicester presented it to the queen in a purple velvet case embroidered with Venetian gold. Miranda Wilson has explained that this gift is "the first evidence we have for a wristwatch, that is, a watch worn against the flesh rather than dangled from a chain, attached to fur, or worn on a ribbon. Dudley's gift is striking not only for its intricacy and beauty, but because it links technological innovation and Elizabeth's body. It is a gift at once unique, intimate, and strange" (Wilson, 45).

From the surviving gift rolls, we know that Elizabeth received at least twenty-four clocks as gifts. Some of them were glamorous and expensive. The same year that Leicester gave the queen her watch, she received a crystal with emeralds on one side and on the other side a clock. In 1574 Elizabeth's cousin, Margaret, Countess of Derby presented Elizabeth with "A white bear of gold and mother of pearl, holding a ragged staff," on a gold stand with diamonds and rubies "wherein is a clock" (Wood, 251). Sir Christopher Hatton's gift to the queen in 1576 was "a rich jewel, being a clock of gold, garnished with diamonds, rubies, emeralds, and pearls" (Wood, 251). Another of Hatton's gifts was an emerald and gold pendant. Seven years after the watch, Leicester gave the queen "A tablet of gold, being a clock fully furnished with small diamonds and rubies; above the same are six bigger diamonds" (Wood, 251–252). He also gave her a gold pendant which on each side was enameled an apple decorated with diamonds and rubies. Two years after that Leicester again repeated the gift of a watch, this one on a gold chain with diamonds. That year Francis Russell, Earl of Bedford gave Elizabeth "a watch set in mother of pearl" as well as three gold pendants. Edward Stafford's gift was "A little clock of gold with a crystal," garnished with sparks of small diamonds, rubies, and emerald" (Wood, 252). On the back side were other diamonds and rubies. Some years later Thomas Knyvet, a Gentleman of the Privy Chamber, gave the queen a small clock in an enameled gold case.

Leicester gave Elizabeth numerous other beautiful gifts as well, including several gold collars and necklaces with many jewels. In 1577 Leicester gave the queen a collar of gold, with thirteen great emeralds and three large pearls. The following year his gift was also very extravagant, a collar of gold, with thirteen large and beautiful emeralds along with pearls and rubies. A second gift was six dozen gold enameled buttons with rubies and in each a pearl. Also in 1578, when Elizabeth was on progress, Leicester gave the queen "one fair cup of crystal fashioned like a slipper, garnished with gold" (Nichols, I, 527–528). It was enameled with a white falcon on the top. Another gift was "a fan of white feathers, set in a handle of gold, the other side thereof garnished with two very fair emeralds." The back side of the handle had diamonds and rubies, "on each side a white bear and two pearls handing, a lion ramping" (Nichols, I, 527). He also gave her a doublet of white satin with 18 clasps that were enameled, every pair set with five diamonds and eight rubies. Another gift was a cross of gold that had thirteen large emeralds and three large pearls.

In 1580 Leicester's gifts were two bodkins, which were long pins or pin-shaped ornaments that women used to fasten up their hair. One had a large diamond surrounded by small rubies and the other a large ruby surrounded by small diamonds. He also gave Elizabeth a cap of black velvet which had a diamond band on it, and fourteen gold and diamond buttons. Two years later it was another rather different necklace than ones he had given previously. On a gold chain was "a little book of gold, enameled, garnished and furnished with small diamonds and rubies, both clasps" (Nichols, III, 528). In 1583 Leicester's gift was especially intricate. It was another gold necklace, which had twenty pieces, which were letters garnished with small diamonds, and between every letter were two pearls, but what they spelled was in code. There was a key to the code in a pendant with diamonds and rubies. He had another unusual gift for the queen in 1585, "a sable skin, the head and four feet of gold, fully garnished with diamonds and rubies" (Nichols, III, 528). The last new year's gifts he gave her were in 1588 the year he died. One was a purse of gold, enameled, and garnished with small diamonds, rubies, and large opals, with a blue sapphire on the top, with two strings, having pendants of large pearls hanging at a small chain of gold. He also gave her a gold bracelet "containing 6 pieces, 4 like crosses, 2 pieces like half crosses, fully furnished with diamonds, rubies, and pearls of sundry bigness, on the one side, with a row of pearls and small rubies on each side of the said bracelet" (Nichols, III, 528). Elizabeth's regular gift to him was 100 ounces of gilt plate.

Another person who worked hard at having special gifts for the queen was Blanche Parry, Gentlewoman of her Privy Chamber, who had known Elizabeth since she was a baby (see Chapter 14). Parry knew how much the queen loved jewelry. On several occasions she gave the queen different gold bracelets. Parry liked the idea of jewelry shaped as flowers. Some of her more unusual gifts included in 1572 a gold rose enameled in red and white and with rubies and diamonds. Two years later her gift was a crystal with Adam and Eve enameled on it and trimmed with gold. And in 1575 there was another gold jewel with three roses and sparks of rubies, and a small gold chain to hang it on. The next year Blanche Parry gave the queen a little box of gold with a gold spoon. In 1581 she gave the queen a gold pendant in the shape of a crane. In 1585 instead of jewelry Blanche Parry gave Elizabeth a girdle of black velvet with gold buttons. The 1587 gift was a pendant enameled in the shape of a serpent's tongue with sparks of rubies and emeralds.

Elizabeth also loved sweets and some of the gifts she received reflected that. In 1562 she received marchpane, what marzipan was then called, from three different people as gifts. At the court of Elizabeth marzipan was fashioned into large and elaborate pieces. One was a model of St. Paul's church, another, given by Richard Hikes, was a tower, with men and artillery, and the third, a gift from George Webster, Master Cook, was a chessboard. Throughout the rest of the reign there were more marchpane gifts, including one in 1579 from her master cook, John Smithson, made into a castle. In 1588 he gave the queen a marchpane with a model of St. George in the middle. The same year her sergeant of the pastry, John Dudley, gave a quince and orange pie made into letters of E and R. She also received, over the years, gifts of candied ginger and sugar-loafs.

Perhaps because of all the sweets she ate, Elizabeth had problems with her teeth. There were times when her teeth ached so much that she had to delay meetings. In 1567 she received instruments for cleaning her teeth from the Italian author and aspiring diplomat, Petruccio Ubaldini. The queen was intrigued and grateful enough that she made sure she could keep this gift by her. This was the first of at least twenty-two gifts related to dental hygiene that she received during her reign. In 1574 Mrs. Snowe gave the queen six small toothpicks made of gold, which Elizabeth clearly used as a gift was annotated with the note that "one of them lost by her Majesty" (Nichols, III, 380). Five years later Sir Edward Horsey gave the queen a toothpick of gold with diamonds.

When Elizabeth went on Progress in 1574 there may have been a coordination of some of the gifts that she was given. Lady Shandowes gave the queen a parrot, the body made of crystal, and the head, tale, legs, and breast were made of gold; there were also sparks of rubies and emeralds, and it hung on a very short gold chain. Sir John Younge, who had given the queen the painting at the beginning of the reign, when she visited him that year, gave her a gold phoenix decorated with rubies and diamonds. Sir John Thin gave the queen a falcon preying on a fowl. There was a large emerald on her breast with sparks of diamonds and rubies. Sir Henry Charington gave Elizabeth a dolphin made of mother of pearl, with a man made of gold upon his back. It was decorated with diamonds and rubies and hung on three short chains. She visited Henry Herbert, Earl of Pembroke at Wilton. The Countess, Catherine, gave the queen a gold mermaid which was decorated with diamonds, rubies, and pearls.

Elizabeth's musicians were diligent at giving the queen New Year's gifts. At the beginning of the reign in 1559 the Bassano family gave the queen two bottles of musk water and a looking glass covered with embroidered crimson satin. Baptista Bassano gave the queen a Venetian lute in 1565. The brothers gave her a fan made of painted feathers in a glass case in 1581. Jeronimo Bassano gave the queen two drinking glasses in 1588. In 1589 the brothers Peter and Joseph Lupo each gave the queen a pair of gloves. In 1600 Joseph and his son Thomas again each gave a pair of perfumed gloves, as did three of the Bassano brothers, and Innocent Comy.

Queen Elizabeth received other particularly interesting gifts over the course of her reign. In 1574 Sir Christopher Hatton gave a gold pendant enameled in colors and set with diamonds, rubies, emeralds, and an opal. In the middle of the jewel were two people and above them a hand holding a garland. That year Thomas Butler, Earl of Ormond gave the queen a large gold pendant with a sapphire surrounded by rubies, emeralds, and diamonds. The back of the pendant was blue crystal engraved with verses, each line beginning with the letters that then spelled out Elizabeth. In 1588 Ormond's gift to the queen was a petticoat of carnation satin embroidered with antique flowers and fishes in gold and silver silk. That year Sir Francis Walsingham also gave the queen clothing that clearly took much time and expense to be created. It was a cloak of velvet in a range of colors pieced together in a pattern with gold lace and silver plate. The cloak was lined with printed silver cloth. He also gave Elizabeth a white satin doublet embroidered with Venetian gold thread. One year Sir Philip Sidney's gift was a jewel encrusted whip. In 1589, the first New Year's after the victory over the Spanish Armada, Lord Burghley's gift to the queen referenced the English victory. It was a plate of gold, engraved on one side with an astronomical design, and on the other side there was a ship called the Triumph.

Peter Bales, a writing master known as "the most famous master in the art of penmanship, or fair writing, and all its relative branches, of his time in our country," did such beautiful calligraphy that he was sometimes hired to do presentation books for the queen, decided when he was at court in March 1575 to give her a present himself. It was a gold and crystal ring in which he had written micrographically the Lord's Prayer and the ten commandments. This brought "the admiration of her Majesty, her Privy Council, and several ambassadors who then saw it" (Kippis, I, 536). Elizabeth often wore the ring. In 1590 he gave a Bible small enough to fit into a walnut shell.

Elizabeth received many gifts from foreign sovereigns. When Tsar Ivan IV wanted to impress the English queen, he sent her "4 pieces of Persian cloth of gold and two whole pieces of cloth of silver of curious work ... a fair large Turkey carpet." He also sent her "rich sables and furs," including white ermines. Elizabeth was so delighted that she "commanded Mrs Mary Skidmore and Mrs May Radcliff, both of Her Majesty's bedchamber, and Mr John Stanhope [Vice-Chamberlain] to help to lay them into Her Majesty's closet" (Arnold, 98). Very late in the reign Elizabeth received a spectacular gift. After Elizabeth in 1599 gave an enormous organ clock and a beautiful coach to Sultan Mehmet III and his family (see Chapter 11), Mehmet's mother, Safiye Sultan, sent the English queen a robe, a girdle, five especially made handkerchiefs, and a necklace. She hoped in return that Elizabeth would send her some gifts as well. Safiye Sultan's private secretary was Esperanza Malchi, a Jewish woman from either Spain or Italy. Malchi, writing in Italian, explained that she "being a Hebrew by law and nation, have from the first hour that it pleased the Lord God to put into the heart of this our most serene Queen mother to make use of my services," she was pleased to have the opportunity to write to the English queen. Malchi wrote how the Sultan's mother "sends to your Majesty by the same illustrious Ambassador a robe and a girdle, and two kerchiefs wrought in gold, and three wrought in silk, after the fashion of this Kingdom, and a necklace of pearls and rubies ... and a wreath of diamonds from the jewels of her Highness, which she says, your Majesty will be pleased to wear for the love of her." Malchi told Elizabeth that the Sultana requested "distilled waters of every description for the face, and odoriferous oils for the hands." Malchi added that

> "Likewise if there are to be had in your Kingdom cloths of silk or wool, articles of fancy suited for so high a Queen as my Mistress, your Majesty may be pleased to send them, as she will be more gratified by such objects than any valuable your Majesty could send her." Malchi ended with the hope that "your Majesty may ever be prosperous and happy." (Ellis, III, 53–55)

The gifts that Elizabeth received throughout her reign on many occasions did make the queen both prosperous and happy.

Entertainers

Elizabeth had many entertainers at her court, and some who might not be professional entertainers but whom she clearly found entertaining. There were also many entertainments planned at court that Elizabeth and her courtiers could attend, as could her foreign ambassadors and other guests. Just as she could be informal with these people as she took them hunting with her, so were there guests who might sit with her during a performance. As well as the many musical events, there were plays and other spectacles performed as well.

There were jesters at court, who were easy to identify because of the ways their heads were shaved. While her father Henry VIII and her successor James I had a range of jesters, they each had one special one who was with the king for much of the reign. In Henry's case it was Will Somers (or Somer), who was a member of Henry VIII's service by July 1535, replacing Sexton, also called Patch, who was banished from court. The ambassador Eustance Chapuys wrote at the time that Henry VIII "the other day nearly murdered his own fool ... who happened to speak well in his presence of the Queen and Princess, and called the concubine 'ribaude' and her daughter 'bastard'" ('Spain: July 1535, 1–31', in *Calendar of State Papers, Spain, Volume 5, Part 1, 1534–1535*, ed. Pascual de Gayangos [London, 1886], pp. 507–523. *British History Online*). Henry felt close enough to Somers that he was included in several portraits. Somers continued as a jester in the reign of Edward VI and Mary, and Somers attended Elizabeth's coronation and died five months later, on June 15, 1559. Archy Armstrong joined James I's court as a royal servant in early 1606. By 1611 he was clearly the royal fool and he was being paid well and naturalized as an English citizen. He was allowed behavior no one else was who was around the king and remained in this privileged position for the rest of the reign, though his career crashed and burned in the reign of James' son Charles. But Elizabeth did not have one major fool. The records mention various jesters or fools at the queen's court but for the most part little is known about them, and they did not have a close relationship with Elizabeth.

Just as Will Somers lived into the reign of Elizabeth and may have entertained her in the first few months of her reign before his death, another fool she inherited was Jane the Fool, one of the few female fools. The first mention of her was that Anne Boleyn in January 1536 ordered her tailor Skutte to make a green satin cap and a mulberry-colored dress for her female fool. But of course by May Anne Boleyn was dead, and Jane the Fool found her way into the household of Henry VIII's daughter Mary by December 1537. Mary's household records show that Jane the Fool had her own horse, and Princess Mary ordered dress, hose, and shoes for Jane, as well as having her head shaved every month. Jane was in the Princess's household until September 1544, when she became the fool of Henry's last wife Katherine Parr, who dropped the head shaving requirement. Both Jane and Will Somers were included in the painting of the royal family that Henry commissioned in 1545. After the death of Katherine Parr, Jane returned to Mary's household. Once Mary was queen, she ordered an extensive and lavish wardrobe for Jane, referring to her as her fool. There was a second female fool at Mary's court, as records show an order for clothes for a female fool named Beden, but we do not know anything else about her. When Jane was ill, Mary hired a nurse for her, and rewarded the nurse with a lavish gift when Jane recovered. Like Will Somers, Jane appears to have died early in Elizabeth's reign.

There were many jesters at Elizabeth's court. Some of them unfortunately we have little more information about beyond their names, and sometimes highly unlikely stories about them. Six of her jesters were called Patch, Pace, Chester, Clod, Hoyden, and Garrett—there was also a Patch, another name for the fool Sexton, at her father's court, but clearly this was a different man. We know little about these jesters. They apparently were able to tease the queen with some impunity, but she sometimes got upset if they were too crude or insulting about those she valued, such as the Earl of Leicester, though she did enjoy some jokes about her courtiers. Pace was known as the "bitter fool," who destroyed items that looked too much like popery. Elizabeth had a crucifix in her private chapel, which was knocked down and destroyed. Though in fact Pace had not been involved, rumors spread that Sir Francis Knollys had paid him to do it. At the end of her reign, according to John Chamberlain in 1602, Garrett made Elizabeth very merry with his fooling during a tournament.

Other court jesters included Jack Green (or Grene), Will Shenton, and Monarcho. Clothing apparently was one of the ways her jesters were paid. The queen gave lavish clothing as gifts—and possible payment—to many of her servants and courtiers. In 1565 and 1567 clothing was ordered for Jack Green, including several hats trimmed with different colored feathers and a number of silver spangles and well decorated breeches. In 1574 and 1575 Shenton received many gifts of clothing, including three complete outfits, made by Thomas Ludwell, the queen's tailor. One was a coat of grey cloth stripped with silk lace, with matching breeches trimmed with multicolored lace, and a doublet was also trimmed with lace. The second outfit was even more lavish and elaborate, with a coat of velvet and taffeta striped in green, yellow, and red. He also received two pairs of breeches, and two hats: a taffeta hat trimmed with multicolored lace and a colored feather with gold spangles and a red felt hat with many colored feathers and gold spangles. His third outfit was a woolen coat with decorative cuts and lace-trimmed breeches line with wool and made with pockets, a new innovation. Shenton also received a bed with blankets, two pairs of sheets, and two quilted night caps. There are no further records of Shenton after 1575. The Italian jester Monarcho, known as fantastical, first appeared at Queen Elizabeth's court in 1568. Ludwell made him a beautiful red gown and Henry Herne made him two pairs of hose. He was also given a hat created by Raphael Hammond, which was made of blue taffeta with gold lace. Another gown was made for him the following year, along with breeches, and two pairs of Spanish leather shoes. He also received a velvet cap, a pair of gloves, and six shirts. In 1574 he received a third blue damask gown, a jacket, and a striped doublet trimmed with silk lace. He received two more pairs of Spanish leather shoes. Monarcho received a fourth gown in 1575 that was apparently made from an old gown of Elizabeth's. There were no more records of Monarcho at court, but he apparently stayed in London, parading around, and claiming to be a sovereign—the king of the world—himself. Thomas Nashe had a feud with Gabriel Harvey that was played out in a pamphlet war, and Nashe compared Harvey to Monarcho, a man of vain praise and glory. Monarcho is also referred to in Shakespeare's play, *Love's Labours Lost*.

The most significant of Elizabeth's jesters was Richard Tarlton (or Tarleton). He was the first jester who was not a permanent resident in a court; he also had a career as a clown on stage. Elizabeth held him in high regard, and he had regular access to the queen. Thomas Fuller, writing in the mid-seventeenth century, explained that "When queen Elizabeth was serious (I dare not say sullen) and out of good humour, he could un-dumpish her at his pleasure." Fuller added that "her highest favorites would, in some cases, go to Tarleton before they would go to the queen, and he was their usher to prepare their advantageous access unto her." But what Fuller found most impressive about Tarlton was that "he told the queen more of her faults than most of her chaplains and cured her melancholy better than all her physicians" (140).

It may well have been Tarlton who invented a joke about Elizabeth that was often told and retold, though today we may not find it laugh out loud funny. A sculler was a small boat that one person alone could sail. Tarlton compared Elizabeth to a sculler, as "neither the Queen nor the sculler hath a fellow" (Doran, *The History of Court Fools*, online). Tarlton would often entertain the queen at dinner wearing his fool's attire. She often took Tarlton with her when she was invited out to dinner, such as with Lord Burghley.

Tarlton also had a stage career, though it is not really known what comedic roles he played. In 1583 Tarlton was the leading comic actor the Queen's Men and named a Groom of Her Majesty's chamber. He also wrote plays, but these have been lost. In early September 1588 he caught the plague and became terribly ill. He made his will, leaving everything to his son Philip, and died soon after. He was lauded after his death by the poet Edmund Spenser, who grieved the loss of jolly merriment. Two jestbooks were published after Tarlton's death: *Tarltons Newes out of Purgatorie* (1590) and *Tarlton's Jests* (1611), though how many of the jokes were actually Tarlton's are not known. In 1643 Sir Richard Baker wrote that it was Tarlton who made comedies complete, for "the Clown's Part, never had his match, never will have" (120).

As well as her actual jesters, Queen Elizabeth had people she found entertaining for whom she also ordered lavish clothing. There was Ippolyta the Tartarian and a dark-skinned boy who served as a page for Elizabeth in the mid-1570s (see Chapter 11). One to whom she was close for some decades was Thomasina de Paris, a dear companion to the queen. Thomasina, known as the queen's dwarf, was apparently from France. The term dwarf was a more expansive term in the Renaissance than it is today, and it meant anyone who was very small. Thomasina was part of the queen's household from the mid-1570s until Elizabeth's death. The queen gave Thomasina many gifts, including gowns, shoes, and jewelry. Elizabeth often had dresses she tired of cut down and made into clothing for her companion, making Thomasina sometimes appear as a miniature queen. The clothing made for Thomasina was extremely elegant. For example, there were dresses of white satin, crimson taffeta, carnation taffeta sleeves, and three petticoats of "red mockeado striped with copper golde" (Arnold, 107). Mockado was fabric similar to velvet. She was also given sheets of lovely cloth, ivory combs, and looking glasses, as well as other treats.

While some considered Thomasina the queen's doll, she was a thoughtful and caring person. Thomasina was a highly intelligent woman who had had a fine education. Elizabeth enjoyed many conversations with her. Elizabeth presented Thomasina with a pen and inkhorn for her letter writing. Thomasina, with two other members of the court, visited John Dee, the astrologer who was very friendly with the queen. Dee had a remarkable library, and Thomasina might have been able to spend some time looking at his books as they stayed overnight. Dee noted the visit in his journal and mentioned only Thomasina by name.

Thomasina was clearly one of the women of Elizabeth's inner circle, someone the queen trusted, and she gave Elizabeth her committed service and her companionship. Elizabeth valued Thomasina so much that when her sister Prudence de Paris came to visit, who may have also been a dwarf, the queen had a violet gown made for her. Another way we know how much the queen valued Thomasina was that, as Janet Arnold explains, Thomasina "was regularly presented with most attractive gowns throughout the reign" (107).

Drama Performed at Court

By the middle of the reign some early theatre companies began presenting plays at court. There were many evenings that plays were performed. The office of the Master of the Revels—Sir Thomas Benger was Master of the Revels from 1560 to 1572 and Sir Edmund Tylney was the Master of the Revels from 1579 through the rest of Elizabeth's reign—organized them and eventually came to license all drama presented in the city as well as at court, censoring material thought to be antithetical to the crown. The plays were put on by a variety of different groups. At the Inns of Court, where lawyers were trained, the law students also acted in plays. Throughout the reign the Children of St. Paul's, a troupe of boy actors educated at the choir school ranging in age from six to about sixteen, presented plays at court. There were also the Children of the Chapel Royal, another group of boy singers who also acted in plays at court. Another troupe was Lord Strange's Men, first developed by Henry Stanley, 4th Earl of Derby. The eldest son of the earl had the title Lord Strange, and the fourth earl began his interest in dramatics prior to becoming earl in 1572. His son Ferdinando, Lord Strange, further developed the troupe with his retainers, and they played at court extensively in the

1580s. The troupe presented many plays at court, though we do not know the names of most of them. The troupe also had tumblers—what we would call acrobats, and they would perform regularly at court as well, though most of the tumblers left Lord Strange's men for the Queen's Men in 1583 after that troupe was established. In 1590 Lord Strange's men became associated with the Lord Admiral's men. This latter troupe was originally known as Lord Howard's men, named after the patron Charles Howard, Earl of Nottingham, and they began presenting at court in December 1576. When Howard was named Lord High Admiral in 1585, the troupe changed its name to honor that. Thomas Radcliffe, Earl of Sussex was another leading courtier who sponsored a troupe of players. Robert Dudley, Earl of Leicester, also had an acting troupe that presented plays at Court as part of the Christmas celebrations during the mid-1570s, including the play *Mamillia* on December 28, 1573. They also performed at the elaborate entertainments when Elizabeth visited Kenilworth. One entertainment was "The Old Coventry play of Hock Tuesday" performed there in July 1575. The play was set in pre-Conquest England, where the Danish forces had invaded. The play showed a series of combats where twice the Danes were victorious, "but at last, by the arrival of the Saxon to assist their countrymen, the Danes were overcome." The women led their captives in triumph. Queen Elizabeth enjoyed the play thoroughly, gave the actors money, and "laughed well" (Chambers, I, 499) (Fig. 16.1).

His brother Ambrose, Earl of Warwick also had a troupe. Sussex and Leicester were rivals at court and their troupes had such a serious rivalry that this may have been why Elizabeth organized the Queen's Men, and various actors left their troupes to join this one. Tarlton had been a member of the Sussex troupe but immediately joined the Queen's Men when it was organized. One of the most important companies of actors who played at court was the Lord Chamberlain's Men. Henry Carey, Baron's Hunsdon, was Lord Chamberlain in 1594; he began the troupe, and after his death, it was continued by his son George. This company was the one in which William Shakespeare was an actor, and, far more importantly, a dramatist. When James I became king, and the troupe's patron, they changed their name to the King's Men.

The records of the plays performed at court are uneven. Sometimes they simply state that a play was performed while sometimes the title of the play possibly with the playwright are listed. Many of the plays listed no longer have existing scripts, so we only have the titles. Others are still available to us today. After the performance of the play there would often be a performance of comic jigs and jokes, and Tarlton was a real star of these. This is a partial list of some the plays that were performed for the queen during her reign.

One of the first plays we know was performed at court was Thomas Norton and Thomas Sackville's *The Tragedie of Gorboduc*, with Norton writing the first three acts, and Sackville the final two. It was performed for Elizabeth at Whitehall in January 1561 by the Gentlemen of the Inner Temple. In some ways it was a precursor of Shakespeare's *King Lear*, as the King of Britain,

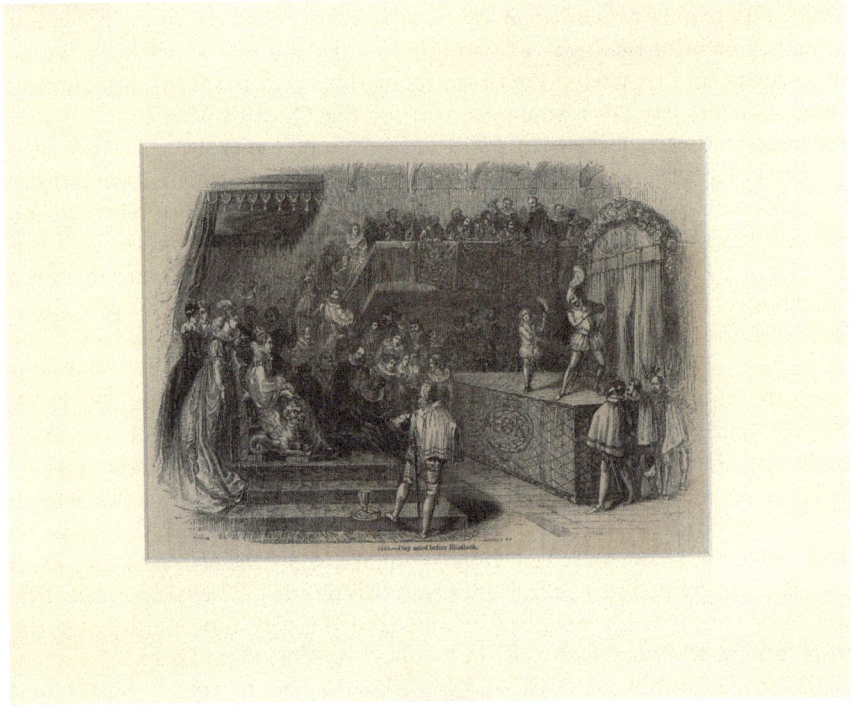

Fig. 16.1 Elizabeth watching play private collection

Gorboduc, divides his kingdom between his two sons during his lifetime with tragic results, one brother murdering the other, and their mother, in revenge, killing the murderous sibling. This led to a rebellion and the death of both the king and queen and ends with Parliament in charge of choosing the next ruler. The play presented a very sensitive issue, as Elizabeth from the beginning of her reign refused to name an heir herself.

Many of the plays presented in the earliest part of the reign were by the Children of St. Paul's, including a play about Solomon and the Queen of Sheba that was performed before Elizabeth and the Swedish Princess Cecilia in 1566 (see Chapter 11). On New Year's Day 1567 the troupe presented *The Historie of Error* at Hampton Court. On Leap Year Day 1568 they presented *Orestes* at Whitehall. Three years later at Whitehall they performed another classical work, *Iphigeneia*.

For the Christmas and New Year's celebrations in 1568 the office of the Revels prepared eight plays, which were *As Plain as Can Be*; *The Painful Pilgrimage*; *Jack and Jill*; *Six Fools*; *Wit and Will*; *Prodigality*; *Orestes*; and *The King of Scots, a tragedy*. Lord Howard's men presented a play called *Tooley* in December 1576, a play called *The Solidary Knight* in February 1577, and another play in January 1578. Other plays presented where we do not know the troupe included also in 1578, *The Rape of the Second Helene*, and *Mask of Amazons*, which Elizabeth watched with Jean de Simier (see Chapter 8). The following March the queen saw the Earl of Sussex's Men's production of *The Knight of the Burning Rock*, and the next January *The History Cipio Africanus*. At the 1578 Christmas holidays the Earl of Warwick's Men put on *Three Sisters of Mantua* and the Earl of Sussex's Men performed *Cruelty of a Stepmother*. Two months later Sussex's Men launched a production of *Murderous Michael*. It is a shame that the scripts for plays with such fascinating titles are unfortunately lost.

Many plays were performed at court in the 1580s, and, again, too often we only have titles, such as on Valentine's Day 1580 Lord Strange's Men performed *The Sultan and the Duke* and around Christmas Leicester's Men presented a play with the one-word title, *Delight*. But we also do have some of the scripts of the plays performed. In January 1584 the Children of the Chapel Royal gave a performance of George Peele's *The Arraignment of Paris*. This extravaganza based on Greek mythology was one of Peele's earliest works. The following month the Children of the Chapel Royal presented Anthony Munday's comedy *Fidele and Fortunio*, a play about relationships and misadventures which includes the character of the sorceress Medusa. Shakespeare may have been influenced by Medusa, as the ingredients she used for casting her spells are very similar to what the witches threw into their cauldron in *Macbeth*. In March the Children of the Chapel Royal joined with the Children of St. Paul's to present John Lyly's comedy *Sappho and Phao*.

The Children of St. Paul's performed several of Lyly's plays; many of Lyly's play used allegory to describe the wonders of Queen Elizabeth. For New Year's Day 1588 they presented Lyly's play *Gallathea*, a play about violence toward women and expansive views of love. In the village the fairest maiden is to be sacrificed to Neptune or he would destroy the village. Galathea's father is sure his daughter is the fairest, and to protect her, sends her to the forest disguised as a boy. So does Phillida's father. The two disguised girls fall in love. Neptune meanwhile rages. Finally, Neptune is convinced not to demand the sacrifice of fair maidens or cause destruction. Gallathea and Phillida are revealed to be females, and still state that they love each other. Venus declares she will change one of them into a man so that they can marry, and their love can continue, though the play ends before either a transformation or a wedding. The following month the same troupe did another Lyly play *Endymion, the Man in the Moon*. It was presented at court with a prologue specifically written for the performance for the queen. Two years later in 1590 the Children of St. Paul's played Lyly's drama *Midas* at Richmond. This was apparently composed to celebrate the defeat of the Spanish Armada, and the character of Midas was a satirical portrait of Philip of Spain. In 1597 Lyly's play *Woman in the Moon* was presented at Court.

Robert Greene was a popular writer of pamphlets, fiction, poetry, and plays, and some of his plays were presented at court in the last decade of Elizabeth's reign. His play *The History of Orlando Furioso* was performed at court in 1593. The Italian epic poem of the same name had been translated into English by Sir John Harington in 1591 for Queen Elizabeth. The story is set in the war between Charlemagne and the Saracen king of Africa, Agramante. *Friar Bacon and Friar Bungay*, set in the reign of Henry III with the heir Edward as a main character, was performed more than once. Another major character, Friar Bacon, is a skilled magician, but inadvertently, his spells cause tragedy, and he renounces magic at the end of the play. Not only was the play very popular but is generally considered his best work. Also presented by the Queen's Men were Greene's play about the Scottish king James IV, and his play in collaboration with Thomas Lodge, *A Looking Glass for London and England*, a play based on Biblical story of Jonah and the debauched city of Nineveh, which, from the title, is clearly a mirror image of London. Other plays presented before Elizabeth include Thomas Dekker's *Shoemaker's Holiday*, about a gentleman who disguises himself as a shoemaker so that he can woo the woman he loves, Rose, the grocer's daughter. Ben Jonson's satirical comedy, *Every Man Out of His Humour*, was also performed at court. There were also a series of Robin Hood plays performed in the 1590s as well.

In 1594 the newly formed Lord Chamberlain's Men started performing at Court. From the list of actors and their pay schedule there is evidence that Shakespeare acted in some of these plays. Because there is not a complete record of all the plays presented at court, we do not know how many different Shakespeare plays the Queen saw, but she certainly saw some. When the plays *The Merry Wives of Windsor* and *Love's Labours Lost* were published, both stated on their title pages that they have been acted before the queen. It also appears very likely that his play *Twelfth Night* was performed at court in the very last years of her reign.

It was not only the actors' troupes that brought entertainment to court. We have seen how members of the Inns of Court participated in entertainment. In the winter of 1594, the junior members of Gray's Inn decided to create some revels for the queen that were highly lavish and intensely elaborate. They became the kingdom of Graius, elected Henry Helmes to be their Prince of Purpoole, and kept up their comic, satiric version of court ceremonial for some weeks. The solemn installation of the prince occurred on December 20. The Prince of Purpoole and his court asked their neighbor in the Inner Temple to send them an ambassador, and of course were obliged with the ambassador from Templaria, who after a rowdy and disorganized revel declared his displeasure and left in a public huff. There were parades and court entertainments including a performance of *The Comedy of Errors*. On January 3 many courtiers went to Gray's Inn Hall to view a masque presented by the Prince of Purpoole and his followers. Members of Elizabeth's court such as Lord Burghley and his son Sir Robert Cecil helped broker a peace between Graius and Templaria. The Prince of Purpoole and his followers came to Greenwich to perform their masque before the queen, who was delighted. The Prince of Purpoole's last appearance in January was a mock tournament in front of the queen, and the prince was so successful against the Earl of Essex that he was won the prize granted by the queen, a jewel set with seventeen diamonds and fourteen rubies. Elizabeth then spoke of her gratitude to Gray's Inn and the mock prince for all the pleasure they had given her.

There was much sorrow and tribulation, hard work, and tragedy for Elizabeth when she was queen. But there were also many ways in which she found pleasure, from hunting, dancing, playing and listening to music, to watching drama, and sometimes participating in the foolery of an imaginary kingdom. It is good to know that the queen did have true moments of pleasure, of joy.

Bibliography

There are a number of online sources that were of great value as I was working on this project, particularly State Papers Online, British History Online, and Folgerpedia. I very much recommend them to anyone interested in Queen Elizabeth I and Renaissance culture. While in the text I gave full citations for British History Online, for State Papers Online since I give year and name in the text the sources are easy for anyone to find. *The Oxford Dictionary of National Biography* is also of greatest value, and many of the people discussed in this book have entries in the ODNB. For Elizabethan music I found Oxford Music Online very useful. There is much great scholarship produced on Elizabeth I. The bibliography is only a resource for the direct quotations.

Abrahams, Israel. "Joachim Gaunse: A Mining Incident in the Reign of Queen Elizabeth." *Transactions: The Jewish Historical Society of England, Sessions 1899–1901* 4 (1903): 92–101.

Alford, Stephen. *The Watchers: A Secret History of the Reign of Elizabeth I*. London: Bloomsbury, 2012.

Allen, William. *An admonition to the nobility and people of England and Ireland concerninge the present warres made for the execution of his Holines sentence, by the highe and mightie Kinge Catholike of Spaine. By the Cardinal of Englande*. Antwerp, 1588.

Andrea, Bernadette. "The 'Presences of Women' from the Islamic World in Sixteenth to Early Seventeenth-Century British Literature and Culture." *Mapping Gendered Routes and Spaces in the Early Modern World*. Merry Wiesner-Hanks, editor. Farnham: Ashgate, 2015, 291–306.

Aske, James. *Elizabetha Triumphans*. London, 1588.

Bajetta, Carlo M. *Elizabeth I's Italian Letters*. New York: Palgrave Macmillan, 2017.

Baker, Richard. *A Chronicle of the Kings of England*. London, 1643.

Bartels, Emily Carroll. "Too Many Blackamoors: Deportation, Discrimination, and Elizabeth I." *SEL Studies in English Literature 1500–1900* 46, no. 2 (Spring 2006): 304–322.

Berry, Steve. *The King's Deception*. New York: Ballantine Books, 2013 [Kindle].

BHO/ British History Online. https://www.british-history.ac.uk/.

Blackwood, Adam. *Martyre de la rayne d'Escosse*. Paris, 1587.

Bossy, John. *Giordanao Bruno and the Embassy Affair.* New Haven: Yale University Press, 2002.
Calendar of Letters and State Papers Relating to English Affairs Preserved Principally in the Archives of Simancas. Martin Hume, editor. London: Printed for H.M. Stationery Office by Eyre and Spottiswoode, 1892–1899.
Calendar of State Papers, Foreign Series, of the Reign of Elizabeth: Preserved in the Public Record Office. Joseph Stevenson, Allan J. Crosby, Arthur John Butler, S. C. Lomas, R. B. Wernham, editors. London: H.M. Stationery Office, 1863–1950.
Calendar of the State Papers Relating to Scotland and Mary, Queen of Scots 1547–1603: Preserved in the Public Record Office, the British Museum, and Elsewhere in England. 12 vols. Edinburgh: H. M. General Register Office, 1898–1969.
Camden, William. *The History of the Most Renowned and Victorious Princess Elizabeth, Late Queen of England.* London, 1688.
Chamberlain, Frederick. *The Sayings of Queen Elizabeth.* London: John Lane, 1923.
Chambers, Robert. *The Book of Days, a Miscellany of Popular Antiquities in Connection with the Calendar, Including Anecdote, Biography, & History, Curiosities of Literature and Oddities of Human Life and Character.* 2 vols. Edinburgh: W. & R. Chambers, 1863.
Chronicle and Romance: Froissart, Malory, Holinshed, William Harrison. John Bourchier Berners, G. C. Macaulay, editors. New York: P.F. Collier & Son, 1910.
Clapham, John. *Elizabeth of England.* Evelyn Plummer Read and Conyers Read, editors. Philadelphia: University of Pennsylvania Press, 1951.
Collinson, Patrick. *Archbishop Grindal, 1519–1583: The Struggle for a Reformed Church.* London: Jonathan Cape, 1979.
Cowan, Samuel. *The Last Days of Mary Stuart and the Journal of Bourgoyne Her Physician.* Philadelphia: J. B. Lippincott Co, 1907.
Cressy, David. *Dangerous Talk: Scandalous, Seditious, and Treasonable Speech in Premodern England.* Oxford: Oxford University Press, 2010.
De Maisse. *A Journal of All That Was Accomplished by Monsieur de Maisse Ambassador in England from King Henri IV to Queen Elizabeth Anno Domini 1597.* G. B. Harrision, editor and translator. London: The Nonesuch Press, 1931.
"Diary of the Journey of Philip Julius, Duke of Stettin-Pomerania, Through England in the Year 1602." Gottfried von Bülow and Wilfred Powell, editors. *Transactions of the Royal Historical Society* 6 (1892): 1–67.
Doran, John. *The History of Court Fools.* Boston: Francis A. Nicolls, 1858. Project Gutenberg eBook.
Doran, Susan. *Elizabeth I & Her Circle.* Oxford: Oxford University Press, 2015.
duc de Sully, Maximilien de Béthune. *Memoirs of Maximilien de Bethune.* Pierre-Mathurin de L'Ecluse de Loges, editor. Edinburgh: Kincaid and Creech, 1773.
Elizabeth I. *Collected Works.* Leah Marcus, Janel Mueller, and Mary Beth Rose, editors. Chicago: University of Chicago Press, 2000.
Elizabeth I. *Translations, 1544–1589.* Janel Mueller and Joshua Scodel, editors. Chicago: The University of Chicago Press, 2009.
Ellis, Henry, editor. *Original Letters, Illustrative of English History: Including Numerous Royal Letters.* London: Harding, Triphook, & Lepard, 1824.
Fletcher, Francis. *The World Encompassed by Sir Francis Drake.* William Vaux, editor. London: Hakluyt Society, 1854.
Folgerpedia, accessed March 16, 2021. http://folgerpedia.folger.edu/.

Fuller, Thomas. *The History of the Worthies of England*. Austin Nuttail, editor, Vol. 3. London: T. Tegg, 1840.

Goodman, Godfrey. *The Court of King James the First*. J. S. Brewer, editor. 2 vols. London: R. Bentley, 1839.

Green, Janet M. "Queen Elizabeth I's Latin Reply to the Polish Ambassador." *The Sixteenth Century Journal* 31, no. 4 (2000): 987–1008.

Green, Robert Lemon, and Mary Anne Everett. *Calendar of State Papers, Domestic Series, of the Reigns of Edward VI, Mary, Elizabeth*. 12 vols. London: Longman, Brown, Green, Longmans, & Roberts, 1856–1872.

Greene, Robert. *The Spanish Masquerado Wherein under a pleasant devise, is discovered effectuallie, in certaine breefe sentences and mottos, the pride and insolencie of the Spanish estate*. London, 1589.

Grossman, Mary Ann. "Steve Berry's Latest Historical Novel Blows the Wig Right Off Queen Elizabeth I." https://www.twincities.com/2014/02/22/steve-berrys-latest-historical-novel-blows-the-wig-right-off-queen-elizabeth-i/.

Habib, Imtiaz H. *Black Lives in the English Archives, 1500–1677: Imprints of the Invisible*. Abingdon, Oxfordshire: Routledge, 2007.

Hackett, Helen. "Dream-Visions of Elizabeth I." *Reading the Early Modern Dream: The Terrors of the Night*. Michelle O'Callaghan, Katharine Hodgkin, S. J. Wiseman, editors. London: Routledge, 2008, 45–65.

The Harleian Miscellany: A Collection of Scarce, Curious, and Entertaining Pamphlets and Tracts, as Well, in Manuscript as in Print. Selected from the Library of Edward Harley, Second Earl of Oxford. Interspersed with Historical, Political Anotaions. Vol. 10. London: White, 1813.

Harrington, John. *Nugae Antiquae: Being a Miscellaneous Collection of Original Papers, in Prose and Verse*. Thomas Park, editor. London: Vernon and Hood, 1804; New York: AMS Press, 1966.

Harrison, G. B. *The Elizabethan Journals: Being a Record of Those Things Most Talked of During the Years 1591–1603. Comprising An Elizabethan Journal, 1591–4, A Second Elizabethan Journal, 1595–8, A Last Elizabethan Journal, 1599–1603*. Ann Arbor: University of Michigan Press, 1955.

Harvey, John. *A discoversive probleme concerning Prophesies, How far they are to be valued, or credited, according to the surest rules, and directions in Divinitie, Philosophie, Astrologie, and other learning: Devised especially in abatement of the terrible threatening*. London, 1588.

Heywood, Thomas. *If You Know Not Me, You Know Nobody, Part I*. Oxford: The Malone Society Reprints at the Oxford University Press, 1934.

Izquierdo, Adrian. "Elizabeth Tudor, the Elephant, and the Mirroring Cases of the Earl of Essex and the Duke of Biron." *The Image of Elizabeth I in Early Modern Spain*. Lincoln: University of Nebraska Press, 2019, 313–43.

Kippis, Andrew, ed. *Biographia Britannica, or, The Lives of the Most Eminent Persons Who Have Flourished in Great Britain and Ireland*. 2nd edn. 5 volumes. London: W. and A. Strahan, 1778–93.

Klarwill, Victor, editor. *Queen Elizabeth and Some Foreigners*. London: John Lane, 1928.

Knecht, R. J. *Catherine de' Medici*. London and New York: Longman, 1998.

Kolkovich, Elizabeth Zeman. *The Elizabethan Country House Entertainment*. Cambridge: Cambridge University Press, 2016.

Leonie, Frieda. *Catherine de Medici*. London: Weidenfeid & Nicholson, 2003.

Letters and Papers, Foreign and Domestic of the Reign of Henry VIII. James Gairdner, R. H. Brodie, editors. 28 vols. London: H.M. Stationery Office, 1862–1920.

Levin, Carole. *Dreaming the English Renaissance: Politics and Desire in Court and Country.* New York: Palgrave Macmillan, 2008.

Levin, Carole. *The Heart and Stomach of a King: Elizabeth I and the Politics of Sex and Power.* 2nd edn. Philadelphia: University of Pennsylvania Press, 2013.

Loomis, Catherine. "Elizabeth's Southwell's Manuscript Account of the Death of Queen Elizabeth [with text]." *English Literary Renaissance* 26, no. 11 (1996): 482–509.

McCullough, Peter E. "Out of Egypt: Richard Fletcher's Sermon Before Elizabeth I After the Execution of Mary Queen of Scots." *Dissing Elizabeth: Negative Representations of Gloriana.* Julia Walker, editor. Durham: Duke University Press, 1998, 118–149.

Michael de Castelnau, and Sieur de Mauvissière. *Memoirs of the Reigns of Francis II and Charles IX of France (English translation).* London, 1724.

The memoires of Sir James Melvil of Hal-hill containing an impartial account of the most remarkable affairs of state during the last age, not mention'd by other historians, more particularly relating to the kingdoms of England and Scotland, under the reigns of Queen Elizabeth, Mary Queen of Scots, and King James: in all which transactions the author was personally and publickly concern. George Scot, editor. London, 1683.

Murdin, William, and Samuel Haynes, editors. *A Collection of State Papers, Relating to Affairs in the Reigns of King Henry VIII. King Edward VI. Queen Mary, and Queen Elizabeth, from the Year 1542 to 1570.* London, 1740–1759.

Neale, J. E. *Elizabeth I and Her Parliaments, 1559–1581.* New York: W. W. Norton, 1958.

Neale, J. E. *Elizabeth I and Her Parliaments, 1584–1601.* New York: W. W. Norton, 1958.

Nichols, John. *The Progresses, and Public Processions, of Queen Elizabeth.* 2 vols. London: J. Nichols and Son, 1823.

Nicolas, Sir Nicholas Harris. *Memoirs of the Life and Times of Sir Christopher Hatton.* London: R. Bentley, 1847.

Osborne, Roger. *The Dreamer of Calle de San Salvador: Visions of Sedition and Sacrilege in Sixteenth-Century Spain.* London: Jonathan Cape, 2001.

Oxford Dictionary of National Biography. https://www.oxforddnb.com.

Paranque, Estelle. *Elizabeth I Through Valois Eyes: Power, Representation, and Diplomacy in the Reign of the Queen, 1558–1588.* New York: Palgrave Macmillan, 2019.

Paranque, Estelle. "Queen Elizabeth I and the Elizabethan Court in the French Ambassadors Eyes." *Queens Matters in Early Modern Studies.* Anna Riehl Bertolet, editor. New York: Palgrave Macmillan, 2018, 267–284.

Platter, Thomas. *Thomas Platter's Travels in England, 1599.* Clare Williams, editor. London: J. Cape, 1937.

Plowden, Alison. *The Elizabethan Secret Service.* New York: St. Martin's Press, 1991.

Richardson, Glenn. "'Your Most Assured Sister': Elizabeth I and the Kings of France." *Tudor Queenship: The Reigns of Mary and Elizabeth.* Alice Hunt and Anna Whitelock, editors. New York: Palgrave Macmillan, 2010, 191–205.

Riehl, Anna. *The Face of Queenship: Early Modern Representations of Elizabeth I.* New York: Palgrave Macmillan, 2011.

Roberts, Richard Arthur, Edward Salisbury, Montague Spencer Giuseppi, and Geraint Dyfnallt Owen, editors. *Calendar of the Manuscripts of the Most Hon. the Marquis of Salisbury, K.G., &c. &c. &c., Preserved at Hatfield House, Hertfordshire*. 24 vols. London: H. M. Stationery Office by Eyre and Spottiswoode, 1883–1976.
Robinson, Richard. *Golden Mirror: Conteining Certaine Pithie and Figurative Visions Prognosticating Good Fortune to England, and All True English Subjectes, with an Overthrowe to the Enemies*. Thomas Corser, editor. Manchester: Chetham Society, 1851.
Rose, John Benson. *A Treatise on the Reign and Times of Queen Catherine de Medici*. London: W. Clowes and Sons, 1871.
Rye, W. B. *England as Seen by Foreigners in the Days of Elizabeth and James the First*. London: Smith, 1865.
Seccombe, Thomas. *Tudor Tracts, 1532–1588*. London: A. Constable and Co, 1903.
Seton-Rogers, Cynthia. "The Exceptions to the Rule: Jews in Shakespeare's England." *European Judaism* 51, no. 2 (2018): 6–12.
Society for the Diffusion of Useful Knowledge, editor. *The Schoolmaster: Essays on Practical Education*. 2 vols. London: Charles Knight, 1836.
Somerset, Anne. *Elizabeth I*. New York: Alfred A. Knopf, 1991.
Speed, John. *The history of Great Britaine under the conquests of ye Romans, Saxons, Danes and Normans*. London, 1611.
State Papers Online, 1509–1714. https://www.gale.com/primary-sources/state-papers-online.
Stow, John. *The chronicles of England from Brute unto this present yeare of Chris*. London, 1580.
Strickland, Agnes. *Letters of Mary, Queen of Scots*. London: H. Colburn, 1843.
Stubbs, John. *Gaping Gulf*. Lloyd E. Berry, editor. Charlottesville: The Folger Shakespeare Library for the University Press of Virginia, 1968.
The Praise of Musicke: Wherein besides the antiquitie, dignitie, delectation, & use thereof in civill matters, is also declared the sober and lawfull use of the same in the congregation and Church of God. Oxford, 1586.
Thomas, Keith. *Religion and the Decline of Magic*. London: Weidenfeld & Nicolson, 1971.
Ungerer, Gustav. "The Presence of Africans in Elizabeth England and the Performance of 'Titus Andronicus' at Burley-on-the- Hill, 1595/96." *Medieval & Renaissance Drama in England* 21 (2008): 19–55.
Valdstejna, Zdenek Brtncky, editor. *The Diary of Baron Waldstein: A Traveller in Elizabethan England*. Trans. G. W. Groos. London: Thames and Hudson, 1981.
Weldon, Sir Anthony. *The Court and Character of King James*, originally published in 1650. London: G. Smeeton, 1817.
White, Francis Overend. *Lives of the Elizabethan Bishops of the Anglican Church*. London: Skeffington, 1898.
Whitelock, Anne. *The Queen's Bed: An Intimate History of Elizabeth's Court*. New York: Farrar, Straus and Giroux, 2013.
Williamson, George Charles, editor. *Lady Anne Clifford, Countess of Dorset, Pembroke & Montgomery, 1590–1676. Her Life, Letters and Work, Extracted from All the Original Documents Available, Many of Which Are Here Printed for the First Time*. Kendal: T. Wilson & Son, 1922.
Wilson, Miranda. "Gifts of Imperfection: Elizabeth I and the Politics of Timepieces." *Explorations in Renaissance Culture* 46 (2020): 44–56.

Wilson, Thomas. *The State of England Anno Dom, 1600.* E. J. Fisher, editor. London: Camden Society, 1936.

Wood, Edward J. *Curiosities of Clocks and Watches from the Earliest Times.* London: Richard Bentley, 1866.

Wright, Thomas. *Queen Elizabeth and Her Times.* 2 vols. London: Henry Colburn, 1838.

Wyatt, Michael. *The Italian Encounter with Tudor England: A Cultural Politics of Translation.* Cambridge: Cambridge University Press, 2005.

Index

0–9

1552 Book of Common Prayer. *See* Book of Common Prayer
1559 Parliament, 6, 26, 33, 51, 70
1563 Parliament, 9, 37, 51–52. *See also* Witchcraft Statute of 1563
1571 Parliament, 6, 43, 52–54, 57, 140. *See also* Thirty-Nine Articles; Treason Bill
1584 Parliament, 54. *See also* Bond of Association
1586 Parliament, 55. *See also* Babington Plot
1589 Parliament, 55
1593 Parliament, 55–56
1597 Parliament, 56, 57
1601 Parliament, 10, 56–57

A

Acts of Supremacy and Uniformity, 6, 33, 51. *See also* Elizabethan Religious Settlement; Oath of Supremacy (1559)
Acts of Succession (1534, 1536, and 1543), 2, 3, 6, 7, 71, 91–92
Allen, Francis, 25
Allen, William, Cardinal, 153–154, 156, 158, 160, 249–250
Alphery, Mikepher, 191–192
Andrea, Bernadette, 203
Anne of Cleves, Queen of England, 70, 235
Arnold, Janet, 282
Ascham, Roger, 2, 260, 271
Ashley, Katherine "Kat", 2–3, 5, 33, 72, 78, 230–232, 236, 242, 243, 257, 259

B

Babington, Anthony. *See* Babington Plot
Babington Plot, 8, 23, 40, 41, 45, 48, 55, 85, 102, 135, 153–155, 253
Bacon, Sir Nicholas, 5, 34, 125, 246
Bancroft, Richard, 55, 67
Beale, Robert, 26–27
Bess of Hardwick. *See* Talbot, Elizabeth "Bess" (formerly Cavendish, formerly St Loe, formerly Barlow, *née* Hardwick), Countess of Shrewsbury
Blount, Lettice (formerly Dudley, formerly Devereaux, *née* Knollys), Countess of Essex & Countess of Leicester, 38, 43, 46, 84, 218
Boleyn, Anne, Queen of England, 1–2, 7, 15, 33, 60, 61, 71, 104, 180, 209, 216–217, 224, 233, 249–250, 251, 272, 279
Boleyn, Mary, 39, 46, 235, 237, 250
Bond of Association, 8, 54, 140

Book of Common Prayer (1549, 1552, 1559), 6, 51, 62, 67
Brandon, Charles, Duke of Suffolk, 93, 98, 147
Brandon, Eleanor. *See* Clifford, Eleanor (*née* Brandon), Countess of Cumberland
Bromley, Sir Thomas, 40, 149
Bond of Association (1584), 8, 54, 140. *See also* Queen's Safety Act of 1585
Brooke, William, Lord Cobham, 41, 210

C

Camden, William, 5, 85, 160, 171, 253, 267
Carey, George, Lord Hunsdon, 47, 186
Carey, Henry, Lord Hunsdon, 39–40, 147, 197, 235, 237, 283
de Carmain, Paul de Foix, French Ambassador, 118–119, 247, 271
Cartwright, Thomas, 62, 63, 66–67
Casimir, John, Count Palatine of Simmern, 79, 122, 181
de Castelnau, Michel, Seigneur de Mauvissière, French Ambassador, 118, 129–132, 149, 249
Catherine de Medici, Queen of France, 6, 23, 41, 47, 79, 102, 115, 118, 119, 128, 133, 142, 215, 261
Cave, Sir Ambrose, 33
Cavendish, Mary. *See* Talbot, Mary (*née* Cavendish), Countess of Shrewsbury
Cecil, Robert, 1st Earl of Salisbury, 9, 10, 24–25, 27–28, 45, 47, 56, 87–88, 104, 108–110, 136, 137, 163–165, 186, 191, 194–197, 200, 205, 206–207, 211–212, 223, 232, 239, 251, 255, 256–257, 263, 286
Cecil, William, 1st Baron Burghley, 3, 4, 5, 8, 9, 16, 21–22, 30, 33–35, 37, 38, 40, 41–42, 62, 63–65, 70, 76–78, 80, 84, 93–95, 98, 114–115, 117, 125–126, 136, 137, 139–140, 142–146, 151, 155–159, 161–162, 170, 185–186, 189, 197–200, 210, 212, 218, 232, 236, 239, 242, 244, 246, 247–248, 261, 271, 277, 281, 286

Charles I, King of England, 19, 46, 96, 279
Charles IX, King of France, 23, 39, 80, 106, 127–128, 129–130, 215
Charles V, Holy Roman Emperor, 3, 126
Charles, Archduke of Austria, 6, 37, 46, 76–79, 80, 117, 118, 120, 124, 262, 266, 268
Charles, Duke of Angoulême, 71
Church of England, 7, 32, 36, 55–56, 62–64, 66–67, 78, 191, 192
Clapham, John, 21, 22, 213, 256
Clifford, Lady Anne. *See* Herbert, Anne (formerly Sackville, *née* Clifford), Countess of Dorset, Pembroke, and Montgomery, Baroness Clifford
Clifford, Eleanor (*née* Brandon), Countess of Cumberland, 93, 98–99, 147
Clifford, George, Earl of Cumberland, 34, 186, 239
Clifford, Henry, 2nd Earl of Cumberland, 98–99, 147
Clifford, Margaret. *See* Stanley, Margaret (*née* Clifford), Countess of Derby
de Clinton, Edward Feinnes, Earl of Lincoln, 31, 147, 168
Count Frederick of Mompelgard, future Duke of Württemberg, 182–184
Courtenay, Edward, Earl of Devon, 26, 72–72
Croft, Sir James, 37
Cromwell, Thomas, 30, 49, 72, 197, 198, 230

D

Davison, William, 24, 37, 41, 155, 218, 238
Dee, John, 13–14, 147, 156, 212, 232, 282
Devereux, Robert, Earl of Essex, 9–10, 23, 24, 28, 42, 45–47, 57, 87–89, 96, 101, 104, 107–108, 109–110, 136–137, 160–161, 162, 163, 182, 187, 196, 224, 265–266, 287
and the Essex Rebellion of 1601, 10, 41–42, 48, 87, 89, 164–165

Douglas, Margaret, Countess of Lennox, 104–105, 106, 107, 123
Drake, Sir Francis, 8, 9, 26, 133–134, 151, 162, 167–170, 178, 199, 203–204, 205–206, 211, 224–225
Dudley, Ambrose, Earl of Warwick, 34, 38–39, 239, 283
Dudley, Amy (*née* Robsart), 6, 82, 234, 243–245. *See also* Dudley, Robert, Earl of Leicester
Dudley, Ann (*née* Russell), Countess of Warwick, 239–240
Dudley, Guilford, 3, 93, 97, 99
Dudley, Lady Jane (*née* Grey), 4, 92–93, 233
  Disputed rule, 38, 82
  Marriage to Guildford Dudley, 93, 97
Dudley, John, Duke of Northumberland, 3, 4, 21, 38, 39, 93, 99
Dudley, Lady Mary. *See* Sidney, Lady Mary (*née* Dudley)
Dudley, Robert, Earl of Leicester, 4, 9, 14–15, 21, 27, 34, 26, 37, 39, 43, 62, 75, 79, 82–85, 91, 94, 102, 107, 114, 122, 123, 129, 140, 141, 143, 145, 155, 165, 217, 231, 237, 239–240, 259, 262, 264, 274, 283
  Marriage to Amy Robsart, 82, 234, 243–245
  Marriage rumors (to Elizabeth), 4, 70–71, 76, 78, 117, 245–250
Dudley, Sir Robert, explorer, 84, 213, 256
Duke of Alva. *See* de Toledo, Fernando Alvarez, Duke of Alva

E
Edward VI, King of England, 2, 3, 4, 17, 22, 25, 27, 29–31, 34, 39, 41, 51, 60, 62, 63, 69, 71, 72, 75, 91–93, 99, 102, 105, 188, 233, 243, 247, 260, 267, 270, 271, 279
Egerton, Sir Thomas, Baron Ellesmere, first Viscount Brackley, 45–46, 196
Elizabeth I, Queen of England, 1–287
  and assassination rumors, plots, & attempts, 1, 23, 40, 44, 76, 84, 88, 99, 100, 115, 127, 139–165, 169, 211, 274
  coronation, 1, 5, 13–17, 32, 36, 44, 46, 64, 113, 236, 265, 269, 279
  and her education, 2, 230–231, 260, 267, 282
  and her favorite palaces. *See* Hampton Court (palace); Richmond (palace); Westminster (palace); Whitehall (palace)
  and Ireland, 9, 10, 26, 39, 44–46, 47, 50, 56–57, 86–89, 115, 133–134, 136, 158, 165, 169–170, 192, 222, 235, 261
  mercy, 13, 16, 36, 37, 39, 45, 53, 75, 147, 150, 211
  progresses, 5, 38, 116, 146, 159, 160, 248–249, 262, 264, 272–273, 275–276
  and relations with France, 29, 42, 46, 114–115, 118–119, 126–132, 136–137, 139, 142
  and relations with Morocco, 193–195
  and relations with Poland, 25, 195–197
  and relations with Spain, 3, 8, 10, 23, 27, 29, 40–41, 46, 50, 55–56, 73, 75–76, 112–115, 119–122, 124–126, 133–136, 146, 156, 158, 162, 165, 167–173, 193–194, 196, 198, 199, 206, 221, 224–225, 253, 262
  relationship with Mary, Queen of Scots, 8, 23–24, 30, 32, 39, 41, 50, 52–53, 55, 84, 92, 100, 101–102, 115–117, 120–121, 129–130, 145, 210, 218, 252, 266–268, 274
  rumors of pregnancy/motherhood, 2, 72, 76, 224, 243, 245–251
  and speeches, 9, 10, 55, 57, 85, 170–171, 196–197
  and the succession, 5–6, 7, 10, 50–52, 70, 85, 87, 91–110, 140, 211, 221
  and suitors/marriage talks, 5–6, 30, 33, 37, 40, 42, 46, 50, 52, 69–80, 82, 84–85, 111, 118–120, 124, 127–133, 147, 148, 189,

218, 231, 246, 249, 252, 260, 266
see also Golden Speech; Tilbury Speech
Elizabethan Religious Settlement, 6, 42, 50, 51, 66. See also Acts of Supremacy and Uniformity
Emmanuel, Charles, Duke of Savoy, 253
Emmanuel, Philibert, Duke of Savoy, 73
Erik XIV of Sweden, 6, 74, 179, 231
Essex Rebellion. *See* Devereaux, Robert and the Essex Rebellion of 1601

F
The Faerie Queene (poem). *See* Spenser, Edmund
Ferdinand II, Archduke of Further Austria, 75, 76–77
Feria, Count of, Spanish Ambassador. *See* Suárez de Figueroa y Córdoba, Gómez, Count and later Duke of Feria, Spanish Ambassador
FitzAlan, Henry, Earl of Arundel, 16, 30–31, 74–75
FitzWilliam, William, Lord Deputy of Ireland, 44, 158
Forman, Simon, 197, 204, 222–223
Fortescue, Sir John, 44, 142, 197
Foxe, John, 63, 98, 238
Francis II, King of France, 8, 71, 77, 102, 105, 106, 122, 129, 244, 261
François, Duke of Alençon, later Duke of Anjou, 6, 80, 118, 129, 130, 132, 147–148, 218, 249, 260, 266

G
Gaunse, Joachim, 198–199
Gérard, Balthasar, 8, 54, 140, 152, 169
Godunov, Boris, 100, 190–191
Golden Speech, 10, 57
Grey, Lady Jane. *See* Dudley, Jane (*née* Grey)
Grey, Lady Mary. *See* Keyes, Mary (*née* Grey)
Grey, Lady Katherine. *See* Seymour, Katherine (formerly Herbert, *née* Grey), Countess of Hertford

Grindal, Edmund, Archbishop of Canterbury, 7, 43, 59, 61, 63–66, 260

H
Hacket, William, 157
Hamilton, James, third Earl of Arran, 6, 71–72, 74
Hampton, Bernard, 25
Hampton Court, 5, 98, 130, 180, 181, 182, 184, 186, 202, 212, 236, 263, 265, 269, 284
Hartgill, William, 53
Hastings, Henry, third Earl of Huntingdon, 92, 93, 190, 240
Hatton, Sir Christopher, 5, 21, 28, 40, 42–44, 55, 67, 85–86, 132, 145, 147–149, 182, 213, 217–218, 224, 232, 234, 247, 266, 274, 277
Heath, Nicholas, Archbishop of York, 13–14, 31–32, 51, 59
Heneage, Sir Thomas, 43, 97, 198, 274
Henri, Duke of Anjou, later Henri III, King of France, 6, 41, 42, 46, 48, 80, 102, 113, 118, 127–130, 133, 215
Henry VII, King of England, 15, 91, 95, 100, 101, 107
Henry VIII, King of England, 1–3, 6, 15–16, 29–31, 33, 35, 36, 39, 44, 47, 49, 51–52, 60, 63, 69, 71–72, 91–93, 97–98, 101, 104, 183, 198, 216, 224, 235, 249–250, 251, 257–258, 260, 264, 267, 271, 279
Hentzner, Paul, 183, 212
Hepburn, James, Lord Bothwell, 8, 102, 105, 107, 117, 254
Herbert, Anne (formerly Sackville, *née* Clifford), Countess of Dorset, Pembroke, and Montgomery, Baroness Clifford, 239–240
Herbert, Sir John, 25
Herbert, William, Earl of Pembroke, 32, 94, 168, 277
House of Commons, 10, 19, 36, 43, 45, 46, 49–56, 67, 70, 145. *See also* Parliament

House of Lords, 19, 32, 49, 51, 53, 67.
    See also Parliament
Howard, Charles, Baron Howard
    of Effingham and later Earl of
    Nottingham, 9, 40–41, 88, 164,
    169–170, 186, 283
Howard, Katherine, Queen of England,
    2
Howard, Katherine (*née* Carey),
    Countess of Nottingham, 237
Howard, Thomas, 4th Duke of Norfolk,
    8, 16, 30, 35–37, 40, 53, 78, 117,
    114, 248, 265
Howard, William, Lord Howard of
    Effingham, 132, 97
Hundred Years War (1337–1453), 4,
    114
Hurault, André, seigneur de Maisse,
    136–137, 254, 264, 265, 267, 268

I
Ignorth, 202–203
Ippolyta, 201–204, 281
Ivan IV, Tsar of Russia, 70, 188–190,
    191, 201, 278

J
James VI and I, King of England,
    Scotland, and Ireland, 10, 28, 29,
    42, 46–48, 52, 54, 84, 87, 92,
    96, 101–104, 105, 107–109, 117,
    122–124, 130, 135, 156, 157,
    162–163, 169, 181–182, 183, 192,
    205, 211, 225, 250–251, 256, 257,
    266, 279, 283
Jane the Fool, 279
Jenkinson, Anthony, 188–190, 201
The Jew of Malta (play). *See* Marlowe,
    Christopher, *The Jew of Malta* (play)
Jesuits, 45, 56, 109, 156–157, 160, 162
Julius, Philip, Duke of Stettin-Pomerania,
    187, 212, 267, 269

K
Keyes, Mary (*née* Grey), 97–98
Knollys, Katherine (*née* Carey), 229,
    235–237

Knollys, Lettice, Countess of Essex. *See*
    Blount, Lettice (formerly Dudley,
    formerly Devereaux, *née* Knollys),
    Countess of Essex & Countess of
    Leicester
Knollys, Sir Francis, 5, 35–36, 46, 236,
    244, 280
Knollys, Sir William, Baron Knollys, Earl
    of Banbury, 46, 162

L
Lopez, Roderigo, 9, 42, 88, 141,
    160–161, 200
Lord Chamberlain's Men, 40, 47, 283,
    286. *See also* Carey, George, Lord
    Hunsdon; Carey, Henry, Lord
    Hunsdon
Lord Stourton's Bill, 53
Lord Strange's Men, 99, 282, 283, 285.
    See also Stanley, Ferdinando, Lord
    Strange; Stanley, William, Earl of
    Derby

M
Maitland, William, of Lethington,
    Scottish Ambassador, 115–117, 122
Manteo, 203–204. *See also* Wanchese;
    Raleigh, Sir Walter; Virginia
Marian Exiles, 4, 7, 23, 62–64, 238
Marlowe, Christopher
    The Jew of Malta (play), 9, 200
Mary I, Queen of England, 1, 2, 3, 14,
    17, 30, 31, 40, 54, 61, 72–73, 74,
    75, 82, 91, 99, 102, 104, 112–113,
    139, 197, 226, 230–231, 236, 241,
    258, 267, 272
    and her rule, 4, 5, 6, 13, 21–22,
        25–26, 28–37, 39, 44, 49, 59,
        63, 92, 94, 105, 198, 220, 233,
        238, 261, 263, 279
Mary of Guise, 71, 101, 116
Mary Stuart, Queen of Scots, 7–8, 38,
    41, 46, 52, 69, 71, 77–78, 79,
    84, 92, 93, 100–102, 104–106,
    109, 111, 114–117, 120–124, 127,
    129–130, 181, 210, 238, 242, 244,
    252–254, 260, 261, 266, 267, 271,
    274

and plotting against Elizabeth, 45, 54, 55, 48, 50, 125–126, 133, 135, 140, 142–145, 148–149, 151, 153–155, 221, 236, 274
and her trial & execution, 23, 24, 40, 41, 43, 53, 86, 135, 169, 216, 218–219, 224–225, 238, 261–262
Mason, Sir John, 31
Maximilian II, Holy Roman Emperor, 77–78, 120, 124
Mehmet III, Sultan of the Ottoman Empire, 193, 278
Melville, James, of Halhill, Scottish Ambassador, 69, 79, 122–124, 238, 263, 266, 267–268
The Merchant of Venice (play). *See* Shakespeare, William, *The Merchant of Venice* (play)
de Mendoza, Don Bernardino, Spanish Ambassador, 26, 27, 133–136, 140, 148–149, 151–156, 167, 169, 249, 253
Mildmay, Sir Walter, 36–37, 53, 55, 219, 245–246
Monarcho, 280
de la Mothe-Fénélon, Bertrand de Salignac, 126–129, 130, 140, 146, 234, 236, 262–263
Murad III, Sultan of the Ottoman Empire, 192–193, 200

N

Norris, Sir Henry, 26, 233–235, 261, 262
Norris (or Norreys), Marjorie Williams, 233–235
North, Lord Roger, 46–47, 84, 128, 271
Northern Rebellion (1569), 8, 30–31, 38, 39, 40, 46, 47, 62, 75, 93, 143–144. *See also* Mary Stuart, Queen of Scots; Neville, Charles, Earl of Westmorland; Percy, Thomas, Earl of Northumberland; de Spes, Guerau, Spanish Ambassador
Notte, Joan, 223–224
Nutioc, 202–203

O

Oath of Supremacy (1559), 13, 22, 32, 33, 59, 61, 157. *See also* Elizabethan Religious Settlement
Oglethorpe, Owen, Bishop of Carlisle. *See* Elizabeth I, Queen of England, coronation
O'Neill, Hugh, Earl of Tyrone, 9, 10, 56, 88–89
Orsini, Virginio, Duke of Bracciano, 185–187, 266, 269

P

de Paris, Thomasina, 210, 281–282
Parker, Matthew, Archbishop of Canterbury, 43, 59, 60–66, 94, 96, 189, 242, 247
Parliament, 1, 3, 6, 10, 13, 19, 25, 26, 28, 30, 33, 35–37, 40, 42, 43, 45, 47, 49–57, 66, 70, 78, 85, 92, 93, 96, 117, 140, 151, 182, 234, 241, 272, 284. *See also* House of Commons; House of Lords
Parr, Katherine, Queen of England, 2, 33, 72, 104, 183, 209, 231, 242, 260, 271, 279
Parr, William, Marquess of Northampton, 35, 179
Parry Plot. *See* Perry, William
Parry, Blanche, 98, 230, 232–233, 236, 238, 276
Parry, Sir Thomas, 2, 3, 33, 44, 72, 108, 243, 257
Parry, William, 54, 151
Parsons, Robert. *See* Jesuits
Paulet, Sir Amias (or Amyas), 29, 41, 154
Paulet, William, Marquess of Winchester, 37
Perrot, Sir John, 44–45, 86, 158
Petre, Sir William, 29, 95
Phillip II of Spain, 3, 4, 6, 8, 39, 41, 44, 25, 55, 73, 74, 75–76, 77, 78, 94, 97, 106, 109, 112–115, 119–120, 122, 124–126, 133, 135, 137, 139–143, 148, 152, 158, 159, 168–170, 222, 224, 225, 241–242,

244, 245, 247–249, 251, 253, 268, 285
Pickering, Sir William, 70, 75, 212
Platter, Thomas, 141, 180, 183–184, 187, 212, 269
Plays Performed at Court, 282–287
Pole, Reginald, Cardinal and Archbishop of Canterbury, 14, 23, 59
Pope Clement VII, 71, 101
Pope Gregory XIII, 148, 149, 153, 255
Pope Pius V, 8, 106, 143, 144
Prince of Purpoole, 286
Privy Council, 1, 5, 19–48, 49, 50, 52, 54, 55, 56, 65–67, 79, 82, 85–86, 95, 100, 107, 115, 134, 135, 140, 141, 147, 149, 155, 160, 162, 164, 167, 171, 179, 196, 197, 199, 205, 212, 236, 242, 277
Puckering, Sir John, 45, 46

Q

de la Quadra, Álvaro, Bishop of Aquila, Spanish Ambassador, 76, 77, 113–115, 119, 142–143, 167, 244, 246
Queen's Safety Act of 1585, 54, 140

R

Radcliffe, Thomas, Earl of Sussex, 5, 21, 30, 33, 37–38, 46, 78, 84, 143, 180, 194, 283
Raleigh, Sir Walter, 10, 86–88, 186, 199, 203, 205
Randolph, Thomas, 189, 210, 215
Reformation Parliament (1529–1536), 49
Renard, Simon, Spanish Ambassador, 4, 70, 73, 74, 272
Richmond (Palace), 5, 120, 132, 145, 182, 191, 240, 247, 256, 285
Ridolfi Plot, 8, 23, 30, 35, 36, 42, 52, 126, 127, 144–145, 247, 274
Roanoke Colony, 86, 202, 203. *See also* Raleigh, Sir Walter
Robsart Amy, Lady Dudley. *See* Dudley, Amy (*née* Robsart)
Rogers, Sir Daniel, 28
Rogers, Sir Edward, 33
Russell, Francis, Earl of Bedford, 34, 125, 148, 239, 275

S

Sackville, Sir Richard, 33–34, 105
Sackville, Thomas, Lord Buckhurst, Earl of Dorset, 42, 186, 283
Sadler, Sir Ralph, 30, 36, 37, 55
Sedition Act of 1581, 54
Seymour, Edward, Duke of Somerset, 2–3, 21, 231, 243
Seymour, Edward, Earl of Hertford, 29, 94, 108
Seymour, Jane Queen of England, 2, 94, 181
Seymour, Katherine (formerly Herbert, *née* Grey), Countess of Hertford, 29, 34, 96, 97, 108, 161. *See also* Seymour, Edward, Earl of Hertford
Seymour, Thomas, Lord High Admiral, 2–3, 33, 72, 231, 242–243
Seymour, William, 96
Shakespeare, William, 9, 10, 42, 101, 149, 187, 193, 281, 283, 285, 286
and *The Merchant of Venice* (play), 9, 193
Sidney, Sir Henry, 39, 244
Sidney, Lady Mary (*née* Dudley), 39
Sidney, Sir Philip, 23, 48, 84, 87, 181, 277
de Silva, Diego Guzman, Spanish Ambassador, 62, 97, 106, 119–122, 124–125, 126, 232, 247, 262, 268
Slavery & Indentured Servitude, 10, 167–168, 178, 193, 201–207
Smith, Sir Thomas, secretary (d. 1577), 4, 22–23, 26
Smith, Sir Thomas, clerk (d. 1609), 28
Smith, William, 26
Snakenborg, Helena, 35, 179–181
Somers (or Somer), Will, 279
Somerset, Edward, Earl of Worcester, 47, 185–186
Somerville, John, or Somerfield, 149–150
Spanish "Invincible" Armada, 8–9, 40, 42, 47, 55, 67, 76, 85, 86, 109,

136, 141, 158, 167–173, 198, 203, 211, 222, 249, 253, 261, 277, 285. See also Tilbury Speech
Spenser, Edmund, 10, 180, 281
de Spes, Guerau, Spanish Ambassador, 25, 113, 121, 124–126, 127, 133, 143, 144–145, 167, 248, 274
St. Bartholomew's Day Massacre, 8, 23, 41, 46, 80, 127, 130, 160, 215, 248, 263
Stafford Plot, 155–156
Stafford, Lady Dorothy, 219, 232, 237–238
Stafford, Douglas (or Douglass) (formerly Sheffield, née Howard), Baroness Sheffield, 38, 84, 256
Stafford, William, 155
Stanhope, Sir John, 47, 278
Stanley, Anne Bridges Touchet, Countess of Castlehaven. See Touchet, Anne (formerly Bridges, née Stanley), Countess of Castlehaven
Stanley, Edward, 3rd Earl of Derby, 32, 99, 144, 205
Stanley, Ferdinando, Earl of Derby, Lord Strange, 99–100, 101, 159–160, 282
  Lord Strange's Men (player company), 99, 285
Stanley, Henry, 4th Earl of Derby, Lord Strange, 41, 99, 148, 160, 282
Stanley, Margaret (née Clifford), Countess of Derby, 99, 147–148
Stanley, William, Earl of Derby, 44–45, 100, 101, 141, 159–160, 186
Star Chamber, 19, 24, 37, 89
Stourton, William, 7th Baron Stourton, 53
Stuart, Lady Arbella, 95–96, 105, 107–109, 242
Stuart, Charles, Earl of Lennox, 107
Stuart, Henry, Lord Darnley, 8, 30, 77, 102, 104, 106–107, 117, 119, 122, 129, 181, 254
Suárez de Figueroa y Córdoba, Gómez, Count and later Duke of Feria, Spanish Ambassador, 73, 75–76, 112–113, 125, 256, 251

Supreme Governor of the Church, 6, 51, 56. See also Elizabethan Religious Settlement

T

Talbot, Elizabeth "Bess" (formerly Cavendish, formerly St Loe, formerly Barlow, née Hardwick), Countess of Shrewsbury, 38, 48, 95, 105, 107, 144, 241–242, 252, 273
Talbot, Francis, Earl of Shrewsbury, 31
Talbot, George, Earl of Shrewsbury, 30, 36, 38, 48, 93, 107, 140, 144, 153, 242, 252
Talbot, Gilbert, Earl of Shrewsbury, 48
Talbot, Mary (née Cavendish), Countess of Shrewsbury, 48, 108
Tarlton (or Tarleton), Richard, 281, 283
Thirty-Nine Articles (1571), 6. See also Book of Common Prayer and Elizabethan Religious Settlement
Thomasina de Paris. See de Paris, Thomasina
Throckmorton, Sir Nicholas, 22, 98, 115, 142, 205, 244, 261
Throckmorton Plot, 40, 54, 135, 148–149, 151
Tilbury Speech, 9, 85, 170–171, 197
de Toledo, Fernando Alvarez, Duke of Alva, 120–121, 133, 144
Touchet, Anne (formerly Bridges, née Stanley), Countess of Castlehaven, 100
Tower of London, 2–4, 15, 24–26, 33, 36–38, 40, 44–45, 50, 53, 56, 72–73, 80, 84, 86, 87, 92, 94–95, 96, 97, 104, 106, 108–109, 142, 144, 146, 149–150, 151, 155–156, 158–159, 161–163, 165, 180, 186, 187, 211, 216, 218, 226, 231, 243, 245, 246, 248, 260, 263, 272
Treason Bill of 1571, 52, 140
Tremayne, Edmund, 26, 134
Tudor, Margaret, Queen of Scots, 6–7, 16, 34, 91, 101, 104, 107
Tudor, Mary, Queen of France, 3, 6, 41, 93, 101, 104, 147, 160

V

Vasa, Cecilia, 35, 179, 284
Virginia, 86, 203–204. *See also* Raleigh, Sir Walter

W

Walsingham, Sir Francis, 4, 5, 7, 9, 21–24, 26–27, 28, 29, 40–43, 46, 48, 54, 65, 67, 85, 127, 133, 139–141, 143, 144–145, 148–149, 151–152, 154, 155, 156–157, 160–161, 169, 170, 180, 198–199, 210, 215, 218, 221, 235, 240, 251, 261, 277
Wanchese, 203–204. *See also* Maneto; Raleigh, Sir Walter; Virginia
von Wedel, Lupold, 181–182, 265
Wentworth, Paul, 50, 52
Wentworth, Peter, 50, 53, 55, 92
Westminster (palace), 16, 19, 36, 49, 105, 164, 273
Whitehall (palace), 5, 13, 15, 16, 17, 132, 137, 180, 181, 183, 185–186, 191, 195, 212, 256, 257, 266, 267, 269, 284
Whitgift, John, Archbishop of Canterbury, 5, 7, 42–43, 62, 66–68, 86
William the Silent, Prince of Orange, 8, 48, 54, 140, 152, 169
Wilson, Thomas, 23, 65, 91
Witchcraft, 52, 141, 146–148
Witchcraft Act of 1542, 10, 52
Witchcraft Act of 1563, 9, 52
Witchcraft Act of 1604, 10, 52
Wolley, Sir John, 43, 55
Wotton, Sir Edward, 48
Wotton, Nicholas, 31
Wyatt, Sir Thomas. *See* Wyatt's Rebellion (1554)
Wyatt's Rebellion (1554), 3, 4, 26, 33, 37, 74, 75, 82, 226

Printed by Printforce, United Kingdom